ATTACHMENT ISSUES
IN PSYCHOPATHOLOGY
AND INTERVENTION

ATTACHMENT ISSUES IN PSYCHOPATHOLOGY AND INTERVENTION

Edited by

Leslie Atkinson
Centre for Addiction and Mental Health

Susan Goldberg
The Hospital for Sick Children

LEA   LAWRENCE ERLBAUM ASSOCIATES, PUBLISHERS
2004   Mahwah, New Jersey   London

Lawrence Erlbaum Associates, Inc., Publishers
10 Industrial Avenue
Mahwah, New Jersey 07430

Cover design by Kathryn Houghtaling Lacey

Library of Congress Cataloging-in-Publication Data

Attachment issues in psychopathology and intervention / edited by Leslie Atkinson,
   Susan Goldberg.
     p. cm.
   Includes bibliographical references and index.
   ISBN 0-8058-3693-4 (alk. paper)
   1. Attachment behavior. 2. Mental illness—Etiology. 3. Object relations
(Psychoanalysis). 4. Attachment behavior in children. I. Atkinson, Leslie, Ph.D.
II. Goldberg, Susan.

RC455.4.A84A885 2003
616.89'071—dc21   2003049132
                                                                         CIP

Books published by Lawrence Erlbaum Associates are printed on acid-free paper,
and their bindings are chosen for strength and durability.

Printed in the United States of America
10 9 8 7 6 5 4 3 2 1

Contents

Preface

The goal of this book is to push forward thinking about the clinical aspects of attachment theory. The need is ironic given that John Bowlby, the founder of attachment theory, was a physician and psychoanalyst whose overriding purpose involved comprehending psychopathology. However, his most influential collaborator, Mary Ainsworth, was a developmental psychologist primarily interested in attachment theory as a key to understanding typical development. In some respects, she and her developmental psychology colleagues "hijacked" the research agenda, such that decades of study focused on typical mother–infant interactions. This hijacking was so successful that two decades after the publication of the first volume of Bowlby's trilogy on attachment, Bowlby wrote an article in the *American Journal of Psychiatry* entitled, "Developmental Psychiatry Comes of Age;" the thrust of the paper rested almost entirely on the work of developmental psychologists studying typical development in non-clinical samples. That same year (1988), Jay Belsky and Teresa Nezworski published an edited book, *Clinical Implications of Attachment*. Although a landmark volume of massive current relevance, the book was about "implications" rather than "applications" because there were virtually no clinical data available. It is true that this situation has changed in the intervening years, but not dramatically; articles combining the clinical interests of Bowlby with the developmental insights spawned by Ainsworth number in the dozens, rather than in the hundreds. And even here, the focus is on understanding psychopathology rather than on treating it.

This book is neatly divided in two parts, with approximately half of the chapters addressing psychopathology per se, and half focusing on intervention. We believe that this balanced coverage alone makes it unique in the literature.

We are delighted to have persuaded so many who have contributed so much to the field to join us in the effort to delineate the ways in which attachment theory can and should inform effective practice. Looking back over the book we have shaped together, we feel confident that it will indeed achieve its goal.

—Leslie Atkinson
—Susan Goldberg

_I_

PSYCHOPATHOLOGY

Applications of Attachment: The Integration of Developmental and Clinical Traditions

Leslie Atkinson
Centre for Addiction and Mental Health and University of Toronto

Susan Goldberg
Hospital for Sick Children and University of Toronto

The notion that early, maladaptive parent-child relations play a causal role in psychopathology has long been central to developmental theorizing. However, it was not until John Bowlby (1969/1982, 1973, 1980) provided a broadly alluring paradigm and Mary Ainsworth (Ainsworth, Blehar, Waters, & Wall, 1978) developed the practical means to verify it that the early relations, later psychopathology hypothesis received concerted empirical attention.

Bowlby and Ainsworth worked in strong partnership. Bowlby (1980) carefully integrated Ainsworth's research findings so as to validate and modify his own theorizing; Ainsworth (1978) drew on the ethology and naturalistic observation that formed the basis of Bowlby's thought. Nevertheless, the emphases of each of these scholars were not entirely complementary: Bowlby focused on the extreme adversities that brought children to clinical care, whereas Ainsworth was concerned with direct mother-child interaction under normative conditions. Methodological differences also underlie each of these approaches: Bowlby drew upon clinical experience to weave inferences and speculations into coherent theory; Ainsworth focused on detailed behavioral observations, which she summarized quantitatively and qualitatively and subjected to statistical test. These contrasts are most evident in efforts to apply attachment theory to clinical populations. The contributors to this volume take up the challenge of integrating these two traditions, that of combining research knowledge and clinical expertise while neither rigidly constraining clinical work nor replacing data and hypothesis testing with clinical intuition. To accomplish this, they reevaluate attachment theory, incorporate diverse approaches in its study, broaden it, qualify it, refocus it, and change it.

ATTACHMENT THEORY: BOWLBY
AND AINSWORTH

As a physician and psychoanalyst, John Bowlby used case study material to construct and verify a theory of extreme adversity and trauma, of abandonment and loss, of psychopathology. For example, Bowlby (1973) drew on case experience to describe the caregivers of school-refusing children (suffering from general anxiety, depression, and psychosomatic difficulties) as immersed in highly conflictual marriages, engaged in role reversal, expressing extreme resentment and anger, and using guilt induction and threats of suicide, abandonment, or expulsion from the family. For Bowlby, issues of protection and distress regulation were paramount to attachment theory. Four characteristics of his approach stand out as most relevant: the use of case study material to develop and validate theory, belief in the extremity of conditions surrounding insecure attachment (and, by inference, belief in the extremity of insecure attachment), a focus on frank psychopathology, and belief in the centrality of protection or distress regulation. Bowlby's work led to a rich clinical literature, wherein attachment theory, as applied to individual cases, is used to understand psychopathology and therapeutic intervention (Holmes, 1993).

As a developmental psychologist, Ainsworth (1978) recognized that separation, both physical and psychological, is a dimensional construct potentially implicit in every mother-child interaction. Ainsworth explored the link between attachment and typical development, observing community samples: (a) in their homes with a set of standardized, context-dependent rating scales of parent-infant interaction and (b) in the "strange situation," a structured laboratory procedure in which the child was observed in an unfamiliar but comfortable setting with the mother, with the mother and a stranger, with a stranger, and alone. The home observations operationalized separation as a psychological construct reflecting the degree to which a mother recognized and responded to her infant's signals, particularly those involving distress (psychological availability). The strange situation operationalized physical separations, but these were brief, not unlike the routine experiences of a typical North American infant. Using these methodologies, Ainsworth discovered three infant attachment patterns: avoidant (A; infant inhibits attachment signals), secure (B; infant expresses attachment needs freely), and ambivalent-resistant (C; infant hyperactivates attachment signals; for description of infant attachment classifications, see Benoit & Coolbear, chap. 3, this volume; Cicchetti, Toth, & Rogosch, chap. 10, this volume; Egeland & Carlson, chap. 2, this volume). These classifications purportedly correspond to three types of parenting: consistently unresponsive, consistently responsive, and inconsistently responsive, respectively. Importantly, although avoidant and ambivalent-resistant strategies involve indirect communication of attachment needs, they are not pathological. Rather, they are normative responses to variation in caregiving environments. In contrast to Bowlby's (1969/1982, 1973, 1980) approach to theory building, Ainsworth adopted a sample-based methodology addressing typical children as they developed a variety of attachment strategies in the context of relatively low-stress environments. Moreover, compared to Bowlby, who emphasized protection and distress regulation, Ainsworth highlighted the relationship, the enduring bond, as central to attachment theory. Ainsworth's research facilitated the comprehension of universal and typical developmental processes, with sample data used to understand the predictors and changing organization of attachment, its stability and variation, its different manifestations across cultures, and its implications for correlated behaviors.

Despite the discrepancies in methodology and emphasis, Bowlby and Ainsworth sustained a long and close collaboration. In succeeding years, however, clinicians and researchers rarely coordinated their efforts to elucidate the clinical implications of attachment. This book reflects a renewed effort toward harmonization, as clinical researchers address issues of extreme adversity using theory and tools developed in clinic and laboratory.

FROM LABORATORY TO CLINIC

The return of attachment from laboratory to clinic has been detailed elsewhere (Atkinson, 1997). Until recently, little research addressed attachment and atypical development. Researchers focused on attachment security as the outcome of normative precursors, such as maternal sensitivity, or as an influence on universal outcomes, such as peer competence (for review, see Bretherton, 1985). Although such studies were relevant to psychopathology, they did not speak to it directly. Within the context of predicting attachment security, it was the study of disturbed and maltreating parents that more immediately bridged the chasm between laboratory and clinic.

For example, Radke-Yarrow, Cummings, Kuczynski, and Chapman (1985) found a greater incidence of insecure attachment (as well as unusual patterns of attachment) among 2- and 3-year-old children of parents experiencing a major affective disorder than among children of a parent

with minor depression or among children whose parents were not de-·
pressed. Not only was demonstration of the link important, but so too was
consideration of the myriad factors that may account for the link. Whereas
Radke-Yarrow et al. invoked mediating factors central to attachment theory, such as unpredictably sensitive caregiving, they also emphasized the
role of disturbed affective communication and maternal sadness, irritability, hopelessness, helplessness, and confusion. In addition, the study of attachment and depression invited consideration of factors like increased
marital conflict, assortative mating (i.e., the tendency of depressed individuals to select partners with psychological difficulties), comorbid diagnoses, and genetic factors, all associated with maternal depression
(Downey & Coyne, 1990) and all potentially related to increased probabil-
ity of insecure attachment. Hence, studies such as that of Radke-Yarrow et
al. made explicit the association between parental psychopathology and
insecure attachment and the complexity of that link. Although constructs
such as maternal sensitivity provided elegantly parsimonious and theoretically powerful main effects in the study of attachment security in typical populations, the preeminence of such constructs, and the main effects
models implicit within them, could not be maintained in the face of numerous additive and interacting influences that are so obvious in clinical
samples. In such research, we see the necessity of amalgamating Bowlby's
(1969/1982, 1973, 1980) complex theory of extreme adversity with
Ainsworth's (1978) elegant model of direct mother-child interaction.

Whereas Radke-Yarrow et al. (1985) and others worked at predicting
attachment security within the clinical context, other investigators attempted to predict behavioral difficulties from attachment in typical samples. In broad terms, the results were similar. For example, Lewis, Feiring,
McGuffog, and Jaskir (1984) showed that attachment security at age 1 predicted degree of psychopathology at age 6. Specifically, insecurely attached boys showed more internalizing behaviors, as reported by their
mothers, than did securely attached boys. However, these results were
heavily qualified, depending on not only the child's gender but also the
child's birth order, whether or not the child was planned, the number of
friends the child had, and the number of family life stress events. Once
again, the complexity of clinical data obtruded itself, belying simple main
effects predictions. Indeed, it is possible that the limitations of attachment
theory, in addition to its strengths, fueled the resurgence of developmental psychopathology. In any case, it was the Feiring et al. (1984) study, and
another study addressing similar issues (Erickson, Sroufe, & Egeland,
1985), that provided direct incentive for the first edited volume dedicated
specifically to the "clinical implications of attachment" (Belsky & Nezworski, 1988).

CLINICAL IMPLICATIONS OF ATTACHMENT

Clinical Implications of Attachment (Belsky & Nezworski, 1988) was the first concerted attempt by attachment researchers to understand the role of insecure attachment in atypical development. Contributors emphasized two complimentary, yet mutually confounding, principles fundamental to all prediction: continuity and context. These twin principles underlie the notion that typical and atypical development are opposite sides of the same coin, explicable with the same set of constructs. Lawful continuity is the "central proposition underlying a developmental perspective" (Sroufe & Rutter, 1984, p. 21), but continuity cannot be understood outside of context. Context renders a given attachment strategy adaptive at one time and place, but maladaptive at another. Change in context leads to lawful change in attachment strategy and its correlates and explains "error" in prediction across time. By altering context, the clinician manipulates attachment strategies or the consequences of those strategies.

Clinical Implications of Attachment (Belsky & Nezworski, 1988) provided significant insight into the common foundations of typical and atypical development. It was, and continues to be, a major milestone in attachment theorizing. However, in spite of these new directions, few chapters included research with clinical populations or attachment-based interventions.

Over the next decade, several interrelated advances occurred that had a profound impact on the study of attachment and psychopathology. First was the discovery of disorganized forms of attachment. As research incorporated risk and clinical samples, investigators found new types of behavior reflecting the collapse of an organized attachment strategy (Main & Solomon, 1986, 1990; Radke-Yarrow et al., 1985). Although diverse, the manifestations of this disorganization have in common the absence of a "readily observable goal, intention, or explanation" (Main & Solomon, 1990, p. 122). Barnett and Vondra (1999, p. 12) summarized:

> Atypicality of attachment can be described at multiple levels: the level of behavioral *systems* (i.e., the coordination of attachment, exploration, affiliation, and fear-wariness systems), the level of social and emotional interactive behavior *patterns* (e.g., mixing avoidance with resistance, distress with avoidance, etc.), and the level of specific behavioral *indices* (e.g., lying prone during reunion, covering mouth or ears when caregiver approaches, dazed facial expression).

The disorganized classification is always assigned with the best fitting organized strategy, such that disorganized individuals are classified as disorganized-avoidant, disorganized-secure, or disorganized-ambivalent-resistant. Disorganization is disproportionately represented in maltreated (Carlson, Cicchetti, Barnett, & Braunwald, 1989; Cicchetti & Barnett, 1991; Lyons-Ruth, Connell, Grunebaum, & Botein, 1990) and other clinical samples (van IJzendoorn, Goldberg, Kroonenberg, & Frenkel, 1992) and improves prediction of subsequent behavior disorder (Lyons-Ruth, Alpern, & Repacholi, 1993; Shaw & Vondra, 1995). Main and Solomon (1986, 1990) hypothesized that disorganization is associated with frightened or frightening caregiver behavior (see Lyons-Ruth, Melnick, Bronfman, Sherry, & Llanas, chap. 4, this volume).

The second major advance in attachment research involved the development of attachment assessment tools beyond infancy. For example, Cassidy and Marvin (1992) developed a coding scheme for scoring preschoolers' behavioral response to separation, with attachment classifications analogous to those manifested in infancy. Main, Kaplan, and Cassidy (1985) did the same for 5- to 7-year-olds. An important clinical finding arising from the use of these schemes is that beyond infancy disorganization manifests itself in varied forms of "controlling" behavior wherein the child inappropriately directs mother-child interaction (see Lyons-Ruth et al., chap. 4, this volume). Another assessment advance was Main's Adult Attachment Interview (AAI; George, Kaplan, & Main, 1984). The AAI represented a move away from behavioral observation in the dyadic context toward the study of individuals' mental representations or states of mind with respect to attachment, as reflected in the coherence of narrative. Nevertheless, the classification scheme remains familiar, illustrating the power of continuity and context. Like the avoidant infant, the adult who is *dismissing* of attachment minimizes the importance of attachment relationships. Analogous to the secure infant, the *autonomous* adult values intimacy and freely expresses her- or himself with respect to attachment. Similar to the ambivalent-resistant infant, the *preoccupied* adult is engrossed in attachment relationships, but cannot modulate stress through them. Finally, like the disorganized-disoriented infant, the *unresolved* adult experiences the periodic collapse of his or her predominant attachment strategy. This occurs in the narration of potentially traumatic events (for a description of adult mental representations, see Benoit & Coolbear, chap. 3, this volume; Cicchetti et al., chap. 10, this volume; Dozier & Bates, chap. 7, this volume; Slade, chap. 8, this volume).

The development of assessment paradigms beyond infancy was important to clinical study because it permitted concurrent exploration of attachment and psychopathology in the childhood and adult years and allowed the study of attachment transmission from one generation to the next. In addition, the parallels between the content of the AAI and clinical

interviews drew clinicians to AAI training institutes, encouraging a significant number of clinician researchers to investigate attachment, many of
them represented in the current volume.

The third major advance in attachment research following the publication of *Clinical Implications of Attachment* (Belsky & Nezworski, 1988) lay in
increased access to or interest in clinical samples. Numerous investigators, some cited previously, studied the issue of maltreatment. From an attachment perspective, this is a particularly informative disturbance of interaction, as it involves an actual threat to the child's well-being. This is
relevant because, as mentioned, Bowlby (1969/1982) stressed the protective function of the attachment system (Goldberg, Grusec, & Jenkins, 1999;
see Cicchetti et al., chap. 10, this volume; Hilburn-Cobb, chap. 5, this volume; Lyons-Ruth et al., chap. 4, this volume). In the maltreating environment, the child is at risk by virtue of extreme neglect or actual abuse, with
the potential "protector" as author of both.

Investigators also studied attachment within the context of parental
psychopathology, anxiety disorders (Manassis, Bradley, Goldberg, Hood,
& Swinson, 1994) being a particularly pertinent sample, given the centrality of fear or anxiety to attachment theory (Greenberg, 1999; Barnett &
Vondra, 1999; see also Hilburn-Cobb, chap. 5, this volume; Lyons-Ruth et
al., chap. 4, this volume). With respect to childhood disorders, oppositional defiant disorder was relatively well studied (DeKlyen, Speltz, &
Greenberg, 1996; Greenberg, Speltz, DeKlyen, & Endriga, 1997; Speltz,
Greenberg, & DeKlyen, 1990), although other disorders, including disturbances as attachment relevant as childhood anxiety and depression, remained unexplored (Greenberg, 1999). In addition, using the AAI, investigators studied older adolescents' mental representations as they related to
depression and antisocial personality disorder (Rosenstein & Horowitz,
1996) and adults' states of mind and depression (Cole-Detke & Kobak,
1996; Fonagy et al., 1996; Patrick, Hobson, Castle, Howard, & Maughan,
1994), bipolar disorder, anxiety disorders (Fonagy et al., 1996), and borderline personality disorder (Fonagy et al., 1996; Patrick et al., 1994).
Taking a life-course approach, Warren, Huston, Egeland, and Sroufe
(1997; see Egeland & Carlson, chap. 2, this volume) predicted anxiety disorder from infant attachment classification. Although few in number,
such studies represent the return of attachment research to the clinic.

In light of these advances, the discovery of disorganized attachment,
the development of assessment methods beyond infancy, and the investigation of bona fide clinical samples, it became evident that the Belsky and
Nezworzki (1988) volume, though continuing to serve as a reference point
with respect to theory, no longer reflected the state of the art to which it
had, in part, contributed. A second compendium was necessary.

ATTACHMENT AND PSYCHOPATHOLOGY

With the passage of a decade, Atkinson and Zucker's (1997) volume incorporated the aforementioned advances. First, disorganization was broadly used. In fact, Goldberg (1997) found a .62 correlation between the proportion of disorganized infants and children and sample status (ranging from typical to at risk to psychopathological). Second, all empirical contributions included assessments of attachment in the early childhood or adult years. Finally, contributors presented data on divorced mothers, chronically ill infants, Romanian adoptees, children of mothers with anxiety disorders, boys with gender identity disorder, preschoolers with appositional defiant disorder, forensic psychiatric inpatients, and inpatients with borderline personality disorder.

Broad themes emerged, all attributable to the clinical application of attachment concepts, including the necessity of at once streamlining, integrating, and expanding theory and the need for more ideographic observation and data-analytic approaches. Thus, Rutter (1997) cautioned that the effects of inconsistent caregiving and loss must be parsed from associated environmental conditions, a consideration of less importance in the study of typical samples, where environmental circumstances are nontoxic. In a related vein, Lieberman (1997) and Zeanah, Finley-Belgrad, and Benoit (1997) implied that overreliance on attachment classification obscures full recognition of the individual or dyad in its broad context. Several authors (Crittenden, 1997; Lieberman, 1997; Zeanah et al., 1997) incorporated psychoanalytic concepts, supplementing them with cognitive attributional (Lieberman, 1997), sociological, and criminological models (Fonagy et al., 1997). In terms of method, contributors advocated closer observation of behavior (Goldberg, 1997), a more individually oriented view of the data (Greenberg, DeKlyen, Speltz, & Endriga, 1997), and detailed review of case study material (Bretherton, Walsh, Lependorf, & Georgeson, 1997; Lieberman, 1997; Zeanah et al., 1997).

In returning to the clinic, attachment researchers exploited the broad scope of issues and methodologies introduced by both Bowlby and Ainsworth. *Attachment and Psychopathology* (Atkinson & Zucker, 1997) reflected the beginnings of a rapprochement between developmental and clinical researchers. All aforementioned themes are continued in the current volume.

Despite advances represented in *Attachment and Psychopathology* (Atkinson & Zucker, 1997), contributors also identified challenges within the field. In terms of research design, Goldberg pointed to the low yield of individuals developing frank psychopathology in longitudinal designs and to confounded etiology when studying attachment and psychopathology concurrently. Rutter's (1997) list of unresolved issues included limitations with respect to theorizing on behavioral control systems, measurement of attachment security, taxonomy of attachment, child's role in influencing attachment, specificity with respect to internal working models, manifestations of attachment after infancy, differentiation of attachment relationships from other forms of relationships, the role of parenting in attachment outcome, and the role of parenting in later disorder. Fonagy et al. (1997) noted the lack of information on ecological factors as they affect attachment. Van IJzendoorn and Bakermans-Kranenburg (1997) discussed the transmission gap, that is, the fact that maternal sensitivity did not explain all the variance in mediating between maternal mental representations and infant attachment security. These challenges are further addressed, if not always resolved, in this volume.

Another difficulty involved the "measurement roadblock" (Greenberg, 1999, p. 486), the fact that no methodology existed for assessing attachment in early and mid-adolescence. This is an important oversight, as adolescence marks the transition from dependent to caregiver (Allen & Land, 1999). Finally, the issue of intervention received little attention (cf. Lieberman, 1997; Zeanah et al., 1997). Again, in the current volume, all these issues are revisited and developed. In particular, every contributor addresses the issue of intervention, whether as a main focus or as one factor among many.

SINCE 1997

Since *Attachment and Psychopathology* (Atkinson & Zucker, 1997) was published, three developments relevant to links between attachment and psychopathology have emerged: (a) rapid expansion of research and theory regarding disorganized attachment, including a focus on parental behaviors that contribute to it; (b) major consolidations of attachment theory and research; and (c) development of attachment-based interventions.

Disorganization

As early as 1990, Main and Hesse speculated that disorganization had its roots in parental behavior that was frightening to the child. Such behaviors, they argued, place the young child in an insoluble dilemma of "fear without solution": both the source of fear and potential comfort reside in the same person. They subsequently developed an observation tool for identifying parental behaviors of this sort (Main & Hesse, 1992), which has since been modified and expanded by others (e.g., Jacobvitz, Hazen, & Riggs, 1997; Schuengel, Bakermans-Kranenburg, & van IJzendoorn, 1999). Lyons-Ruth and colleagues (Lyons-Ruth & Block, 1996; Lyons-

Ruth, Bronfman, & Parsons, 1997) and Solomon and George (1999) further elaborated the hypothetical processes contributing to disorganized attachment, noting that lack of response can be as frightening as directly threatening or frightening behavior. Lyons-Ruth and Block (1996; see Lyons-Ruth et al., chap. 4, this volume) expanded the Main and Hesse (1992) tool to include five dimensions of caregiver behavior considered to disrupt attachment formation: affective errors, role reversals, fearful or disoriented behavior, intrusive behavior, and withdrawing behaviors. The coding tools resulting from these efforts are now used as research instruments in normative (e.g., Schuengel et al., 1999), risk (Lyons-Ruth et al., 1999), and clinical (Benoit et al., 2001) populations with informative results that are relevant to understanding attachment-psychopathology links.

Research with clinical populations identified other atypical forms of attachment in infants and young children (e.g., Crittenden, 1999). There has been interest in identifying subtypes of disorganized attachment and explicit efforts to identify unique precursors and sequelae of these (e.g., Lyons-Ruth et al., 1999; Solomon & George, 1999; Vondra & Barnett, 1999). In addition, there were efforts to distinguish neurological conditions contributing to atypical behavior from relationship-based experiences that disrupted attachment (e.g., Atkinson et al., 1999; Barnett, Butler, & Vondra, 1999; Pipp-Siegel, Siegel, & Dean, 1999). Much of this work was summarized and evaluated in an edited monograph on "atypical attachment in infancy and early childhood" (Vondra & Barnett, 1999).

Interest in the sequelae of disorganized attachment also expanded with publications linking early disorganization to subsequent cognitive (e.g., Moss, St. Laurent, & Parent, 1999) and behavioral (Lyons-Ruth, 1996) problems as well as to dissociative experiences (Carlson, 1998). Notable publications that summarized these developments include a meta-analysis of disorganized attachment (van IJzendoorn, Schuengel, & Bakermans-Kranenburg, 1999) and an edited book (Solomon & George, 1999) on disorganization. Many chapters of the latter volume draw upon work with clinical populations (e.g., Barnett et al., 1999; Jacobsen & Miller, 1999; Pianta, Marvin, & Morog, 1999), but the primary purpose is to report research bearing on clinical issues, rather than to discuss or evaluate attachment-based clinical interventions. Thus, although these developments clearly demonstrate the relevance of attachment research to clinical issues, clinical interventions per se received minimal attention.

Consolidation

Important volumes that survey and consolidate the larger field of attachment theory and research have recently been published. The first and most comprehensive is the *Handbook of Attachment* (Cassidy & Shaver,

1999), comprised of 37 chapters on a range of attachment topics. These chapters represent varied approaches to the assessment, study, and application of attachment. Seven chapters form a section labeled "Clinical Applications of Attachment Theory and Research." Three of these are reviews of research. The first two summarize what is known about the contributions of early attachment to psychopathology in childhood (Greenberg, 1999) and adulthood (Dozier, Stovall, & Albus, 1999) and the third summarizes the work on disorganization referred to earlier (Lyons-Ruth & Jacobvitz, 1999). The remaining chapters are contributions from clinician-researchers, two focusing primarily on clinical interventions that use attachment constructs and one a theoretical review that compares and contrasts attachment and psychoanalytic theories.

The Cassidy and Shaver (1999) volume is a landmark in the attachment field, a state-of-the-art overview that draws together work from the two broad streams of attachment research, one arising in developmental research on parent-child relationships and the other in the social psychology of adult-adult relationships. It also marks the first time that attachment-based interventions were afforded such prominence in the field. Nevertheless, in the "Emerging Topics and Perspectives" section, only one of ten chapters, on "grief work" following loss and bereavement (Fraley & Shaver, 1999), is clinical in orientation. Among the "18 points" and future studies outlined by Main (1999) in the concluding chapter, clinical applications and implications are not mentioned. Thus, even though clinical applications receive their share of attention, the main thrust of this volume is oblique to the expanding field of attachment and psychopathology.

The *Handbook of Attachment* (Cassidy & Shaver, 1999) is directed primarily at professionals in the attachment field. In the year following its publication, a more accessible (though less comprehensive) overview of the field in the form of a textbook for university-level students appeared (Goldberg, 2000). Like the *Handbook of Attachment*, this volume drew upon and attempted to integrate the two different streams of attachment research. Unlike the *Handbook of Attachment*, though it made efforts to represent divergent opinions, it contained the perspective of a single author and therefore is less representative of the full range of research and theory. Because it was addressed to those taking academic developmental courses, limited attention was given to clinical issues. Nevertheless, it included a chapter on "attachment and mental health," which discussed applications to diagnosis, treatment, and prevention. It also included a chapter on "attachment and physical health," which drew attention to potential applications of attachment theory and research in medical settings. The rapid succession of publication of these monographs, review papers, and volumes testifies to an important period of consolidation in the field of attachment: a time when the field is engaged in summarizing and taking stock of where it stands.

Intervention

The third development, the increasing application of attachment theory to clinical interventions, was well reviewed by Lieberman and Zeanah (1999), Slade (1999), and Byng-Hall (1999). These reviewers reminded us that there is no comprehensive approach to attachment and intervention. Rather, it is often idiosyncratic (Erickson, Korfmacher, & Egeland, 1992), "rudimentary" (Lieberman & Zeanah, 1999, p. 561), and poorly studied (Byng-Hall, 1999; Slade, 1999); efficacy remains controversial (cf. Lieberman, 1999; van IJzendoorn, Juffer, & Duyvesteyn, 1995; but cf. Cicchetti et al., chap. 10, this volume). Nevertheless, the principles of attachment theory are being more broadly applied to pragmatic interventions, infant- and toddler-parent psychotherapy, individual psychotherapy, and couples and family therapy. As Slade (1999) argued, "an understanding of the nature and dynamics of attachment *informs* rather than *defines* intervention and clinical thinking" (p. 577). The last several years, then, have seen the exciting development of a rich and diverse literature on attachment as an intervention framework.

APPLICATIONS OF ATTACHMENT

The contributors to this volume struggle with a variety of clinical challenges across at least three dimensions: (a) form of psychological difficulty (including failure to thrive, social withdrawal, aggression, anxiety, depression, bipolar disorder, dissociation, trauma, schizo-affective disorder, narcissistic personality disorder, eating disorders, and comorbid disorders); (b) life stage (infancy, childhood, adolescence, and adulthood); and (c) application (risk, psychopathology, and intervention). This is a remarkably ambitious agenda.

Consonant with trends to consolidate what is already known, to apply attachment theory in the clinic, and to bring varied research paradigms to light, the contributors adopt several strategies to realize their agenda. First, they reiterate and recombine first principles in order to develop new directions, a sort of *reculer pour mieux sauter* strategy. Second, they study phenomena or circumstances that in fact magnify these first principles, what might be described as a "writ large" strategy. Third, they integrate attachment theory with other frameworks in an effort to expand the explanatory reach of these models. Finally, they bring to bear a comprehensive armamentarium of research technologies. In what follows, we review these strategies.

Return to First Principles

Perhaps the most basic principle of attachment involves the fact that relationships take place in the broader context. Egeland and Carlson (chap. 2) present attachment in its full complexity. They remind us that attachment is just one of a network of influences, including genetic, physiological, psychological, and environmental, that are involved in child development. Moreover, they define attachment itself as a "dynamic multidetermined process based on the interaction of constituents over the course of development." Operating within this changing matrix, the individual is conceptualized as both agent and object. The diversity of human functioning and the probabilistic (as opposed to deterministic) nature of development can only be understood as researchers unravel the issues of continuity and context within this matrix. Egeland and Carlson's data elucidate the continuity of development from infancy to adolescence, the contextual factors that disrupt that continuity and, in fact, the context that influences the impact of those disruptive factors. It is the complexity of Egeland and Carlson's conceptualization of attachment, as one system operating within a complicated matrix, that accounts for their success in prediction across large parts of the lifespan.

Benoit and Coolbear (chap. 3) approach the issue of attachment from the context of disorder, rather than vice versa, but, like Egeland and Carlson, they point to multifactorial etiology and outcome, noting the biological, nutritional, and environmental origins, the biological and socioemotional outcomes, and the interactions amongst these factors, in failure to thrive. The probabilistic, as opposed to deterministic, nature of development is also implicit in Benoit and Coolbear's work; they note that whether attachment plays a role in any given case of failure to thrive, and what the nature of that role is, depends on a host of other factors and relations in the matrix within which attachment operates.

Cicchetti et al. (chap. 10) also underscore the importance of context in their study of intervention for mothers with major depression. These authors recognize the impact of broad ecological factors, such as low socioeconomic status, on mother-child attachment relations. They also discuss factors that are more immediately associated with depression and that affect parenting and attachment, including more frequent parenting hassles, poorer marriages, less social support, less self-validation, and greater emotional difficulties.

Lyons-Ruth et al. (chap. 4) and Hilburn-Cobb (chap. 5) discuss attachment within the matrix of goal-corrected behavioral systems. These authors reiterate that attachment is just one such system. This assumption is pivotal to the metapsychology of attachment theory (Bowlby, 1969/1982) but remains peripheral to research and applied considerations. Lyons-Ruth et al. remind us that most interactions between child and parent, even in infancy, do not involve the attachment system. Hilburn-Cobb points out that, just as attachment involves proximity seeking, so too do other behavioral control systems, such as affiliation, sexuality, caregiving, subordination or submission, and dominance: Different systems subsume the same behaviors and the same behaviors serve different systems. However, Lyons-Ruth et al. and Hilburn-Cobb identify another basic premise that renders the confound of behavioral systems manageable: Attachment serves a protective function and as such is the preemptive distress-regulating behavioral system (see also chaps. by Benoit & Coolbear, Cicchetti et al., and Johnson). Therefore, by studying individuals and dyads under protection- and distress-relevant circumstances, one can magnify distinctions between systems (as discussed later) and better identify the system under consideration.

Kobak and Esposito (chap. 6) review multiple findings and constructs that are central to attachment theory but that are not well integrated with one another. These include internal working models, attachment strategies, open communication, states of mind, and reflective function. Based on the assumption that parents and children process attachment information at multiple levels, Kobak and Esposito systematize and reframe these constructs to develop a Levels of Processing model, which integrates the major findings from the past two decades of attachment research.

In a chapter complementing that of Kobak and Esposito, Dozier and Bates (chap. 7) return to first principles to examine interpersonal interaction, particularly between client and clinician, from the perspective of interacting internal working models. Dozier and Bates point out that the client-clinician relationship is an attachment relationship, the clinician representing someone stronger and wiser who provides caregiving and treatment often aimed at modifying the way the client processes attachment-relevant information. Along with other pertinent information, Dozier and Bates present data on the clinical interaction of clients and clinicians with varying attachment representations. These data show that the interaction between clients' and clinicians' states of mind influences the shape of the intervention and perhaps client outcomes.

Slade begins chapter 8 with four basic assumptions of attachment theory (the baby is motivated from birth to form primary relationships, the infant will do what is necessary to maintain these relationships and their disruption can lead to lifelong disturbance, the child's adaptations to the caregiver lead to stable patterns of defense and affect regulation, and the caregiver's organization of attachment profoundly influences the child's representations), some data on the morphology of insecure attachment, and the construct of metacognitive modeling. Neatly incorporating and instantiating these simple premises, Slade presents two case studies, one demonstrating the extremes of the dismissing attachment strategy and its consequences, the other the extremes of the preoccupied strategy. Here again the power and parsimony of first principles are shown to clarify, deepen, and advance our understanding of theory and application.

Johnson (chap. 9) takes as her starting point two definitions of attachment: attachment as a tie or bond, perhaps most closely associated with Ainsworth's (1978) theorizing, and attachment as a protective and distress-regulating system, reflecting Bowlby's (1969/1982, 1973, 1980) original formulation. Johnson combines these definitions in the remarkably fitting context of emotionally focused couples therapy for posttraumatic stress disorder. Emotionally focused couples therapy is designed to foment the protective, emotionally regulating aspect of the love relationship. As do other contributors, Johnson illustrates that the reexamination of basic attachment principles in the clinical context leads to diverse new approaches and insights.

Amplifying the Signal

As discussed previously (see also Rutter, 1997), the complicated context within which attachment relations take place can serve to confound the study of attachment itself. However, the contributors to this book adopt a variety of strategies to magnify the attachment process so that it can be scrutinized over and above its context. The first of these strategies was reviewed earlier, namely isolation and reintegration of basic principles.

Contributors also select populations that magnify attachment principles and processes. Several authors take advantage of the protective and distress-regulating role of attachment to study relationship issues. Lyons-Ruth et al. (chap. 4) and Hilburn-Cobb (chap. 5) examine these dynamics where they are distorted or blocked, in disorganized attachment. In studying failure to thrive, Benoit and Coolbear (chap. 3) scrutinize the attachment relations of mothers and infants whose physical well-being is actually under threat. Egeland and Carlson (chap. 2) also include such populations by predicting adolescent anxiety disorders and dissociation from attachment status in infancy in a socially disadvantaged sample.

In studying posttraumatic stress disorder resulting from relationship violations, Johnson (chap. 9) notes that "trauma increases the need for protective attachment and, at the same time, renders those attachments direct sources of danger." This, of course, is identical to the dynamics of disorganization, as described by Main and Hesse (1990; see chaps. by Lyons-Ruth et al. and Hilburn-Cobb) and explains the link between disorganization and posttraumatic stress disorder reported by Egeland and Carl-son (chap. 2).

Cicchetti et al. (chap. 10) investigate infants of depressed mothers, whose lack of maternal availability is over determined by extreme psychological difficulty, probable maternal absences, and the adverse familial correlates of major depression. However, to further amplify the issue of attachment per se and, more specifically, the role of maternal mental representations and behavior, Cicchetti et al. confine their sample to mothers without co-occurring poverty and associated risk factors. In this way, they ensure that treatment advantages derive from attachment-relevant intervention and that they influence attachment-relevant constructs.

Integration and Theory Expansion

Challenged by observations within the clinic and by the need not just to study attachment processes but also to change them, contributors integrate attachment theories with other paradigms to expand and refine existing theory. Egeland and Carlson (chap. 2) make predictions within the context of ecological and developmental psychopathology frameworks. Similarly, Benoit and Coolbear (chap. 3) utilize the attachment framework to explain failure to thrive, but, respecting the extant biological, nutritional, and ecological data, they resist simple conclusions, arguing that the causes of failure to thrive, are likely multiple and varied. Lyons-Ruth et al. (chap. 4) argue that ecological factors influence the way in which disorganized parents interact with their infants and, consequently, the manifestation of infant disorganization. Kobak and Esposito (chap. 6) incorporate ecological factors into their assessment and treatment protocol.

Hilburn-Cobb (chap. 5) draws on British social psychology to argue for the hierarchical interaction of attachment, affiliation, and subordination-submission control systems within all insecure attachment relationships. Kobak and Esposito (chap. 6) compare internal working models to the core cognitive schemas that form the basis of cognitive behavioral therapies. They also point out the utility of structural family therapy conceptions and techniques. Dozier and Bates (chap. 7) refer to techniques (i.e., paradoxical injunction) borrowed from family systems therapists.

Several investigators augment attachment theory with psychodynamic principles. Egeland and Carlson (chap. 2) couch (if we may use the term) their intervention recommendations in psychoanalytic terms, noting the centrality of the therapeutic alliance to attachment-based therapy. Hilburn-Cobb (chap. 5) cites Winnicott on the necessity of patience in waiting for some clients to reexperience a need for primary attachment within a significant therapeutic regression. Dozier and Bates (chap. 7) highlight the issue of transference in attachment-relevant therapy. Slade (chap. 8) outlines the ways in which attachment research influences her psychoanalytically oriented practice and Cicchetti et al. (chap. 10) evaluate the efficacy of toddler-parent psychotherapy, Lieberman's "iteration" (Lieberman & Zeanah, 1999, p. 562) of Fraiberg's (1980) psychoanalytic Child Development Project. Although the reintegration of attachment and psychoanalytic theories is not without critics (Rutter, 1997), it does represent the combination of two rich paradigms.

Contributors also work within the constraints of attachment theory, but unravel its implications in novel ways. Lyons-Ruth et al. (chap. 4) and Hilburn-Cobb (chap. 5) reexamine the issue of disorganization, devilicating the construct to augment its explanatory power. Puzzled by the different manifestations of disorganization in the preschool years, Lyons-Ruth et al. describe two groups of parents of disorganized infants, one group "hostile or self-referential," the other "helpless or fearful" regarding attachment. Lyons-Ruth et al. argue that these parents have different attachment histories and demonstrate that they interact differently with their babies. These infants, in turn, manifest their attachment through different forms of controlling behavior, such as punitive and caregiving, respectively. Hilburn-Cobb distinguishes among adolescents who are "disorganized," "controlling," and "frankly disorganized." She maintains that disorganized adolescents struggle to maintain attachment relations, however ineffectually; controlling adolescents forsake attachment altogether in favor of other behavioral control systems; and frankly disorganized adolescents lack any control system whatsoever.

Kobak and Esposito (chap. 6) integrate a variety of central attachment constructs in their Levels of Processing model and demonstrate how this model can be used to distinguish among secure, anxious, and distressed parent-teen relationships and to establish treatment goals to promote relationship security.

Johnson (chap. 9) molds basic attachment tenets into emotionally focused couples therapy (EFT), an intervention that "focuses on partners' emotional responses and how these responses organize attachment behaviors.... EFT sees marital distress through the lens of separation distress and insecure attachment and helps couples shift their interactional positions in the direction of accessibility and responsiveness so that a secure bond can be established." In combination, the aforementioned theory integration and expansion reflect a remarkable set of advances.

Data Analysis Strategies

By combining laboratory and clinical research, the contributors generate a proliferation of research methodologies. Egeland and Carlson (chap. 2) use a quantitative longitudinal design to predict behavior disorder in childhood and adolescence from attachment in infancy. Their success in doing so is astonishing. Benoit and Coolbear (chap. 3) and Hilburn-Cobb (chap. 5) use concurrent designs to study attachment relationships in clinical samples. Each is remarkable for different reasons. Failure to thrive is a bona fide disorder of infancy. Despite the huge empirical literature on early attachment, developmentalists have almost universally studied caregiving environments and insecure attachment as risk factors for subsequent disorder. Benoit and Coolbear show that failure to thrive provides the researcher with an opportunity to study the origins of attachment insecurity and disorder in the emergent stage. Hilburn-Cobb addresses the neglected area of adolescence, developing an observational method for coding attachment and applying it to adolescents as they relate to both mother and father. Cicchetti et al. (chap. 10) completed a randomized clinical trial to evaluate the efficacy of toddler-parent psychotherapy. They demonstrate the efficacy of this intervention and begin to disentangle the causal roles of maternal sensitivity and mental representations in the child's attachment security. This is the first intervention for mothers with depression that has been shown to modify attachment security.

Almost all authors include case study material. Lyons-Ruth et al. (chap. 4) and Hilburn-Cobb (chap. 5) instantiate the practical implications of their theoretical and quantitative findings with case studies. Dozier and Bates (chap. 7) and Slade (chap. 8) present cases detailing the role of attachment theory in case formulation. Johnson (chap. 9) illustrates the working principles of EFT with material excerpted from therapy. Cicchetti et al. (chap. 10) include discussion of two cases in addition to the randomized clinical trial.

In this book, we see the integration of Bowlby's (1969/1982, 1973, 1980) clinical theory and methodology, Ainsworth's (1978) developmental conceptions and empirical method, and the advances subsequently constructed on their foundations. Bowlby's dream has truly come full circle (Cicchetti, Toth, & Lynch, 1995). We hope that the vision of the contributors with differing emphases, frameworks, populations, and methodologies engaged in a common pursuit will inspire developmentalists and clinicians, researchers and practitioners alike.

REFERENCES

Ainsworth, M. D. S., Blehar, M. C., Waters, E., & Wall, S. (1978). *Patterns of attachment: A psychological study of the strange situation.* Hillsdale, NJ: Lawrence Erlbaum Associates.
Allen, J. P., & Land, D. (1999). Attachment in adolescence. In J. Cassidy & P. R. Shaver (Eds.), *Handbook of attachment: Theory, research and clinical applications* (pp. 319–335). New York: Guilford Press.

Atkinson, L. (1997). Attachment and psychopathology. In L. Atkinson & K. Zucker (Eds.), *Attachment and psychopathology* (pp. 3–16). New York: Guilford Press.

Atkinson, L., Chisholm, V. C., Scott, B., Goldberg, S., Vaughn, B. E., Blackwell, J., Dickens, S., & Tam, F. (1999). Maternal sensitivity, child functional level, and attachment in Down Syndrome. In J. I. Vondra & D. Barnett (Eds.), *Atypical attachment in infancy and early childhood among children at developmental risk* (Society for Research in Child Development Monograph No. 238, pp. 45–66). New York: Guilford Press.

Atkinson, L., & Zucker, K. (Eds.). (1997). *Attachment and psychopathology.* New York: Guilford Press.

Barnett, D., & Vondra, J. I. (1999). Atypical patterns of early attachment: Theory, research and current directions. In J. I. Vondra & D. Barnett (Eds.), *Atypical attachment in infancy and early childhood among children at developmental risk* (Society for Research in Child Development Monograph No. 238, pp. 1–24). Malden, MA: Blackwell.

Barnett, D., Butler, C. M., & Vondra, J. I. (1999). Atypical patterns of early attachment: Discussion and future directions. In J. I. Vondra & D. Barnett (Eds.), *Atypical attachment in infancy and early childhood among children at developmental risk* (Society for Research in Child Development Monograph No. 238, pp. 172–192). Malden, MA: Blackwell.

Barnett, D., Hunt, K. H., Butler, C. M., McCaskill IV, J. W., Kaplan-Estrin, M., & Pipp-Siegel, S. (1999). Indices of attachment disorganization among toddlers with neurological and non-neurological problems. In J. Solomon & C. George (Eds.), *Attachment disorganization* (pp. 189–212). New York: Guilford Press.

Belsky, J., & Nezworski, T. (Eds.). (1988). *Clinical implications of attachment.* Hillsdale, NJ: Lawrence Erlbaum Associates.

Bowlby, J. (1973). *Attachment and loss: Vol. 2. Separation: Anxiety and anger.* New York: Basic Books.

Bowlby, J. (1980). *Attachment and loss: Vol. 3. Loss: Sadness and depression.* New York: Basic Books.

Bowlby, J. (1982). *Attachment and loss: Vol. 1. Attachment.* New York: Basic Books. (Original work published 1969)

Bretherton, I. (1985). Attachment theory: Retrospect and prospect. In I. Bretherton & E. Waters (Eds.), *Growing points in attachment theory and research* (Society for Research in Child Development Monograph No. 209, pp. 3–36). Malden, MA: Blackwell.

Bretherton, I., Walsh, R., Lependorf, M., & Georgeson, H. (1997). Attachment networks in postdivorce families: The maternal perspective. In L. Atkinson & K. Zucker (Eds.), *Attachment and psychopathology* (pp. 97–134). New York: Guilford Press.

Byng-Hall, J. (1999). Family and couple therapy: Towards greater security. In J. Cassidy & P. R. Shaver (Eds.), *Handbook of attachment: Theory, research and clinical applications* (pp. 625–645). New York: Guilford Press.

Carlson, E. A. (1998). A prospective longitudinal study of attachment disorganization/disorientation. *Child Development, 69,* 1107–1129.

Carlson, V., Cicchetti, D., Barnett, D., & Braunwald, K. (1989). Disorganized/disoriented attachment relations in maltreated infants. *Developmental Psychology, 25,* 525–531.

Cassidy, J., & Marvin, R. S., with the MacArthur Working Group on Attachment. (1992). *Attachment organization in three and four year olds: Procedures and coding manual.* Unpublished manuscript, University of Virginia, Charlottesville.

Cassidy, J., & Shaver, P. R. (Eds.). (1999). *Handbook of attachment: Theory, research and clinical applications.* New York: Guilford Press.

Cicchetti, D., & Barnett, D. (1991). Attachment organization in maltreated preschoolers. *Development and Psychopathology, 4,* 397–411.

Cicchetti, D., Toth, S. L., & Lynch, M. (1995). Bowlby's dream comes full circle: The application of attachment theory to risk and psychopathology. In T. H. Ollendick & R. J. Prinz (Eds.), *Advances in clinical child psychology* (Vol. 17, pp. 1–75). New York: Plenum Press.

Cole-Detke, H., & Kobak, R. (1996). Attachment processes in eating disorder and depression. *Journal of Consulting and Clinical Psychology, 64,* 282–290.

Crittenden, P. M. (1997). Patterns of attachment and sexual behaviour: Risk of dysfunction versus opportunity for creative integration. In L. Atkinson & K. Zucker (Eds.), *Attachment and psychopathology* (pp. 47–93). New York: Guilford Press.

Crittenden, P. M. (1999). Danger and development: The organization of self-protective strategies. In J. I. Vondra & D. Barnett (Eds.), *Atypical attachment in infancy and early childhood among children at developmental risk* (Society for Research in Child Development Monograph No. 238, pp. 145–171).

DeKlyen, M., Speltz, M. L., & Greenberg, M. T. (1996, January). *Predicting early starting behaviour disorders: A clinic sample of preschool appositional defiant boys.* Paper presented at the International Society for Research in Child and Adolescent Psychopathology, Santa Monica, CA.

Downey, G., & Coyne, J. C. (1990). Children of depressed parents: An integrative review. *Psychological Bulletin, 108,* 50–76.

Dozier, M., Stovall, K. C., & Albus, K. (1999). Attachment and psychopathology in adulthood. In J. Cassidy & P. R. Shaver (Eds.), *Handbook of attachment: Theory, research and clinical applications* (pp. 497–519). New York: Guilford Press.

Erickson, M. F., Korfmacher, J., & Egeland, B. (1992). Attachments past and present: Implications for the therapeutic intervention with mother-infant dyads. *Development and Psychopathology, 4,* 405–504.

Erickson, M. F., Sroufe, L. A., & Egeland, B. (1985). The relationship between quality of attachment and behaviour problems in preschool in a high risk sample. In I. Bretherton & E. Waters (Eds.), *Growing points in attachment theory and research* (Society for Research in Child Development Monograph No. 209, pp. 147–186). Blackwell.

Fonagy, P., Leigh, T., Steele, M., Steele, H., Kennedy, R., Mattoon, G., Target, M., & Gerber, A. (1996). The relation of attachment status, psychiatric classification, and response to psychotherapy. *Journal of Consulting and Clinical Psychology, 64,* 22–31.

Fonagy, P., Target, M., Steele, M., Steele, H., Leigh, T., Levinson, A., & Kennedy, R. (1997). Morality, disruptive behaviour, borderline personality disorder, crime and their relationship to security of attachment. In L. Atkinson & K. Zucker (Eds.), *Attachment and psychopathology* (pp. 223–274). New York: Guilford Press.

Fraiberg, S. (1980). *Clinical studies in infant mental health: The first year of life.* New York: Basic Books.

Fraley, R. C., & Shaver, P. R. (1999). Loss and bereavement: Attachment theory and recent controversies concerning "grief work" and the nature of detachment. In J. Cassidy & P. R. Shaver (Eds.), *Handbook of attachment: Theory, research and clinical applications* (pp. 735–769). New York: Guilford Press.

George, C., Kaplan, N., & Main, M. (1984). *Adult Attachment Interview.* Unpublished manuscript, University of California at Berkeley.

Goldberg, S. (1997). Attachment and childhood behaviour problems in normal, at-risk and clinical samples. In L. Atkinson & K. Zucker (Eds.), *Attachment and psychopathology* (pp. 171–195). New York: Guilford Press.

Goldberg, S. (2000). *Attachment and development.* London: Arnold.

Goldberg, S., Grusec, J., & Jenkins, J. (1999). Confidence in protection: Arguments for a narrow definition of attachment. *Journal of Family Psychology, 13,* 475–483.

Greenberg, M. T. (1999). Attachment and psychopathology in childhood. In J. Cassidy & P. R. Shaver (Eds.), *Handbook of attachment: Theory, research and clinical applications* (pp. 469–496). New York: Guilford Press.

Greenberg, M. T., DeKlyen, M., Speltz, M. L., & Endriga, M. C. (1997). The role of attachment processes in externalizing psychopathology in young children. In L. Atkinson & K. Zucker (Eds.), *Attachment and psychopathology* (pp. 196–222). New York: Guilford Press.

Greenberg, M. T., Speltz, M. L., DeKlyen, M., & Endriga, M. C. (1991). Attachment security in preschoolers with and without externalizing problems: A replication. *Development and Psychopathology, 3,* 413–430.

Holmes, J. (1993). *John Bowlby and attachment theory.* London: Routledge.

Jacobson, T., & Miller, L. J. (1999). Attachment quality in young children of mentally ill mothers: Contribution of maternal caregiving abilities and foster care context. In J. Solomon & C. George (Eds.), *Attachment disorganization* (pp. 347–378). New York: Guilford Press.

Jacobvitz, D., Hazen, N., & Riggs, S. (1997, April). Disorganized mental processes in mothers, frightening/frightened caregiving, and disoriented/disorganized behaviour in infancy. Symposium paper presented at the Meeting of the Society for Research in Child Development, Washington, DC.

Lewis, M., Feiring, C., McGuffog, C., & Jaskir, J. (1984). Predicting psychopathology in six-year-olds from early social relations. *Child Development, 55,* 123–156.

Lieberman, A. F. (1997). Toddlers' internalization of maternal attributions as a factor in quality of attachment. In L. Atkinson & K. Zucker (Eds.), *Attachment and psychopathology* (pp. 277–291). New York: Guilford Press.

Lieberman, A. F., & Zeanah, C. H. (1999). Contributions of attachment theory to infant-parent psychotherapy and other interventions with infants and young children. In J. Cassidy & C. George (Eds.), *Handbook of attachment: Theory, research and clinical applications* (pp. 555–574). New York: Guilford Press.

Lyons-Ruth, K. (1996). Disorganized/disoriented attachment in the etiology of dissociative disorders. *Dissociation, 4,* 196–204.

Lyons-Ruth, K., Alpern, L., & Repacholi, B. (1993). Disorganized infant attachment classification and maternal psychosocial problems as predictors of hostile-aggressive behaviour in the preschool classroom. *Child Development, 64,* 572–585.

Lyons-Ruth, K., & Block, D. (1996). The disturbed caregiving system: Relations among childhood trauma, maternal caregiving, and infant affect and attachment. *Infant Mental Health Journal, 17,* 257–275.

Lyons-Ruth, K., Bronfman, E., & Parsons, E. (1999). Maternal frightened frightening or atypical behaviour and disorganized infant attachment patterns. In J. Vondra & D. Barnett (Eds.), *Atypical attachment in infancy and early childhood* (Society for Research in Child Development Monograph No. 209, pp. 67–96). Malden, MA: Blackwell.

Lyons-Ruth, K., Connell, D., Grunebaum, H., & Botein, S. (1990). Infants at social risk: Maternal depression and family support services as mediators of infant development and security of attachment. *Child Development, 61,* 85–98.

Lyons-Ruth, K., & Jacobvitz, D. (1999). Attachment disorganization: Unresolved loss, relational violence, and lapses in behavioral and attentional strategies. In J. Cassidy & C. George (Eds.), *Handbook of attachment: Theory, research and clinical applications* (pp. 520–554). New York: Guilford Press.

Main, M. (1999). Attachment theory: Eighteen points with suggestions for future studies. In J. Cassidy & P. R. Shaver (Eds.), *Handbook of attachment: Theory, research and clinical applications* (pp. 845–888). New York: Guilford Press.

Main, M., & Hesse, E. (1990). Parents' unresolved traumatic experiences are related to infant disorganized attachment status: Is frightened and/or frightening behaviour the linking mechanism? In M. T. Greenberg, D. Cicchetti, & E. M. Cummings (Eds.), *Attachment in the preschool years* (pp. 161–182). Chicago: University of Chicago Press.

Main, M., & Hesse, E. (1992). Disorganized/disoriented infant behaviour in the strange situation, lapses in the monitoring of reasoning and discourse during the parent's Adult Attachment Interview and dissociative states. In M. Ammaniti & D. Stern (Eds.), *Attachment and psychoanalysis* (pp. 161–184). Rome: Guis, Laterza, & Figli.

Main, M., Kaplan, N., & Cassidy, J. (1985). Security in infancy, childhood and adulthood: A move to the level of representation. In I. Bretherton & E. Waters (Eds.), *Growing points of attachment theory and research* (Society for Research in Child Development, Monograph No. 209, pp. 66–104). Blackwell.

Main, M., & Solomon, J. (1986). Discovery of a new, insecure-disorganized/disoriented attachment pattern. In M. Yogman & T. B. Brazelton (Eds.), *Affective development in infancy* (pp. 95–124). Norwood, NJ: Ablex.

Main, M., & Solomon, J. (1990). Procedures for identifying infants as disorganized/disoriented during the Ainsworth Strange Situation. In M. T. Greenberg, D. Cicchetti, & E. M. Cummings (Eds.), *Attachment in the preschool years: Theory, research, and intervention* (pp. 121–160). Chicago: University of Chicago Press.

Manassis, K., Bradley, S., Goldberg, S., Hood, J., & Swinson, R. P. (1994). Attachment in mothers with anxiety disorders and their children. *Journal of the Academy of Child and Adolescent Psychiatry, 33,* 1106–1113.

Moss, E., St. Laurent, D., & Parent, S. (1999). Disorganized attachment developmental risk at school age. In C. George & J. Solomon (Eds.), *Attachment disorganization* (pp. 160–188). New York: Guilford Press.

Patrick, M., Hobson, R. P., Castle, D., Howard, R., & Maughan, B. (1994). Personality disorder and the mental representation of early social experience. *Development and Psychopathology, 6,* 375–388.

Pianta, R. C., Marvin, R. S., & Morog, M. C. (1999). Resolving the past and present: Relations with attachment organization. In J. Solomon & C. George (Eds.), *Attachment disorganization* (pp. 379–398). New York: Guilford Press.

Pipp-Siegel, S., Siegel, C. H., & Dean, J. (1999). Neurological aspects of the disorganized/disoriented attachment classification system: Differentiating quality of the attachment relationship from neurological treatment. In J. I. Vondra & D. Barnett (Eds.), *Atypical attachment in infancy and early childhood among children at developmental risk* (Society for Research in Child Development Monograph No. 238, pp. 25–44).

Radke-Yarrow, M., Cummings, E. M., Kuczynski, L., & Chapman, M. (1985). Patterns in attachment in two- and three-year-olds in normal families and families with parental depression. *Child Development, 29,* 358–545.

Rosenstein, D. S., & Horowitz, H. A. (1996). Adolescent attachment and psychopathology. *Journal of Consulting and Clinical Psychology, 64,* 244–253.

Rutter, M. (1997). Clinical implications of attachment concepts: Retrospect and prospect. In L. Atkinson & K. Zucker (Eds.), *Attachment and psychopathology* (pp. 17–46). New York: Guilford Press.

Schuengel, C., Bakermans-Kranenburg, M. J., & van IJzendoorn, M. H. (1999). Frightening maternal behaviour linking unresolved loss and disorganized infant attachment. *Journal of Consulting and Clinical Psychology, 67,* 54–63.

Shaw, D. S., & Vondra, J. I. (1995). Infant attachment security and maternal predictors of early behaviour problems: A longitudinal study of low-income families. *Journal of Abnormal Child Psychology, 23,* 335–357.

Slade, A. (1999). Attachment theory and research: Implications for the theory and practice of individual psychotherapy with adults. In J. Cassidy & P. R. Shaver (Eds.), *Handbook of attachment: Theory, research and clinical applications* (pp. 575–594). New York: Guilford Press.

Solomon, J., & George, C. (Eds.). (1999). *Attachment disorganization.* New York: Guilford Press.

Speltz, M. L., Greenberg, M. T., & DeKlyen, M. (1990). Attachment in preschoolers with disruptive behaviour: A comparison of clinic-referred and nonproblem children. *Development and Psychopathology, 2,* 31–46.

Sroufe, L. A., & Rutter, M. (1984). The domain of psychopathology. *Child Development, 55,* 17–29.

van IJzendoorn, M. H., & Bakermans-Kranenburg, M. J. (1997). Intergenerational transmission of attachment: A move to the contextual level. In L. Atkinson & K. Zucker (Eds.), *Attachment and psychopathology* (pp. 135–170). New York: Guilford Press.

van IJzendoorn, M. H., Goldberg, S., Kroonenberg, P. M., & Frenkel, O. J. (1992). The relative effects of maternal and child problems on the quality of attachment: A meta-analysis of attachment in clinical samples. *Child Development, 59,* 147–156.

van IJzendoorn, M. H., Juffer, F., & Duyvesteyn, M. G. C. (1995). Breaking the inter-generational cycle of insecure attachment: A review of the effects of attachment-based interventions on maternal sensitivity and infant security. *Journal of Child Psychology and Psychiatry, 36,* 225–248.

van IJzendoorn, M. H., Schuengel, C., & Bakermans-Kranenburg, M. J. (1999). Disorganized attachment in early childhood: Meta-analysis of precursors, concomitants and sequelae. *Development and Psychopathology, 11,* 225–249.

Warren, S. L., Huston, L., Egeland, B., & Sroufe, L. A. (1997). Child and adolescent anxiety disorders and early attachment. *Journal of the American Academy of Child and Adolescent Psychiatry, 36,* 637–644.

Zeanah, C. H., Finley-Belgrad, E., & Benoit, D. (1997). Intergenerational transmission of relationship psychopathology: A mother-infant case study. In L. Atkinson & K. Zucker (Eds.), *Attachment and psychopathology* (pp. 292–318). New York: Guilford Press.

2

Attachment and Psychopathology

Byron Egeland
Elizabeth A. Carlson
University of Minnesota

Attachment theory (Bowlby, 1969/1982) from its beginning was concerned with the implications of atypical patterns of attachment as well as the formation and course of normal infant-parent relationships. Bowlby (1944) formulated his ideas of personality development in part to explain the link between early emotional deprivation and later pathology in the lives of 44 thieves and as a guide for the diagnosis and treatment of emotionally disturbed children and families. Thus, attachment theory is a theory of both psychopathology and normal development.

Central to Bowlby's (1969/1982) theory was the notion of process. Bowlby posited specific propositions regarding the manner in which early experience might contribute to later psychological well-being or pathology. He began by distinguishing the idea of individual differences from causal traits, conceptualizing attachment as a pattern of organized behavior developed over time within a caregiving relationship, not a trait that infants have in varying quantity (Sroufe & Waters, 1977). He considered early experience to be a foundation for later development, but one transformed by subsequent experience. Bowlby wrote that individual development "turns at each and every stage of the journey on an interaction between the organism as it has developed up to that moment and the environment in which it then finds itself" (1969/1982 p. 364). Psychopathology and normal functioning are conceived as dynamic multideter-mined processes based on the interaction of constituents over the course of development (e.g., Sameroff, 1989).

In this chapter, we elaborate on the theoretical implications of the Bowlby-Ainsworth attachment theory for developmental psychopathology, illustrating the links between attachment and psychopathology using data drawn primarily from the Minnesota Longitudinal Study of Parents and Children.

PSYCHOPATHOLOGY AS DEVELOPMENTAL CONSTRUCTION

According to attachment theory and consistent with ecological perspectives, children develop within a network of influences operating on many levels (e.g., genetic, physiological, psychological, environmental; Bronfenbrenner, 1986). Whereas some factors influence the child directly, others have an indirect impact through their influence on parenting. Developmental context is emphasized because "changes in circumstances can lead to changes in interaction and therefore to changes in relationships" (Vaughn, Waters, Egeland, & Sroufe, 1979, p. 974). Within this process the individual is viewed as an active participant in shaping and creating experience and the child's history of experience is a critical part of the developmental context. The child brings to each new developmental challenge all of his or her prior experience, and the child and context become mutually transforming (cf. Sameroff & Chandler, 1975).

Bowlby's ideas regarding the roles of prior experience and current circumstances in adaptation and psychopathology are summarized in the concept of developmental pathways (Bowlby, 1969/1982, 1973). The model (often depicted as a railyard or branching tree) incorporates several key ideas (Sroufe, 1991, 1997). First, there is great diversity even in normality. Second, prior to the onset of psychopathology, certain developmental pathways represent adaptational failures that probabilistically forecast later pathology. However, outcomes of given pathways may vary; some may be related to pathology and others not (multifinality). Ongoing circumstances may support the individual following potentially deviating developmental pathways or deflect the individual back toward more normal functioning. Early development on a particular pathway does not determine final outcome, but instead initiates a set of possibilities. Third, psychopathology results from a series of successive adaptations. Risk factors (e.g., anxious attachment in infancy) may initiate a process of disturbance, however, psychopathology becomes likely only if subsequent adaptations continue to represent deviation from positive functioning. Fourth, change is possible at each phase of development. Change is constrained by prior adaptation, however, and alterations in some forms of adaptation may be more likely for certain individuals than for others.

Role of Early Experience

Attachment theory encompasses an organizational perspective on development wherein adaptation in each developmental period builds upon and transforms preceding functioning (Sroufe, 1996). From this view, early experience has special significance because it provides the foundation for the child's subsequent transactions with the environment. The child interprets and creates new experiences based on experiences of emotional closeness in the earliest relationships (Bowlby, 1988). Early experiences derive special significance from their nature: They are preverbal, not accessible to verbal recall, and less readily modified by subsequent experience (Sroufe, Carlson, Levy, & Egeland, 1999). These early variations in quality of emotional connectedness, confidence regarding the availability of others, and feelings of self-worth may be the legacy of infancy (Sroufe, Levy, & Carlson, 1998).

Continuity in Adaptation

From the perspective of attachment theory, continuity in adaptation and functioning in later relationships may be supported by several mechanisms, including stability in quality of care, broader environmental influences, and prior history of development. In the Minnesota longitudinal study, stability and change in caregiving quality were related to contextual factors both within and across developmental periods. For example, continuity in maternal sensitivity was found in infancy (Egeland & Farber, 1984) and from infancy to preschool (Pianta, Sroufe, & Egeland, 1989). Across both developmental periods, maternal stress accounted for declines in sensitivity, whereas social support was related to increases in maternal sensitivity. In turn, quality of caregiving was related to child adaptation across periods of early development. Continuity in attachment classification between 12 and 18 months was found for 60% of the sample in infancy (Egeland & Farber). Change in classification from anxious to secure for boys was related to improvement in mother-child interactions, increased stability in mothers' close relationships, and decreases in life stress. For girls, discontinuity was related to maternal personality characteristics.

From an organizational perspective, continuity in child adaptation is also supported by the child's prior history of relationship experiences. The child actively participates in constructing experience in at least three ways: (a) by behaving in ways that elicit responses that support prior adaptation, (b) by making choices that selectively engage aspects of the environment supporting a particular adaptive style, and (c) by interpreting new and ambiguous situations in ways that are consistent with earlier experience.

Bowlby (1973) employed the concept of "internal working model" to explain the manner in which individuals make use of prior history in constructing experience. He proposed that children extract from their experience expectations regarding the likely behavior of others and themselves in relationships. Substantial research confirms the idea that children with varying early histories construe the environment differently. Attachment-related differences have been revealed in the completions of stories with separation themes (Bretherton, Ridgeway, & Cassidy, 1990), symbolic play (Rosenberg, 1984), reactions to cartoons depicting potential social conflict (Suess, Grossmann, & Sroufe, 1992), reactions to family photographs (Main, 1993), family drawings (Fury, Carlson, & Sroufe, 1997; Main), and memories for affective-cognitive stimuli (Belsky, Spritz, & Crnic, 1996; Rieder & Cicchetti, 1989). These studies show that children with insecure histories are more likely to attribute negative intent in ambiguous social situations and less likely to bring fantasized conflicts to successful resolution and to see themselves as connected to others, especially family members. Furthermore, these studies, based on cognitive frameworks, are compatible with literature on the significance of early experience for brain system development (e.g., Cicchetti & Tucker, 1994; Schore, 1994) and for basic patterns of emotional regulation (Sroufe, 1996, 1997).

EARLY RELATIONSHIP DISTURBANCE

Bowlby's work emphasizing the quality of early adaptation and continuity in experience provides a framework for conceptualizing early relationship disturbances and their links to psychopathology (Sroufe, 1989). Disturbed early relationships are viewed as markers of a process that leaves individuals vulnerable to normative stresses and the development of pathology (Sameroff & Emde, 1989). Although disturbance within the child may manifest itself at an early age (infancy or toddlerhood) in the context of extreme deprivation or maltreatment, in most cases early disturbance lies within the dyadic relationship and only gradually takes the form of enduring disturbance within the child.

From an attachment theory perspective, anxious attachment patterns are viewed as dyadic regulatory patterns that maximize infant opportunities for closeness with the primary caregiver in the context of unavailable or intermittently available parenting (Sroufe et al., 1999). Avoidant infants maintain proximity to the caregiver by minimizing signals of distress and negativity that may alienate a rejecting caregiver (Main, 1981). Infants classified as resistant employ heightened distress signals to maintain the attention of intermittently responsive caregivers. Behaviors associated with the disorganized category (e.g., stereotypies, unusual behavioral sequences) enable infants to maintain proximity in the context of frightening caregiver behavior and internal conflict (Main & Hesse, 1990).

Relationship patterns from infancy are carried forward as characteristic modes of affective regulation and core expectations, attitudes, and beliefs. The variations and distortions in early regulatory patterns provide the basis for differences in strategies for coping with normative stresses, eliciting support from others, and making use of internal signals (Carlson & Sroufe, 1995). As a result, individuals with histories of insecure attachment may be more likely to form relationships that are unsupportive and easily disrupted. For the child with an avoidant history, early experiences support a view of the self as unworthy of care and unable to achieve emotional closeness and a behavioral style of isolation. For the child with a history of unpredictable or inconsistent caregiving experiences, negative emotions disrupt rather than restore relationships, inhibiting the development of stable close relationships. Individual continuity in such patterns results, in part, because nonconscious, underlying processes are no longer a part of conscious social interchange and subject to environmental feedback and revision (Sroufe et al., 1999).

For children with avoidant or resistant histories, emotions that would have facilitated affective communication and exchange are defensively modified or cut off (Carlson & Sroufe, 1995; Kobak, Ruckdeschel, & Hazan, 1994). As a result, when experiencing distress children may fail to signal directly a need for support, become embroiled in negative emotion, and be unable to draw upon potentially supportive social relationships. For individuals with histories of disorganized attachment relationships, processes of regulation and the integration of behavioral and emotional states may have been disrupted by extremely harsh or chaotic caregiving contexts (Carlson & Sroufe). In the context of inadequate caregiving or recurring trauma, the level of arousal and the need to separate or compartmentalize overwhelming affects and memories may result in dissociative phenomena (Putnam, 1994).

In summary, early disturbances in attachment relations, not generally viewed as pathology or directly causing pathology, lay the foundation for disturbances in developmental processes that can lead to psychopathology. Understanding the processes that begin as relationship disturbance and that may lead in time to individual disorder through their impact on neurophysiological and affective regulation is a central task for the field of developmental psychopathology (Sameroff & Emde, 1989).

EMPIRICAL LINKS BETWEEN ATTACHMENT
AND MALADAPTATION

In this section, we illustrate links between attachment and general indicators of maladaptation in preschool, middle childhood, and adolescence. These studies illustrate the importance of early history in establishing a pattern of adaptation (or maladaptation) from which subsequent patterns evolve. The studies demonstrate that, when caregiving and contextual factors remain relatively constant, children tend to develop along pathways established by early experience. Changes in developmental trajectories are associated with lawful changes in ongoing circumstances, such as caregiving interactions and contextual factors that influence caregiving.

Infancy to Early Childhood

Early results from the longitudinal study demonstrated an association between anxious attachment in infancy and behavior problems in preschool (Erickson, Egeland, & Sroufe, 1985). Based on observer ratings, anxious-avoidant and anxious-resistant children were found to be more teacher dependent and less agentic (i.e., confident, assertive), respectively, than children with secure attachment histories. Both anxious groups were found to have poorer social skills than securely attached infants in preschool. Analyses based on teacher ratings indicated that anxious-avoidant children were withdrawn and gave up easily compared with securely attached children, were more hostile than anxious-resistant children, and were more exhibitionistic and impulsive than children in either the secure or anxious-resistant groups. Anxious-avoidant children received higher total scores on both the Preschool Behavior Questionnaire and the Behavior Problem Scale (Behar & Stringfield, 1974) than either anxious-resistant or securely attached children, suggesting more and varied behavior problems in the avoidant group.

From the 96 children observed in preschool (Erickson et al., 1985), two groups of children with behavior problems were identified: acting out/inattentive ($n = 20$; 14 boys and 6 girls) and withdrawn ($n = 7$; 3 boys and 4 girls). A comparison group of competent preschoolers ($n = 22$; 12 boys and 10 girls) was selected from the same sample. Children in the acting-out group were described by teacher checklists and rated by observers as disobedient, inconsiderate, easily irritated, and verbally and physically aggressive with peers or adults or both. The withdrawn children were passive, showing little interest in their surroundings, usually not engaged in play, and sometimes daydreaming, and low on positive affect. Chi-square analyses of the combined behavior problem groups by attachment classification at 12 and 18 months were significant ($p < .001$ and $p < .04$, respectively), confirming the hypothesis that children with histories of anxious attachment were more likely to have behavior problems in preschool. These data were analyzed by stability of attachment classification from 12 to 18 months, and results were consistent with expectations. Of the 14 stable anxiously attached children, only 2 were in the well-functioning group in preschool. In contrast, 15 of 21 stable secure children were in the competent preschool group. For children with classification changes, preschool group membership was hard to predict: Four of 10 were in the group without behavior problems.

Although results supported continuity between attachment quality and preschool behavior, exceptions to predicted relations were also examined. Results of these analyses were quite coherent but they must be considered tentative due to the small sample size. Change from anxious attachment in infancy to competent functioning in preschool was related to quality of caregiving. At 42 months, mothers of children without behavior problems were found to be respectful of children's autonomy, allowing the child to explore and attempt tasks without intrusion. Mothers were warm and supportive, structuring tasks carefully, providing well-timed cues to help the child, and setting firm, consistent limits without being hostile. Home environments of these children provided the stimulation necessary to foster healthy development through appropriate play materials and active parental involvement. The occurrence of stressful life events did not distinguish anxiously attached children with and without behavior problems in preschool, although mothers of children without behavior problems reported better emotional support. Change from secure attachment in infancy to behavior problems in preschool was related to less effective caregiving in intermediate stages of toddlerhood and early childhood. Based on laboratory observations, mothers of these children were found to be less supportive of their children's efforts to solve problems at 24 months and less effective in structuring tasks and establishing consistent standards at 42 months. Home observations at 30 months revealed deficits in age-appropriate play materials and mother-child interaction for these children compared with preschool children without behavior problems.

The preschool findings (Erickson et al., 1985) suggest that attachment quality is not only an indicator of the quality of care and support provided in the first year of life, but also a predictor of subsequent care. We assume continuity of care and support across time that, in turn, serves to perpetuate expectations and behavioral organization developed during the attachment phase. Thus, we assume continuity between quality of attachment in infancy and adaptation in preschool. In cases where the outcome changes, where the quality of the child's adaptation in preschool is not predicted by quality of attachment in infancy, we expect changes in quality of care and in the environment influencing the quality of care to account for discontinuity. Our findings support these hypotheses.

Middle Childhood to Adolescence

Consistent with the developmental pathways model, longitudinal data demonstrated that adaptation and maladaptation in early development were related to functioning in middle childhood and adolescence, and that change was lawful. For example, of the preschool behavior problem groups described earlier, 80% of the acting-out group, 71% of the withdrawn group, and only 27% of the competent group showed significant behavior problems in 2 of the first 3 years of elementary school as rated by teachers (Egeland, Kalkoske, Gottesman, & Erickson, 1990). Furthermore, as expected, deflections in expected pathways (decline as well as improvement in individual functioning) between preschool and elementary school were related to changes in maternal stressful life events, overall maternal functioning (i.e., psychopathology), family relationship status, and organization in the home. Specifically, decline in functioning was related to family stressful life events and maternal depression as well as poor quality of stimulation and organization of the home environment. Improved functioning was related to higher scores on the measures of the home environment and low levels of maternal depression. These findings demonstrate that, when caregiving and contextual factors remain stable, children tend to develop along pathways established by early experience. Changes in caregiving and contextual factors are likely to be associated with changes in developmental trajectories (Egeland et al.).

Study of the relations between behavior problems in middle childhood and psychopathology in adolescence demonstrated the pathogenic effect of a cumulative history of maladaptation (Egeland, Pianta, & Ogawa, 1996). Of children with no behavior problems identified in early elementary school, 33% were diagnosed with problems at age 17.5 based on the Kiddie Schedule of Affective Disorders and Schizophrenia measure (K-SADS; Ambrosini, Metz, Prabucki, & Lee, 1989). Using composite scores from teacher ratings on the Child Behavior Checklist (CBCL; Achenbach & Edelbrock, 1986) administered in grades 1, 2, and 3, children were placed in pure internalizing, pure externalizing, and mixed internalizing-externalizing groups; 78% of the internalizers, 69% of the externalizers, and 63% of the mixed group received K-SADS diagnoses in adolescence.

EMPIRICAL LINKS: LASTING EFFECT
OF EARLY EXPERIENCE

The relations between attachment and later adaptation are obviously complex and our findings regarding continuity and change do not lead to the conclusion that the effects of early experience are erased, even for the minority of children who change substantially. Rather, we expect that children with histories of early maladaptation whose lives have improved remain differentially vulnerable, at least for a time. Likewise, we would expect that securely attached infants who later show maladaptive functioning would rebound quickly should life supports improve. Attachment theory suggests that, despite change in development, early experience remains influential in later functioning. Our longitudinal data demonstrate the lasting impact of early history even in the context of current or intermediate experience.

To investigate the continued impact of early experience and adaptation given subsequent experience or developmental change, we compared two groups of children in elementary school on teacher judgments of peer competence and emotional health (Sroufe, Egeland, & Kreutzer, 1990). Children in both groups had been functioning (equivalently) poorly on three assessments across the 42- to 54-month period. One group, however, had shown consistently positive adaptation during the infant and toddler periods, including secure attachment, whereas the other had functioned poorly throughout. In this study, children showing positive adaptation in the infant-toddler period showed greater rebound in the elementary school years, despite poor functioning in the intervening preschool period. In addition, a series of regression analyses was performed in which variance related to near-in or contemporary predictors of adaptation in middle childhood was removed before adding earlier adaptation measures. These analyses revealed some incremental power of early predictors with intermediate predictors removed, supporting the organizational developmental thesis that current adaptation is a product of both current circumstances and developmental history (Bowlby, 1980).

We demonstrated similar predictability in behavior problem change from the late elementary years to adolescence (Sroufe et al., 1999). To parallel and expand on the preschool study, we created groups of children who were functioning comparably in terms of behavior problems during elementary school, but who had differed in their attachment histories. A total of four groups were created, including children with stable secure histories (at 12 and 18 months) who were functioning well or poorly in middle childhood and children with stable insecure histories who were functioning well or poorly in middle childhood (based on the CBCL in grades 1–3; Achenbach & Edelbrock, 1986). Peer competence and emotional health rankings made by teachers paralleled behavior problem status in middle childhood.

Analyses of subsequent adolescent adaptation included critical comparisons between groups of children who functioned equivalently in middle childhood, but who differed in their early attachment status. These groups differed with respect to later psychopathology and competence in

ways predictable from their early histories. Among the children functioning well in middle childhood, those with secure attachment histories received lower scores on pathology indices derived from the K-SADS at age
17½ and significantly higher global ratings of competence at age 19 based
on functioning across work, school, and relationship domains (Sroufe et
al., 1999). For children functioning poorly in middle childhood, those with
histories of secure attachment received lower total and past pathology
scores as measured by the K-SADS. As evidenced in early development,
individuals showing positive change (now in adolescence), following a
period of maladaptation, appeared to draw upon a more positive foundation in infancy.

For all four groups in this study, level of functioning in adolescence appeared to depend on both early and later experience. For example, children
with histories of secure attachment who were also functioning well in middle childhood consistently received significantly higher ratings of social
competence and lower ratings of psychopathology than all other groups.
Conversely, children with insecure histories and behavior problems in middle childhood received lower ratings of social competence and higher ratings of psychopathology than all other adolescent groups. Notably, the two
groups of children with mixed histories (secure attachment and later behavior problems or insecure attachment and later positive functioning)
were comparable with respect to adolescent competence and behavior
problems. A positive early foundation appeared to be a protective factor for
some children, allowing them to rebound somewhat from a difficult middle
childhood. These findings suggest a special role for early experience. Not
only were the effects of early history apparent following a long passage of
time, but early experience seemed as potent as later experience in predicting adolescent outcomes. At the same time, children with insecure histories
were amenable to positive change: Those who were doing well in middle
childhood were also functioning fairly well in adolescence.

Throughout the longitudinal study, our findings have consistently emphasized quality of early parent-child relationships as an important protective factor in later functioning. For children living in poverty, parents
and caregivers serve as mediators of the effects of poverty, potentially
harmful community values, social isolation, psychosocial pathology, and
difficult relationships with family and societal networks (Musick, Bernstein, Percansky, & Stott, 1987). In several studies, we examined the relationships between life stressors and child outcomes and attempted to
identify protective factors for individuals who experienced high life stress
but were functioning in a competent fashion (Egeland & Kreutzer, 1991;
Pianta, Egeland, & Sroufe, 1990).

Pianta et al. (1990) found that stressful family events (experienced during the preschool period) were predictive of outcomes in the socioemo-

tional-behavioral domains in first grade, even after accounting for maternal and child IQ. To identify protective factors, these authors compared competent to less competent children of highly stressed mothers (based on the results of a hierarchical cluster analysis). Competent boys of highly stressed mothers were differentiated from their incompetent peers by higher language ability, more structured, responsive, and organized home environments, and positive mother-child interaction at 42 months. The data suggest that competence in these boys may be due in part to the mothers' ability to buffer their sons from the effects of stress by providing good quality care. Like the boys, the more competent girls had better language skills and lived in more organized home environments. For girls, however, competence was most highly related to positive maternal personality characteristics and was unrelated to observed quality of mother-child interaction. Competence for girls may have depended on their mothers' personal adjustment, which may have had the double benefit of buffering the daughters from the negative effects of stress and providing a role model for positive coping. Child IQ measured by the WPPSI (Wechsler Preschool and Primary Scale of Intelligence; Wechsler, 1967) was not found to be a protective factor for boys or girls. Early history of competence observed during the infancy, toddler, and preschool periods has also been identified as a protective factor against the negative effects of high family life stress, especially for boys (Egeland & Kruetzer, 1991).

EMPIRICAL FINDINGS: LINKS BETWEEN ATTACHMENT AND SPECIFIC PSYCHOPATHOLOGY

Relations between early experience and maladaptive socioemotional patterns across development demonstrate not only the enduring impact of early relationships but also the divergent consequences of differences in early dyadic patterns. Links between attachment and both global and specific indices of psychopathology in adolescence also highlight these relations. For example, attachment disorganization measured in infancy was significantly related to a global index of psychopathology in adolescence (r = .36) and increased the likelihood or risk of psychopathology in adolescence even within the context of intermediate measures of behavior problems in grades 1 through 6 and quality of care at age 13 (Carlson, 1998). In regression analyses predicting adolescent pathology, behavior problems and quality of care at age 13 accounted for 16% and 3% of the variance, respectively. Entered subsequently, infant attachment history (avoidant and disorganized) accounted for an additional 14% of the variance. Our research and the literature in general provide preliminary data regarding hypotheses of special vulnerabilities or particular domains of impact from early experience. In a series of studies, we explored relations posited by

Bowlby (1969/1982, 1973, 1980) and others regarding early experience and later anxiety, conduct disorder, depression, and dissociative phenomena.

Anxiety Disorders

Explanations for the etiology of anxiety disorders in children and adolescents include genetically based theories (Biederman, Rosenbaum, Bolduc, Faraone, & Hirshfeld, 1991) as well as those emphasizing the role of temperament (Kagan, 1994). From an attachment theory perspective, disorders of anxiety evolve from distortions in the adaptive functioning of anxiety in early development. Bowlby (1973) noted that infant anxiety regarding brief caregiver separations in the first year of life serves the evolutionary purpose of infant protection. Anxiety prompts infant distress signals and proximity-seeking behavior that, in turn, elicits regulatory assistance from the caregiver, reducing the likelihood of harm. Thus, separation distress may be adaptive in the context of responsive, sensitive caregiving. In the context of inconsistent caregiver response to infant signals, however, chronic vigilance and anxiety may establish a response pattern that becomes generalized to multiple sources of fear (including fear aroused by developmental challenges), leaving the child vulnerable to the development of anxiety disorders. Thus, infants whose needs have been met in an inconsistent fashion would be anxious about their needs being met in other situations. Chronic hypervigilance and anxiety resulting from inconsistent care may set the stage for later anxiety disorders.

Using longitudinal data, we explored the relations between anxious-resistant attachment and anxiety disorders incorporating available familial and temperament measures (Warren, Huston, Sroufe, & Egeland, 1997). The study included: (a) a measure of maternal anxiety (Anxiety Scale Questionnaire; Cattell, 1963) as a surrogate for familial predisposition; (b) measures of temperament chosen to correspond to Kagan's "highly reactive temperament" including nurses' ratings of newborns in the newborn nursery and the Neonatal Behavioral and Neurological Assessment Scale (NBAS; Brazelton, 1973) assessments of motor activity, range of state, regulation of state, and habituation; and (c) strange situation classifications as measures of infant attachment. Childhood and adolescent anxiety disorders were assessed using the K-SADS (Ambrosini et al., 1989), the outcome variable being the total number of past and present anxiety disorder diagnoses.

Using hierarchical regression analyses we examined the contributions of anxious-resistant attachment beyond the contributions of maternal anxiety and infant temperament. No relation was found between the measure of maternal anxiety and the presence of child or adolescent anxiety disorders in the next generation. Three variables indexing temperament (nurses' ratings of temperament, range of state, and habituation) significantly predicted later anxiety disorders, however, in each case, anxious-resistant attachment contributed to the prediction of anxiety disorders above and beyond the contribution of temperament. The importance of these findings derive in part from the theoretical precision underlying the prediction. As specified by attachment theory, only anxious-resistant attachment and not avoidant attachment predicted later anxiety disorders. Although the variance accounted for by anxious-resistant attachment was modest, this prediction was made over a 16-year period.

Antisocial Behavior

Bowlby's (1973) attachment theory linked the origins of aggression and delinquency with early experiences of insecurity and detachment (defined by Bowlby as an apparent lack of trust and caring for significant others). He observed that, although children were made angry by experiences such as adverse parental attitudes, harsh treatment, separation, and threats of abandonment, expressions of anger toward caregivers regarding such treatment would only exacerbate parent-child disruption. Bowlby (1973, pp. 225, 246) suggested that, in despair, anger is redirected toward the environment in the form of "aggressive detachment" in early childhood and antisocial acts in later developmental periods. For boys, an early history of avoidant attachment has been related to aggression in childhood based on teacher ratings of aggression in grades 1, 2, and 3 ($r = .23, p < .05$). Combining avoidant attachment with negative affect at 24 and 42 months yielded correlations of .41 and .29 for boys and girls, respectively (Renken, Egeland, Marvinney, Mangelsdorf, & Sroufe, 1989). Similar results occurred in predicting aggression ($r = .20, p < .05$) and delinquency ($r = .30, p < .001$) in adolescence measured by the Teacher Report Form (Achenbach & Edelbrock, 1986). Adolescent findings were especially strong for aggression ($r = .34, p < .001$) and delinquency ($r = .40, p < .001$) for boys.

Bowlby's (1969/1982, 1973, 1980) emphasis on the role of early history is also reflected in the longitudinal study of dual types of adolescent antisocial behavior (Aguilar, Sroufe, Egeland, & Carlson, 2000). In this study, based on parent, child, and teacher reports of behavior (Achenbach, 1991), four groups were defined: never antisocial ($n = 34$, males $= 21$), cases classified as "not antisocial early" and "not antisocial in adolescence"; childhood limited ($n = 13$, males $= 7$), cases classified as "antisocial early" and "not antisocial in adolescence"; adolescent onset ($n = 35$, males $= 13$), cases classified as "not antisocial early" and "antisocial in adolescence"; and childhood-onset life-course persistent ($n = 38$, males $= 21$), cases classified as "antisocial early" and "antisocial in adolescence." Antisocial group differences were examined with respect to temperamental, neuropsychological, and psychosocial factors.

Overall, the results supported the presence of childhood-onset life-course persistent and adolescence-onset antisocial behavior groups. The groups were most reliably and significantly distinguished by indices of socioemotional history within the first 3 years, however, no significant differences were found on measures of early temperament or neuropsychological functioning. Early psychosocial environment was operationalized as an index of seven risk factors: single parenthood, mother's reported depression, mother's reported overall life stress from the child's birth to 48 months, observed maternal sensitivity to infant signals at 3 and 6 months, attachment quality, indices of maltreatment, and mother's support and involvement with the child at 24 and 42 months. Compared with the adolescent-onset and never antisocial groups, the childhood-onset antisocial adolescents experienced significantly more early risk factors. The effects of these risk factors appeared to be cumulative in the development of antisocial behavior.

Examination by individual risk factor also revealed consistent group differences between the early onset group and other groups. Individuals in the early onset life-course persistent group were more likely to have been avoidantly attached at 12 and 18 months compared to the never anti-social group. These findings are consistent with the findings of Greenberg, Speltz, and DeKlyen (1993), who argued that avoidant attachment in combination with other life stress and risk factors promotes the development of antisocial behavior.

Depression

Bowlby (1973) reserved a central place in his theory of socioemotional development for childhood experiences of separation and loss in the production of defensive mechanisms, depressive symptoms, and distortions in personality organization. He conceptualized depressive disorders in terms of core experiences of hopelessness or helplessness resulting from early loss and the chronic inability to make or maintain affectional relationships. Bowlby reasoned that particular patterns of depressive disorders are likely to turn on particular patterns of childhood caregiving experiences, citing experiences consistent with those of anxious-avoidant, resistant, and disorganized attachment. For example, childhood experiences of never having attained a stable secure relationship despite repeated efforts to fulfill caregiving demands or unrealistic expectations (experience of resistant attachment) may lead children to interpret later difficulties or loss as yet another failure to affect the environment, specifically to maintain affectional relationship. Depression for these children is likely to take the form of helplessness. Through repeated experiences of psychologically unavailable or punitive caregiving, of being told verbally or through behavior that they are unlovable or inadequate (experiences of avoidant attachment), children learn to expect others to be hostile and negative rather than helpful or supportive. From these experiences, children may carry forward fundamental experiences of alienation and hopelessness. Finally, Bowlby reasoned that experiences of parental loss or trauma without auxiliary support (experiences related to disorganized attachment) would predispose children to interpret later challenges as insurmountable and the self as impotent in the face of adversity. Based on these formulations, Bowlby argued that child and adolescent dejected mood states result from schemas and expectations about the self and others developed through early caregiving experiences and maintained through environmental choices.

Using longitudinal data, we examined the antecedents of childhood-onset depression versus adolescent-onset depression that may approximate the adult phenomenon (Duggal, Carlson, Sroufe, & Egeland, 2001). In this study, depression was assessed using three Achenbach measures: Teacher Report Form (grades 1, 2, and 3 and high school), the parent Child Behavior Checklist (grade 1), the Youth Self-Report (high school), two versions of the Children's Depression Rating Scale-Revised (mother version, grades 2 and 3, and child version, grade 3), and a depression summary score derived from the Kiddie Schedule for Affective Disorders and Schizophrenia (age 17½). The K-SADS depression summary score consisted of 12 items related to mood, anhedonia, fatigue, suicidal ideation, psychomotor retardation or agitation, and sleep or appetite disturbances. Continuous depression scores in childhood and adolescence were derived by standardizing the scores (7 in childhood, 4 in adolescence) and using the highest rating for each time period.

In childhood, depression group status was determined by first examining depression for grades 1, 2, and 3 separately, using the criteria of clinical cutoff on at least one measure and at least 75% of the threshold score on the remaining measure(s). Overall, childhood depression group status was assigned if depression criteria were met for any one of the three time periods assessed. Adolescent group status was evaluated for ages 16 and 17½ separately, with the same criteria as childhood for age 16 and a clinical cutoff criterion at age 17½. Adolescent depression status was assigned if criteria were met for one of the two time periods. A control group consisted of individuals not assigned to either depression group.

Antecedents examined included maternal depression (higher rating of two assessments of Beck Depression Inventory when the child was 7 and 8 years old and parent-child relationship factors: mother's early emotional support of the child measured in observations from 12 to 42 months (including infant attachment at 12 and 18 months), emotional support available to the parent from 12 to 64 months, history of abuse from 24 to 64 months, and maternal life stress for two time periods (children ages 12 to 64 months and ages 6 to 17).

Regression analyses and group comparisons yielded similar results in this study (Duggal et al., 2001). In childhood, maternal depression, early emotional support of the child, parental emotional support, and life stress variables each accounted for unique variance in the hierarchical regression, together accounting for 19% of the childhood depression variance. In adolescence, maternal depression and early emotional support of the child accounted for 19% of the variance. Together, the analyses suggested that psychosocial factors including child emotional support significantly contribute to the development of depressive symptomatology in both childhood and adolescence. In the teenage years, however, emotional support of the child and the interaction of emotional support of the child and mother's history of depression best accounted for the onset of adolescent depression.

Extracted from the early childhood composite variable and examined independently, insecure attachment significantly predicted adolescent symptomatology with all other factors controlled ($t = 3.10$, $p < .01$). The findings suggest that early childhood experiences of dysregulation have an enduring effect on depressive symptomatology. Early experiences may be more powerful than subsequent life events and relationship support in accounting for total variance because early experiences influence the interpretation of subsequent experiences.

Dissociation

Disorganized-disoriented attachment and a history of trauma have been linked to the evolution of dissociative symptoms. Disorganized patterns of attachment in infancy are thought to result from frightening or confusing parental behavior. Because frightened infants are biologically disposed to approach caregivers, when the caregiver is the source of fear, infants are placed in an unresolvable paradox. Being unable to simultaneously approach and flee, the infant may engage in contradictory or attention-shifting behaviors or rapid changes in state that represent the earliest origins of dissociation. The child is challenged to manage extreme arousal at a time when infant capabilities are insufficient to ensure self-regulation (when organization depends upon dyadic regulation).

Liotti (1992) argued that the combination of disorganizing early caregiving and later trauma may be a particularly devastating developmental pattern. In response to internal conflict or pain, infants with histories of attachment disorganization may sequester certain aspects of experience and fail to evolve coherent organization of self and other in relationships. In the face of later trauma, these children are likely to respond with established patterns of disconnecting disturbing stimuli from normal cognitive and emotional processing. In addition, they may fail to develop the adaptive coping capacities of young children, those based on expectations that others are available for support and a belief in their own effectiveness at eliciting that support. What begins as a potential for dissociation in early patterns of disorganization-disorientation may become crystallized into dissociative symptoms in the context of severe or repeated trauma.

Using longitudinal data to examine dissociative phenomena, we expected that disorganized attachment, independently and in combination with indices of chronic trauma, would be related to later dissociation. Disorganized attachment status was derived from infant attachment assessments. Severity and chronicity of trauma were documented using indices of trauma from infancy to adolescence (i.e., physical abuse of the child, witnessing family violence, death of a family member, catastrophic illness of a family member, prolonged parent-child separations). Dissociation was assessed across time, using teacher, parent, and child reports of behavior problems in childhood, a diagnostic interview at age 17½, and the Putnam Child Dissociative Checklist (DES) at age 19 (Putnam, Helmers, & Trickett, 1993).

As predicted, both disorganized attachment and trauma were related to later dissociative symptoms (Carlson, 1998; Ogawa, Sroufe, Weinfield, Carlson, & Egeland, 1997). Disorganized attachment, assessed at 12 and 18 months of age, was related to dissociation across childhood and through adolescence, including clinical assessments at age 17½ and the DES at age 19. Trauma at each age was related to concurrent dissociation and to symptoms at the next period, and chronicity of trauma, prospectively assessed, showed an especially strong relation to dissociation. An interactive model proposed by Liotti (1992), wherein early disorganization creates susceptibility to the effects of trauma, was clearly confirmed (Ogawa et al.). The most pronounced dissociative symptoms were associated with this developmental pathway. Findings from this study may help to explain why trauma is not always associated with dissociation and why certain individuals may be especially vulnerable to the dissociative effects of trauma. First, dissociative symptoms may be likely in the context of chronic trauma. Second, some individuals may be especially vulnerable to dissociating in the face of trauma because early patterns of protodissociation have been established within disorganizing caregiving relationships.

INTERVENTION

The importance of the early relationship experience (the increased likelihood of negative child outcomes resulting from an anxious parent-infant attachment relationship and the positive developmental outcomes associated with secure attachment) provides a strong rationale for attachment-based interventions for the purpose of preventing later behavior problems and psychopathology. Attachment interventions for parents and their infants exist, and, like parenting interventions in general, they are quite varied in terms of program approach and goals, recipient of program services (e.g., child, parent, or parent-child relationship), method of service delivery (e.g., home-based services), and quantity and timing of services as well as characteristics and training of intervenors. In addition, there is variation in the characteristics of the participants, although most attachment interventions conducted in the U.S. have involved high-risk parents and infants (Egeland, Weinfield, Bosquet, & Cheng, 2001).

Attachment-based interventions have included programs designed to enhance maternal sensitivity (e.g., van den Boom, 1994), provide social support (Beckwith, 1988), and promote change in parents' inner working models of attachment. This latter approach can be traced to the infant-parent psychotherapy movement and the work of Selma Fraiberg (1980). There are also broad-based, comprehensive attachment-based interventions such as STEEP (Steps Toward Effective Enjoyable Parenting) that incorporate components related to maternal representation, maternal sensitivity, and social support. This program also focuses on parents' perspective taking, including their beliefs, expectations, and understanding of the baby and their relationship with their baby. In addition, the program focuses on issues of crisis management and empowerment (Egeland et al., 2001).

The STEEP program, like most of the attachment interventions, did not result in a greater number of securely attached infants. However, the overall findings of these interventions have been positive. For example, Lieberman, Weston, and Pawl (1991) did not find a difference between treatment and control mother-infant pairs on attachment classification, but did find differences on certain attachment dimensions, such as significantly less avoidance for the infants in the intervention group. In the STEEP evaluation, differences were found on a variety of variables indirectly related to quality of attachment, such as mothers' beliefs, attitudes, and well-being (lower depression scores), as well as the quality of the home environment (Egeland et al., 2001). We hope that attachment theory and research findings will be incorporated into parenting and home visitation programs and we strongly recommend that more attachment intervention research be conducted. The importance of the early parent-infant relationship for later development provides an excellent rationale for implementing attachment-based interventions.

From the perspective of attachment theory, psychopathology is viewed as a developmental construction, resulting from ongoing transactive processes between the evolving individual and the environment. Individuals both transform and are transformed by the environment in which they find themselves. From this perspective, early attachment variations are not generally viewed as pathology or even as directly causing pathology. Rather, varying patterns of attachment serve as initiating conditions (Sroufe et al., 1999). Patterns of infant-caregiver attachment play a dynamic role in the development of pathology by establishing tendencies and expectations that shape subsequent environmental engagement and by influencing basic neurophysiological and affective regulatory systems. Early developmental paths are probabilistically related to later disorder and are dependent on subsequent experience to maintain their trajectories. Change remains possible at numerous points in development, although both theory and data suggest that such change is more readily accomplished early in the process or at least when there is a foundation of early support (Egeland, Weinfield, Bosquet, & Cheng, 2001).

Attachment theory and research findings regarding continuity and opportunities for change in developmental pathways provide clear implications for prevention and intervention. Research results highlight the importance of environmental factors in the ongoing transactive process, in particular infant-caregiver relationships that provide a foundation for later development. In addition, research suggests that prevention and intervention strategies begin early, provide comprehensive care, and follow relationships through the demands and changes of early development.

REFERENCES

Achenbach, T. M. (1991). *Integrative guide for the 1991 CBCL/4-18, YSR, and TRF profiles.* Burlington, VT: University of Vermont Department of Psychiatry.

Achenbach, T. M., & Edelbrock, C. S. (1986). *Manual for the teacher's report form and teacher version of the child behavior profile.* Burlington, VT: University of Vermont.

Aguilar, B., Sroufe, A. L., Egeland, B., & Carlson, E. A. (2000). Distinguishing the early-onset/persistent and adolescence-onset antisocial behavior types: From birth to 16 years. *Development and Psychopathology, 12,* 109–132.

Ambrosini, P. J., Metz, C., Prabucki, K., & Lee, J. (1989). Videotape reliability of the third revised edition of the K-SADS. *Journal of the American Academy of Child and Adolescent Psychiatry, 28,* 723–728.

Beckwith, L. (1988). Intervention with disadvantaged parents of sick preterm infants. *Psychiatry, 51,* 242–247.

Behar, L., & Stringfield, S. (1974). A behavior rating scale for the pre-school child. *Developmental Psychology, 10,* 601–610.

Belsky, J., Spritz, B., & Crnic, K. (1996). Infant attachment security and affective-cognitive information processing at age 3. *Psychological Science, 7,* 111–114.

Biederman, J., Rosenbaum, J. F., Bolduc, E. A., Faraone, S. V., & Hirshfeld, D. (1991). A high-risk study of young children of parents with panic disorder and agoraphobia with and without comorbid depression. *Psychiatry Research, 37,* 333–348.

Bowlby, J. (1944). Forty-four juvenile thieves: Their characters and home life. *International Journal of Psychoanalysis, 25,* 19–52, 107–127.

Bowlby, J. (1973). *Attachment and loss: Vol. 2. Separation.* New York: Basic Books.

Bowlby, J. (1980). *Attachment and loss: Vol. 3. Loss.* New York: Basic Books.

Bowlby, J. (1982). *Attachment and loss: Vol. 1. Attachment.* New York: Basic Books. (Original work published 1969)

Bowlby, J. (1988). *A secure base: Parent-child attachment and healthy human development.* New York: Basic Books.

Brazelton, T. B. (1973). *A neonatal assessment scale.* Philadelphia: Lippincott.

Bretherton, I., Ridgeway, D., & Cassidy, J. (1990). Assessing internal working models of the attachment relationship: An attachment story completion task for 3-year-olds. In M. T. Greenberg, D. Cicchetti, & E. M. Cummings (Eds.), *Attachment in the preschool years: Theory, research, and intervention* (pp. 273–308). Chicago: University of Chicago Press.

Bronfenbrenner, U. (1986). Ecology of the family as a context for human development: Research perspectives. *Developmental Psychology, 22,* 723–742.

Carlson, E. A. (1998). A prospective longitudinal study of attachment disorganization/disorientation. *Child Development, 69,* 1107–1128.

Carlson, E. A., & Sroufe, L. A. (1995). The contribution of attachment theory to developmental psychopathology. In D. Cicchetti & D. Cohen (Eds.), *Developmental processes and psychopathology: Vol. 1. Theoretical perspectives and methodological approaches* (pp. 581–617). New York: Cambridge University Press.

Cattell, R. B. (1963). *Anxiety symptom questionnaire.* Champaign, IL: Institute for Personality and Ability Testing.

Cicchetti, D., & Tucker, D. (1994). Development and self regulatory structures of the mind. *Development and Psychopathology, 6,* 533–549.

Duggal, S., Carlson, E. A., Sroufe, L. A., & Egeland, B. (2001). Depressive symptomatology in childhood and adolescence. *Development and Psychopathology, 13,* 143–164.

Egeland, B., & Farber, E. A. (1984). Infant-mother attachment: Factors related to its development and changes over time. *Child Development, 55,* 753–771.

Egeland, B., Kalkoske, M., Gottesman, N., & Erickson, M. F. (1990). Preschool behavior problems: Stability and factors accounting for change. *Journal of Child Psychology and Psychiatry, 31,* 891–910.

Egeland, B., & Kreutzer, T. (1991). A longitudinal study of the effects of maternal stress and protective factors on the development of high-risk children. In A. L. Green, E. M. Cummings, & K. H. Karraker (Eds.), *Life-span developmental psychology: Perspectives on stress and coping* (pp. 61–84). Hillsdale, NJ: Lawrence Erlbaum Associates.

Egeland, B., Pianta, R., & Ogawa, J. (1996). Early behavior problems: Pathways to mental disorders in adolescence. *Development and Psychopathology, 8,* 735–749.

Egeland, B., Weinfield, N. S., Bosquet, M., & Cheng, V. K. (2001). Remembering, repeating and working through: Lessons from attachment-based interventions. In D. J. Osofsky & H. E. Fitzgerald (Eds.), *Infant mental health in groups at high risk* (Vol. 4, pp. 35–89). New York: Wiley.

Erickson, M., Egeland, B., & Sroufe, L. A. (1985). The relationship between quality of attachment and behavior problems in preschool in a high-risk sample. In I. Bretherton & E. Waters (Eds.), *Growing points in attachment theory and research* (Society for Research in Child Development Monograph No. 209, pp. 147–186). Chicago, IL: University of Chicago Press.

Fraiberg, S. (1980). *Clinical studies in infant mental health: The first year of life.* New York: Basic Books.

Fury, G., Carlson, E., & Sroufe, L. A. (1997). Children's representations of attachment relationships in family drawings. *Child Development, 68,* 1154–1164.

Greenberg, M. T., Speltz, M. L., & DeKlyen, M. (1993). The role of attachment in the early development of disruptive behavior problems. *Development and Psychopathology, 5,* 191–213.

Kagan, J. (1994). *Galen's prophecy.* New York: Basic Books.

Kobak, R. R., Ruckdeschel, K., & Hazan, C. (1994). From symptom to signal: An attachment view of emotion in marital therapy. In S. M. Johnson & L. S. Greenberg (Eds.), *The heart of the matter* (pp. 46–71). New York: Brunner/Mazel.

Lieberman, A. F., Weston, D. R., & Pawl, J. H. (1991). Preventive intervention and outcome with anxiously attached dyads. *Child Development, 62,* 199–209.

Liotti, G. (1992). Disorganized/disoriented attachment in the etiology of the dissociative disorders. *Dissociation, 4,* 196–204.

Main, M. (1981). Avoidance in the service of attachment: A working paper. In K. Immelmann, G. Barlow, L. Petrinovich, & M. Main (Eds.), *Behavioral development: The bielefeld interdisciplinary project* (pp. 651–693). New York: Cambridge University Press.

Main, M. (1993). Discourse, prediction, and recent studies in attachment: Implications for psychoanalysis. *Journal of the American Psychoanalytic Association, 41,* 245–260.

Main, M., & Hesse, E. (1990). Parents' unresolved traumatic experiences are related to infant disorganized attachment status: Is frightened and/or frightening parental behavior the linking mechanism? In M. T. Greenberg, D. Cicchetti, & E. M. Cummings (Eds.), *Attachment in the preschool years* (pp. 161–182). Chicago: University of Chicago Press.

Musick, J. S., Bernstein, V., Percansky, C., & Stott, H. (1987). A chain of enablement: Using community based programs to strengthen relationships between teen parents and their infants. *Zero to three. Bulletin of the National Center for Clinical Infant Programs, 7,* 1–6.

Ogawa, J., Sroufe, L. A., Weinfield, N. S., Carlson, E., & Egeland, B. (1997). Development and the fragmented self: A longitudinal study of dissociative symptomatology in a nonclinical sample. *Development and Psychopathology, 9,* 855–1164.

Pianta, R., Egeland, B., & Sroufe, L. A. (1990). Maternal stress in children's development: Predictions of school outcomes and identification of protective factors. In J. E. Rolf, A. Masten, D. Cicchetti, K. Neuchterlen, & S. Weintraub (Eds.), *Risk and protective factors in the development of psychopathology* (pp. 215–235). New York: Cambridge University Press.

Pianta, R., Sroufe, L. A., & Egeland, B. (1989). Continuity and discontinuity in maternal sensitivity at 6, 24, and 42 months in a high-risk sample. *Child Development, 60,* 481–487.

Putnam, F. W. (1994). Development and dissociative disorders. In D. Cicchetti & D. J. Cohen (Eds.), *Developmental psychopathology: Vol. 2. Risk, disorder, and adaptation* (pp. 581–608). New York: Wiley.

Putnam, F. W., Helmers, K., & Trickett, P. K. (1993). Development, reliability, and validity of a child dissociation scale. *Child Abuse and Neglect, 17,* 731–741.

Renken, B., Egeland, B., Marvinney, D., Mangelsdorf, S., & Sroufe, L. A. (1989). Early childhood antecedents of aggression and passive-withdrawal in early elementary school. *Journal of Personality, 57,* 257–281.

Rieder, C., & Cicchetti, D. (1989). Organizational perspective on cognitive functioning and cognitive-affective balance in maltreated children. *Developmental Psychology, 25,* 382–393.

Rosenberg, D. (1984). *The quality and content of preschool fantasy play: Correlates in concurrent social-personality function and early mother-child attachment relationships.* Unpublished doctoral dissertation, University of Minnesota, Minneapolis.

Sameroff, A. (1989). General systems and the regulation of development. In M. Gunnar & E. Thelen (Eds.), *Minnesota Symposia in Child Psychology* (Vol. 22, pp. 219–235). Hillsdale, NJ: Lawrence Erlbaum Associates.

Sameroff, A., & Chandler, M. (1975). Reproductive risk and the continuum of care-taking casualty. In Horowitz, Hetherington, Scarr-Salapatek, & Siegal (Eds.), *Review of child development research* (Vol. 4, pp. xx–xx). Chicago: University of Chicago Press.

Sameroff, A., & Emde, R. (1989). *Relationship disturbances in early childhood*. New York: Basic Books.

Schore, A. (1994). *Affect regulation and the origin of the self: The neurobiology of emotional development*. Hillsdale, NJ: Lawrence Erlbaum Associates.

Sroufe, L. A. (1989). Relationships and relationship disturbances. In A. J. Sameroff & R. N. Emde (Eds.), *Relationship disturbances in early childhood: A developmental approach* (pp. 70–94). New York: Basic Books.

Sroufe, L. A. (1991). Considering normal and abnormal together: The essence of developmental psychopathology. *Development and Psychopathology, 2*, 335–347.

Sroufe, L. A. (1996). *Emotional development: The organization of emotional life in the early years.* New York: Cambridge University Press.

Sroufe, L. A. (1997). Psychopathology as outcome of development. *Development and Psychopathology, 9*, 251–268.

Sroufe, L. A., Carlson, E. A., Levy, A. K., & Egeland, B. (1999). Implications of attachment theory for developmental psychopathology. *Development and Psychopathology, 11*, 1–13.

Sroufe, L. A., Egeland, B., & Kreutzer, T. (1990). The fate of early experience following developmental change: Longitudinal approaches to individual adaptation in childhood. *Child Development, 61*, 1363–1373.

Sroufe, L. A., Levy, A. K., & Carlson, E. (1998, March). *Resilience in adolescence: Changing the odds.* Paper presented at the biennial meeting of the Society for Research on Adolescence, San Diego, CA.

Sroufe, L. A., & Waters, E. (1977). Attachment as an organizational construct. *Child Development, 48*, 1184–1199.

Suess, G. J., Grossmann, K. E., & Sroufe, L. A. (1992). Effects of infant attachment to mother and father on quality of adaptation in preschool: From dyadic to individual organization of self. *International Journal of Behavioral Development, 15*, 43–66.

van den Boom, D. C. (1994). The influence of temperament and mothering on attachment and exploration: An experimental manipulation of sensitive responsiveness among lower-class mothers with irritable infants. *Child Development, 65*, 1457–1477.

Vaughn, B., Waters, E., Egeland, B., & Sroufe, L. A. (1979). Individual differences in infant-mother attachment at 12 and 18 months: Stability and change in families under stress. *Child Development, 50*, 971–975.

Warren, S. L., Huston, L., Sroufe, L. A., & Egeland, B. (1997). Child and adolescent anxiety disorders and early attachment. *Journal of the American Academy of Child and Adolescent Psychiatry, 36*, 637–644.

Wechsler, D. (1967). *Wechsler Preschool and Primary Scale of Intelligence.* New York: The Psychological Corporation.

Disorders of Attachment and Failure to Thrive

Diane Benoit
University of Toronto and The Research Institute, Hospital for Sick Children

Jennifer Coolbear
The Hospital for Sick Children

Failure to thrive (FTT) is a common and serious problem of infancy that is believed to have multifactorial etiology, including biological, nutritional, and environmental contributors (see Fig. 3.1), and is associated with poor long-term developmental, growth, health, and socioemotional outcomes (Pollitt, 1987; Pollitt et al., 1996). FTT is a condition that is particularly interesting to those working in the fields of attachment and developmental psychopathology because of the hypothesized interplay between the individual, biological characteristics of the infant and the caregiving environment in determining the onset, perpetuation, and resolution of FTT. Over the past several decades, researchers have focused on an increasingly controversial question: Does FTT reflect a disturbed caregiver-infant relationship and suboptimal caregiving or does it reflect problems within the infant, independent of the caregiving environment? Despite the controversy and the consideration of factors within the infant, many researchers in the field of FTT have continued to focus primarily on the caregiver-infant relationship. The objectives of this chapter are to: (a) briefly review research documenting the epidemiology, definition, etiology, and outcome of FTT to highlight the nature and significance of this problem; (b) review empirical evidence supporting or challenging the long-held belief that FTT is associated with a problematic caregiver-infant relationship, specifically the attachment relationship; (c) review empirical evidence pertaining to the question of whether infants with FTT could be at risk for disorders of attachment; and (d) examine new data regarding the possible association

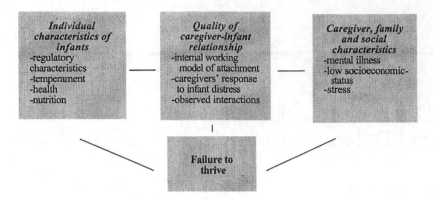

FIG. 3.1. Pathways to failure to thrive.

between infant regulatory problems and FTT. As a problem of infancy that occurs within the broader context of the parent-infant relationship, understanding the risk and protective factors within the infant, the caregiver, and the relationship that are associated with FTT presents a particular challenge.

FAILURE TO THRIVE (FTT)

Definition

There is no universally accepted definition of FTT (Benoit, 1993a, 1993b, 2000a). However, since the mid-1980s researchers and clinicians have frequently used anthropometic criteria to determine growth status. One of the more frequent definitions used by other research groups, and the one used in the study discussed in a later section of this chapter, includes the following criteria: (a) weight for age at or below the fifth percentile on standardized growth charts, (b) weight less than expected (i.e., less than 90% of ideal body weight), and (c) a deceleration in the rate of weight gain from birth to the present (weight decrease of at least two major centiles on standardized growth charts; Altemeier et al., 1979; Benoit, Zeanah, & Barton, 1989; Drotar & Eckerle, 1989; Gorman, Leifer, & Grossman, 1993). Unfortunately, the lack of a universally accepted definition of FTT has made research findings difficult to compare across studies.

Epidemiology

Studies conducted in the United States show that FTT affects up to 30% of infants seen in ambulatory care and inner city emergency room settings, 22% of infants born prematurely with low birth weight, 1% to 5%

of those admitted to a hospital, and 10% of infants living in poverty (Casey et al., 1994; Frank & Zeisel, 1988; Powell, Low, & Speers, 1987). Studies conducted in Great Britain show that: (a) Nearly 2% of infants from inner city, community samples and nearly 3% of those born full term and appropriate for gestational age develop FTT, (b) less than one in three affected children is ever referred to hospital services for assessment or treatment, and (c) children from lower socioeconomic backgrounds are two to three times more likely than children from more affluent backgrounds to develop FTT (Skuse, Gill, Reilly, Wolke, & Lynch, 1995; Skuse, Wolke, & Reilly, 1992; Wright, Waterston, & Aynsley-Green, 1994). A community-based study conducted in Israel showed that nearly 4% of full-term infants develop FTT (Wilensky et al., 1996). In summary, whatever various definitions are used to describe it, FTT is a common problem of infancy and early childhood.

Etiology

Numerous etiological factors have been described and grouped under three major categories: organic (when an underlying health problem, in addition to undernutrition, is present; approximately 25% of cases), nonorganic (when no underlying health problem, other than undernutrition, is identified), and mixed (when both organic and nonorganic problems are present; approximately 20% of cases). Although these percentages might explain the strong emphasis that researchers have historically placed on elucidating the role of various nonorganic factors on the onset and perpetuation of FTT, it is important to point out that all infants with FTT suffer from a serious medical condition, specifically, malnutrition. The nonorganic factor that has been most extensively studied over the past several decades is the quality of the caregiver-infant relationship. In fact, FTT has long been viewed as a sign of suboptimal parental care and neglect, although this belief was based on clinical opinions and impressions rather than on clear and solid empirical evidence. This clinical belief is reflected by the use of terms such as "psychosocial dwarfism," "maternal deprivation syndrome," and "environmental FTT" to describe FTT (Barbero & Shaheen, 1967; Berkowitz & Senter, 1987; Chatoor, Egan, Getson, Menvielle, & O'Donnell, 1987; Shapiro, Fraiberg, & Adelson, 1976; Stanhope, Wilks, & Hamill, 1994; Wright et al., 1994). More recently, however, researchers and clinicians have generally acknowledged that there are multiple pathways leading to malnutrition and FTT. Factors associated with characteristics of the infant, the caregiver, the unique fit between the caregiver and infant, and the environment all likely play a role in the development, maintenance, and severity of FTT. Unfortunately, despite several decades of research in the field, no definitive answer has yet been provided about the contribution of these various possible factors to FTT.

Outcome

Developmental, Health, and Growth Sequelae Associated with FTT. Serious short- and long-term developmental, health, and growth sequelae have been documented. The developmental and health sequelae are believed to result from permanent damage to the developing nervous system and impairment of defenses against disease that occur when severe undernutrition goes uncorrected (Bithoney et al., 1991; Casey et al., 1994). The damage to the nervous system may take the form of reduced neural cell growth and delayed neural maturation, leading to hypotonia (Mathisen, Skuse, Wolke, & Reilly, 1989; Wilensky et al., 1996), developmental delays, attentional problems, and learning disabilities (Black, Dubowitz, Hutcheson, Berenson-Howard, & Starr, 1995; Dowdney, Skuse, Heptinstall, Puckering, & Zur-Szpiro, 1987; Puckering et al., 1995; Raynor & Rudolf, 1996; Wilensky et al., 1996; Wolke, Skuse, & Mathisen, 1990). Studies that have examined long-term outcome, ranging from 1 to over 10 years after the onset of FTT, have shown that, irrespective of the presence of prematurity or type of recruitment site (e.g., community vs. hospital vs. pediatric primary care clinic), infants with FTT have lower intelligence than children without a history of FTT, show declines in their reading and language skills and in their cognitive and intellectual functioning over time, including one third being "seriously retarded" at age 4 (Black et al., 1995; Dowdney et al., 1987; Drotar & Sturm, 1988; Kristiansson & Fallstrom, 1987; Pollitt et al., 1996; Puckering et al., 1995).

The impairment of defenses against disease is manifested by more frequent bouts of illness, more severe forms of illness, and longer convalescent periods for infants with FTT compared to thriving infants. In fact, infants with FTT are twice as likely to be hospitalized in the first year of life than their matched counterparts without FTT (Wilensky et al., 1996). With respect to growth outcome, studies have shown that children with a history of FTT generally remain shorter and weigh less than children without such a history (Kristiansson & Fallstrom, 1987; Puckering et al., 1995).

Behavioral and Emotional Characteristics and Outcomes. Studies that have compared the behavioral and emotional characteristics of infants with FTT to those of infants without FTT have documented significant maladjustment problems both at the time of diagnosis and up to several years later. These problems include more demanding, more fussy, and less sociable behaviors and less task-oriented and persistent behavioral styles (Wilensky et al., 1996; Wolke et al., 1990), more general inactivity, expressionless face, hyperalertness, gaze avoidance, rumination (i.e., repeated self-induced vomiting and reswallowing of the vomitus), thumb sucking, disproportionate hand and finger activity, lack of vocalization and smile, and unusual body posture, compared to infants without FTT (Powell et al., 1987). Regulatory difficulties (e.g., sleep problems) have also been associated with FTT, although these difficulties have been less extensively studied (Benoit, 2000b; Raynor & Rudolf, 1996; Wilensky et al., 1996).

Unfortunately, many studies in the field have serious methodological problems, including lack of prospective, longitudinal designs, correlational findings that do not allow researchers to determine the direction of effects, and lack of consideration of other possible mediating factors. In the next section, we review one such possible factor, the parent-infant attachment relationship, although other factors could be contributing.

ATTACHMENT AND FTT

A review of all aspects of the caregiver-infant relationship as they relate to FTT is beyond the scope of this paper.[1] Briefly, researchers have identified aspects of the play and feeding interactions between infants with FTT and their caregivers that are problematic and have concluded, perhaps without sufficiently strong empirical evidence, that FTT is attributable to a disordered caregiver-infant relationship. Other researchers, however, have failed to replicate these findings and have raised serious questions about the role of the caregiver-infant relationship in FTT (e.g., Wolke, 1996). In the present section, we focus on the caregiver-infant attachment relationship in the context of FTT. We examine each side of the caregiver-infant attachment relationship (infant and adult) in general, then specifically as it relates to FTT.

Caregiver-Infant Attachment Relationship

The Infant's Side of the Caregiver-Infant Attachment Relationship. The purpose of attachment in a caregiver-infant relationship is to make the infant safe and protected (Bowlby, 1969/1982, 1973, 1980). Whenever an infant's attachment system becomes activated (i.e., when the infant is ill, physically hurt, or emotionally upset), the infant exhibits attachment behaviors (i.e., cries, seeks proximity, and tries to maintain contact with the attachment figure). The role of the attachment figure is to provide the

---

[1]For a more detailed description of studies pertaining to aspects of the caregiver-infant relationship other than the attachment relationship, see Benoit (2000a).

protection, nurturance, warmth, and support necessary for the infant's attachment system to become deactivated (which signals that the infant feels safe and protected). Bowlby (1969/1982, 1980) hypothesized that, when caregivers are emotionally available and respond sensitively to infants when the infants' attachment system is activated, infants construct internal representations or working models of their caregivers as available and responsive (or loving). Internal working models provide infants with the basic framework for experiencing, interpreting, and anticipating current and later attachment-relevant events (Bowlby, 1969/1982, 1980). When their internal working model of the attachment relationship with that caregiver is formally assessed using the strange situation procedure (SS; Ainsworth, Blehar, Waters, & Wall, 1978), infants whose caregivers have consistently responded to them in loving ways approach or greet their caregivers following brief separations (which activate the attachment system) and maintain contact with their caregivers until they feel safe (Ainsworth et al.). These infants' behaviors toward loving caregivers reflect internal working models of the attachment relationship with their caregivers that are considered secure.

Infants whose caregivers do not respond to their attachment behaviors with nurturance, warmth, and support develop working models of attachment that are considered insecure. For instance, when caregivers consistently respond to their infants' distress by ridiculing, ignoring, or becoming annoyed, these infants develop internal working models of their caregivers as unavailable, unresponsive, and rejecting, and of themselves as unworthy of love and affection (Sroufe, 1988; van IJzendoorn, 1995; van IJzendoorn, Schuengel, & Bakermans-Kranenburg, in press). In the SS, some infants classified as insecure reacted to the stress of the separation from their caregivers by avoiding or ignoring their caregivers upon being reunited (Ainsworth et al., 1978). These infants have an internal working model labeled "insecure-avoidant." Infants whose caregivers respond unpredictably in times of need or expect the infant to worry about their own (i.e., caregivers') psychological needs develop internal working models of their caregivers as inconsistently responsive and of themselves as inefficient in generating care and protection from their caregivers (Lojkasek, Cohen, Durek, & Zbogar, 1998; van IJzendoorn et al., in press). In the SS, these infants become extremely distressed by brief separations from their caregivers and are unsoothable and overly focused on their caregivers during the reunion episodes (Ainsworth et al.). These infants have an internal working model labeled "insecure-ambivalent-resistant."

In addition to the secure, insecure-avoidant, and insecure-resistant-ambivalent categories, infants' behavior in the SS can also be classified as insecure-disorganized-disoriented if they exhibit unusual behaviors in the presence of the caregivers (Main & Hesse, 1990, 1992). Examples of such unusual behaviors include stilling or freezing for long periods, displaying fear or apprehension when caregivers enter the room or approach them, confusing caregiver and stranger, or simultaneously displaying contradictory behaviors (Main & Hesse, 1990, 1992).

Infant Attachment and FTT. Given the long-held belief that FTT reflects suboptimal parental care or neglect, one would expect that the internal working model of the attachment relationship of infants with FTT toward their primary caregivers would be characterized by insecure attachment as assessed by the SS. Table 3.1 illustrates four controlled studies and one noncontrolled study that have used the SS to test this hypothesis. As can be seen from Table 3.1, only the three most recent studies have used the insecure-disorganized-disoriented attachment classification and all three of these studies show that an overwhelming majority of infants with FTT have insecure working models of attachment to their caregivers. These findings suggest that infants with FTT may generally perceive their caregivers either as inconsistently and unpredictably responsive or as unavailable emotionally, lacking in affection and warmth, and rejecting in times of emotional upset, physical pain, or illness. What remains unclear, however, is whether the FTT status of the child is an outcome of an insecure attachment to the primary caregiver, or the child's growth problems or other factors predate the insecure attachment. Before one can definitely conclude that FTT is due to a relationship problem between the FTT infant and his or her caregiver, an experimental design is needed, one that includes random assignment of two interventions (one focusing exclusively on the relationship and one focusing exclusively on something other than

TABLE 3.1
Studies of Infant Attachment in Failure to Thrive (FTT)
Using the Strange Situation Procedure

Study	n	% Disorganized-disoriented per Group	% Insecure per Group	p
Gordon and	12 FTT	Not assessed	50% FTT	a
Jameson (1979)	12 controls		17% controls	
Drotar et al. (1985)	68 FTT	Not assessed	45% FTT	N/A
Crittenden (1987)	18 FTT	45% FTT	92% FTT	a
	21 controls	b	33% controls	
Valenzuela (1990)	42 FTT	32% FTT	93% FTT	< .0001
	43 controls	5% controls	50% controls	
Ward, Kessler, and	26 FTT	46% FTT	65% FTT	< .01
Altman (1993)	28 controls	7% controls	36% controls	

[a]p value not given. [b]p value not mentioned for control group.

the relationship) and measures the effect of each intervention on growth parameters (which could be used as a primary outcome measure). If an intervention focused exclusively on specific aspects of the relationship (e.g., attachment) is associated with weight gain, then one could definitely conclude that specific aspects of the caregiver-infant relationship (i.e., those targeted by the intervention) have a direct impact on growth parameters and FTT. Until strong empirical evidence is available to demonstrate the role of the caregiver-infant relationship, including the attachment relationship, in the onset and perpetuation of FTT, researchers and clinicians should be cautious about making premature conclusions that FTT is the result of a disordered caregiver-infant relationship.

Regardless of the role of insecure attachment in the etiology of FTT, there is a clear association between FTT and insecure attachment. This is of concern because insecure attachment, particularly disorganized attachment, has been associated with a risk of emotional and behavioral problems and psychopathology. Insecure attachment in infants with FTT has been related to long-term socioemotional problems, above and beyond those reported in thriving infants. For example, infants with FTT who were classified as insecurely attached at 12 months have been described as more rigid under stress and less competent, skillful, and creative at 42 months, compared to their non-FTT counterparts (Brinich, Drotar, & Brinich, 1989). Insecure attachment in infants with or without FTT has also been related to severity of malnutrition and long-term health outcome (Goldberg, 2000). For example, Valenzuela (1990) reported that infants with FTT classified as both avoidant and ambivalent (one type of insecure-disorganized-disoriented classification) presented the most severe degrees of malnutrition within the underweight group. In another study, Simmons and his colleagues (Simmons, Goldberg, Washington, Fischer-Fay, & MacLusky, 1995) showed that infants with cystic fibrosis classified as insecure-avoidant at 12 months had significantly poorer nutritional status at 1, 2, and 3 years of age, compared to infants with cystic fibrosis who received any of the other SS classifications. Chatoor, Ganiban, Colin, Plummer, and Harmon (1998) used a continuous rating of security based on SS observations and found that attachment security was correlated with weight for height. Finally, Brinich et al. (1989) showed that infants with FTT who had been classified as insecurely attached at 12 months were rehospitalized twice as often between the time of diagnosis and 42 months, compared to infants with FTT classified as securely attached. Findings from these studies suggest that the vulnerability of insecurely attached infants (with or without FTT) may not be limited to socioemotional adjustment and mental health, but may encompass physical health as well. These findings highlight that, although insecure attachment as assessed by the SS is not synonymous with psychopathology, it does represent a marker for later socioemotional maladjustment, in both FTT and non-FTT infants (Zeanah, Mammen, & Lieberman, 1993).

Although a majority of infants with FTT are classified as insecurely attached to their caregivers in the SS, there is a proportion of infants who have secure internal working models of their attachment relationships with their primary caregivers, as assessed by the SS. These children and caregivers have not yet been studied extensively, but the findings suggest that factors other than quality of attachment may play a role in the etiology of FTT. For example, some infants with FTT, whether they have insecure attachment or not, may also have varying degrees of physiological, regulatory difficulties (Benoit, 2000b). Although much research related to the caregiver-infant relationship has been conducted in the last few decades, the conclusions from these studies appear to be based on interpretation of results and opinions, rather than on solid empirical evidence. In fact, in nearly every study, the interpretations provided could have alternate, equally plausible interpretations. We do not advocate that the caregiver-infant relationship, including the attachment relationship, is irrelevant to the study of FTT. To the contrary, we advocate and encourage researchers in the fields of attachment and FTT to use stringent empirical design to prove (or disprove) what can now be considered only a belief that FTT is caused by difficulties in the caregiver-infant relationship.

The Adult's Side of the Caregiver-Infant Attachment Relationship. Adults' internal working models of attachment (or states of mind with respect to attachment) are usually assessed by the Adult Attachment Interview (AAI; George, Kaplan, & Main, 1984), which could be viewed as the adult equivalent of the SS. In this structured interview, caregivers are repeatedly asked for their assessment of attachment-relevant experiences with their attachment figures during childhood and for their appraisal of the impact of these early experiences on themselves as individuals and as parents. Verbatim transcripts of the interview are rated and patterns of responses are then categorized into secure-autonomous (corresponding to the secure classification in infants), insecure-dismissing (corresponding to the insecure-avoidant classification in infants), insecure-preoccupied (corresponding to the insecure-resistant classification in infants), insecure-unresolved for mourning or trauma (corresponding to insecure-disorganized-disoriented in infants).

Caregivers who respond to the questions of the AAI in thoughtful ways, have access to both positive and negative memories and emotions, have convincingly forgiven their parents for unfortunate experiences, are at peace with imperfections in themselves and others, and value attachment relationships are usually assigned a secure-autonomous classification. Caregivers who depict their childhood attachment experiences in mostly positive or even glowing terms but fail to recall specific incidents to support these general, positive impressions or contradict the positive descriptors with specific memories usually receive a classification of insecure-dismissing. These caregivers typically dismiss the importance of attachment experiences on the self and parenting. Individuals who demonstrate ongoing preoccupation with pleasing their parents, ongoing, unsuccessful struggles to separate from their parents, or an inability to provide a coherent and succinct description of childhood experiences and their effects upon the self usually receive a classification of insecure-preoccupied. Finally, the discourse of individuals classified as insecure-unresolved shows the characteristics of the other three classifications but, in addition, it shows evidence of confusion or disorientation (or failure in metacognitive monitoring) when discussing traumatic experiences of loss or sexual and physical abuse.

Adult Attachment and FTT

To date, only two studies have examined primary caregivers' attachment as assessed with the AAI and FTT (Benoit et al., 1989; Coolbear & Benoit, 1999). Findings from these two studies are summarized in Table 3.2. Although one would assume primary caregivers' attachment would be stable and predate the onset of FTT, there is no empirical evidence to support this conclusion.

DISORDERS OF ATTACHMENT AND FTT

Zeanah et al. (1993) cautioned against viewing insecure attachment assessed in the SS as synonymous with a disorder of attachment. They describe disorders of attachment as profound disturbances in a child's feelings of safety and security within the relationship with a primary caregiver. The question of whether infants with FTT suffer from such disorders of attachment has never been tackled directly, partly because of the lack of a

TABLE 3.2
Studies of Adult Attachment and Failure to Thrive (FTT)

Study	n	% Insecure[a]	p
Benoit, Zeanah, and Barton (1989)	25 FTT	96% FTT	.003
	25 non-FTT	60% non-FTT	
Coolbear and Benoit (1999)	28 FTT	93% FTT	< .01
	27 non-FTT	67% non-FTT	

[a]Using the three-way attachment classification of the Adult Attachment Interview (secure-autonomous, insecure-dismissing, and insecure-preoccupied).

universally accepted method for assessing disorders of attachment in infancy. In an attempt to address this issue, however, Coolbear and Benoit (1999) developed the following empirical definition of "risk for a clinical disturbance of attachment": (a) presence of nonautonomous state of mind with respect to attachment in the caregiver (assessed by the AAI), (b) nonbalanced caregivers' representation and subjective experience of their child,[2] (c) problematic play interactions, and (d) problematic feeding interactions. They tested this empirical definition with 57 infants (30 with FTT and 27 matched controls), aged 4 to 36 months, recruited from outpatient clinics from a tertiary care pediatric hospital in a large Canadian metropolitan area. Using logistic regression analysis, Coolbear and Benoit demonstrated that the four elements of the empirical definition reliably distinguished between the FTT and non-FTT groups with an overall success rate of 75%. However, they also demonstrated that: (a) the knowledge of the internal working models measures (items [a] and [b] of the empirical definition) predicted membership into the FTT group with a success rate of 86% and into the non-FTT group with a success rate of 67% and (b) the knowledge of the quality of play and feeding interactions did not help to decide whether an infant was at risk for a clinical disturbance of attachment. The authors indicated that a significant problem in their study design, which should be addressed in future research, was the absence of a measure for infants' internal working models of attachment. Again, these data are somewhat ambiguous as each aspect of the data could be interpreted differently. Clearly, more research is needed to address the question of whether some or all infants with FTT are at risk for disorders of attachment, and whether an intervention that targets these aspects of the relationship results in the amelioration of growth difficulties.

ROLE OF REGULATORY CHARACTERISTICS OF INFANTS IN FTT

Another possible explanation for the lack of differences in the observed play and feeding interactions between caregivers and their infants with and without FTT is that the basic difficulty in FTT may not reside exclusively in the caregiver-infant relationship. In fact, infants' regulatory difficulties may represent a significant challenge to any caregiver-infant relationship. Regulation disorders consist of difficulties in any combination of physiological domains that require internal regulation (e.g., thermoregu-

---

[2]The description of the instrument used to assess caregivers' subjective experience and relationship with the child is beyond the scope of this paper. See Coolbear and Benoit (1999) for details.

lation, hunger-satiety cycles, sleep-wake cycles, elimination, mood, social interaction, cuddling), sensory integration (e.g., olfactory, gustatory, vestibular, auditory, visual, tactile, proprioceptive), or motor planning (e.g., swallowing textured foods, running). Infants with regulatory difficulties or disorders usually have a history of difficult temperament, colic, difficulty soothing, and lack of cuddliness (Greenspan & Wieder, 1993). Furthermore, studies have shown that infants with FTT are more likely to have lower birth weights compared to thriving infants, suggesting that some infants with FTT are born with a vulnerability and predisposition to poor growth and maturational problems (Mathisen et al., 1989; Wilensky et al., 1996). One cannot help but wonder whether these characteristics could also reflect poor self-care in the mothers during pregnancy. Studies that have examined individual characteristics of infants with FTT (see Benoit, 2000a, for details) have pointed out interesting behavioral characteristics that could be viewed as regulatory difficulties. However, here again, an alternate explanation is possible. Research has shown that attachment may play a major role in various aspects of self-regulation, including the more subtle aspects of regulation such as that of emotion and social interactions. The question of whether aspects of attachment and self-regulation are independent phenomena or overlap, especially in infants with FTT, is still not clear.

In support of the hypothesis that some infants with FTT suffer from regulatory difficulties or disorders, one needs to consider that a subgroup of infants with FTT have histories of feeding difficulties starting at birth (e.g., difficulties such as latching and remaining alert). Furthermore, Wolke et al. (1990) found that 12-month-old infants with FTT were more demanding, fussy, and unsociable than their matched counterparts. This finding of more negative affect was also reported by Polan and colleagues (1991b). In another study, Powell et al. (1987) described unusual postures (e.g., general inactivity, infantile posture, flexed hips) that could possibly signal the motor tone problems reported in some regulatory disorders. Powell et al. also described "problematic interactive behaviors" (e.g., hyperalertness, gaze avoidance) that could signal state, reactivity, and sensory problems encountered in children with regulatory disorders. Other symptoms consistent with regulatory difficulties include fearfulness and apprehension (Wilensky et al., 1996) and sleep and feeding problems (Benoit, 2000b; Wilensky et al.). However, many of these behaviors have also been described in infants who have insecure or disorganized attachment and some have been described in infants who suffer from malnutrition. To date, no study has definitely answered the question of whether these behavioral signs are characteristics of the infant (e.g., nutritional status, regulatory characteristics) or characteristics of the caregiver-infant attachment relationship or both, or even some other factor.

To address the question of whether regulatory characteristics of infants might distinguish infants with FTT from those without FTT, we reexamined data collected in a recent study of 57 infants (30 with FTT and 27 without FTT), ages 4 to 36 months, and recruited from outpatient clinics of a tertiary care pediatric hospital in a large Canadian metropolitan area (Coolbear & Benoit, 1999). Because a prerequisite to the diagnosis of regulatory disorder is a difficult temperament (Greenspan & Wieder, 1993), we first examined whether primary caregivers' reports of infant temperament (assessed using the difficultness factor on the Infant Characteristics Questionnaire; Bates, Freeland, & Loundsbury, 1979) differed between the FTT and non-FTT groups. No differences were detected. To determine whether an independent coder's more objective assessment of how difficult the infant was perceived to be by the primary caregiver would yield different results, the mean group scores were compared on a subscale of the working model of the child interview (the infant difficulty scale). The caregivers of infants with FTT came across to the independent coder as perceiving their infants as more burdensome and difficult, compared to the non-FTT group ($t = 3.89$, $p < .001$). Thus, what mothers reported (via questionnaires) and what they believed subconsciously is inconsistent, which could suggest that maternal reports of their infants' temperaments need to be disregarded because they are biased by their own attributions. Findings from studies examining temperamental characteristics of infants with FTT partially support the hypothesis that infants with FTT might be more challenging than infants without FTT. These findings also highlight the importance of using more objective measures of perceived infant difficulty than the standard paper-and-pencil tests in this population.

Finally, another common problem described in regulatory disorders is developmental delay. We compared the FTT and non-FTT groups on cognitive development, (measured using the Bayley Scales for Infant Development, second edition, or BSDI-II; Bayley, 1993). Infants with FTT obtained significantly lower scores on the mental development scale of the BSDI-II, compared to their counterparts ($M_{FTT} = 89.45$, $SD = 10.45$ vs. $M_{non-FTT} = 98.44$, $SD = 10.33$, $t(54) = 3.24$, $p < .01$). These data are in line with other findings documenting an association with FTT and suboptimal development. The reasons for these developmental delays, however, remain unclear. Again, the question of whether these delays result from malnutrition or lack of stimulation due to a suboptimal caregiving environment or both, or from some other factor, remains unanswered.

FTT is a serious problem of infancy and early childhood that has significant short-term and long-term sequelae. Although there is controversy surrounding its definition and debate regarding the role of the caregiver-infant relationship in the onset and perpetuation of FTT, caregiver-infant attachment relationship could play a significant role. The question of whether FTT represents one form of disorder of attachment has not yet been answered and should be addressed in future research. Similarly, the role of specific infant regulatory characteristics in the onset and perpetuation of FTT has not yet been elucidated. Solid empirical research to disentangle which infant factors (e.g., regulation, nutritional status) and which relationship factors (e.g., attachment) uniquely contribute to the final clinical picture of an infant with FTT is sorely needed in the field. Clinicians dealing with infants with FTT and their families simply cannot wait until such evidence becomes available before they provide any assistance and intervention. For these clinicians, the knowledge of various aspects of the caregiver and infant relationship, including the attachment relationship, can be invaluable in shaping an intervention program that is individually tailored to the needs of a specific caregiver and infant with FTT dyad. It is possible that a focus on the caregiver-infant attachment relationship might have benefits, but the main question remains: Would an intervention focusing on the caregiver-infant attachment relationship eliminate the infant's FTT?

REFERENCES

Ainsworth, M. D. S., Blehar, M. C., Waters, E., & Wall, S. (1978). *Patterns of attachment: A psychological study of the Strange Situation.* Hillsdale, NJ: Lawrence Erlbaum Associates.

Altemeier, W. A., III, Vietze, P. M., Sherrod, K. B., Sandler, H. M., Falsey, S., & O'Connor, S. (1979). Prediction of child maltreatment during pregnancy. *Journal of the American Academy of Child Psychiatry, 18,* 205–219.

Barbero, G., & Shaheen, E. (1967). Environmental failure to thrive: A clinical interview. *Journal of Pediatrics, 73,* 690–698.

Bates, J. E., Freeland, C. A., & Loundsbury, M. L. (1979). Measurement of infant difficultness. *Child Development, 50,* 794–803.

Bayley, N. (1993). *Bayley Scales of infant development* (2nd ed.). San Antonio, TX: The Psychological Corporation.

Benoit, D. (1993a). Feeding disorders and failure to thrive. In C. H. Zeanah (Ed.), *Handbook of infant mental health* (pp. 317–331). New York: Guilford Press.

Benoit, D. (1993b). Phenomenology and treatment of failure to thrive. *Child and Adolescent Psychiatric Clinics of North America, 2,* 61–73.

Benoit, D. (2000a). Feeding disorders, failure to thrive, and obesity. In C. H. Zeanah (Ed.), *Handbook of infant mental health* (2nd ed., pp. 339–352). New York: Guilford Press.

Benoit, D. (2000b). Regulation and its disorders. In C. Violato, E. Oddone-Paolucci, & M. Genuis (Eds.), *The changing family and child development* (pp. 149–161). Aldershot, England: Ashgate.

Benoit, D., Zeanah, C. H., & Barton, M. L. (1989). Maternal attachment disturbances in failure to thrive. *Infant Mental Health Journal, 10,* 185–202.

Berkowitz, C. D., & Senter, S. A. (1987). Characteristics of mother-infant interactions in nonorganic failure to thrive. *Journal of Family Practice, 25,* 377–381.

Bithoney, W. G., McJunkin, J., Michalek, J., Snyder, J., Egan, H., & Epstein, D. (1991). The effect of a multidisciplinary team approach on weight gain in nonorganic failure to thrive children. *Developmental and Behavioral Pediatrics, 12,* 254–258.

Black, M. M., Dubowitz, H., Hutcheson, J., Berenson-Howard, J., & Starr, R. H. (1995). A random-ized clinical trial of home intervention for children with failure to thrive. *Pediatrics, 95,* 807–814.

Bowlby, J. (1973). *Attachment and loss. Vol. 2: Separation.* New York: Basic Books.

Bowlby, J. (1980). *Attachment and loss. Vol. 3: Loss.* New York: Basic Books.

Bowlby, J. (1982). *Attachment and loss. Vol. 1: Attachment.* New York: Basic Books. (Original work published 1969)

Brinich, E., Drotar, D., & Brinich, P. (1989). Security of attachment and outcome of preschoolers with histories of nonorganic failure to thrive. *Journal of Clinical Child Psychology, 18,* 142–152.

Casey, P. H., Kelleher, K. J., Bradley, R. H., Kellogg, K. W., Kirby, R. S., & Whiteside, L. (1994). A multifaceted intervention for infants with failure to thrive: A prospective study. *Archives of Pediatrics and Adolescent Medicine, 148,* 1071–1077.

Chatoor, I., Egan, J., Getson, P., Menvielle, E., & O'Donnell, R. (1987). Mother-infant interac-tions in infantile anorexia nervosa. *Journal of the American Academy of Child and Adolescent Psychiatry, 26,* 535–540.

Chatoor, I., Ganiban, J., Colin, V., Plummer, N., & Harmon, R. J. (1998). Attachment and feed-ing problems: A re-examination of non-organic failure to thrive and attachment security. *Journal of the American Academy of Child and Adolescent Psychiatry, 37,* 1217–24.

Coolbear, J., & Benoît, D. (1999). Failure to thrive: Risk for disturbance of attachment? *Infant Mental Health Journal, 20,* 87–104.

Dowdney, L., Skuse, D., Heptinstall, E., Puckering, C., & Zur-Szpiro, S. (1987). Growth retar-dation and development delay amongst inner-city children. *Journal of Child Psychology and Psychiatry, 4,* 529–541.

Drotar, D., & Eckerle, D. (1989). The family environment in nonorganic failure to thrive: A controlled study. *Journal of Pediatric Psychology, 14,* 245–257.

Drotar, D., & Sturm, L. (1988). Prediction of intellectual development in young children with early histories of nonorganic failure to thrive. *Journal of Pediatric Psychology, 13,* 281–296.

Frank, D. A., & Zeisel, S. H. (1988). Failure to thrive. *Pediatric Clinics of North America, 35,* 1187–1206.

George, C., Kaplan, N., & Main, M. (1984). *Adult Attachment Interview.* Unpublished manu-script, Department of Psychology, University of Berkeley, California.

Goldberg, D. (2000). *Attachment and development.* London: Arnold.

Gorman, J., Leifer, M., & Grossman, G. (1993). Nonorganic failure to thrive: Maternal history and current maternal functioning. *Journal of Clinical Child Psychology, 22,* 327–336.

Greenspan, S. I., & Wieder, S. (1993). Regulatory disorders. In C. H. Zeanah (Ed.), *Handbook of infant mental health* (pp. 280–290). New York: Guilford Press.

Kristiansson, B., & Fallstrom, S. (1987). Growth at the age of four subsequent to early failure to thrive. *Child Abuse and Neglect, 11,* 35–40.

Lojkasek, M., Cohen, N., Durek, D., & Zbogar, H. (1998, April). *Maternal responses to infant emotional expressions relate to infant attachment.* Paper presented at the Biennial Meeting of the International Society of Infant Studies, Atlanta, GA.

Main, M., & Hesse, E. (1990). Parents' unresolved traumatic experiences are related to infant disorganized attachment status: Is frightened and/or frightening parental behavior the linking mechanism? In M. Greenberg, D. Cicchetti, & E. M. Cummings (Eds.), *Attachment in the preschool years: Theory, research and intervention* (pp. 161–184). Chicago: University of Chicago Press.

Main, M., & Hesse, E. (1992). *Frightening, frightened, or disorganized behavior on the part of the parent: A coding system for parent-infant interactions.* Unpublished manuscript.

Mathisen, B., Skuse, D., Wolke, D., & Reilly, S. (1989). Oral-motor dysfunction and failure to thrive among inner-city children. *Developmental Medicine and Child Neurology, 31,* 293–302.

Polan, H. J., Kaplan, M. D., Kessler, D. B., Shindledeker, M. N., Stern, D. N., & Ward, M. J. (1991). Psychopathology in mothers of children with failure to thrive. *Infant Mental Health Journal, 12,* 55–64.

Polan, H. J., Leon, A., Kaplan, M. D., Kessler, D. B., Stern, D. N., & Ward, M. J. (1991). Disturbances of affect expression in failure to thrive. *Journal of the American Academy of Child and
Adolescent Psychiatry, 30,* 897–903.

Pollitt, E. (1987). A critical review of three decades of research on the effects of chronic energy undernutrition on behavioral development. In B. Schurch & N. S. Scrimshaw (Eds.),
Chronic energy deficiency: Consequences and related issues (pp. 77–93). Lausanne, Switzer-
land: International Dietary Energy Consultative Group.

Pollitt, E., Golub, M., Gorman, K., Grantham-McGregor, S., Levitsky, D., Schurch, B., Strupp,
B., & Wachs, T. (1996). A reconceptualization of the effects of undernutrition on children's biological, psychosocial, and behavioral development. *Social Policy Report (Society
for Research in Child Development), 10,* 1–22.

Powell, G. F., Low, J. F., & Speers, M. A. (1987). Behavior as a diagnostic aid in failure to
thrive. *Journal of Developmental and Behavioral Pediatrics, 8,* 18–24.

Puckering, C., Pickles, A., Skuse, D., Heptinstall, E., Dowdney, L., & Zur-Szpiro, S. (1995).
Mother-child interaction and the cognitive and behavioural development of four-year-
old children with poor growth. *Journal of Child Psychology and Psychiatry and Allied Disciplines, 36,* 573–595.

Raynor, P., & Rudolf, M. C. J. (1996). What do we know about children who fail to thrive?
Child: Care, Health, and Development, 22, 241–250.

Shapiro, W., Fraiberg, S., & Adelson, E. (1976). Infant-parent psychotherapy on behalf of a
child in critical nutritional state. *Psychoanalytic Study of the Child, 31,* 461–491.

Simmons, R. J., Goldberg, S., Washington, J., Fischer-Fay, A., & MacLusky, I. (1995). Infant-
mother attachment and nutrition in children with cystic fibrosis. *Journal of Developmental
and Behavioral Pediatrics, 16,* 183–186.

Skuse, D. H., Gill, D., Reilly, S., Wolke, D., & Lynch, M. A. (1995). Failure to thrive and the risk
of child abuse: A prospective population survey. *Journal of Medical Screening, 2,* 145–149.

Skuse, D., Wolke, D., & Reilly, S. (1992). Failure to thrive: Clinical and developmental aspects. In H. Remschmidt & M. H. Schmidt (Eds.), *Developmental psychopathology* (pp.
46–71). Lewiston, NY: Hogrefe & Huber.

Sroufe, L. A. (1988). The role of infant-caregiver attachment in development. In J. Belsky & T.
Nezworski (Eds.), *Clinical implications of attachment* (pp. 18–38). Hillsdale, NJ: Lawrence
Erlbaum Associates.

Stanhope, R., Wilks, K., & Hamill, G. (1994). Failure to grow: Lack of food or love? *Professional Care of Mother and Child, 4,* 234–237.

Valenzuela, M. (1990). Attachment in chronically underweight young children. *Child Development, 61,* 1984–1996.

van IJzendoorn, M. H. (1995). Adult attachment representations, parental responsiveness,
and infant attachment: A meta-analysis on the predictive validity of the Adult Attachment Interview. *Psychological Bulletin, 117,* 387–403.

van IJzendoorn, M. H., Schuengel, C., & Bakermans-Kranenburg, M. J. (in press). Disorganized attachment in early childhood: Meta-analysis of precursors, concomitants, and
sequelae. *Development and Psychopathology.*

Wilensky, D. S., Ginsberg, G., Altman, M., Tulchinsky, T. H., Yishay, B., & Auerbach, J. (1996).
A community based study of failure to thrive. *Archives of Disease in Childhood, 75,* 145–148.

Wolke, D. (1996). Failure to thrive: The myth of maternal deprivation syndrome. *The Signal, 4,* 1–6.

Wolke, D., Skuse, D., & Mathisen, B. (1990). Behavioral style in failure-to-thrive: A preliminary investigation. *Journal of Pediatric Psychology, 15,* 237–253.

Wright, C. M., Waterston, A., & Aynsley-Green, A. (1994). Effect of deprivation on weight
gain in infancy. *Acta Paediatrica, 83,* 357–359.

Zeanah, C. H., Mammen, O. K., & Lieberman, A. F. (1993). Disorders of attachment. In C. H.
Zeanah (Ed.), *Handbook of infant mental health* (pp. 332–249). New York: Guilford Press.

Hostile–Helpless Relational Models and Disorganized Attachment Patterns Between Parents and Their Young Children: Review of Research and Implications for Clinical Work

Karlen Lyons-Ruth
Sharon Melnick
Elisa Bronfman
Susannah Sherry
Lisa Llanas
Harvard Medical School

In this chapter, we begin to elucidate the lawful relations between frightened, frightening, or contradictory maternal caregiving behaviors and the infant's disorganized behavioral responses to this caregiving. In the study results, two profiles of parenting behaviors were identified among mothers of disorganized infants that we describe as "hostile" and "helpless" subgroups. Parents with the first profile tended to override the infant's cues with a combination of negative-intrusive and role-reversed, self-referential behaviors. Students of the attachment literature will recognize that this combination of parental behaviors combines attachment cues that are both involving and rejecting of infant approach behaviors. We termed this group "hostile-self-referential regarding attachment." Not surprisingly, the correlations between infant and parent behavior showed that infants of these parents combined avoidant and resistant behaviors with other disorganized behaviors toward the parent. These infants were classified as disorganized, with a subclassification of insecure (D-insecure, see Main & Solomon, 1990, for subclassification procedures).

The second subgroup of parents of disorganized infants looked very different from the first, and this second subgroup is quite important because parents and children in this subgroup are likely to be more prevalent in middle socioeconomic status (SES) samples. Mothers in this subgroup were more fearful, withdrawing, and inhibited and sometimes appeared particularly sweet or fragile. They were unlikely to be overtly hostile or intrusive and they usually gave in to their infants' concerted bids for contact. However, they often failed to take the initiative in greeting or approaching their infants and they often hesitated, moved away, or tried to deflect their infants' requests for close contact before giving in. We termed this group "helpless-fearful regarding attachment."

Infants in this subgroup also differed in that they all continued to express their distress, approach their mothers, and gain some physical contact with them, even though they also displayed disorganized behaviors such as freezing, huddling on the floor, disoriented wandering, or interrupted approaches toward their mothers. These infants were classified disorganized with a subclassification of secure (D-secure), because the outlines of a secure comfort-seeking strategy could still be seen, even though it was overridden by disorganized behaviors.

In this chapter, we first describe the empirical work that led to the identification of these two profiles of parent and infant behavior. We then integrate this work in infancy with other work during the preschool period that identifies two forms of controlling attachment behavior—punitive control and caregiving control—that are predicted by infant disorganization. We offer a model of the intergenerational cycle of disorganized-controlling parent–child interaction patterns and we relate these patterns theoretically to a hostile–helpless internal working model of attachment relationships. The second section of the chapter describes a parent–child case and draws some implications of this body of work for treating parents with hostile–helpless relational models and their young children.

INTRODUCTION

This chapter provides an overview of recent work charting the developmental pathways and family processes associated with disorganized forms of attachment behaviors in infancy. These research findings both converge with and expand on earlier, less systematic clinical observations that have variously described inconsistency, role reversal, or coercive discipline in the parenting behaviors of parents of clinically referred children.

Attachment research provides one scientific foundation for positing relational as well as biological contributions to many forms of psychopathology. However, attachment theory also advances a more specific model within the broader relational framework. We describe some of the more specific tenets of attachment theory regarding the development of psychopathology and then present a brief overview of recent findings regarding the development of disorganized and controlling forms of attachment behavior.

First, from a research perspective, the attachment system is only one of a number of goal-corrected behavioral or motivational systems and all or most of the interactions between parents and children will not be integral to the attachment system even in infancy. For example, interactions around play, teaching, or even routine caregiving are not necessarily engaging attachment motivations or affects.

The attachment system can be thought of as the psychological version of the immune system, in that the attachment system is the preadapted behavioral system for combating and reducing stress, or fearful arousal, just as the immune system is the biological system for combating physical disease. Under normal conditions, an adequately functioning attachment relationship will serve to buffer the infant (and adult) against extreme levels of fearful arousal. However, the attachment system itself may also malfunction, just as the immune system may develop autoimmune disorders. Based on accumulated research findings, disorganized and controlling forms of attachment behavior are now thought to represent signs of maladaptive functioning of the attachment relational system.

An emphasis on fearful arousal and the relational modulation of that arousal lies at the heart of attachment theory and is clearly a departure from an emphasis on libidinal and aggressive drives as the central motivational systems. Instead, it regrounds clinical theory in the developmental dynamics of fear. In addition, attachment research has illuminated the ontogeny of defensive adaptations to caregivers' refusals or failures to provide the needed soothing responses to infant fear or distress. These infant defensive adaptations involve alterations of both attention and affect expression and are reliably observed by the end of the first year of life, much earlier than previous clinical theory had predicted. The early appearance and systematic use of defensive strategies by 1-year-olds was one of Mary Ainsworth and colleagues' (1978) crucial scientific contributions.

In addition, attachment theory is a two-person theory of conflict and defense. It emphasizes the coping or defensive processes required to deal with fearful arousal within a particular set of attachment relationships. In contrast to an intrapsychic theory of defense, attachment theory and research locates the ontogeny of defenses in an intersubjective field. Defense formation occurs at the interface between individual fearful arousal and the responses of central attachment partners. Therefore, both infant individual differences and caregiver differences will contribute to the infant–caregiver negotiations that occur around distress and comfort, as well as to the potential defensive adaptations that may result from those negotiations.

Although the attachment relational system is viewed as only a single circumscribed motivational system among other systems, it is also regarded as preemptive when aroused, because it mobilizes responses to fear or threat. In that sense, the quality of regulation of fearful affect available in attachment relationships is foundational to the developing child's freedom to turn attention away from issues of threat and security toward other developmental achievements, such as exploration, learning, and play. Therefore, attachment security has far-reaching consequences for development for at least two separable reasons. First, at all ages the regulation of fearful arousal is a preemptive motivational system. Second, fearful arousal is a prominent affect from the beginning of life so that later developmental acquisitions are partially dependent on this early-functioning system. Buffering by others is needed from birth and the prolonged immaturity of the human infant leaves the infant unusually dependent on the security-providing responses of others for a long period in early development.

Recent neuroscience research with both rats and rhesus macaques is suggesting that an even stronger statement regarding the foundational nature of the early attachment relationship may be warranted. These studies are demonstrating that both infant neurotransmitter systems and the infant stress response system mediated by the hypothalamic-pituitary-adrenal (HPA) axis are open systems at birth that depend on the patterning of caregiver behavior to set enduring parameters of their functioning across the life span. Therefore, the attachment system may also be foundational at a physiological level in setting up relatively irreversible patterns of neurotransmitter activity and levels of HPA axis responsivity to stress or threat. For example, when caregiving behavior is impaired among macaque mothers due to uncertainty about the ease of obtaining food, macaque infants develop enduring fearful behaviors and elevated levels of corticotropin-releasing factor that do not wane after a predictable food supply is reestablished (Coplan et al., 1996; Nemeroff, 1996). In addition, using a cross-fostering design with newborn rat pups, Francis, Diorio, Liu, and Meaney (1999) recently demonstrated that both the quality of parent–pup interaction and the pup's associated physiological stress responses mediated by the HPA axis may be passed on intergenerationally, independent of genetic influence. These findings converge with findings from human attachment studies that have also documented the link between disorganized attachment strategies and elevated cortisol levels to stressors (Hertsgaard, Gunnar, Erickson, & Nachmias, 1995; Spangler & Grossmann, 1993). In addition, human attachment studies have documented the intergenerational transmission of attachment strategies over two and three generations (van IJzendoorn, 1995). More research will be needed to assess how closely human brain and HPA-axis development reflects the effects of caregiver responsivity documented in animal research.

A large body of research on fearful arousal has documented the range of individual coping responses to pain or fear, captured by the summary label "fight or flight" (e.g., Jansen, Nguyen, Karpitskiy, Mettenleiter, & Loewy, 1995). In addition, Seligman (1975) and others have described "freezing" and "learned helplessness" as responses occurring when more active responses are unavailable or ineffective. Recently, Shelly Taylor and colleagues (Taylor et al., 2000) have advanced an alternative "tend or befriend" hypothesis regarding primary responses to threat among social primates, arguing that fight or flight may be more relevant to the stress responses of males, whereas various forms of affiliative responses may be more common stress responses of females. From an attachment point of view, however, we would expect affiliative responses to threat to be available to all social primates, without regard to gender. As we will show later, this entire array of coping or defensive responses appears in some form in the behaviors that are part of the disorganized-controlling spectrum of attachment behaviors.

PARENTAL AFFECTIVE COMMUNICATION PATTERNS RELATED TO INFANT DISORGANIZATION

If caregiver responsivity is indeed implicated in guiding early brain development, what has been learned about caregiver–infant interactions among infants displaying disorganized attachment responses when under stress? All of the parental factors shown to predict infant disorganization, such as parental psychosocial risk factors or parental unresolved loss or trauma on the Adult Attachment Interview, suggest that aspects of parent–infant interaction contribute to the development of infant disorganization (for review, see Lyons-Ruth & Jacobvitz, 1999). In relation to insecure infant behavior that is avoidant or ambivalent, it has already been documented that parental behavior that is somewhat insensitive, that is, somewhat rejecting and intrusive or somewhat inconsistent and self-preoccupied, is related to the infant's display of avoidant or resistant behavior when needing comfort. However, parental behavior that is somewhat insensitive is not correlated with infant disorganized attachment behavior, because studies using Ainsworth's global rating scale for sensitivity have generated only a small association between parental behavior and infant disorganization (van IJzendoorn, 1995). On the other hand, maltreatment is clearly associated with infant disorganization (Carlson, Cicchetti, Barnett, & Braunwald, 1989). However, that criterion for problematic parental behavior is too extreme given that 15% of infants in low-risk families display disorganized attachments (van IJzendoorn,

Schuengel, & Bakermans-Kranenburg, 1999). How can the parental behaviors most implicated in the process of disorganization be captured?

Recent research in our lab has focused on exploring the family contexts
and later correlates of disorganized attachment behavior as first observed
in infancy. To this end, we have been conducting a 19-year longitudinal
study of low-income families, half of whom were referred to a clinical infant service because of concerns about the quality of parent–infant interaction. The other half were socioeconomically matched nonreferred families
from the same communities. Here we focus on only one aspect of this
work, namely, the types of parent–infant affective communication processes that we have found associated with infant disorganized attachment
behaviors.

Main and Hesse (1990) advanced the hypothesis that disorganization of
infant attachment strategies is related to parental unresolved fear, fear
that is transmitted to the infant through parental behavior that appears
frightened or that is frightening to the infant. According to Main and
Hesse's reasoning, if the parent arouses the infant's fear, this will place the
infant in an unresolvable paradox regarding whether to approach the parent for comfort. This is because the parent becomes both the source of the
infant's fear and the haven of safety.

Along with others, we have explored Main and Hesse's (1990) hypothesis that the parent's frightened or frightening behavior is the distinctive element associated with disorganization of infant attachment strategies.
Prior to the development of the Main and Hesse (1992) coding instrument
for frightened or frightening behavior, however, our pilot work had led us
to advance two additional hypotheses regarding the parental behaviors
that might be disorganizing to the infant. First, we reasoned that parents
might display competing or contradictory caregiving strategies, much as
the disorganized infant displays competing or contradictory attachment
strategies. Second, we reasoned that the parent's overall regulation of the
infant's fearful arousal might be more important than specific behaviors,
so that failures to respond to the infant's attachment bids might be as important as more obviously frightened or frightening parental behaviors.
In this view, parental withdrawing or role-confused behaviors that left the
infant without adequate parental regulation of fearful affect would also be
potentially disorganizing, whether or not the parent's own behaviors
were directly frightened or frightening to the infant (Lyons-Ruth, Bronfman, & Parsons, 1999).

Therefore, in addition to specific frightened or frightening behavior, we
also coded five broader aspects of disrupted parental affective communication with the infant. These five aspects included: (a) parental withdrawing responses, (b) negative-intrusive responses, (c) role-confused responses, (d) disoriented responses, and (e) a set of responses we termed

affective communication errors, which included both simultaneous con-flicting affective cues to the infant and failures to respond to clear affective signals from the infant. Examples of these behaviors are given in Table 4.1.

Infants classified as disorganized in their attachment behavior were also subclassified into two subgroups according to standard coding pro-cedures, based on the type of organized attachment strategy their behav-ior most closely resembled. These two subgroups are usually labeled dis-organized-secure (D-secure) and disorganized-insecure (D-insecure). Here we will use the more behaviorally descriptive labels D-approach and D-avoid-resist.

As predicted, the frequency of these five aspects of disrupted parental affective communication was significantly related to the extent of the in-fant's disorganized attachment behaviors. In addition, these disrupted maternal behaviors, which were coded during a series of separations and reunions, demonstrated cross-situational stability in that they were also

TABLE 4.1
Dimensions of Disrupted Maternal Affective Communication

Affective errors
    Contradictory cues
        Invites approach verbally then distances
    Nonresponse or inappropriate or mismatched responses
        Does not offer comfort to distressed infant; mother smiling while infant angry or distressed
Disorientation (including items from Main & Hesse, 1992)
    Confused or frightened by infant
        Exhibits frightened expression; quavering voice or high, tense voice
    Disorganized or disoriented
        Sudden loss of affect unrelated to environment; trance-like states
Negative-intrusive behavior (including frightening items, Main & Hesse, 1992)
    Verbal negative-intrusive behavior
        Mocks or teases infant
    Physical negative-intrusive behavior
        Pulls infant by the wrist; bared teeth; looming into infant's face; attack-like posture
Role confusion (includes items from Sroufe, Jacobvitz, Mangelsdorf, DeAngelo, & Ward, 1985; Main & Hesse, 1992)
    Role reversal
        Elicits reassurance from infant
    Sexualization
        Speaks in hushed, intimate tones to infant
    Self-referential statements
        "Did you miss me?"; "OK, he doesn't want to see me."
Withdrawal
    Creates physical distance
        Holds infant away from body with stiff arms
    Creates verbal distance
        Does not greet infant after separation

related to similar behaviors observed at home. Higher levels of disrupted maternal communication in the separation procedure were also associated with increased infant distress at home. Neither infant gender nor cumulative demographic risk was significantly related to maternal disrupted communication (Lyons-Ruth, Bronfman, & Parsons, 1999).

When examined separately, the frightened or frightening behaviors described by Main and Hesse (1992) showed the same relation to infant disorganized attachment classification as did overall disrupted communication. However, the specific behaviors described by Main and Hesse constituted only 17% of the behaviors included in our larger coding protocol as disrupted. With all frightened or frightening behaviors removed from the total disrupted behavior score, the remaining disrupted behaviors still reliably distinguished between mothers of organized and disorganized infants. These findings indicate that frightened or frightening behaviors are embedded in a broader context of disrupted affective communication between mother and infant (Lyons-Ruth, Bronfman, & Parsons, 1999).

HOSTILE OR HELPLESS PROFILES OF PARENTING

There were two additional aspects to the findings that were also quite interesting from a clinical perspective. The first finding was that, of the five classes of disrupted communication coded, parental affective communication errors were particularly strongly related to infant disorganized behaviors. These errors often included simultaneous conflicting affective signals to the infant, such as speaking soothingly but stepping out of reach, so that the parent's attachment-related behaviors toward the infant also displayed some of the same contradictory, unintegrated quality as the infant's disorganized attachment behaviors toward the parent. In addition to predicting disorganized infant behaviors, maternal affective communication errors also predicted infant crying and infant proximity-seeking behavior. These mixed disorganized yet approaching infant behaviors appeared to mirror the mixed affective signals of the parent, which included positive cues mixed with subtle or muted negative cues (e.g., speaking soothingly while stepping away from the infant).

The more surprising finding, however, was that there were substantial differences in maternal behavior within the disorganized infant group, differences that were correlated with the subtypes of infant disorganized behavior mentioned earlier (D-approach, D-avoid-resist). Statistically, mothers of the two subtypes of disorganized infants differed more from one another than they did from the other mothers in the study whose infants were not disorganized. Mothers in the two D subgroups did not differ significantly in frequency of affective communication errors or in frequency of disoriented behaviors. However, mothers of disorganized infants who also exhibited avoidance or resistance (D-avoid-resist infants) displayed significantly higher rates of both role confusion and negative-intrusive behavior than did mothers of disorganized infants who continued to approach their mothers. Negative-intrusive and role-confused behaviors were strongly correlated as well, so these mothers were displaying a contradictory mix of rejecting behaviors and behaviors that sought attention from their infants. We termed this group "hostile or self-referential regarding attachment."

In contrast, mothers of D-approach infants exhibited significantly higher rates of withdrawal than mothers of D-avoid-resist infants. Infants of more withdrawing mothers continued to approach them for contact but also displayed signs of conflict, apprehension, uncertainty, helplessness, or dysphoria. Mothers in this subgroup were more fearful, withdrawing, and inhibited and sometimes appeared particularly sweet or fragile. They were very unlikely to be overtly hostile or intrusive and they usually gave in to the infants' concerted bids for contact. However, they often failed to take the initiative in greeting or approaching the infant and they often hesitated, moved away, or tried to deflect the infant's requests for close contact before giving in. We termed this group "helpless-fearful regarding attachment." Infants of "helpless" mothers also looked different from infants of "hostile" mothers in that they all continued to express their distress, approach their mothers, and gain some physical contact with them, even though they also displayed disorganized behaviors, including behaviors such as freezing, huddling on the floor, apprehension, or avoidance while in contact with their mothers. The helpless-fearful parental profile is described in more detail in Table 4.2.

Additional subject-based analyses added to this emerging picture of the behaviors of mothers of D-approach infants. Based on Main and Hesse's (1990) hypothesis that frightened, as well as frightening, maternal behavior should be disorganizing to the infant, we examined the small group of mothers who displayed frightened behavior only. Among their infants, 43% displayed the D-approach profile, compared to only 9% of infants whose mothers displayed any frightening behavior. When the frightened and withdrawing variants of parental behavior were included together, they accounted for 80% of the mothers of D-approach infants, discriminating those mothers both from mothers of organized infants and from mothers of D-avoid-resist infants (Lyons-Ruth, Bronfman, & Atwood, 1999). Figure 4.1 displays the frequency of the two subtypes of maternal behavior by infant attachment classification.

Accurate identification of patterns of caregiving received by infants classified as D-approach is important for at least two reasons. First, there

TABLE 4.2
Helpless/Fearful of Attachment: Attachment-Related Behaviors of Mothers
of Disorganized-Approach (D-Secure) Infants During Reunions

1. Delayed responsiveness or ignored cues, usually followed by compliance to infant's continued demands (e.g., greets or hugs infant only after persistent bids by the infant).

2. Withdrawal or distancing (e.g., fails to greet, interacts from a distance, stands at a distance, circles around the infant, holds infant facing out).

3. Cursory responsiveness (e.g., gives quick hug then moves away; "hot potato" quality to treatment of infant).

4. Directs infant away from self to toys; uses toys to soothe.

5. Hesitation or tension at moments of heightened attachment, such as greetings or contact seeking by the infant (e.g., parent hesitates, freezes, passes by infant, backs away, teases infant, or voice quavers, cracks, stutters).

6. Little physical contact between mother and infant unless infant demands.

7. Vacating parental role (e.g., little sense of authority, little collaboration of mother with baby's initiative, little parental direction or protection).

8. May seem subtly fearful, submissive, or placating with regard to infant (e.g., high frightened voice when greeting; hesitation, then compliance with infant's cues).

9. May show little overt negative affect or intrusiveness; not ominous or threatening.

10. Positive behaviors not often seen among fearful mothers (e.g., unsolicited warmth or affection expressed toward child that does not have delayed, hesitant, forced, or strained feel such as overbright smile, high strained voice; sustained sharing of positive affect and interest in play that feels fluid, spontaneous; taking responsibility for initiating and guiding the interaction with the child in an appropriate parental manner when enters room, even if interaction is not carefully attuned to infant's signals).

11. Negative behaviors not usually seen among fearful mothers (e.g., persistently seeking affection or attention from child; persistent self-referential behavior; looming into infant's space; sustained intrusive, controlling behavior toward child).

are repeated indications in the literature that parents in this group are harder to identify because their more withdrawing and fearful but non-hostile behaviors are harder to discriminate from more confident and structuring parental behaviors. Second, this fearful but nonhostile behavior pattern is likely to be particularly prevalent in low-risk middle-income samples, where 15% of infants are still classified disorganized. Finally, there is repeated evidence that, compared to D-avoid-resist infants, D-approach infants are at equal risk for a variety of negative outcomes, including elevated cortisol secretion to mild stressors in infancy (Hertsgaard et al., 1995; Spangler & Grossmann, 1993), elevated hostile-aggressive behaviors toward peers in kindergarten and second grade (Lyons-Ruth, Alpern, & Repacholi, 1993; Lyons-Ruth, Easterbrooks, & Cibelli, 1997), and elevated rates of controlling attachment patterns toward parents by age 6 (Main & Cassidy, 1988; Wartner, Grossmann, Fremmer-Bombik, & Suess, 1994). Figure 4.2 displays the percentage of children in

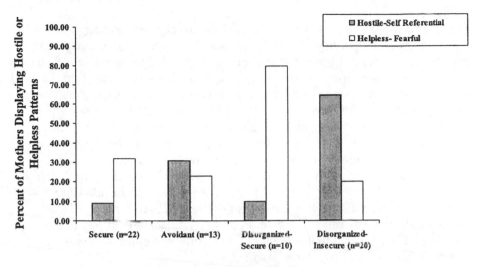

FIG. 4.1. Percentage of mothers displaying hostile-self-referential or help-less-fearful patterns by infant attachment classification.

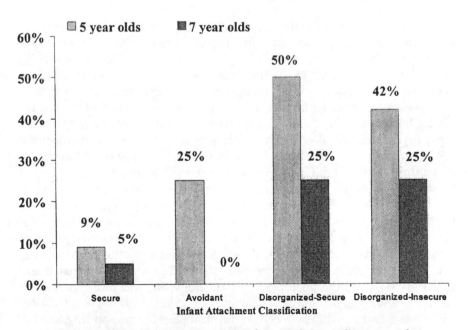

FIG. 4.2. Percent of children in each infant attachment subgroup rated over clinical cut-off points for hostile behavior by teachers in kindergarten and second grade.

our own sample in each disorganized subgroup at age 5 and age 7 rated by teachers as displaying clinically significant aggressive, externalizing behaviors. We would predict that mothers in the helpless-fearful group would show more appropriate caregiving behavior when the child's attachment system is not aroused and would become more fearful, hesitant, contradictory, or withdrawn when the infants' fearful and distressed attachment affects are more directly aroused and expressed. At such times, one would expect the mother's own underlying sense of helplessness to become more pronounced. As the infant begins to react with conflict and apprehension to the mother's hesitancy and fear in responding to attachment affects, the mother's sense of helplessness would be likely to increase. This transactional process might lead to the more obvious dysregulation in the relationship and compensatory controlling behavior on the part of the child that is evident by the time the child is seen during the preschool period (see later discussion).

UNDERSTANDING INTERGENERATIONAL CYCLES: THE EMERGENCE OF CONTROLLING ATTACHMENT BEHAVIORS

As children develop over the preschool years, many formerly disorganized infants reorganize their attachment behaviors into controlling behaviors toward the parent by the time they reach school age (Main & Cassidy, 1988; Wartner et al., 1994). Again, these new controlling behaviors can take two very different forms: either controlling through more punitive, coercive behaviors or controlling through more solicitous, directing, caregiving behaviors. These controlling behaviors appear to become increasingly organized over the preschool years. Solomon, George, and DeJong (1995) also reported differences in the fantasy play behavior of caregiving and punitive children: Caregiving children tend to inhibit their fantasy play while punitive children exhibit more chaotic play scenarios, with themes of unresolved danger and blocked access to care and safety. We have speculated that the two organizations of parenting behavior described earlier also provide the relational context for the emergence of these two distinct forms of controlling behavior during the preschool period. We speculate further that the two infant subgroups, D-approach and D-avoid-resist, are the precursors to the caregiving and punitive stances observed among controlling children at age 6. Along with others, we view these two stances as different behavioral strategies for responding to similar core representational and affective themes, namely a disruption in the regulatory function of the caregiving system that exposes the child to inadequately modulated fear. We hypothesize further that, without intervention, these punitive or caregiving behavioral manifestations become consolidated and are reflected in the parenting constellations we have termed *hostile* and *helpless* parenting stances. Longitudinal data to evaluate these postulated longitudinal links between the two D subgroups in infancy and the two controlling subgroups during the preschool period, and these two observed parenting profiles, are still lacking.

HOSTILE–HELPLESS INTERNAL WORKING MODELS OF RELATIONSHIPS

Although the two polarized behavioral profiles observed among mothers whose children were disorganized appear superficially to be quite different, we have advanced the theory that these two different constellations of parenting behavior can be meaningfully explained as alternate behavioral expressions of a single underlying hostile–helpless dyadic internal model (Lyons-Ruth, Bronfman, & Atwood, 1999).

In what follows, we briefly outline a model of how hostile–helpless internal models of attachment relationships are thought to contribute to the emergence of disorganized attachment behaviors in infancy (Lyons-Ruth, Bronfman, & Atwood, 1999). Our thoughts about the role of contradictory hostile–helpless internal models began with our data on the severity of trauma in the mother's childhood and its relation to her own interactive behaviors with her infant at home (Lyons-Ruth & Block, 1996). Those data revealed that the severity of trauma in the mother's childhood predicted her own increased withdrawal from responsive affective engagement with her infant when observed at home. In addition to the withdrawal noted among mothers with more severe trauma, a second finding specifically related physical violence or abuse in the mother's childhood to increased covert hostility and intrusive behavior toward her infant. However, this increased subtle hostility and interference was not displayed by mothers who had experienced sexual abuse without associated physical abuse: Those mothers displayed only emotional and physical withdrawal. Because clinical treatment of sexual abuse survivors clearly reveals the underlying fear and rage of those who have been victimized (cf. Terr, 1991), we felt that both groups of mothers were likely to have experienced unbalanced victim or aggressor relational patterns in their families of origin. However, sexually abused mothers appeared more likely to manage their negative affects by withdrawing from interaction with the infant, whereas mothers who had been exposed to violence or physical abuse appeared to handle their underlying fear by identifying with an aggressive style of interaction.

We view hostile–helpless relational models as influenced by parents' own experiences in their families of origin, models that then guide similar patterns of behavior with their own children. According to this hypothesis, in the mother's own childhood her needs for protection and comfort when fearfully aroused or distressed were not adequately met. Indeed, her own caregivers may have displayed frightened, frightening, or other contradictory or atypical behaviors toward her in moments of her greatest need for physical closeness and soothing. The result of this repeated lack of adequate comfort and protection was a dysregulation of arousal, which over time led to the development of chronic mechanisms of fight (e.g., anger, aggression) or flight (e.g., dissociation, withdrawal). At a more relational level, these hostile or helpless stances were also likely to have been displayed by her own parents, both in relation to one another and in relation to her as a child. Therefore, these preadapted individual responses to fearful arousal were likely to have been further consolidated by established patterns of family interaction.

According to this model, as a woman makes the transition from emphasizing the fulfillment of her own attachment needs to becoming the attachment figure for her own child (e.g., from "protected" to "protector," George & Solomon, 1996), her experience of being comforted will inform her ability to comfort her children. If a parent has not experienced comfort in relation to her own fear-evoking experiences, then her infant's pain, distress, or fear may evoke her own physiological arousal, painful memories, and negative emotion related to reexperiencing her early vulnerability and lack of comfort. She thus comes to see her own child as triggering these vulnerable affects (e.g., feelings of being helpless, enraged, or out of control) and herself as helpless to protect or control her child. George and Solomon first described the pervasive sense of helplessness in relation to the child that was evident in the caregiving interviews of parents whose children were classified in the disorganized category. These experiences of helplessness were related either to a sense of the child as "larger than life," that is, as especially smart or gifted, or to a sense of the child as impossible to control or influence.

We theorize further that, when parents become aroused by fearful stimuli, they may be caught in a dilemma of needing to seek resolution for their own unresolved attachment needs as well as needing to tend to those of their children. This underlying conflict may give rise to contradictory caregiving behaviors that may be internalized by the vulnerable infant as contradictory and unintegrated models of the parent and of the parent–infant relationship. Other parents may suppress the contradictory elements of the internal model and act only in the role of either the hostile or the helpless party in the relationship. In such asymmetric dyadic interactions, in which one partner's attachment-related goals or initiatives are elaborated at the expense of the other's, the resulting dyadic internal model is also contradictory in that the relationship is unbalanced and encompasses two polar roles, for example, hostile child and helpless adult or controlled child and controlling adult. Importantly, what is represented is the entire dyadic relational pattern of controlled self and controlling other, even though as adults the parents may disavow their identification with one of the roles (e.g., the controlled child) and behave according to only one of the positions (e.g., the controlling adult).

Entering parenthood with a hostile–helpless internal working model of relationships should place a parent at risk for acting from the extreme stance of one of these unbalanced behavioral positions or for showing contradictory behaviors that reflect his or her experience and conflict around both relational roles. In the current study, we found support for both of these theoretical assertions. Mothers of children with disorganized attachments could be subgrouped into either those displaying negative-intrusive and self-referential behaviors, or those showing fearful and withdrawn behaviors, whereas mothers in both groups tended to show some form of contradictory affective communications.

In the hostile subtype, parents may be identified with a malevolently represented caregiver from childhood, an identification that is maintained through unintegrated, or split, internal models that hold in place a contradictory, polarized model of relationships. Caregivers who display a hostile interaction pattern appear to be attempting to master unbearable feelings of vulnerability by denying their own feelings of fear and helplessness. This denial may be accomplished through suppression of conscious experience of vulnerable emotions and through consistently controlling others in relationships. Behaviorally, parents in this group may reenact discipline by coercion, suppression of children's anger, and premature encouragement of children's autonomy. In these families, both researchers and clinicians note extreme attempts to control children's behavior, with subsequent chains of reciprocal coercive behavior and negative affectivity between parents and children (e.g., Patterson, 1982).

In the helpless-fearful subtype, parents may have adopted a lifelong caregiving adaptation characterized by paying attention to the needs of others (e.g., their own parent) at the expense of having their own attachment needs met. Clinically, mothers in this category appear to be fearful and easily overwhelmed by the demands of others. Their longtime focus on others may be based on a coping strategy of dissociating from their own affect life and withdrawing from closer emotional contacts with others, so that they feel powerless to control their children when their own affects are aroused. Their anxiety and fear of close emotional contact may be noted by their children, who, in turn, develop caregiving strategies to support their parents, thus perpetuating intergenerational cycles. However,

mothers in the helpless subgroup do not seem to display the more pervasive suppression of emotional life and adoption of the tough, invulnerable
stance that characterizes the hostile subgroup.

To avoid becoming flooded by their overwhelming affects, mothers
may need to engage in behaviors that appear either frightening (e.g., suppressing children's emotions, yelling) or frightened (dissociating, withdrawing) to the child. Mothers' preoccupation with regulating their own
affect states and the extreme nature of their distancing behaviors may interfere with their ability to repair miscommunications once they occur. Infants and children are likely to be frightened by the lack of comfort when
their attachment needs are activated and confused by the disproportionate intensity of their parents' responses. They appear to adapt to the
irresolvable paradox produced by their caregivers' behaviors with a mix
of approach-avoidance, frozen-dissociative, and other atypical behaviors.

We speculate that hostile or helpless parental stances may reflect alternative expressions of a single unbalanced dominant-submissive relationship prototype experienced in the parent's own attachment history. As a
single dyadic prototype, we would expect that individuals displaying disorganized or controlling strategies would have access to both the hostile
and helpless aspects of this single representational model. The degree to
which either the hostile or helpless position in this dyadic organization is
identified with the self may depend on situational, temperamental, and
cultural factors, as well as aspects of the individual's particular relationship history, and we would expect that a single individual could display
either or both of these relational stances at different times or in different
situations or relationships.

Unresolved parental loss or trauma has also been empirically associated with disorganized attachment patterns in infancy (Main et al., 1985;
van IJzendoorn et al., 1999). A hostile–helpless relational process is proposed to contribute to the transmission of disorganized attachment
through four mechanisms, as shown in Fig. 4.3. First, hostile–helpless interactions are directly related to disorganized behaviors in infancy; second, the cumulative trauma of hostile–helpless interaction patterns that
continue throughout childhood will maintain controlling attachment behaviors into adulthood, whether or not the child experiences more dis-
crete forms of loss or trauma; third, traumatic loss or abuse will be more
likely to occur in the context of hostile–helpless family interaction patterns
because of the parents' difficulty in closely monitoring and responding to
their own and their child's vulnerabilities; and, fourth, these traumatic experiences are less likely to be resolved by a child or adult in a hostile–helpless relationship because they will usually not have access to adequate
comfort and protection from an attachment figure. This theoretical model
is elaborated in more detail in Lyons-Ruth, Bronfman, and Atwood (1999).

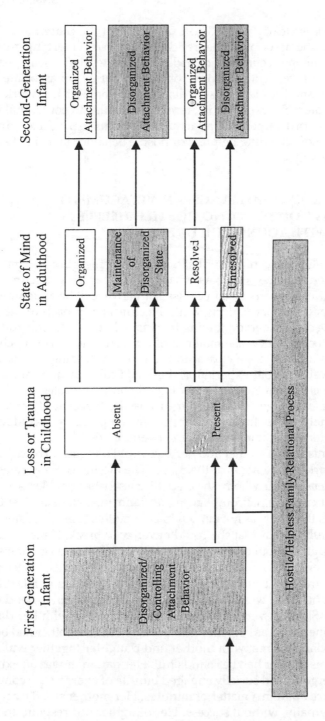

FIG. 4.3. Proposed contributions of a hostile–helpless relational diathesis to the inter-generational transmission of disorganized/controlling attachment.

More work is clearly needed to examine both the maternal behavior patterns and the associated theoretical hypotheses emerging from this work. However, the accumulated evidence indicates that researchers need to continue to investigate the developmental pathways associated with both helpless and hostile forms of disorganization. Further work is also needed to explore the experiential, temperamental, and contextual factors that interact with disorganized attachment patterns to produce a differential likelihood of activating helpless or hostile behavior in intimate attachment relationships.

COMFORT AND COMPLIANCE: AN ATTACHMENT PERSPECTIVE ON TREATING HOSTILE–HELPLESS PARENTS WITH YOUNG CHILDREN

What are some of the clinical implications of this emerging understanding of the relational contexts associated with disorganized attachment patterns? Here we focus on one clinical issue that we feel the attachment perspective illuminates particularly well: the clinical approach to the parent whose young child is demonstrating increasingly coercive, controlling behavior. We focus on the case material of a parent with a young child because that is the age range closest to the research findings we have presented. However, in our experience, these clinical principles are relevant whether the child is a toddler, school aged child, or adolescent. We first sketch out a case vignette and then discuss how recent attachment research can help focus the clinical approach. To preserve confidentiality, the case material is composited from several cases.

The patients were a mother and her 2-year-old daughter. The child's parents both worked long hours at their jobs. The mother came in referred by her pediatrician, with whom she had discussed her problems with her daughter's increasing noncompliance and tantrums. Her statement of her problem was that she was not cut out to be a mother. Her daughter was so demanding all the time that she could never get a break. If she tried to say "no" her daughter would have a screaming fit and she was getting so frustrated with her that she really did not like her. In her words, "I feel like I'm really a bad mother. I probably shouldn't have had kids at all." She also said that her husband was always angry at her for giving in to her daughter all the time. She was very afraid that her relationship with her daughter would become as bad as her relationship with her own mother had been.

The clinician also met with mother and daughter together and understood that this mother had her hands full. Her daughter was an extremely curious, energetic, and socially engaged bundle of energy who completely took the office apart in a matter of minutes. Her mother stood by trying to intervene verbally, without success. Her daughter did respond to the clinician stepping in and structuring the play while participating in it with her, and with guiding help the child was able to play with one toy at a time and put each toy away, partly as a game, before taking out the next one. This experience left the therapist able to talk with the mother in positive terms about both the demands and the rewards that her daughter's energy and curiosity were likely to present and to empathize with the challenges she might experience in setting limits with her daughter.

Whereas the surface problem appeared to be one of setting limits effectively with her daughter, an attachment perspective suggests that a more complex set of issues needs to be evaluated and addressed. The first step was to take a developmental and family history and establish that other issues such as recent family changes, substance abuse, marital conflict, or problems with extrafamilial childcare providers were not likely contributors to the problem.

After a thorough evaluation, an attachment perspective offered several guidelines for approaching the problem. First, for parents with hostile–helpless relationship histories, attachment needs become entangled with role-boundary confusions, hostility, and fears of abandonment. This knot of confused feelings and contradictory responses must be identified and sorted out if the parent is to find his or her way to both meeting the child's attachment needs and setting limits effectively. Second, attachment research has demonstrated that the quality of the attachment relationship is influenced by internal models of the parenting the parents themselves received as a child (van IJzendoorn, 1995). Other research has established that the same process of intergenerational transmission occurs in relation to disciplinary practices (Elder, Caspi, & Downey, 1986; Ge, Fan, & Wenk, 2000). Thus, the parent's own childhood experiences and his or her evaluation of those experiences needs to be explored. Third, clinicians must be mindful of the degree to which their own responses to parents are in the service of constructing a current secure base for the parents so that the parents feel safe to explore their own life histories and current parenting experiences. Conveying these principles implicitly, by modeling them in one's own manner of relating to the parents, may be the best way to convey the possibility of a different way of responding to anger or vulnerability. We discuss these guidelines in reverse order.

Therapist as Secure Base for Exploration

The attachment literature can guide therapists in attempting to provide a secure therapeutic base from which parents can both explore the problem and simultaneously internalize a security-promoting model for parenting their own children. Arguably, the parent is the most important patient. Therefore, clinicians need to approach parents the way they would want

TABLE 4.3
Therapist as Secure Base: Providing an Implicit
Model for the Parent–Child Dialogue

1. Listen to the parent.
2. Express approval and positive regard for the parent.
3. Encourage communication about all kinds of affects.
4. Respond to hostility with increased attention, openness to listening, and problem solving. In the attachment literature, anger and distress are understood as attachment behaviors. These attachment behaviors are often expressed in heightened form if the parent or child has had a parent who was reluctant or inconsistent in responding to less dramatic signals.
5. Join with parent empathically around the complexities of parenting, pointing out that: (a) All children are different, thus, there are no cookie-cutter answers; (b) all children are complicated, thus, simple answers often do not work; (c) every parent struggles to figure out how best to be the parent of this particular child—if you as a parent are trying to figure that out, you are on the right track; (d) one of the tougher problems of parenting is in figuring out when to give more love and when to be firm about limits.
6. Encourage a patient but hopeful problem-solving approach (e.g., "Let's spend some time thinking together about exactly where the problems come up and what might be contributing to them").
7. Maintain an active, balanced, collaborative dialogue with the parent.

the parents to approach their children. This involves maintaining a balance between attentive responsiveness to the parents' feelings and goals and offering helpful structure and direction around those goals. Although most therapists arrive at a helpful, empathic stance intuitively, it can be conceptually useful to spell out some elements of such a responsive dialogue that are also supported by parent–child research. The salient point is to be aware that there are always at least two levels to the parent–therapist transactions—the overt content and the implicit modeling of how a variety of problems and vulnerable affects can be approached and problem solved together. What therapists do with the parent is likely to speak louder than what they say and can potentially be transferred by the parent into the dialogue with the child. Table 4.3 outlines some of the elements that the developmental literature would indicate are important ingredients of secure parent–child relationships and that also contribute to an open and balanced therapeutic dialogue (see Bretherton, 1988; Baldwin, Cole, & Baldwin, 1982).

The Parents' Childhood History of Comfort, Sharing, and Discipline

The parents' own childhood experiences around both comforting interactions and discipline need to be elicited and explored in the process of establishing the parents' goals for the work. How were closeness, cuddling, and comforting handled when they were young (the child's age now)? What did they like and not like about their parents' ways of handling things? How would they like to be similar to or different from their own parents? Most often, parents can identify ways that they felt as a child that they do not want their child to feel. However, they often cannot make the links between their own negative feelings, the problematic parental behaviors they experienced, and an alternative way of approaching the interaction that might feel differently. Constructing a joint sense of what the parent wants to accomplish is the first piece of work. An extensive research literature on autonomous, dismissing, and preoccupied models of attachment, as well as the hostile–helpless models discussed in this chapter, is available to guide the clinician in understanding the different models of parenting parents might bring to treatment, as well as their long-term correlates in child behavior (for reviews, see Bretherton, 1988; Hesse, 1999; Main, 1993).

If the parent is espousing a somewhat distanced encouragement of independence, competition, and discipline, at the expense of a closer, more open responsiveness to the child's anger or distress, and if this is a consistent, nonconfusing stance that the parents agree on, research indicates that this parental style is not predictive of behavior problems per se. Escalating tension between children and parents is likely to be a sign that this organized stance favoring restricted emotional expression is not consistent and is punctuated by angry outbursts or complete withdrawal on the part of the parent.

Similarly, if the parents' style is somewhat heightening of emotional responses to others and tends to draw the child's attention to family relationships and, mildly, to the concerns of the parent, this can also be a nonproblematic cultural variation, as long as the parent does not abdicate a parental role. If the parent can provide appropriate parental structure and distress regulation for the child and does not unduly exacerbate the child's fearful responses to the world, a somewhat self-involved or family-enmeshed parenting style has not been correlated with behavior problems or psychopathology.

Not until parental stances approach the helpless, childlike, or excessively fearful stances associated with role reversal as the child becomes older, or the contradictory push–pull of the hostile but self-referential parent, who rejects the child's vulnerable feelings while simultaneously asking for the child's attention, are clear correlations found with child problem behavior. Parents with young children who present for treatment are often at the beginning of an escalating coercive process where the child is becoming more and more demanding in an increasingly frantic attempt to feel comforted and safe with the parent and the parent is feeling increasingly helpless and angry.

THE TANGLED KNOT AT THE HEART
OF HOSTILE–HELPLESS RELATIONSHIPS

The Emerging Conflict of Wills Between Parent and Toddler

Winnicott (1969) described most eloquently the normal developmental imperative behind a young child's need to test parents' convictions about the rules they set. Although he worded this developmental push in terms of earlier psychoanalytic models of development, he captured very well the developmental thrust behind children's need to explore the limits that the world will place on the expression of their wills and the need to explore, in particular, the balance that will be struck between the expression of the child's will and the expression of the parent's will. All 2- to 4-year-olds will test the parent's convictions and explore the balance of wills that characterizes their relationship.

However, this is not a new drama that emerges in toddlerhood, as is often portrayed. Toddlers' ability to hold their own desire in mind over an extended period and resist distractions is new as is their ability to verbalize a "no" (e.g., Kagan, 1981). In addition, they have a new ability to think about, and therefore to want to identify, those qualities of the world or of behavior that are labeled "bad" and "good" (Emde, Johnson, & Easterbrooks, 1987; Kagan, 1981). All of these new abilities lend a different quality to the parent's negotiations with the toddler.

However, children's wish to be on the "good" side, that is, to stay in the parents' good graces and comply with their rules, is a function of the positive relationship between them, not primarily a function of the severity of the discipline (Matas, Arend, & Sroufe, 1978; Patterson, 1982). Moreover, the balance of initiative between parent and child has been negotiated between them since the first moments of life. Because the child's earliest initiatives are attachment-related, that is, related to regulating distress by seeking contact, comfort, and pleasurable exchanges with the parent, this balance of initiatives is first worked out in relation to the infant's attachment initiatives. To the extent that the infant's attachment behaviors and affects have been responded to with fear, nonresponse, or contradictory behaviors, the child enters toddlerhood with less investment in maintaining a positive tie to the caregiver, with more anticipation of a noncooperative response from the parent, and with atypical heightened or numbed physiological responses to stressors that make affect regulation more difficult. These difficulties on the part of the child, in turn, make the parent's task more difficult. Not surprisingly, parents often react by feeling even more helpless to satisfy and guide their child and by becoming increasingly enraged at the child and frightened by the intensity of their anger.

Parents with a hostile–helpless relational model are then faced with a painful emotional dilemma. First, they can suppress their own anger and helplessly capitulate to the child's will to avoid hostile retaliation and feared further loss of any possibility of a positive attachment relationship. However, this helpless stance on the part of the parent does not assuage the child's anger at the parent's underlying emotional unavailability and is only likely to fuel escalating coercive or punitive behaviors by the child. In addition, some parents, consciously or unconsciously, admire the child's angry, punitive behaviors as evidence that the child is not stuck in the same helpless position as they are. From an intrapsychic psychodynamic perspective, one would say that parents project their own hostile impulses onto the child and receive unconscious gratification when those impulses are expressed by the child. From the perspective of internalized relational models, the child may be experienced as, and then gradually inducted into, the role of the admired and hated dominating or abusive figure in the parent's own childhood. Child characteristics will play a role in the degree to which the child more plausibly elicits this identification with a domineering parent. Alternately, parents can identify with the hostile parent in their own past and reenact the painful cycles of anger, aggression, and emotional abandonment from the position of the person with greater power. Faced with these two available but equally unsatisfactory models, parents may also shift from one to the other in their approaches to the child.

Parents are often caught between these two fears, either that they will assert limits and become the hated, domineering parent of their own childhood, or that they will fail to set limits and the child will become the hated, emotionally abusive figure from the past. Research indicates that this dilemma around limit setting and assertive behavior is often related to a deeper dilemma surrounding attachment and abandonment. Research findings and clinical insight suggest that parents in disorganized attachment relationships are likely to have experienced some degree of emotional abandonment in relation to their own parents. It is likely, then, that they will be particularly fearful of losing the child's love and reexperiencing emotional abandonment, as well as fearful of their own anger about their frustrated attachment needs and the potential for experiencing that anger in destructive or abusive ways toward the child. Needless to say, parents may not be aware of these many conflicting emotions. How can the clinician help parents to unravel some of the strands of this increasingly tangled knot at the heart of the relationship with their child?

SEPARATING THE STRANDS OF THE KNOT

In working with parents of coercive or punitive children, we have found it important to help the parent clearly distinguish between the attachment needs and feelings of the child and the nonattachment components of the child's self-assertive behaviors, and to adapt different models for understanding these two sets of behaviors. Confusion between these two domains often occurs in the thinking of both clinicians and parents and this confusion is also evident in the parent-advice literature, where advocates of consistent limit setting vie with advocates of responsive understanding of the child's needs. One group stresses that responding to anger or distress or noncompliant behavior reinforces the behavior, whereas the other group points out that basic needs, if not fulfilled, will increase the child's escalating angry or distressed behavior.

Clearly, both reinforcement models and need-fulfillment models are compelling and relevant to a full understanding of human behavior, particularly for attachment and limit setting in early childhood. However, a continual challenge of parenting lies in understanding which model is relevant to which behaviors and at what times. Moreover, finding the relevant model for understanding a particular parenting dilemma can be particularly challenging for parents who have themselves experienced hostile–helpless relationship patterns in their families of origin.

In hostile–helpless interactions, in particular, research indicates that attachment and limit-setting interactions have gone awry and have become entangled with one another. Clinically significant problems during the preschool period are likely to involve disorganization of the attachment relationship (Greenberg, Speltz, DeKlyen, & Endriga, 1991; Lyons-Ruth et al., 1993; Moss, Parent, Gosselin, Rousseau, & St. Laurent, 1996) as well as overly harsh, overly timid, or inconsistent limit setting. Therefore, the clinician does not need to choose between limit-setting and need-fulfillment models of behavior. However, it is important to sort out when each model is most appropriate for guiding the approach to the child. Disentangling these two components is particularly important for parents with a hostile–helpless relational model because aggression and emotional abandonment have become intertwined in their thinking. This makes it difficult to imagine how not only to become more emotionally supportive and available to the child but also to feel comfortable and effective in saying "no" when necessary.

In our clinical experience, the first priority is to help parents feel more confident and hopeful about their ability to make an emotional connection with their child before useful progress can be made in combining closeness with limits. This requires developing the conceptual distinction between fulfilling attachment needs and setting limits so that each component can be worked on separately.

This conceptual distinction needs to be worked out in relation to both the child's behaviors and the kinds of penalties or limits the parent might impose. For example, child behaviors such as "he clings to me all the time" or "she always has to get up to get extra hugs at bedtime" are more closely attachment related than "she kicks and bites her younger sister." Setting limits on attachment behaviors is likely to exacerbate the oppositional behavior rather than lead to increased closeness and security.

Similarly, some types of threats or penalties are more likely to exacerbate the child's attachment insecurity than others, for example, penalties such as "I won't read to you and put you to bed if you treat me like that" or threats such as "If you keep that up, I'll send you to grandma's for the whole summer," are more threatening to the attachment relationship than penalties such as losing TV or dessert privileges. Making these distinctions during the initial evaluation period, as the current problems in the relationship are formulated and goals for the work are set, begins to help the parent to conceptualize the attachment domain separately from the domain of limits, which have more to do with respecting the rights of others.

These distinctions are not easy to make, of course, partly because anger and distress are important attachment affects and behaviors for children. In other words, these emotions may be expressed or even exaggerated to signal to the parent that her attention and care are needed. The less consistently responsive the parent, the more likely the stronger signal of anger will be added to the child's expressive attachment behavior (Cassidy & Berlin, 1994).

Attachment need fulfillment and limit setting are also difficult to disentangle because behavior is multidetermined and many of the child's emotional reactions, such as hitting a sibling, have an attachment component. The challenge of uncovering the meaning of the child's behavior is one of the primary difficulties shared by all parents. Therapists can explicitly acknowledge this difficulty and commiserate with the parent around it, while also communicating confidence that the parent can still ultimately understand the child's behavior well enough to develop a positive relationship.

Exploring Current Interactions Around Comfort, Emotional Sharing, and Limit Setting

These points can best be illustrated by returning to the clinical illustration of the mother and her 2-year-old daughter. After getting a developmental and family history and finding no other serious family dysfunction, the therapist asked the mother about her experiences growing up, her relationships with her own parents, and in what ways she wanted to parent similarly to or differently from them. She was frank about how critical her own mother was of her, how immature and unreliable her mother was, and how little structure her mother was able to provide for the household. The patient had had undue responsibility for the care of her younger sister, which she resented. She considered herself both neglected and emotionally abused and had particularly hated some of her mother's boyfriends, who were alcoholic and explosive, though not abusive to her. She was very afraid that her relationship with her daughter was now on the same deteriorating path as her own relationship with her mother.

The therapist then began to explore very carefully exactly which behaviors of her daughter were problematic and when they occurred. (In our experience, clinical meaning is often revealed in the details.) As mother and therapist delineated the various incidents of the past week, they also constructed a picture of the family schedule and routines. It emerged that a particularly difficult time occurred at the end of the parents' long work days, when the mother would come home at 7:00 or 7:30 and her daughter would follow her around and cling to her. When the mother tried to set limits on her clinging behavior, her daughter would throw increasingly out-of-control tantrums. The tantrums also began occurring at nap time and at other times when the parents needed to ask for her compliance with household routines. The daughter's behavior was angering the father, who became increasingly critical of his wife for not setting limits with her. The mother, however, sensed the increasing alienation between her daughter and herself and feared replaying the lack of love in her relationship with her own mother, while at the same time becoming more and more angry and helpless in relation to her daughter. The therapist discussed the possibility that either attachment insecurity or inconsistent limits or both were contributing to her daughter's escalating behavior and examined these issues in relation to how the mother remembered experiencing these kinds of interactions in her own childhood and what would have felt better to her as a child.

The therapist suggested, and she agreed, that they should first focus on strengthening the positive relationship between mother and daughter and see what they could learn before thinking more about limit setting. The mother and therapist talked more about the nature of the child's attachment needs and about how important the mother was to her child, and they explored how often the two had close, positive, quiet time together. This led to an exploration of how much time she could set aside to be with her child, given the business that she ran out of her home. The therapist empathized with the dilemma the mother faced about the relative pressures of income, achievement, and parenthood, and explored what kind of problem solving could be done given the life pressures that the mother felt confined her. Initially, she could see little possibility of spending any more time with her child. However, she very much wanted the relationship to be better and she did decide that she could be more understanding and more patient with her daughter's need for her company when she was at home, despite her husband's pressure. Implicit aspects of this phase of the treatment were the therapist's (a) permission and encouragement to share close moments with her child, (b) confidence that their relationship could improve, and (c) assurance that responsiveness to the child's attachment needs was not the same as spoiling her child and, in fact, could lead to an easier time in setting limits on non-attachment-related behaviors.

A fortunate piece of serendipity in the treatment came about when a long-planned vacation week occurred after the first few weeks of treatment. The mother felt she would be able to spend a lot of time with her daughter, without the need to come and go several times a day as she did with her work at home, and she agreed that this was a good chance to see whether her daughter's behavior was less tense and noncompliant when she had more relaxed, positive time with her parents.

The week went very well and the mother came back from it saying that, for the first time in months, she really loved her daughter again. They had all gotten along well, she felt like a loving and competent parent, and, most importantly, she could see how important she was and how much her daughter was reacting partly out of insecurity about her mother's availability. Although the mother's job situation could not change, her attitude toward her daughter when she was with her did change, which began to ease the daughter's outbursts.

The therapist then began to talk about the complexities of setting limits and the mother's fears and concerns about either losing her daughter's love or being defeated by her daughter's noncompliance. However, once she began to see how to be closer to her daughter and to sense when her daughter needed more comfort and quiet time with her, saying "no" to her daughter lost much of the anxiety that before had been related to becoming a rageful parent like her own mother and losing her daughter's love. Mother and therapist problem solved finding ways of setting limits that the mother felt confident were not too punitive and were not ultimately damaging of the mother-daughter relationship. They also explored how to choose methods that the mother knew she could follow through on without becoming defeated and helpless. They also worked out how the mother could take the initiative in becoming friends with her child again after she had had to say "no." Once she began to feel that she could be firm and step in before her own anger had escalated and that her ways of stopping the behavior were not ultimately damaging to her child or to their relationship, she decided to enforce naptime firmly, rode through the first tantrum with great trepidation but did not back down, and was surprised and relieved to find that she and her daughter were friends again after the nap was over. After this, she steadily gained confidence in herself as a parent, in the ultimate goodness of her child, and in the solidity of their relationship together.

REFERENCES

Ainsworth, M. D. S., Blehar, M., Waters, E., & Wall, S. (1978). *Patterns of attachment*. Hillsdale, NJ: Lawrence Erlbaum Associates.

Baldwin, A. L., Cole, R. E., & Baldwin, C. P. (Eds.). (1982). Parental pathology, family interaction, and the competence of the child in school. *Monographs of the Society for Research in Child Development, 47*, 90.

Bretherton, I. (1988). Open communication and internal working models: Their role in the development of attachment relationships. In R. A. Thompson (Ed.), *Nebraska Symposium on Motivation: Socio-emotional development* (pp. 57–113). Lincoln: University of Nebraska Press.

Carlson, V., Cicchetti, D., Barnett, D., & Braunwald, K. (1989). Disorganized/disoriented attachment relationships in maltreated infants. *Developmental Psychology, 25*, 525–531.

Cassidy, J., & Berlin, L. (1994). The Insecure/ambivalent pattern of attachment: Theory and research. *Child Development, 65*, 971–991.

Coplan, J., Andrews, M., Rosenblum, L., Owens, M., Friedman, S., Gorman, J., & Nemeroff, C. (1996). Persistent elevations of cerebrospinal fluid concentrations of corticotropin-releasing factor in adult nonhuman primates exposed to early-life stressors: Implications for the pathophysiology of mood and anxiety disorders. *Proceedings of the National Academy of Sciences, USA, 93*, 1619–1623.

Elder, G., Caspi, A., & Downey, G. (1986). Problem behavior and family relationships: Life course and intergenerational themes. In A. Sorensen, F. Weinert, & L. Sherrod (Eds.), *Human development: Interdisciplinary perspectives* (pp. 293–340). Hillsdale, NJ: Lawrence Erlbaum Associates.

Emde, R. N., Johnson, W. F., & Easterbrooks, M. A. (1987). The do's and don'ts of early moral development: Psychoanalytic tradition and current research. In J. Kagan & S. Lamb (Eds.), *The emergence of morality in young children* (pp. 245–276). Chicago: University of Chicago Press.

Francis, D., Diorio, J., Liu, D., & Meaney, M. (1999). Non genomic transmission across generations of maternal behavior and stress responses in the rat. *Science, 286*, 1155–1158.

Ge, X., Fan, J., & Wenk, E. (2000, March). *Trajectories of criminal offending of serious juvenile offenders*. Paper presented at the Psychopathology Across Time: Studying Trajectories of Maladaptive Functioning from Adolescence Through Early Adulthood Symposium, Chicago, IL.

George, C., & Solomon, J. (1996). Representational models of relationships: Links between caregiving and attachment. *Infant Mental Health Journal, 17*, 198–216.

Greenberg, M. T., Speltz, M. L., DeKlyen, M., & Endriga, M. C. (1991). Attachment security in preschoolers with and without externalizing problems: A replication. *Development and Psychopathology, 3*, 413–430.

Hertsgaard, L., Gunnar, M., Erickson, M. F., & Nachmias, M. (1995). Adrenocortical response to the Strange Situation in infants with disorganized/disoriented attachment relationships. *Child Development, 66*, 1100–1106.

Hesse, E. (1999). The adult attachment interview: Historical and current perspectives. In J. Cassidy & P. R. Shaver (Eds.), *Handbook of attachment: Theory, research, and clinical applications*. New York: Guilford Press.

Jansen, A., Nguyen, X., Karpitskiy, V., Mettenleiter, T., & Loewy, A. (1995). Central command neurons of the sympathetic nervous system: Basis of the fight-or-flight response. *Science, 270,* 644–646.

Kagan, J. (1981). *The second year: The emergence of self-awareness.* Cambridge, MA: Harvard University Press.

Lyons-Ruth, K., Alpern, L., & Repacholi, B. (1993). Disorganized infant attachment classification and maternal psychosocial problems as predictors of hostile-aggressive behavior in the preschool classroom. *Child Development, 64,* 572–585.

Lyons-Ruth, K., & Block, D. (1996). The disturbed caregiving system: Relations among childhood trauma, maternal caregiving, and infant affect and attachment. *Infant Mental Health Journal, 17,* 257–275.

Lyons-Ruth, K., Bronfman, E., & Atwood, G. (1999). A relational diathesis model of hostile–helpless states of mind: Expressions in mother-infant interaction. In J. Solomon & C. George (Eds.), *Attachment disorganization* (pp. 33–70). New York: Guilford Press.

Lyons-Ruth, K., Bronfman, E., & Parsons, E. (1999). Atypical maternal behavior and disorganized infant attachment strategies: Frightened, frightening, and atypical maternal behavior and disorganized infant attachment strategies. In J. Vondra & D. Barnett (Eds.), *Atypical patterns of infant attachment: Theory, research, and current directions* (Society for Research in Child Development, Monograph No. 258, pp. 67–96). Blackwell.

Lyons-Ruth, K., Easterbrooks, M. A., & Cibelli, C. D. (1997). Infant attachment strategies, infant mental lag, and maternal depressive symptoms: Predictors of internalizing and externalizing problems at age 7. *Developmental Psychology, 33,* 681–692.

Lyons-Ruth, K., & Jacobvitz, D. (1999). Attachment disorganization: Unresolved loss, relational violence, and lapses in behavioral and attentional strategies. In J. Cassidy & P. Shaver (Eds.), *Handbook of attachment: Theory, research, and clinical implications* (pp. 520–554). New York: Guilford Press.

Main, M. (1993). Discourse, prediction and recent studies in attachment: Implications for psychoanalysis. *Journal of the American Psychoanalytic Association, 61*(Supplement on Research in Psychoanalysis), 209–243.

Main, M., & Cassidy, J. (1988). Categories of response to reunion with the parent at age 6: Predictable from infant attachment classifications and stable over a 1-month period. *Developmental Psychology, 24,* 415–426.

Main, M., & Hesse, E. (1990). Parents' unresolved traumatic experiences are related to infant disorganized attachment status: Is frightened and/or frightening parental behavior the linking mechanism? In M. Greenberg, D. Cicchetti, & E. M. Cummings (Eds.), *Attachment in the preschool years: Theory, research and intervention* (pp. 161–184). Chicago: University of Chicago Press.

Main, M., & Hesse, E. (1992). *Frightening, frightened, dissociated, or disorganized behavior on the part of the parent: A coding system for parent–infant interactions.* Fourth Edition, Unpublished.

Main, M., & Solomon, J. (1990). Procedures for identifying infants as disorganized/disoriented during the Ainsworth Strange Situation. In M. T. Greenberg & D. Cicchetti (Eds.), *Attachment in the preschool years: Theory, research, and intervention.* The John D. and Catherine T. MacArthur Foundation Series on mental health and development (pp. 121–160). Chicago: University of Chicago Press.

Matas, L., Arend, R. A., & Sroufe, L. A. (1978). Continuity of adaptation in the second year: The relationship between quality of attachment and later competence. *Child Development, 49,* 547–556.

Moss, E., Parent, S., Gosselin, C., Rousseau, D., & St. Laurent, D. (1996). Attachment and teacher-reported behavior problems during the preschool and early school-age period. *Development and Psychopathology, 8,* 511–526.

Nemeroff, C. (1996). The corticotropin-releasing factor (CRF) hypothesis of depression: New findings and new directions. *Molecular Psychiatry, 1,* 336–342.

Patterson, G. R. (1982). *A social learning approach to family intervention: Vol. 3. Coercive family process.* Eugene, OR: Castalia.

Seligman, M. E. D. (1975). Helplessness: On depression, development, and death. *A series of books in psychology.* New York: W.H. Freeman/Times Books/Henry Holt & Co.

Solomon, J., George, C., & DeJong, A. (1995). Children classified as controlling at age six: Evidence of disorganized representational strategies and aggression at home and at school. *Development and Psychopathology, 7,* 447–463.

Spangler, G., & Grossmann, K. E. (1993). Biobehavioral organization in securely and insecurely attached infants. *Child Development, 64,* 1439–1450.

Sroufe, L. A., Jacobvitz, D., Mangelsdorf, S., DeAngelo, E., & Ward, M. J. (1985). Generational boundary dissolution between mothers and their preschool children relational systems approach. *Child Development, 56,* 317–325.

Taylor, S. E., Klein, L. C., Lewis, B. P., Gruenewald, T. L., Gurung, R. A., & Updegraff, J. A. (2000). Biobehavioral responses to stress in females: Tend-and-befriend, not fight-or-flight. *Psychological Review, 107,* 411–429.

Terr, L. C. (1991). Childhood traumas: An outline and overview. *American Journal of Psychiatry, 148,* 10–20.

van IJzendoorn, M. H. (1995). Adult attachment representations, parental responsiveness, and infant attachment: A meta-analysis on the predictive validity of the Adult Attachment Interview. *Psychological Bulletin, 117,* 387–403.

van IJzendoorn, M. H., Schuengel, C., & Bakermans-Kranenburg, M. K. (1999). Disorganized attachment in early childhood: Meta-analysis of precursors, concomitants and sequelae. *Development and Psychopathology, 11,* 225–249.

Wartner, U. G., Grossmann, K., Fremmer-Bombik, E., & Suess, G. (1994). Attachment patterns at age six in south Germany: Predictability from infancy and implications for preschool behavior. *Child Development, 65,* 1014–1027.

Winnicott, D. W. (1969). The use of an object. *International Journal of Psychoanalysis, 50,* 711–716.

Adolescent Psychopathology in Terms of Multiple Behavioral Systems: The Role of Attachment and Controlling Strategies and Frankly Disorganized Behavior

Cathron Hilburn-Cobb
Northside Mental Health Clinic, Atlanta
Formerly, Hincks-Dellcrest Centre, Toronto, and University of Toronto

Myths from numerous cultures compare human efforts to achieve a sense of felt security through attachments with efforts to establish security through instrumental tools, supplies, privileges, and agents. Consider these two examples:

1. From the Mediterranean tradition, there is Midas, a man so preoccupied with material wealth, he believed his fondest wish would be to turn all he touched into gold. But no sooner did the gods grant him this power than he unthinkingly transformed his own daughter into solid metal by giving her a loving embrace. Without hesitation he prayed to have the power reversed and gladly renounced all his gains in order to have her restored to him as she had been. The theme that is represented here is the realization of the irreplaceable value of loving relationships and the pointlessness of material acquisition without the bonds of attachment and caregiving.

2. In the second myth from the Norse tradition, there is Alberecht, the Niebelung dwarf who has been tantalized, spurned, and ridiculed by the silly Rhine maidens he has tried to love. In a spiteful rage, Alberecht forswears all love in order to gain the secret to power over others. He then enslaves his own kinsmen to increase his wealth. The theme here is more complex and may be considered in three aspects: (a) Those who ridicule and reject another's love become responsible for a cascading chain of harmful events; (b) those who cannot feel themselves to be lovable will

simply renounce affection at some point, in favor of survival by material gain and power; and (c) those who do forswear love are powerful precisely because they are not limited in their actions by the one thing that would stop others from exploitation and cruelty, that is, the valuing of human attachments.

Both stories illustrate a universal recognition that relationships involving attachment goals have a special and preferred status (the ethological base); however, in some cultures, it is represented as an obvious truth that attachment relationships outweigh worldly rank and acquisitions. In others, a deliberate choice to depend on instrumental tools and supplies is represented as regrettable but conceivable and the processes that bring this about become the stuff of mythology.

The central argument of this chapter is that one route toward psychopathology involves an effort to preserve one's felt security (an experience of internal regulation) mainly by instrumental means when attachments have chronically failed in this task. This forms the core of a proposed theoretical model for the link between certain forms of adolescent psychopathology and behavior that has been described by attachment research as disorganized, controlling, or both. A distinction is made here between disorganized attachments, controlling behavior, and frank disorganization. The model proposes that controlling behavior should be understood not as a special type of anxious attachment, but as a strategy of an alternate behavioral system that is recruited to obtain instrumental supplies; frank disorganization is understood as the failure of organization by any system.

Disorganization has repeatedly been connected to psychopathology, but ordinary anxious attachments, free of significant disorganization, have not been directly linked to concurrent psychopathology during the early childhood and latency years (Greenberg, DeKlyen, Speltz, & Endriga, 1997; Moss, Parent, Gosselin, Rousseau, & St. Laurent, 1996; Solomon, George, & DeJong, 1995; Sroufe, Carlson, Levy, & Egeland, 1999). The present model lays out a process by which chronically anxious but well-organized attachments become direct risk factors for either controlling or frankly disorganized functioning during adolescence, if not earlier. I suggest specific conditions under which an inflexible, hierarchical organization among those systems supporting anxious attachments may lead to psychopathology such as behavior disorders, depression, or dissociative states.

The model expands on previous attachment-based hypotheses regarding psychopathology (Greenberg, Speltz, DeKlyen, & Endriga, 1991). There are two aspects to the model: (a) an emphasis on attachment behavior as only one part of the general theory of behavioral control systems originally outlined by Bowlby (Ainsworth, 1978, 1990) and (b) an emphasis on multiple behavioral systems to explain any type of behavior under stress (Bretherton, 1987; Cicchetti, Cummings, Greenberg, & Marvin, 1990).

In particular, I propose a hierarchical interaction of the attachment, affiliation, and subordination-submission control systems within all anxious attachment relationships, whether associated with outright psychopathology or with normal living. For this task, the model makes use of certain constructs from the work of British social psychologists who have concerned themselves with ethological and neurobiological aspects of social hierarchy theory and the distinction between attachment and other social behaviors (Allan & Gilbert, 1997; Gilbert, 1992; Gilbert & Allan, 1998; Gilbert, Allan, & Trent, 1995). The purpose of this model is to clarify how attachment theory can inform therapy with depressed or highly distressed, hard-to-reach adolescents.

ATTACHMENT AND OTHER MEANS TO FELT SECURITY

Three propositions form the basis of my arguments. They are discussed in the following sections.

First Proposition

Survival depends on the regulation of internal states, which, for our species, must include cognitive and emotional regulation. In a regulated state, individuals are most able to mobilize their best problem-solving efforts, whether the solution is fight, flight, protection seeking, endurance, or working through. Therefore, a dysregulated cognition or emotional state can be as much a survival threat as dysregulated body temperature or lack of food (McGuire, 1988; McGuire, Raleigh, Fawzy, Spar, & Troisi, in press; McGuire & Troisi, 1987a, 1987b). If dysregulation approaches the level of frank disorganization, the individual will mobilize any resource at its disposal to reinstate internal equilibrium. Any means for achieving regulation will be better than none. On the other hand, the most effective and comprehensive regulation may be achieved by nurturing contact with a maternal caregiver (Cassidy, 1994; Hofer, 1994, 1995; Kraemer, 1992). For very young mammals, such contact may be a necessary condition for regulation or even survival (Bowlby, 1951; Harlow & Harlow, 1969; Spitz, 1946). Therefore, this proposition emphasizes caregiver contact as a unique and preferential regulator of internal states on physiological, emotional, and cognitive levels.

Second Proposition

The behavioral control system for attachment serves the regulatory goal of the organism, not simply by maintaining a safe physical proximity, but by eliciting a cooperative, caregiving state of mind in specific and irreplaceable caregivers, so that they will regulate internal states (conferring felt security) through contact comfort or its emotional equivalent. In other words, in humans (and perhaps other higher order species) the emotional relationship itself acts as an intrinsic regulator (Hofer, 1984). As an example, consider this reunion episode in a Strange Situation: An avoidant young child hides his inner distress behind the smooth offering of a toy to the caregiver. The caregiver, proud of her child's self-contained behavior during the separation, gladly allows this play-focused proximity. Although this caregiver happens to be dismissive, she is now particularly well disposed toward the child and, should a mishap occur in the vicinity, she would very likely offer a spontaneous and adequate response without the child's needing to signal distress. Within this safe zone of current positive regard, the child's unseen turmoil gradually subsides.

The "safe zone of current positive regard" refers to the child's awareness that, for the time being, the caregiver is emotionally disposed to be protective. Although an unreliable history of contact comfort may have prolonged the current recovery time (Spangler & Grossmann, 1993) and created a predisposition for stress response in the future, the child does recover because of the mother's return. Therefore, what made the behavior a successful (avoidant) attachment strategy was not that the child concealed his distress, nor simply that he avoided rejection (Main & Weston, 1982), but that the stoic behavior elicited his mother's willingness to be at her most available and responsive despite her tendency to minimize or dismiss distress signals. This proposition emphasizes the attachment goal of mobilizing the attachment figure's caregiving system and the child as an active organizer of his caregiver's state of mind or availability (see Kobak, 1999, for review).

Third Proposition

In contrast to the attachment goal, an instrumental security goal would be acquisition of tools or supplies to achieve a sense of regulation. These tools and supplies might include soothing toys and entertainment, foods, wealth, drugs or alcohol, the social status that gives access to these, or simply the narcotic of hard work. Several different behavioral systems can organize the acquisition of instrumental supplies (Ainsworth, 1990, p. 474). Strategies to obtain instrumental means of regulation may or may not involve other persons and are not defined by specific persons. Personal agents whose assistance may be used to acquire these supplies are relatively interchangeable and replaceable.

A word must be said about the terms *goal, function,* and *outcome.* The convention is to differentiate control systems by these terms, but theorists have used the words in different ways. First, a brief review of the concept of a behavioral system is in order. This ethological construct proposes that, for higher order species, in contrast to instinctual routines, a number of primary motives become the foci of flexible, electively organized, and cybernetic behavioral strategies that serve an evolutionary (survival or reproductive) function. Some systems organize behavior to acquire survival resources (including reproductive resources), some to defend what is acquired, and others to recruit the assistance of conspecifics (Gilbert, 1997, 2000). For example, the attachment system organizes strategies to elicit a specific kind of assistance from special figures. A primary motivation and its control system are always in a state of activation, that is, the central motive is inextinguishable, causing the brain to monitor the environment for signs that would alert the self, and the self, in turn, sets goal-corrected behavior in motion (see Bretherton, 1987). Specific behavioral strategies may be implemented or discarded, hyperactivated or deactivated, as feedback is received within the system (Main, 1990). In other words, feedback about how a strategy is working, relative to the goal, is an essential component of the control system. The strategy selection process may be unconscious or automatic (Main), but increasing anxiety may cause greater attention to feedback and goal-corrected behavior. No control system can be identified by particular behaviors (such as proximity seeking) because a behavior may serve several systems.

Ainsworth (1990) stated that the goal of the attachment system was proximity (to a special figure), extended to include emotional access. Earlier, she had stated that the outcome is proximity, the function is protection or safety, and the goal is the physical distance required to deactivate the system (Ainsworth, 1978). Cicchetti et al. (1990) defined the goal as security, the function as protection, and the outcome as proximity. The present model defines goal as hyperactivating the caregiving system in the attachment figure, function as regulation through an intrinsically valued relationship, and outcome as the attachment figure's degree of willingness to personally protect.

These definitions should not be taken as innovations, however; they are simply restatements in terms that include the behavior of both partners in the relationship, because attachment is a property of a dyad, not an individual personality trait. It is also important for the therapeutic use of attachment theory that the construct be formulated in terms that clarify how this ethological factor is manifested distinctively in human beings (see Hinde, 1970). Because we are a species capable of a theory of mind, feedback about the caregiver's state of mind can activate goal-corrected behavior and it can be comforting to believe that a caregiver is willing to do whatever he or she can, even when realistic obstacles prevent the most effective action. This mental representation (or internal working model) of the positive, emotional partnership becomes an intrinsic regulator.

Therefore, when behavior is organized by the attachment system, it is classified as "secure" if it is characterized by direct, appropriate signals for assistance that, in turn, successfully enlist the caregiver's willingness to regulate arousal under stressful conditions. Behavior organized by the attachment system is classified as "anxious" if signals are either suppressed (avoidant) or distorted (ambivalent-preoccupied) in order to maximize the attachment figure's willingness to provide ultimate protection. However, in the latter case, the need to suppress or distort means that no strategy on the child's part will result in the caregiver conferring as much real comfort (regulation of internal states) as would be conferred in a secure dyad (Cobb, 1996; Lyons-Ruth, 1996).

Individuals who enjoy secure attachments with their caregivers may be unaware of the need for regulation, because its provision is well enough assured; they plan their activities on the basis of contingencies that have little to do with regulation. However, those individuals whose attachments are anxious often feel that the most ordinary contingencies of daily life have survival significance and regulation is always an issue hovering, unspoken, behind emotional reactions to daily mishaps (see Spangler & Grossmann, 1993).

To summarize, attachment has been defined conventionally in terms of a simple proximity- or contact-seeking goal or in terms of maintaining the caregiver's availability under stress. However, by virtue of this analysis, it is clear that the construct of attachment may be understood in terms of a specific means to a general homeostatic goal: to achieve synchronized, physiological, cognitive, and emotional regulation by eliciting care from a unique relationship. This concept can include the idea of striving for some type of proximity in order to gain protection from stress or danger, yet it is more specific about the purpose of proximity and what would qualify as protection. Regulation is experienced as protection or felt security (Cobb, 1996; Hofer, 1984; Lyons-Ruth, 1996; Sroufe & Waters, 1977). Ainsworth (1990, pp. 473–474) resisted Sroufe's (1977) redefinition of the goal of attachment as felt security on the grounds that, as maturation proceeds, felt security can be obtained through the operations of many other behavioral systems besides attachment. That is indeed the position taken in the present model, with the additional stipulation that it is precisely the means by which attachment accomplishes felt security that defines its unique function, that is, by emotional access to the attachment figure. Ainsworth also objected to Sroufe and Waters' definition on the grounds that it entails that the child planned how he would become secure, rather than planning the conditions that, if successful, would make him secure (Kobak, 1999).

The present model does indeed propose that by the preschool years the child has already begun to choose how to obtain felt security: The place of attachment can change within a growing hierarchy of recourse systems under stress.

THE PLACE OF SELF-REGULATION

In addition to attachment and instrumental tools, supplies, and activities, there is, of course, another important means for achieving internal regulation, and this is the maturing capability for self-regulation through natural biofeedback mechanisms in which an individual may exert some control over breathing, heart rate, and so forth, even affective intensity. Such feedback mechanisms are often cognitively mediated (e.g., self-talk, meditation, etc.), but may also be subconscious and automatic. The capacity for self-regulation depends in part on temperamental factors (how easily one's stress response can be activated) and in part on opportunities to practice self-soothing in small enough doses. What is needed for the development of a child's self-control or self-regulating capacity is caregiving that does not (a) hyperactivate the attachment system, encouraging high dependency on attachment figures for regulation or (b) overstimulate the child's efforts to obtain and depend upon instrumental supplies for regulation. Self-regulatory competence is therefore likely to be more developed in secure attachments, where the caregiver scaffolds independent learning and self-care and, at the same time, does not leave the child to overrely on instrumental supplies when arousal is high. Table 5.1 summa-

TABLE 5.1
Comparison of Attachment, Instrumental, and Self-Regulated Security

Survival Requirement	Means	Essential Aspects	Strategies
Regulation of internal states (felt security)	Attachment (personalized protection, contact comfort)	Bonding with irreplaceable figure(s)	Direct signals of distress or need
		Gain emotional access, elicit caregiving state of mind in attachment figures	Submissive and affiliative signals
	Tools and supplies (instrumental protection and comfort)	Selection of convenient (replaceable) providers or agents	Direct signals of desire Deception or forceful seizure
		Exploration, for new sources	Self-reliance
	Self-regulation	Biofeedback processes	Focused concentration or self-talk

rizes the comparison between attachment, instrumental, and self-regulated security.

I return now to the two mythical stories introduced in the beginning. The first is an illustration that attachment is ultimately more valued by human beings than material supplies; the second is a warning about the possibility that there may be circumstances in which material supplies rather than attachment will be the main choice, regardless of the value of attachment or, even in a perverse way, because of it. In other words, attachment regulation is so unique that, if it is not available, an individual may become obsessed with regaining felt security by instrumental means, driven by the need to feel as secure as when attachments did function as regulators. The possibility of renouncing attachment behavior reveals what I believe to be a necessary addition to the theory.

Main (1990) greatly enhanced researchers' ethological understanding of attachment behavior by employing the concepts of primary and secondary "conditional" strategies from general biology (see also Hinde, 1970). A primary strategy is the most direct behavior that expresses the goal of a particular control system; secondary strategies are those that are enacted when the primary strategy fails or would not be adaptive for the context. Main and Hesse (1990) described an outcome when both primary and secondary attachment strategies fail in their objective of regulating anxiety, that is, behavior becomes disorganized.[1] The indices of disorganization lead to a category of "disorganized attachments" (Main & Solomon, 1990). In addition, however, children's behavior in a reunion that appears relatively organized but negative and controlling has also been labeled as a form of disorganized attachment and in research findings these organized strategies have been combined with the more obvious disorganized behaviors (Cassidy & Marvin, 1992; Main & Cassidy, 1988). The argument has been that neither type of behavior accomplishes the goal of attachment competently, but the very activation of an attachment strategy has remained unquestioned.

Now, it is true that the underlying attachment motivation cannot be entirely overridden (Main, 1990): There will always be a stress-related impulse to seek regulation through human contact. However, it is known that the behavior of any survival system can be suppressed even under conditions that should act as a natural activator. One particularly startling

---

[1]This is a restatement of Main and Hesse's (1990) hypothesis that disorganization is the consequence of frightened or frightening behavior on the part of the caregiver: A state in which both primary and secondary attachment strategies chronically failed to regulate anxiety in daily life would be sure to occur if the caregiver was the source of anxiety. However, there may be additional circumstances that cause all attachment possibilities to fail, thereby producing disorganized behavior in relation to any current caregiver, such as intractable pain, the traumatic loss of primary caregivers, and so on.

example occurs when an anorexic suppresses food intake, even though the hunger motivation continues during starvation and drives food-obsessed activities. Nevertheless, current attachment theory does not contain an account of attachment strategies, either primary or secondary, being chronically suppressed in close relationships that have been attachments at one time. The assumption seems to be that the attachment-caregiving relationship cannot be set aside and therefore any stress-related effort to gain access to a caregiver must be motivated by the goal of attachment, even if the behavior is negative.

However rare, it is possible that, as in the Niebelungen myth, attachment behavior is virtually abandoned by an individual who must survive under highly unfavorable emotional circumstances (i.e., when attachments no longer regulate), even though an attachment figure may still be physically on the spot. The behavior of oppositional, defiant, or disruptive children and adolescents could be consistent with an attempt to achieve regulation mainly (if not entirely) through instrumental tools and supplies and to acquire these through other control systems driven by other motivations and goals than those of attachment.

In such cases, the context in which regulatory supplies are sought is usually still the set of relationships within the family and the parents are most often the agents selected to supply the means for instrumental regulation. Children often increase attention seeking, enacting temper outbursts to get what they want. Although the commonly offered explanation is that this negative attention seeking is a cry for love and affection (and certainly long-standing deprivation is the origin of the trouble), what is now accepted as love is not a caress, but an object; the child continues to agitate until the instrumental demand is met. Therefore the family relationships per se are not abandoned; in fact, the child does appear more clinging and needy, but the child's functional goal within the relationship has altered. The shift in goals may be hard to discern for an observer, especially when all family members use the language of emotional care in relation to giving and receiving tools and supplies, for example, "I do care, didn't I do _____ for you?"

More often, of course, no absolute choice must be made between attachment and instrumental security. Even individuals in secure relationships derive additional felt security from instrumental supplies. Successful anxious attachments often include the use of instrumental tools and supplies to compensate for the residual anxiety that is a part of those relationships. Parents and children may concentrate their relationship around construction of toys or games, learning of things, achievement, and success instead of emotions. Instrumental supplements chosen by an anxiously attached individual are not alienating and should increase the emotional access to the caregiver, for instance, a shared absorption in a sport

or even drinking together. By such means the functioning of the attachment system—internal regulation through an intrinsically valued relationship—is preserved.

But what about the situation when instrumental means, not attachment, become the main means for achieving felt security? Furthermore,
if the individual in a relationship continues to manifest behaviors such
as an apparent fear of loss, proximity seeking, or separation protest
(Weiss, 1991; West, Rose, & Sheldon, 1993), how would one conclude
that instrumental security is sought more than, or rather than, the comfort of the emotional relationship? One clue would be provided if the instrumental supplies sought are not a means to accord with the parent (or
partner), but instead supply seeking becomes grounds for continually
escalating antagonism and rejection: "No you can't have a bigger allow-
ance, you'll just spend it on cigarettes!" or "No, you can't stay in the
house while we're away, you'll just bring those deadbeat friends in
here." A close analysis of the relationship outcome (Ainsworth, 1978) of
behavior is required. If the outcome is that the adolescent's behavior
achieves physical proximity and access but does not create a protective,
positive, and willing state of mind in the caregiver, the outcome is not
consistent with the attachment goal. Furthermore, as the adolescent continues to agitate for supplies or privileges, the resulting parental anger
or rejection does not instigate a goal-corrected change in adolescent
strategy. This is also inconsistent with the attachment functioning. Call-
ing this behavior "maladaptive attachment" cannot solve the problem.
Even malfunction must involve an attempt to increase the caregiver's
positive state of mind. Maladapted attachment would more properly refer to a mismatch between child strategy and caregiver state of mind
(e.g., an avoidant child with a preoccupied parent).[2]

The phenomenon of attachment behavior being set aside where it
would be expected has been described in Robertson and Bowlby's (1952)
stage of "detachment." Bowlby mentioned the possibility of attachment
behavior "rendered . . . permanently incapable of being activated" (Bowlby, 1988, pp. 33–34), but gave his attention to a temporary period of detachment followed by a more intensified form of proximity seeking,
which he described as an anxiety-ridden return of attachment behavior.
However, he did not address the fact that the anxious, often angry and
clinging or demanding behavior is not goal corrected to obtain emotional

---

[2]A maladapted attachment strategy still uses feedback from caregivers to gain their willing cooperation, even though the child's basic approach creates more difficulties for the partnership (e.g., the avoidant child finds ways to amuse the preoccupied parent or impress the
parent with academic success, a marginally successful way of distracting from emotional demands).

access to the caregiver. Instead, it is chronic, immoderate, and usually noxious in its persistence.

Continual anger, insults, and violence are paradoxical as attachment behaviors because, even if they were initially intended to dissuade the caregiver from future abandonment or to force care from abdicating parents, they nevertheless consistently result in loss of the attachment figure's tender and supportive disposition (see also Speltz, 1990, p. 404).[3] Cause-and-effect learning in the service of attachment should prevent persistence in a strategy that discourages a cooperative and accepting state of mind in the caregiver, but another control system may be quite consistent with coercive disregard for the parent's anger, especially if the child has discovered that instrumental supplies are more reliable regulators than concern from the attachment figure. The child's persistently offputting behavior may make sense if the goal is an object or service, not a comforting relationship; anxious and angry attacks can then be readily explained as actions intended to intimidate an unsatisfactory agent. In other words, a situation of chronic emotional assault by a child against a parent is a paradox only if it is assumed that the behavior was governed by the attachment system.

In order to explain the phenomenon of chronic behavior that would otherwise be an attachment paradox, researchers must develop a systematic theory about when the attachment system controls behavior under stress and when it does not. When is proximity seeking under stress and separation protest not attachment behavior? When will an individual turn to some other behavioral system entirely to try to ensure its own regulation and even survival? It must be made clear that the biological goal of the organism is regulation and survival (for reproduction), not the perpetuation of attachment; soon after infancy, attachment falls into place as the ultimate among many biological means. Bowlby's model assumes the interaction of many behavioral systems, each with a unique survival-enhancing goal and each of which should become the primary organizer

---

[3]There have been at least two significant attempts to explain this type of situation in terms of conventional attachment theory (i.e., without reference to other systems; Crittenden, 1997; Greenberg, Speltz, DeKlyen, & Endriga, 1991; Speltz, 1990). Speltz and Greenberg simply suggested that attachment organizes punitive behavior because it achieves attention and proximity, even though it is not adaptive in the long term. Crittenden had a more complicated rationale in terms of alternating strategies to get the parent to give first proximity, then protection (never both at the same time), which must be recycled continually. The model proposed in the present chapter achieves consistency in definitions and parsimony by reassessing the goal of the behavior as regulation that may be achieved by a number of other systems that also require proximity and may even involve gaining assistance from others (who are agents rather than attachment figures).

of an individual's behavior in different situations (Bowlby, 1988, pp. 5–6; see also Ainsworth, 1990; Cicchetti et al., 1990).

I now briefly consider a small selection of alternative behavioral systems, their goals, and their functions. These functions are outlined in Table 5.2; I consider four in particular. Note that, although survival depends on the regulation of internal states, because we are social animals, social hierarchy functioning also constitutes an ethological requirement (Gilbert, 1993, 1997).

The general goal of the subordination system is to defuse specific attacks or exclusion by dominant members of a social group. This system functions through voluntary or involuntary signaling of "no threat," a noncombative state, and a yielding behavioral subroutine (Gilbert, 1992; Price, 1988; Price & Sloman, 1987; Price, Sloman, Gardner, Gilbert, & Rhode, 1994; Trower & Gilbert, 1989). In other words, various signals of yielding and submission are primary subordination strategies. Rather than being one pole of a dominance-submission dimension, subordination strategies can constitute a unique continuum in their own right, ranging from appeasing (obsequious) forms of approach to a readiness to give ground as required (partial escape), in order to stimulate acceptance from higher ranking members.

The goal of the dominance system is to increase access to supplies (and reproductive rights) and defend what is acquired. The system functions

TABLE 5.2
Simple Proximity-Seeking Behavioral Control Systems

System	Goal	Function
Attachment	Mobilizing caregiving in unique figures	Regulation of internal states through intrinsic properties of relationship
Affiliation	Gain social status through hedonic interactions (not coercion)	Display of personal attractions, formation of alliances
Sexuality	Gene enhancement and reproduction	Acquiring suitable mate(s)
Caregiving	Protection of the young and helpless	Regulate stress and foster autonomy Organize care for multiple dependents
Subordination or submission	Diffuse threat or attacks by dominants, stimulate social inclusion	Ingratiation, acceptance of lower status, or keeping distance to signal no threat
Dominance	Increase access to resources and reproductive rights, defend acquisitions	Intimidation, discouraging challengers, eliminating rivals

by threats and force designed to eliminate rivals, enforce the subordination of weaker members, or discourage challengers (Gilbert, 1992, 1997). Strategies range from crude and primitive force to sophisticated displays of power that depress status opposition.

The evolutionary goal of affiliation is to increase social status by attracting alliances and eliciting assistance, by displaying pleasing qualities about the self rather than by threats or force (Gilbert, 1992, 1997). An individual may develop highly preferred allies (including friends, insofar as numbers of loyal friends and supporters confer status), but their loss, though sometimes as grievous as loss of a special possession, is not a dysregulating and destabilizing event (Ainsworth, 1991; Weiss, 1982, 1991)[4] and allies do not have to be regulatory or wiser, just able to give assistance in some way.

In contrast, the goal of attachment is to gain emotional access to an irreplaceable caregiver who is seen as stronger (regulating) and wiser, not just helpful (Bowlby, 1980, 1988) and whose accessibility will confer regulation of stressed states, not necessarily social status. In order for a behavior to have an attachment function, it is essential that it dispose the caregiver to give sufficient protection to regulate internal states: No true attachment strategy should discourage a caring state of mind in the attachment figure. It follows that any customary behavior with a caregiver that succeeds in engagement, but continually forestalls a receptive and protective state of mind in that caregiver, is unlikely to be attachment-driven behavior.[5]

---

[4]Ainsworth (1991) and Greenberg and Marvin (1982) proposed the demarcation of a separate "sociable system" to describe the tendency to seek proximity with peers for the benefits of companionship but whose association does not contribute to social status and whose loss is grieved, but is not destabilizing.

[5]It is possible that, when a child has his or her first or second tantrum, the primary goal is just to get contact comfort through a primitive sort of attachment functioning in which dominance is recruited in the service of the attachment goal. However, unless the mind is disorganized or neurologically impaired and thus prevented from learning through experience, this sort of attempt should soon be dropped because the attachment goal is almost never achieved (i.e., caregivers are not more willing to give comfort if it is forced out of them). The author has observed one child with obsessive-compulsive disorder (OCD) persist in forcing the mother to give contact comfort despite her impatience and rejection. Here the OCD prevented learning new strategies and in any case the main means of regulation was still instrumental tools and supplies. The raging child, like the lover who threatens violence if he is not loved, is primarily operating in a dominance mode at that moment and the first objective is to subordinate the object (for here the relationship is treated like a tool), indicating a real confusion between emotional and instrumental relationships. An attempt to force contact comfort is doomed to be insufficient as a means to regulation because the physical provider is not in an emotionally protective state of mind and, in terms of emotional access, will provide fear and resentment instead of confidence and selfless protectiveness. One or two experiences of being held by a figure who is afraid and angry should be so unsatisfactory that either the strategy is changed or the goal is changed to forcing the figure to donate instrumental

Returning to the example from the strange situation, if another behavioral routine, such as tantrums, were to be the habitual approach to gain this mother's attention, but the attention was accompanied by the mother's frustration and helplessness and she consistently resorted to some pacifier (a candy, toy, blanket, etc., "to shut him up"), we would have to say the child's strategy fulfilled the survival requirements for regulation, but did not fulfill the requirements for attachment behavior. For the latter, the child's strategy (a) must not habitually incite the caregiver to turn her back in resentment or disgust, justifying small or accidental lapses in protection ("It serves you right!"); and (b) must not so overwhelm the caregiver's resources that it incites the substitution of an instrumental pacifier for personal comfort giving. Unless the attachment behavior mobilizes a special caregiver to be personally and willingly protective, the relationship and its internal working model will not function as an intrinsic regulator.

INTERACTING BEHAVIORAL SYSTEMS AND THE RISK OF PSYCHOPATHOLOGY

As maturation proceeds, the behaviors at the disposal of any system may become much more sophisticated and the interaction among systems becomes more complex. One reasonable concept of system interaction would be that the primary strategies of one system (along with the goal of that system) may be seconded in the service of other systems to produce more civilized strategies for meeting social and survival needs. For instance, many systems may recruit affiliative behaviors in order to better adapt to social contexts. For example, affiliation in the service of subordination in the service of attachment appears as an appealingly dependent and compliant personal style that would be quite adaptive for eliciting caregiving from strong-minded parents, whereas affiliation in the service of sexuality in the service of dominance appears as an attractive and exciting but controlling style that could be adaptive for maintaining cooperation and task adherence from subordinates in a workplace. In those cases, the affiliative goal of increasing social status and the self-promoting strategies to achieve that goal become a means to another system's goal: Feedback about social status is secondary, whereas feedback relating to the

---

supplies. One cannot have unilateral power in a secure attachment relationship: This is learned in the socialization of secure attachments. Nevertheless, for younger children, their persistent attempts to gain access to supplies by dominance may require remedy through repeated offering of attachment regulation: The caregiver who paradoxically imposes a hug on a raging child may be doing exactly the right thing that would reactivate the attachment goal into primacy.

goal of the primary or originating system pilots behavior. System goals may be layered in either a flexible hierarchy of choice among unlimited systems or a rigid hierarchy in which some systems may not be available for organizing social behavior, regardless of persisting motivations.

I argue that a significant risk for psychopathology lies in the coincidence of two factors: (a) An individual becomes restricted to a rigid hierarchy of systems he or she may choose for adaptation and (b) when coping with stress, that individual attempts to gain felt security by renunciation (or suppression) of the attachment goal, in favor of impersonal instrumental supplies obtained by recourse to the next system in the hierarchy, although the substitution confers even less regulation than attachment relationships had done in the first place. In other words, the substitution of systems (and change of functional goals) in relation to former attachment figures becomes pathological if it requires a level of instrumental competence beyond one's actual abilities and particularly if reliance on the substituted system prevents the continued development of competencies that would be essential for mature autonomy. There is a particular risk of this happening during adolescence because at that time the young individual, popular culture, and even some professionals (e.g., Blos, 1979; Douvan & Adelson, 1966) assert that this would be an appropriate time to move away from dependency on childhood attachments, even though the various other behavioral systems are usually still too immature to support competent functioning without assistance from a stronger, wiser, and well-adapted attachment figure (Ryan & Lynch, 1989).

In reality few individuals suppress attachment functioning to the point where instrumental regulation is the main means to obtain felt security. Ordinarily, the attachment motive seems to develop greater strength the more it is frustrated and it requires either an exceptional will or inebriation to renounce it on a consistent basis. (Note that Greenberg & Speltz, 1990, described unexpected character strength in controlling, defiant children.) In most chronic, anxiety-provoking circumstances, neurotic or characterological problems mark the attempt to retain attachment functioning within relationships that give little comfort or protection. However, I believe that formulating at least some adolescent psychopathologies in terms of a premature and maladaptive renunciation of early attachments and recourse to other systems will allow an understanding of the relationship between psychopathology and behavior that has been classified as controlling, as well as disorganized behaviors.

In the remainder of this chapter, I further develop the theoretical argument about when attachment might be set aside in a hierarchy of survival choices and when the individual might turn to some other behavioral system to support regulation or gain a sense of security. I then link this argument to the distinction between frankly disorganized versus controlling behavior. I present some of the indices of adolescent disorganization and controlling behavior that I have developed and some data from a study applying these criteria to a new sample. Finally, I suggest different treatment implications for frankly disorganized and controlling behavior.

CIRCUMSTANCES IN WHICH ORGANIZATION OF BEHAVIOR BY THE ATTACHMENT SYSTEM WOULD NOT BE ADAPTIVE: THE DEVELOPMENT OF A FLEXIBLE HIERARCHY OF RECOURSE

Attachment functioning is not always the most adaptive behavior, even under conditions of stress: For instance, in adulthood (Fig. 5.1), when individuals become parents, the caregiving system motivating giving protec-

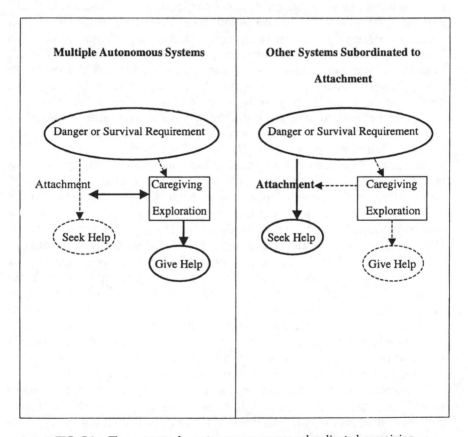

FIG. 5.1.   The outcome for autonomous versus subordinated caregiving and exploratory systems under conditions that could hyperactivate attachment functioning.

tion to helpless young should preempt parents' own impulse to seek protection for themselves when danger threatens. Parents might run into a burning building to save their child rather than wait for help. This happens, of course, only if the caregiving system has been able to mature in its own right and operate according to its own goal instead of being subordinated to an insecure attachment system (Fig. 5.1). In another example, an individual with highly developed exploratory skills may set aside the impulse to stay close to protective relationships in order to serve the society by exploring new territories, rocketing off into space, pursuing dangerous enemies, and so forth.

In other words, when instrumental skills have reached truly matured levels of competence, they may support regulation and survival by way of nonattachment behavioral systems and without the immediate protection of an attachment figure. It may be adaptive, at that point, for a person to deliberately set aside overt attachment behavior in favor of other adaptive goals for self or the social group. During such extended periods, protection and regulation available from the mental representation of attachments are augmented by other means, perhaps largely self-regulation.

The ability to do this depends on whether a person's recourse to many behavioral systems has become elective and flexible: By adulthood, one should be able to make a rational choice about whether attachment motives or other concerns organize one's immediate behavior. Thus, there must be continual opportunities during the course of maturation to temporarily suppress the impulse to signal distress or seek emotional support from attachment figures, in order to develop the skills and competencies one would need for isolated or altruistic functioning.

In infancy, when mobility and exploratory motives place the child at risk of harm, survival is enhanced if, under conditions of stress, the attachment motivation takes precedence over the motives of every other behavioral system (Bowlby, 1969/1982; Bretherton, 1987). At this stage one would say that all behavioral systems should be organized in a rigid hierarchy, with the attachment system always the first recourse under stress. Note that this has nothing to do with attachment security: Either secure or anxious attachment strategies will be the preemptive recourse under elevated stress. It is for this reason that personal development of exploratory skills (and other skill systems) depends on how much the parent can guarantee lower stress conditions during the earliest years.

As the child matures, however, there is an adaptive advantage if attachment functioning becomes less preemptive, so that behavior within other systems can be undertaken and practiced even when situations involve high stress. In other words, the rigid hierarchy among systems from earlier years should be relaxed. While learning life skills relevant to other behavioral systems, the child cannot always be running to its mother or relating to peers or other adults as if they were attachment figures whenever stress increases. The process of beginning to relax the behavioral hierarchy should set in as early as school entrance when it becomes more adaptive for juveniles to organize behavior with peers within primitive dominance and submissive systems so that these strategies can also mature (Gilbert, 1997; Gilbert, Allan, & Trent, 1996; Gilbert & Trower, 1990). This is depicted in Fig. 5.2.

The momentum to relax the infantile hierarchy of organizing systems should be accelerated during adolescence, when a much greater potential for self-regulation and for developing skill within a variety of other systems is coming on line. In particular, there may now be an intense concentration on personal development within the affiliative system in order to organize social status relations with peers.

However, despite the maturational advances, behavioral systems like exploration, affiliation, caregiving, and sexuality are still in an immature state during adolescence and still operate to best advantage under conditions of lesser stress where the course of one's life is not actually at stake (Eccles et al., 1993; Paikoff & Brooks-Gunn, 1991). Reciprocal attachment and caregiving continue to mature more effectively in practice attachments with peers and in dating relationships, where only limited regulation is required of the partner. Dominance and subordination strategies also gain sophistication more effectively if they are practiced within peer groups that do not have a permanent effect on one's future. Practicing these behaviors is stressful nevertheless and it is usually the primary caregiver from childhood who, by virtue of experience and history, should be

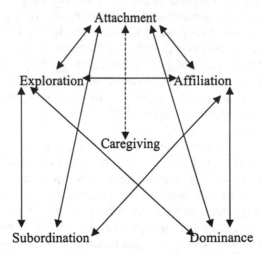

FIG. 5.2. Early stage of development for a flexible hierarchy among multiple systems.

able to offer the most intimately knowledgeable, safest, and wisest support and regulation during these trials. The adolescent may not turn to the parent first, but access to the parent for ultimate assuagement can ideally ensure minimal disruption in development (Fulingi & Eccles, 1993; Greenberg, Siegel, & Leitch, 1983; Kobak, Sudler, & Gamble, 1992; Ryan & Lynch, 1989; Smetana, 1988; Smetana & Asquith, 1994).

Even in competent maturity (represented in Fig. 5.3), the hierarchy of systems remains most flexible when the stress of day-to-day functioning can be relieved by recourse to the comfort of an effective attachment relationship (Bowlby, 1988). Therefore, at any stage, it is most adaptive if the attachment system always occupies an ultimate position within a flexible hierarchy of systems.

PERSISTENT RIGIDITY IN THE HIERARCHY OF RECOURSE AMONG SYSTEMS

The Attachment Figure in Anxious Relationships Is Perceived as a Social Dominant

If stress can be only partially assuaged through attachment relationships, that is, if the attachments are anxious, then the individual will become preoccupied with the task of maintaining an accessible disposition on the part of the caregiver. Although the attachment system does not evolve to organize social hierarchy goals, within anxious attachments caregivers' dominant power and status become salient through their predisposition to limit comfort. In ethological terms, the most adaptive means of maintaining access to a threatening dominant is subordination or submissive behavior.

Crittenden (1996, 1997) drew our attention to the role of certain submissive behaviors in ambivalent attachments from the preschool age onward. I suggest that we recognize the equally subordinate or submissive quality of avoidant behavior as well. There are in fact a variety of strategies (Gilbert, 2000) within the subordination-submission control system that may be recruited by the attachment system to increase caregiver good will. Overdependence, coy ingratiation, and role reversal are examples of what ethologists would call "reverted escape" strategies (Gilbert). The prototype is a threatened individual who tries to gain social inclusion by appeasing or groveling instead of attempting to flee. These submissive strategies require the caregiver's active approval and therefore even role reversal actually leaves the caregiver in the dominant position (parents who need care still have the power to criticize if it is not done to their own satisfaction, e.g., "You're not doing enough to save me from worry"). Because they involve extra efforts to solicit approval,

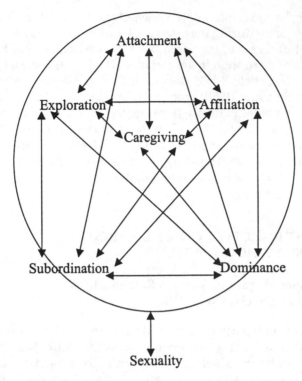

FIG. 5.3.   Matured stage of flexible hierarchy among systems for adaptation.

these strategies qualify as hyperactivating and, in the conventional Ainsworth-Main classification scheme, would refer to passive, preoccupied attachments. Angry ambivalent strategies oscillate between paying this price of inclusion and episodic but temporary struggles against subordination. (Securely preoccupied strategies [B_4, F_4] also concede status and solicit acceptance by submitting to the dominant figure, but successfully use affiliative appeals to obtain consistent and effective care.) On the other hand, there are strategies that appear to be based less on placating submissiveness and more on deactivating one's alternative impulse to flee from a threatening dominant figure. They take up a nondramatized subordination and thereby preserve a sense of independence while avoiding exile. The tactical principle appears to be, "If you run, there is greater risk of attack." Strategies minimizing affective appeals that could incite social rejection are called "enclosed avoidance" and those that virtually cease displays are called strategies of "arrested escape" (Gilbert). Both strategies accept subordination but deactivate the impulses to either beg for more or go elsewhere. They are the avoidant or dismissive attachments in conventional terminology.

Therefore, all anxious attachment strategies can be described as an override of the primary attachment strategy by varieties of submissive behavior, with or without the finesse of affiliative behaviors (Hilburn-Cobb, Gotlieb, Pye, & Mann, 2000). In other words, this model proposes that all secondary attachment strategies are based on strategies evolved primarily for a subordination-submission control system, but now recruited to serve an attachment goal instead of a social hierarchy goal.

Subordination or Submission in the Service of the Attachment Goal and Limitations on Developing Competence

When attachment relationships are secure and can efficiently assuage stress from various daily activities, the attachment system operates, as nature intended, only in a circumscribed, stress-triggered set of circumstances. Once a stress is resolved, other behavioral systems (including subordination and affiliation) continue to develop freely according to their unique goals. They will not be distorted though recruitment to furnish second, third, or fourth layers to secondary attachment strategies.[6]

However, the more conditional (i.e., threatening) the caregiver's attitude about being available, the more adaptive it becomes to subordinate oneself to the caregiver's wishes in a wide variety of activities, not just matters of distress and safety. This would increase the likelihood of the attachment figure being well disposed and offering regulatory protection whenever needed. Therefore, when attachments are anxious, the motive to mobilize caregiving may come to organize many domains of everyday life, such as recreation, work, learning skills, and social choices, even when situations are not particularly stressful. The hierarchy among systems retains its infantile rigidity, with the attachment goal constantly preempting the strategies and functioning of other systems, and therefore the development of competencies within those other systems suffers restriction, matures more slowly, or does not mature at all. For instance, if affiliative self-promoting behaviors were employed constantly to engage an attachment figure's willingness to comfort, the consequence could be poor development of affiliative behaviors appropriate for negotiating so-

---

[6]For instance, in cases where there is stable, secure attachment to parents, peer relations may come to have a greater statistical association with personality variables than with parent variables because other behavioral systems (fostered in peer groups and other institutional associations) are free to develop regardless of parental ideas (see Bretherton, Golby, & Cho, 1997). However, in the case of anxious attachments, child personality should show a greater association with parent variables than with peers', but this will not show up as a main effect for a general population in which most attachments are secure. This would make sense of Harris's (1998) findings.

cial status relations with peers. Alternatively, if exploration were restricted to areas approved by the attachment figure, many other talents,
skills, and interests that would make one attractive to peers or increase
self-regulatory competence might not be developed.

THE PARTICULAR PROBLEM FOR ANXIOUS
ATTACHMENTS AND A RIGID HIERARCHY
AMONG SYSTEMS DURING ADOLESCENCE

By the time of adolescence, cultural pressure reinforces the innate drive to
develop autonomous competence in various life skills. Because anxious
attachments are characterized by a generalized, competence-restricting
subordination to the caregiver's state of mind, the shortfall in competence
can create new, dysregulating levels of anxiety. What limited powers of
assuagement were available by way of anxious attachments in younger
years can now be overridden by the adolescent's increased sense that he
or she is falling behind in social and cognitive maturity. Anxiety is particularly acute about establishing one's social status, which depends on the
adolescent's ability to gain and maintain alliances with others through attractiveness and skills (social attention holding power or SAHP; Gilbert,
1992, 1997). If an anxious attachment to parents has left an adolescent uncertain about his or her basic worthiness and there are no external relationships (work, school, sports) in which the adolescent can receive acknowledgment for competence, then the adolescent may simply form
alliances with peers who are unselective on any criteria except the demand for loyalty. Continuing association with "a bad type of friends" is
one of the frequent presenting complaints of parents of adolescents with
behavior problems. The relentless parental disapproval further intensifies
the adolescent's reliance on those very friends, in a vicious downward spi-
ral that seldom allows further positive skill development or genuine mas-
tery (Fulingi & Eccles, 1993).

Therefore, by the time of adolescence if not earlier, regulation through
chronically anxious attachments may have required too much sacrifice of
competence development. This, of course, would be a truly individual difference: No two anxiously attached individuals, even using the same general strategy, necessarily make the same sacrifice of autonomy in their re-
spective families. Only under specific conditions, then, might chronic
anxious attachments trigger an attempt to suppress attachment functioning in relation to former attachment figures, or suppress it altogether.
These conditions would be: (a) Childhood attachments can no longer assuage anxiety (the adolescent's anxiety now exceeds the caregiver's usual
level of response or the parents cannot increase their sensitivity and re-

sponsiveness at this time in their own lives); (b) the adolescent has insufficient experience of being independently valued outside the home for some competence that is also valued by the parent(s); and (c) the partnership with the parent is felt to be an impediment to growth (perhaps the adolescent senses that his or her subordination has prevented his or her developing in the same way as his peers). These adolescents may try to gain material supplies or privileges for instrumental security from their parents and use the supplies both to self-regulate and to share with their peer group to increase their status, believing that this can be a better route to maturing social status and competence.

For example, 13-year-old Henry enabled a friend to steal Henry's mother's car for a joy ride, then Henry forced his parents to drop charges against the friend by threatening to abandon the family and accusing them of disloyalty to him if they prosecuted (he exploited their continued valuing of the relationship). Without remorse for the damage or gratitude for the reprieve and without being deterred by his parents' increasing rejection and threats of boarding school, Henry continued to come and go without parental consent, but took every opportunity to extract sums of money from them that were used for clothes, drugs, alcohol, and gifts to the friends.

THE MODEL FOR SUBSTITUTION OF BEHAVIORAL SYSTEMS (AND FUNCTIONAL GOALS) WITHIN A RIGID HIERARCHY OF RECOURSE

The rigid hierarchy of choices is illustrated in Fig. 5.4. To summarize the previous arguments, if primary attachment strategies consistently fail to regulate internal states during stress, the child or adolescent first attempts to salvage attachment security through one or more secondary strategies of either voluntary subordination or involuntary submission to the caregiver's state of mind. This would be a normal and adaptive development. (Success at this point depends greatly on the child's temperamental suitability for a submissive role, but also the readiness of the caregiver to accept a subordinate, submissive, or ambivalently submissive approach.) In any event, subordination must be continually reinforced to solve the problem of attachment and status insecurity impels the child to become preoccupied with maintaining the caregiver's readiness, not just in objectively dangerous situations, but in situations of many sorts. Then the alternative behavioral systems (dominance, exploration, affiliation, even caregiving) that should have developed sophisticated strategies for obtaining appropriate tools or supplies are distorted by being used mainly to serve the goal of the attachment system.

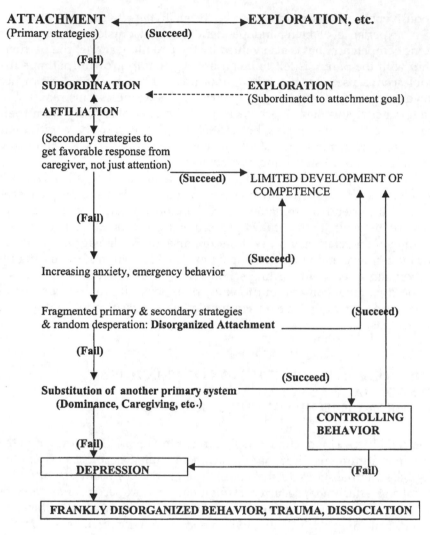

FIG. 5.4.   Model of rigid hierarchy of systems with risk points for psychopathology.

By adolescence, these individuals have only immature strategies to use
on their parents or peers when trying to organize social behaviors even at
the best of times: For example, caregiving is practiced by intrusive ob-
sessionality rather than by appropriate goal-corrected partnership (West &
Sheldon, 1988, 1994); exploration is practiced with considerable risk taking
rather than systematic or disciplined problem solving (Bretherton, 1985);
and dominance is practiced by sheer force and poor judgment rather than
persuasive leadership and reciprocity of rights and privileges.

As depicted in Fig. 5.4, if well-established submissive strategies fail to confer sufficient regulation, the first manifestation of the failure is various emergency tactics to regain the caregiver's favor. The observer could note fragmented efforts to return to the primary attachment strategy, alternating with remnants of the secondary strategy and more random desperation behavior. This would be the state of a true disorganized attachment. However, if this obvious distress cannot reinstate the caregiver's comfort, children must reinstate internal organization for themselves and take recourse in the next system in the hierarchy to prevent dysregulation. Whether the new organizing system is dominance, caregiving, or some other system, caring continues to exist, but the interpersonal goal is different: Now the dependent cares about the relationship as the means to acquire instrumental tools and supplies. The adolescent controls the relationship by a display of attractive, seductive, or caregiving attributes at best, or by threats and force at worst. The parent often senses that there has been a shift in the nature of the child's emotional investment. The more hierarchically challenging behaviors do not pass undisputed by the caregiver, especially if the child has resorted to dominance in order to gain supplies through intimidation. Being subjected to primitive dominance threats by one's own child may make even an abdicating parent angry enough to counter with equally unpracticed control and a coercive cycle is established (Patterson, 1982). With adolescent anxiety at a new height, if the parent blocks all ill-conceived attempts to bypass attachment but offers no other relief, the adolescent with a rigid hierarchy of recourse runs out of organized options. This may be experienced as a massive personal defeat with consequent depression. If the depression does not finally elicit sensitive parenting and reinstate attachment functioning, and instead brings more criticism, the ultimate consequence could be frankly disorganized fear.

THE DISTINCTION BETWEEN FRANK DISORGANIZATION AND CONTROLLING BEHAVIOR

For young infants, there are few behavioral systems other than attachment and exploration available for organizing behavior, so in cases of overwhelming anxiety it is easy to run out of options and fall into completely unorganized behavior. Main and Solomon (1990) identified indices for such disorganization in infant strange situations, but similar frank disorganization may be seen at any point in life when all available systems for achieving regulation are exhausted or blocked, and cause-and-effect reasoning cannot be made to serve the situation. Distressed and traumatized adults can go in circles, wring or flap their hands, cover their faces with palms outward as if to ward off the blow of terrible information, seem unable to carry even brief action plans through to completion, and so on. When this happens, it is clear not only that the attachment system has ceased to operate effectively, but also that cognition is too disrupted for any system to organize a coherent behavioral response. A distinction can therefore be made between disorganized attachments, in which the signs of disorganization are minor and do not disrupt act completion or goal correction, and frank disorganization, where the indices of trauma outweigh the fragmentary remnants of any behavioral control system.

In contrast, controlling behavior forestalls disorganization by suppressing attachment behavior and substituting another organizing system into the preemptive position in the rigid hierarchy. Mainstream developmental research has accepted controlling behavior as an anomalous but disorganized attachment strategy (Cassidy & Marvin, 1992; Main & Cassidy, 1988), because many formerly disorganized infants develop into controlling children. My own observations suggest that controlling behavior almost always contains elements of behavioral incompetence or disorganization (after all, it must be disorienting to suppress attachment functioning within an ongoing relationship). However, although controlling strategies are proximity maintaining and attention holding, these effects are not sufficient to define attachment functioning and several critical distinctions between controlling behavior and any possible strategy of the attachment system can now be summarized:

1. Instead of soliciting a receptive state of mind and emotional access, controlling almost always ensures some resistant or negative parental reaction.

2. The goal is acquisition of instrumental tools and supplies, not emotional, relationship-based assuagement; the outcome is a power struggle over material rewards, not a goal-corrected partnership for personalized regulation, protection, and security.

3. Most essentially, the attachment figure has become functionally interchangeable with any other resource holder and is not treated as emotionally irreplaceable. The parent has been recast in the role of agent rather than being an intrinsic, emotional regulator. These adolescents try to get their parents to submit to their demands only because most children have greater access to the supplies controlled by their parents than to those from any other source. If they have come to depend on access to supplies as essential regulators, they will become desperate if their best source threatens to escape their range of dominance. Therefore, there may be fear of loss and separation protest (Bowlby, 1988, pp. 30–31), but it is better understood as the distress a con artist might experience when the mark leaves town or the terror any bully feels if there are no sycophants in attendance. The replaceable nature of these adolescent-parent relation-

ships is revealed when it becomes evident that a better supplier will mean the adolescent abandons the attempt to get more out of the parents and virtually disappears. Older adolescents may use gang membership to capture supplies rather than continue the struggle with their families.

But what is the alternative for an individual whose primary attachment figures simply abdicate a protective function? An adaptive solution for profoundly inadequate caregivers would involve reorganizing one's attachment system in relation to a new figure or set of figures who are truly stronger and wiser, much as should happen in normal mourning after a loss. However, human attachments must include cognitive protection, for instance, wisely interpreting the meaning of experiences and events and fostering coherent reasoning (Cobb, 1996; Kobak, Cole, Ferenz-Gillies, Fleming, & Gamble, 1993). In adolescence, fiercely loyal friends can keep each other from feeling alone and abandoned, but although adolescents who suppress attachment functioning with their parents may try reorganize their attachment system around peers, the regulation available from peers rarely supports further development of problem solving and reasoning and therefore fails to function more protectively than the original attachments. In fact, the desperate, exclusive dependence often seen among teen peers usually results in the whole group landing in serious forms of trouble and social defeat. Without conscious choice, the group adopts a mode of instrumental alliances focused on obtaining tools and supplies for regulation. Although it may seem that the priority they place on loyalty and mutual trust is a way of preserving attachment, the outcome of this bonding is often admission of boredom while relying on drugs, alcohol, and sometimes sex. Reorganizing attachments around more suitable adult figures might have a different outcome, but most controlling adolescents, gun-shy from chronic parental struggles, do not want to become closer to other adults they know, nor are they encouraged to model themselves after wise cultural heroes with whom symbolic identification might offer a template for safe, productive learning, thereby regulating anxiety.

OBSERVATIONAL INDICES FOR CLASSIFYING CONTROLLING AND FRANKLY DISORGANIZED BEHAVIOR IN ADOLESCENCE

Adolescent attachment, controlling, and frankly disorganized behavior can be assessed using the Attachment Behavior Classification Procedure (ABCP; Cobb, 1996; Hilburn-Cobb, 1998). The method involves each adolescent-parent dyad watching an upsetting film together, answering questions that focus on the film's attachment themes of separation and loss, and engaging in three different discussion tasks that continually focus on attachment issues. The videotaped discussions and reunions with each parent allow classification of either direct indices of secure-based interaction with the parent or the defenses against impact of attachment feelings. Extensive observation of adolescent behavior in this protocol confirms that most teens are able to maintain at least a veneer of cooperation with their parents' authority even if the idea of participating in research was not their own. Secure adolescents demonstrate that a relaxed, mutually open, and personally relevant conversation about attachment situations and feelings is possible in the teen years. Avoidant adolescents also preserve interested, sociable interaction as long as they steer the topic away from the effects of attachment on the self; preoccupied adolescents may engage in intensely emotional exchanges or passive deference to the parent's views (Cobb, 1993, 1996).

The original, three-way ABCP classification scheme was expanded to include indices for disorganized and controlling behavior (Hilburn-Cobb, 1998), relying heavily on the theoretical principles behind Main and Solomon's (1990) indices for disorganization in infancy and Main and Cassidy's (1988) and Cassidy and Marvin's (1992) indices for controlling behavior. There are four categories of extreme behavior in the ABCP: three classes of frankly disorganized behavior and one category of maladaptive organization. Disorganization in task behavior can be seen in inexplicable behaviors, extreme anxiety symptoms, sudden unwillingness to engage with the discussion task despite informed consent, self-harming behavior or threats during the discussions, and inappropriate or bizarre affect mismatched with the parent. Disorganization in information processing involves unusual misunderstandings of information in the film or scenarios under discussion or insisting on contents that were not included or were explicitly ruled out in the protocol in order to solve attachment issues. Finally, disorganization of event representation includes references to bizarre or violent images or acts or nonplayful references to harm or danger from the research setting. In contrast, the strategies in the category of maladaptive organization, or controlling behavior, represent a relatively organized, hierarchical challenge or role reversal initiated by the adolescent rather than induced or encouraged by the parent. In fact, the parent's attitude usually ranges from helpless accommodation to hostile unwillingness to accept the adolescent's authority. One 13-year-old boy continually gave his mother directions to make him some tea, to drink it a certain way, to double his privileges if she could not deliver one privilege on time, and so on while openly taunting her that there was nothing she could do about his power over her. The mother struggled against her helplessness by trying to point out her son's logical fallacies, while she automatically followed his series of orders.

Adolescents might show lack of enthusiasm for the research experience they have agreed to, but those with adequate attachments do so in a relatively careful manner, not directly defying parental authority. An adolescent who engages in controlling behavior shows little regard for the parent's state of mind and focuses on acquiring concessions or simply reducing the parent to submission. The theme of material supplies, money, and privileges is almost never absent. In short, the adolescent's behavior does little to maintain the parent's protective state of mind.

For example, 13-year-old Sabrina consented to participate in the research protocol but, when the film ended, she immediately asked her mother what time it was, obviously counting the minutes until her stipulated period of cooperation would be over. This triggered the mother to assert that they would not go on a promised shopping trip unless she cooperated. Sabrina flew into a rage and refused to continue, screaming that her mother had "lied," always lied, and worse; she refused to simply honor her personal agreement with the researchers. She insisted she would continue only if her mother promised the researcher that the shopping trip would take place. Needless to say, the session was terminated.

Because dominance skills are still rather crass and unsophisticated, adolescents who try to use a dominance-organized controlling strategy are often unsuccessful in getting what they want from the parent and their anxiety is not well regulated by the few instrumental supplies they do garner. Still, adolescents do not have the judgment to see the inadequacy of the strategy they have used and evaluate it as self-defeating.

Data from ABCP Classification of Frankly Disorganized and Controlling Behavior

From a sample of 70 adolescents (ages 11 to 18) recruited from a clinical assessment service and community advertising, a subsample of 48 received acceptable scores on a scale for social desirability responding in Gibbs, Barriga, and Potter's (1992) How I Think (HIT) questionnaire and were also classified for attachment strategy with their primary attachment figures (48 with mothers and 42 with fathers or mothers' long-term partner). Three-way attachment classifications were expressed quantitatively on a 9-point scale for emotional proximity seeking or exploration with the parent, ranging from limiting or avoidance at the low end to preoccupied entanglement at the high end. Separate Disorganization (D) scores (0–9) were also assigned for each of the controlling and disorganized behaviors within each relationship. Some controlling adolescents also showed indices of disorganization and received a notable rating on both scales. (D scores less than 5 are considered disorganized attachment and classified in one of the three basic categories; any D score greater than 5 is classified as a fourth category.)

Sixty percent of subjects received scores above the clinical cutoff on the Child Behavior Checklist (CBCL) or Youth Self-Report (Achenbach, 1991). All adolescents completed a questionnaire battery including Davis's Interpersonal Reactivity Index (IRI; Davis, 1983, 1994), which includes a scale for empathic concern, and the HIT (Barriga & Gibbs, 1996) as a measure of cognitive distortion and predicted pathology. All but five mothers completed the CBCL (Achenbach) as a measure of behavior disorder. Most details of the study and the sample will be published elsewhere. Correlation results that have bearing on this model are given in Table 5.3. The correlations for the continuous ABCP scale with the outcome measures indicate that secure and preoccupied attachments are moderately associated with higher self-reported empathic concern and avoidant attachments with lower empathic scores, as would be predicted in attachment theory. Adolescents who are avoidant with their father are more likely to minimize, otherwise the basic attachment scales are not related to the psychopathology or maternal CBCL (Child Behavior Checklist) scores. However, controlling scores in relation to mother are strongly related to blaming of others, Oppositional Defiant Disorder, and externalizing behavior disorder, in addition to various cognitive distortions. There appears to be no significant relation between controlling behavior with fathers and psychopathology. On the other hand, frankly disorganized behavior in relation to mothers has no relation to be-

TABLE 5.3
Pearson Correlations for Attachment Strategy, Controlling Behavior,
and Frankly Disorganized Behavior with Empathy,
Reasoning, and Psychopathology

	Continuous Scale Attachment		Controlling Behavior		Frankly Disorganized Behavior	
	Mother	Father	Mother	Father	Mother	Father
Empathic concern	.341*	.363*	−.087	.043	.032	−.295
Self-centered	−.118	−.281	.325*	.109	.229	.455**
Minimizing or mislabeling	−.173	−.323*	.317*	.240	.242	.409**
Assuming the worst	−.140	−.142	.311*	.158	.286*	.468**
Blaming others	−.032	−.206	.390**	.183	.234	.366*
Aggression	−.121	−.260	.355*	.111	.369**	.509**
Opposition or defiance	.008	.179	.415**	.252	.265	.417**
Maternal CBCL internalizing	.102	.144	.205	.104	.273	.123
Maternal CBCL externalizing	.137	.191	.398**	.176	.266	.338*

$*p < .05.$ $**p < .01.$

havior disorders, whereas disorganized behavior with fathers is very strongly associated with all pathological behaviors and also is associated with mothers' higher externalizing scores. It appears that disorganizing fear in relation to fathers is most strongly associated with adolescent behavior disorder, but that these teens are able to gather together some organizing control in the relationship with their mothers, even if disorganization is also evident in those controlling strategies.

Tables 5.4 and 5.5 show ANOVAs by three- and four-way attachments that confirm that the D's had been, as a group, the worst of the avoidants. All six cases that were frankly disorganized in relation to their fathers had

TABLE 5.4
ANOVA Effect of Separating Disorganized and Controlling
Subjects From Simple Attachments to Mother

	Three-Way				Four-Way			
Variable	n	Means		F	Scheffe	n	Means		F	Scheffe
Empathic	29	A	16.2	4.99**	B > A	20	A	15.1	4.48**	B > A
concern	5	B	23.7			5	B	23.7		
	11	C	18.8			8	C	19.1		
						12	D	18.4		
Self-centered	29	A	2.5	1.1		20	A	2.5	1.2	
	5	B	1.9			5	B	1.9		
	11	C	2.4			8	C	2.2		
						12	D	2.7		
Minimizing	29	A	2.4	2.0		20	A	2.4	1.6	
or misla-	5	B	1.6			5	B	1.6		
beling	11	C	2.3			8	C	2.1		
						12	D	2.6		
Assuming	29	A	2.5	.84		20	A	2.4	1.4	
the worst	5	B	1.9			5	B	1.9		
	11	C	2.3			8	C	2.1		
						12	D	2.7		
Blaming oth-	29	A	2.4	1.3		20	A	2.3	2.1	
ers	5	B	1.7			5	B	1.7		
	11	C	2.5			8	C	2.2		
						12	D	2.7		
Aggression	29	A	2.4	1.9		20	A	2.3	3.1*	—
	5	B	1.5			5	B	1.5		
	11	C	2.2			8	C	1.8		
						12	D	2.8		
Opposition	29	A	2.5	.57		20	A	2.5	.68	
or defiance	5	B	2.1			5	B	2.2		
	11	C	2.7			8	C	2.5		
						12	D	2.8		

Note. This analysis excludes three cases classified as A/C with mother.
*$p < .05$. **$p < .01$.

TABLE 5.5
ANOVA Effect of Separating Disorganized and Controlling
Subjects from Simple Attachments to Father

Variable			Three-Way					Four-Way		
	n		Means	F	Scheffe	n		Means	F	Scheffe
Empathic	26	A	16.3	8.03***	B > A	20	A	16.9	5.8***	B > A, D
concern	3	B	26.5			3	B	26.5		
	11	C	20.0			11	C	20.0		
						6	D	14.5		
Self-centered	26	A	2.5	3.0		20	A	2.3	4.8**	D > B, C
	3	B	1.4			3	B	1.5		
	11	C	2.0			11	C	2.0		
						6	D	3.2		
Minimizing or	26	A	2.4	5.1**	—	20	A	2.3		D > B, C
mislabeling	3	B	1.1			3	B	1.1	6.2***	
	11	C	1.9			11	C	1.9		
						6	D	3.1		
Assuming the	26	A	2.4	1.7		20	A	2.2	3.7*	D > B
worst	3	B	1.5			3	B	1.5		
	11	C	2.1			11	C	2.1		
						6	D	3.1		
Blaming	26	A	2.3	4.3*		20	A	2.2	4.6**	D > B
others	3	B	1.2			3	B	1.2		
	11	C	2.1			11	C	2.1		
						6	D	2.7		
Aggression	26	A	2.3	4.0*		20	A	2.1	5.4***	D > B, C
	3	B	1.1			3	B	1.1		
	11	C	1.7			11	C	1.7		
						6	D	3.0		
Opposition or	26	A	2.5	1.4		20	A	2.3	3.43*	—
defiance	3	B	1.8			3	B	1.7		
	11	C	2.3			11	C	2.2		
						6	D	3.3		

Note. This analysis excludes two cases classified as A/C with father.
*p < .05.   **p < .01.   ***p < .005.

been given an avoidant three-way classification; 75% of adolescents who
were controlling with their mothers were classed as avoidant. The mean
scores for (combined) controlling and disorganized adolescents are consistently more negative than for other classifications in father-related analyses or in mother-related analyses, except for empathic concern, which is
due to a single extreme case. If highly anxious attachment strategies represent reverted (preoccupied) and arrested (avoidant) escape strategies,
then it makes sense that the combined D classifications represent individuals who have moved from curtailed to full escape from the caregiver to
gain regulation through instrumental means, and the outcome has been

either controlling behavior to secure supplies or, failing that, utter chaos (frank disorganization).

Table 5.3 correlations support the notion that controlling behavior may be distinct from frank disorganization and from behavior organized mainly by the attachment system. The scores assigned for basic attachment showed statistical behavior different from the scores for frankly disorganized and controlling behavior, within the same individuals. Behavior problems and cognitive distortions were associated with teens who were controlling with mothers but disorganized with fathers, which may indicate that fathers are more likely than mothers to squash hierarchical challenge, thus cutting off an adolescent's recourse with him and leaving no alternative but disorganization or depression.

SUMMARY OF ARGUMENT

1. Attachment relationships are the preemptive mechanism for regulation during infancy. The attachment system is therefore paramount in a rigid hierarchy of recourse under stress at this period.

2. As a child matures, the hierarchy among systems should gain flexibility in order to allow instrumental and social competencies to develop within other behavioral control systems, even under conditions of stress.

3. When attachments are secure, the hierarchy of recourse more readily relaxes. However, when attachments are anxious, preoccupation with obtaining regulation maintains the hierarchy in a state of infantile rigidity. All other systems are subordinated to serve an attachment goal rather than their own unique goals. If this continues, those systems produce only limited or distorted competence in social and instrumental domains.

4. If both primary and secondary attachments chronically fail to assuage anxiety, a new stressful situation is first met with random desperation tactics, interspersed with attempts to return to the preferred attachment strategy. This would appear as the disorganized attachment strategy identified in existing attachment research.

5. If signs of disorganized attachment fail to mobilize the caregiver, the individual facing chronic stress will either (a) experience disorganizing fear, labeled frank disorganization where no system organizes behavior; or (b) suppress attachment functioning and turn to another behavioral system to force caregivers to provide supplies for instrumental regulation. The latter is labeled controlling behavior.

6. At this stage, alternative systems only offer primitive strategies for acquiring regulatory supplies. Controlling strategies are powerful precisely because they are not self-limited by valuing the relationship with parents as

an irreplaceable attachment. Nevertheless, because they are primitive, controlling strategies may not be effective in obtaining sufficient instrumental supplies to regulate for further growth of competence. Primitive and incompetent attempts to coerce parents are vulnerable to defeat.

7. A final failure to ensure security by alternative systems may lead to severe depression or frankly disorganized behavior manifesting itself as traumatized or dissociative states.

IMPLICATIONS OF DISORGANIZATION
AND CONTROLLING BEHAVIOR FOR TREATMENT

Jane was 14 when she came with her mother and brother for family therapy. Jane was angry and distrustful because of her mother's series of unsuitable boyfriends, who were punitive and rejecting toward the children, and because of the mother's inability to look after even her own interests. Jane denied any type of abuse. In family sessions there was an intense struggle between herself and her mother over Jane's efforts to correct and direct her mother's behavior. As a support to the family work, Jane entered individual therapy and made excellent use of the opportunity to explore her own thoughts and feelings about her relationships, including a rich use of dream material that she delighted in analyzing. She maintained good grades and the practice of an artistic talent. However, Jane's contempt for the mother's judgment became acute as the mother did not mend her ways. She began to request the therapist's help to leave her home. The therapist tried a temporizing and delaying strategy, because there did not seem to be actual abuse or danger and the home did offer her the opportunity to continue all of her developing skills.

Jane left therapy without warning and would not return calls. She obtained student welfare assistance through her school and did leave her home, dropped her artistic endeavors, got a part-time job, but remained in school, graduated, and attended a university. She came back to see the therapist on the eve of her senior prom to let the therapist know that she had been successful and was looking forward to her future. Several years later she contacted the therapist again. She had gotten her B.A., but had not found a career that claimed her commitment; she was a temporary secretarial worker and seemed to be drifting from one part of the country to another and from one relationship to another, all with individuals who were rootless and directionless. She seemed more vague and immature than she had been during her adolescence. The therapist had the sense of seeing someone who had almost made a heroic save, but, for want of some overlooked but essential factor, had missed the catch after all.

As a general rule, there is no reason to expect any other control system to secure safer, more maturity-promoting, regulatory support than the attachment system during the adolescent years. Therefore, the ultimate goal for therapy with adolescents whose behavior represents a maladaptive choice for organizing regulation is a reinstatement of the attachment system to a meaningful status within the adolescent's hierarchy of recourse. This would imply that therapy with controlling adolescents should employ the therapeutic relationship as a bridging partnership or transitional attachment, aimed at encouraging the adolescent to either (a) reinvest in discarded family attachments, if these can become more sensitive and regulatory, or (b) reorient the attachment system around some other appropriately regulatory figure. If there is no hope of family rehabilitation (or the parents definitely reject the adolescent, as in many failed adoptions) or the adolescent insists on being detached from the original parents, a therapeutic effort to reorganize adolescent attachments around new, appropriately helpful figures may be the only attachment option that circumstances allow. Attachment to new figures may be especially necessary in cases of remorseless abuse by former caregivers.

However, once attachment functioning has been suppressed on a habitual basis, the therapist cannot assume that it will be reinstated as soon as a kindly person offers emotional access: My argument has been that controlling behavior still represents a very rigid hierarchical solution. The controlling child or adolescent has only substituted a less adaptive system into the unyielding, preemptive position that attachment had previously occupied within a rigid hierarchy of recourse. Felt security is sought by instrumental means, through the operation of the substituted system in almost all circumstances. Controlling behavior therefore represents an inflexible instrumental recourse that is resistant to redirection. As long as it seems to adolescents that a controlling strategy is an adequate resort in an inadequate and threatening environment, they will be terrified of handing over control in order to rely only on regulation from a relationship with a therapist or any other transitional attachment figure.

Of course, the attachment motivation is never extinguished and continues to tempt the controlling individual to try regulation and protection through relationships, just like hunger continues to tempt the anorexic. However, if the adolescent has come to believe that control of such temptation is essential for survival, a therapeutic approach that continually offers and actively encourages forming new attachments will be treated as dangerous by the young client. Furthermore, a push to reconsider attachment security (to discuss feelings about losses, to acknowledge caring, to hope for more responsive caring, etc.) carries the message that the competence of the client's own solution is not appreciated (by the therapist). This does not constitute a good beginning for a therapeutic alliance with someone whose great fear is the discovery of his or her own incompetence.

What may be more helpful, in a prolonged initial phase of treatment, is acceptance of the adolescent's instrumental emphasis. Comments that reflect and interpret instrumental supplies and tools in terms of their genuine security value and normalizing comments that emphasize that everyone needs to be reasonably certain of regulation and a sense of such security, although they may use different methods, may be helpful in educating the client into the language of thoughts, feelings, and emotional needs. This approach does not demand that security needs be met in any particular way. A cognitive-behavioral approach that leaves control of the goals and pace of therapy in the hands of the client may be indicated for this period. If the therapeutic alliance can be sustained on this basis, the relationship may become tempting enough to elicit a transitional attachment.

For example, 15-year-old Jesse had experienced the traumatic deaths of his family members but refused to discuss those events or the effect of loss on his current behavior. He was placed in a group home where he was described as immature and highly attention seeking, often monopolizing conversations to talk about his own accomplishments and interests, but uninterested in others. Jesse agreed that he ruined relationships by wanting to become friends but withdrawing whenever the friendships threatened to involve emotional closeness. At the same time, he showed exceptional mathematical talent and spent considerable time on the internet corresponding with unseen others who shared his abstract interests.

Although the residential staff were trained to set goals that would involve retrospective grief work, discussion of emotions, and learning to consider and empathize with the needs of others, it was recognized that all these goals presupposed either anxious or secure attachment functioning. Given that Jesse's world did not currently contain any stronger or wiser figure who could have offered a stable, long-term attachment relationship, his egocentric social behavior was accepted as a rigidly controlling attempt at adaptation. He was understood to be organizing his behavior mainly in terms of exploratory (abstract mathematics) and affiliative systems (compulsive displays of personal qualities) in order to gain status and the regulatory supplies that would come with status, rather than attempting to gain security through emotional connections. A new therapeutic approach was recommended, based on recognizing and supporting the instrumental, security-enhancing aspects of his work and his commitment to social-affiliative rather than (dominance-based) hostile, offensive methods. The longer term goal involved finding a permanent individual therapist who would be willing to engage in a therapeutic alliance based on instrumental issues. This would allow the therapist to be available for a transitional attachment at some indefinite future time when Jesse might be willing to allow this to happen.

Winnicott (1958, 1965), working with adults who rigidly controlled their own lives through what he called a "false-self" personality, argued that it would be necessary to wait for a considerable period for the patient's decision to hand over control of the therapy to the therapist, and only then would the patient be able to allow themselves to reexperience a need for primary attachment within a significant therapeutic regression and, in turn, only then could they rebuild genuine attachments in their outside lives.

In other words, a disorganized (regressed) state may be necessary before there can be a reorganization among the behavioral systems that constitute a rigid hierarchy of adaptive recourse. Although the renunciation of attachment in favor of dominance or any other survival system often contains elements of disorganization (fear), a system substitution is still an organized effort to adapt to a dysregulating environment and, in that sense, controlling behavior may appear on the surface to represent a lesser form of psychopathology than the personal chaos of frankly disorganized functioning. However, for clients who present in a state of frank disorganization, no behavioral system has primacy for the time being and they are no longer rigidly restricted to behavioral control within any particular system. The attachment system should be as available as any other for reorganizing a search for felt security. Therefore, frank disorganization may offer greater immediate potential for reorganizing through new attachment experiences than would be the case for individuals who present with controlling forms of behavior.

REFERENCES

Achenbach, T. M. (1991). *Child behavior checklist for ages 4–18*. Burlington, VT: University of Vermont, Department of Psychiatry.

Ainsworth, M. (1978). Theoretical background. In M. Ainsworth, M. Blehar, E. Waters, & S. Wall (Eds.), *Patterns of attachment: A psychological study of the Strange Situation* (pp. 3–28). Hillsdale, NJ: Lawrence Erlbaum Associates.

Ainsworth, M. (1990). Epilogue: Some considerations regarding theory and assessments relevant to attachments beyond infancy. In M. Greenberg, D. Cicchetti, & E. M. Cummings (Eds.), *Attachment in the preschool years* (pp. 463–488). Chicago: University of Chicago Press.

Ainsworth, M. (1991). Attachment and other affectional bonds across the life cycle. In C. Parkes, J. Stevenson-Hinde, & P. Marris (Eds.), *Attachment across the life cycle* (pp. 33–51). London: Routledge.

Allan, S., & Gilbert, P. (1997). Submissive behavior and psychopathology. *British Journal of Clinical Psychology, 36,* 467–488.

Barriga, A., & Gibbs, J. (1996). Measuring cognitive distortion in antisocial youth: Development and preliminary validation of the "How I Think" questionnaire. *Aggressive Behavior, 22,* 333–343.

Blos, P. (1979). *The adolescent passage*. New York: International Universities Press.

Bowlby, J. (1951). *Maternal care and mental health*. New York: Columbia University Press.

Bowlby, J. (1982). *Attachment and loss. Vol. 1: Attachment*. London: Pelican Books. (Original work published 1969)

Bowlby, J. (1988). *A secure base: Parent-child attachment and healthy human development*. New York: Basic Books.

Bretherton, I. (1987). New perspectives on attachment relations: Security, communication, and internal working models. In J. Osofsky (Ed.), *Handbook of infant development* (pp. 1061–1100). New York: Wiley.

Bretherton, I., Golby, B., & Cho, E. (1997). Attachment and the transmission of values. In J. Grusec & L. Kuczynski (Eds.), *Handbook of parenting and the socialization of values* (pp.). New York: Wiley.

Cassidy, J. (1994). Emotion regulation. *Influences of attachment relationships*.

Cassidy, J., & Marvin, R. (1992). *Attachment organization in three and four year olds: Coding guidelines*. Unpublished manuscript, MacArthur Attachment Working Group.

Cicchetti, D., Cummings, E. M., Greenberg, M., & Marvin, R. (1990). An organizational perspective on attachment beyond infancy. In M. Greenberg, D. Cicchetti, & E. M. Cummings (Eds.), *Attachment in the preschool years* (pp. 3–49). Chicago: University of Chicago Press.

Cobb, C. (1996). Adolescent-parent attachments and family problem-solving styles. *Family Process, 35*, 57–82.

Crittenden, P. (1996). Attachment and psychopathology. In S. Goldberg, R. Muir, & J. Kerr (Eds.), *Attachment theory: Social, developmental, and clinical perspectives* (pp. 367–406). New York: Analytic Press.

Crittenden, P. (1997). Attachment and sexual behavior. In L. Atkinson & K. Zucker (Eds.), *Attachment and psychopathology* (pp. 47–93). New York: Guilford Press.

Davis, M. (1983). Measuring individual differences in empathy: Evidence for a multidimensional approach. *Journal of Personality and Social Psychology, 44*, 113–126.

Davis, M. (1994). *Empathy: A psychological approach*. Madison, WI: WCB Brown & Benchmark.

Douvan, E., & Adelson, J. (1966). *The adolescent experience*. New York: Wiley.

Eccles, J., Midgley, C., Wigfield, A., Buchanan, C., Reuman, D., Flanagan, C., & MacIver, D. (1993). Development during adolescence: The impact of stage-environment fit on young adolescents' experience in schools and in families. *American Psychologist, 48*, 90–101.

Fulingi, A., & Eccles, J. (1993). Perceived parent-child relationships and early adolescents' orientation toward peers. *Developmental Psychology, 29*, 622–632.

Gibbs, J., Barriga, A., & Potter, G. (1992). *The How I Think Questionnaire*. Unpublished manuscript, Ohio State University, Ohio.

Gilbert, P. (1992). *Depression: The evolution of powerlessness*. New York: Guilford Press.

Gilbert, P. (1993). Defense and safety: Their function in social behavior and psychopathology. *British Journal of Clinical Psychology, 32*, 131–153.

Gilbert, P. (1997). The evolution of social attractiveness and its role in shame, humiliation, guilt and therapy. *British Journal of Medical Psychology, 70*, 113–147.

Gilbert, P. (2000). Varieties of submissive behavior as forms of social defense: Their evolution and role in depression. In L. Sloman & P. Gilbert (Eds.), *Subordination and defeat: An evolutionary approach to mood disorders and their therapy* (pp. 3–45). Mahwah, NJ: Lawrence Erlbaum Associates.

Gilbert, P., & Allan, S. (1998). The role of defeat and entrapment (arrested flight) in depression: An exploration of an evolutionary view. *Psychological Medicine, 28*, 1–14.

Gilbert, P., Allan, S., & Trent, D. (1995). Involuntary subordination or dependency as key dimensions of depressive vulnerability? *Journal of Clinical Psychology, 15*, 740–752.

Gilbert, P., Allan, S., & Trent, D. (1996). A short measure of social and separation anxiety. *British Journal of Medical Psychology, 69*, 155–161.

Gilbert, P., & Trower, P. (1990). Social anxiety: Evolution and manifestation. In R. Crozier (Ed.), *Shyness and embarrassment: Perspectives from social psychology* (pp. 144–177). New York: Cambridge University Press.

Greenberg, M., DeKlyen, M., Speltz, M., & Endriga, M. (1997). The role of attachment processes in externalizing psychopathology in young children. In L. Atkinson & K. Zucher (Eds.), *Attachment and psychopathology* (pp. 196–222). New York: Guilford Press.

Greenberg, M., & Marvin, R. (1982). Reactions of preschool children to an adult stranger. *Child Development, 53,* 481–490.

Greenberg, M., Siegel, J., & Leitch, C. (1983). The nature and importance of relationships to parents and peers during adolescence. *Journal of Youth and Adolescence, 12,* 373–388.

Greenberg, M., Speltz, M., DeKlyen, M., & Endriga, M. (1991). Attachment security in preschoolers with and without externalizing behavior problems: A replication. *Development and Psychopathology, 3,* 413–430.

Harlow, H., & Harlow, M. (1969). Effects of various mother-infant relationships on rhesus monkey behaviors. In B. Foss (Ed.), *Determinants of infant behavior* (Vol. 4, pp. 15–36). London: Methuen.

Harris, J. (1998). *The nurture assumption.* New York: Free Press.

Hilburn-Cobb, C. (1997). *Adolescent attachment, self-conscious emotion, moral reasoning and social behavior.* Unpublished manuscript.

Hilburn-Cobb, C. (1998). *Coding manual and scoring directions for adolescent attachment behavior, 5th revision.* Unpublished manuscript.

Hilburn-Cobb, C., Gotlieb, H., Pye, R., & Mann, S. (2000). Modeles d'attachement des parents et comportements d'attachement des adolescents: un arrimage avec les modeles multiples d'attachement. In G. M. Tarabulsy, S. Larose, D. R. Pederson, & G. Moran (Eds.), *Attachement et developpement: Le role des preemieres relations dans le developpement humain* (pp. 267–300). Sainte-Foy, Quebec: l'Universite du Quebec.

Hinde, R. (1970). *Animal behavior: A synthesis of ethology and comparative psychology* (2nd ed.). New York: McGraw-Hill.

Hofer, M. (1984). Relationships as regulators: A psychobiologic perspective on bereavement. *Psychosomatic Medicine, 46,* 183–197.

Hofer, M. (1994). Hidden regulators in attachment, separation, and loss. In N. Fox & J. Campos (Eds.), *The development of emotion regulation: Biological and behavioral considerations* (Society for Research in Child Development Monograph No. 59 [2–3], pp. 192–207). MA: Blackwell.

Hofer, M. (1995). Hidden regulators: Implications for a new understanding of attachment, separation, and loss. In S. Goldberg, R. Muir, & J. Kerr (Eds.), *Attachment theory: Social, developmental, and clinical perspectives* (pp. 203–230). New York: Analytic Press.

Kobak, R. (1999). The emotional dynamics of disruptions in attachment relationships: Implications for theory, research, and clinical intervention. In J. Cassidy & P. Shaver (Eds.), *Handbook of attachment* (pp. 21–43). New York: Guilford Press.

Kobak, R., Cole, H., Ferenz-Gillies, R., Fleming, W., & Gamble, W. (1993). Attachment and emotion regulation during mother-teen problem-solving: A control theory analysis. *Child Development, 64,* 231–245.

Kobak, R., Sudler, N., & Gamble, W. (1992). Attachment and depressive symptoms during adolescence: A developmental pathways analysis. *Development and Psychopathology, 3,* 461–474.

Kraemer, G. (1992). A psychobiological theory of attachment. *Behavioral and Brain Sciences, 15,* 493–541.

Lyons-Ruth, K. (1996). Attachment relationships among children with aggressive behavior problems: The role of disorganized early attachment patterns. *Journal of Consulting and Clinical Psychology, 64,* 64–75.

Main, M. (1990). Cross-cultural studies of attachment organization: Recent studies, changing methodologies, and the concept of conditional strategies. *Human Development, 33,* 48–61.

Main, M. (1991). Metacognitive knowledge, metacognitive monitoring, and singular (coherent) vs. multiple (incoherent) models of attachment. In C. Parkes, J. Stevenson-Hinde, & P. Marris (Eds.), *Attachment across the life cycle* (pp. 127–159). London: Routledge.

Main, M., & Cassidy, J. (1988). Categories of response to reunion with parent at age 6: Predictable from infant attachment classification and stable for a one month period. *Developmental Psychology, 24,* 415–426.

Main, M., & Hesse, E. (1990). Parents' unresolved traumatic experiences are related to infant disorganized attachment status: Is frightened and/or frightening parental behavior the linking mechanism? In M. Greenberg, D. Cicchetti, & M. Cummings (Eds.), *Attachment in the preschool years* (pp. 161–184). Chicago: University of Chicago Press.

Main, M., Kaplan, N., & Cassidy, J. (1985). Security in infancy, childhood, and adulthood: A move to the level of representation. In I. Bretherton & E. Waters (Eds.), *Growing points of attachment theory and research* (Society for Research in Child Development Monograph No. 209, pp. 66–104). MA: Blackwell.

Main, M., & Solomon, J. (1990). Procedures for identifying infants as disorganized/disoriented during the Strange Situation. In M. Greenberg, D. Cicchetti, & M. Cummings (Eds.), *Attachment in the preschool years* (pp. 121–160). Chicago: University of Chicago Press.

Main, M., & Weston, D. (1982). Avoidance of the attachment figure in infancy: Descriptions and interpretations. In C. Parkes & J. Stevenson-Hinde (Eds.), *The place of attachment in human behavior* (pp. 31–59). New York: Basic Books.

McGuire, M. (1988). On the possibility of ethological explanations of psychiatric disorders. *Acta Psychiatrica Scandinavica, 77*(Suppl.), 7–22.

McGuire, M., Raleigh, M., Fawzy, F., Spar, J., & Troisi, A. (in press). Dysthymic disorder, regulation-disregulation theory, CNS blood flow, and CNS metabolism. In P. Gilbert, L. Sloman, & J. Price (Eds.), *Subordination and mood disorders.* Mahwah, NJ: Lawrence Erlbaum Associates.

McGuire, M., & Troisi, A. (1987a). Physiological regulation-dysregulation and psychiatric disorders. *Ethology and Sociobiology, 8,* 9S–12S.

McGuire, M., & Troisi, A. (1987b). Unrealistic wishes and physiological change. *Psychotherapy and Psychosomatics, 47,* 82–94.

Moss, E., Parent, S., Gosselin, C., Rousseau, D., & St. Laurent, D. (1996). Attachment and teacher-reported behavior problems during the preschool and early school-age period. *Development and Psychopathology, 8,* 511–525.

Paikoff, R., & Brooks-Gunn, J. (1991). Do parent-child relationships change during puberty? *Psychological Bulletin, 110,* 47–66.

Patterson, G. (1982). *A social learning approach to family intervention: Vol. 3. Coercive family process.* Eugene, OR: Castalia.

Price, J. (1988). Alternative channels for negotiating asymmetry in social relationships. In M. R. A. Chance (Ed.), *Social fabrics of the mind.* Hillsdale, NJ: Lawrence Erlbaum Associates.

Price, J., & Sloman, L. (1987). Depression as yielding behavior: An animal model based on Schjelderup-Ebbe's pecking order. *Ethology and Sociobiology, 8*(Suppl.), 85–98.

Price, J., Sloman, L., Gardner, R., Gilbert, P., & Rhode, P. (1994). The social competition hypothesis of depression. *British Journal of Psychiatry, 164,* 309–315.

Robertson, J., & Bowlby, J. (1952). Responses of young children to separations from their mothers. *Courrier Centre International Enfancie, 2,* 131–142.

Ryan, R., & Lynch, J. (1989). Emotional autonomy versus detachment: Revisiting the vicissitudes of adolescence and young adulthood. *Child Development, 60,* 340–356.

Smetana, J. (1988). Adolescents' and parents' conceptions of parental authority. *Child Development, 59,* 321–355.

Smetana, J., & Asquith, P. (1994). Adolescents' and parents' conceptions of parental authority and personal autonomy. *Child Development, 65,* 1147–1162.

Solomon, J., George, C., & DeJong, A. (1995). Children classified as controlling at age six: Evidence of disorganized representational strategies and aggression at home and at school. *Development and Psychopathology, 7,* 447–463.

Spangler, G., & Grossmann, K. (1993). Biobehavioral organization in securely and insecurely attached infants. *Child Development, 64,* 1439–1450.

Speltz, M. (1990). The treatment of preschool conduct problems. In M. Greenberg, D. Cicchetti, & E. M. Cummings (Eds.), *Attachment in the preschool years* (pp. 399–426). Chicago: University of Chicago Press.

Spitz, R. (1946). Anaclitic depression. *The Psychoanalytic Study of the Child, 2,* 313–342.

Sroufe, L. A., Carlson, E., Levy, A., & Egeland, B. (1999). Implications of attachment theory for psychopathology. *Development and Psychopathology, 11,* 1–13.

Sroufe, L. A., & Waters, E. (1977). Attachment as an organizational construct. *Child Development, 48,* 1184–1199.

Trower, P., & Gilbert, P. (1989). New theoretical conceptions of social anxiety and social phobia. *Clinical Psychology Review, 9,* 19–35.

Weiss, R. (1982). Attachment in adult life. In C. Parkes & J. S. Stevenson-Hinde (Eds.), *The place of attachment in human behavior* (pp. 171–184). New York: Basic Books.

Weiss, R. (1991). The attachment bond in childhood and adulthood. In C. Parkes, J. Stevenson-Hinde, & P. Marris (Eds.), *Attachment across the life cycle* (pp. 66–76). London: Routledge.

West, M., Rose, M., & Sheldon, A. (1993). Anxious attachment as a determinant of adult psychopathology. *Journal of Nervous and Mental Disease, 181,* 422–427.

West, M., & Sheldon, A. E. (1988). Classification of pathological attachment patterns in adults. *Journal of Personality Disorders, 2,* 153–159.

Winnicott, D. W. (Ed.). (1958). *Through pediatrics to psycho-analysis* (pp. 300–305). London: Hogarth Press.

Winnicott, D. W. (1965). *The maturational processes and the facilitating environment.* London: Hogarth Press.

II

INTERVENTION

Levels of Processing in Parent-Child Relationships: Implications for Clinical Assessment and Treatment

Roger Kobak
University of Delaware

Alison Esposito
University of Delaware

During the past decade, attachment research has shed new light on the nature of parent-child relationships and their potential contribution to child and adolescent psychopathology. Researchers have linked insecure states of mind in the Adult Attachment Interview to increased risk for a variety of symptoms in adults (Dozier, Stovall, & Albus, 1999) and patterns of insecure parent-infant attachment have been associated with increased risk for child and adolescent psychopathology (Greenberg, 1999). Despite the progress in understanding the relation between attachment and psychopathology, research findings have had several notable limitations for clinicians working with children and their parents. First, available research methods for assessing attachment are labor intensive and often beyond the resources of most practicing clinicians. Second, and perhaps most important, research methodologies such as the "strange situation" and Adult Attachment Interview provide a narrow and rather limited understanding of how attachment processes contribute to the emergence of psychopathology. More specifically, both methodologies focus on the individual child or parent and fail to describe or account for the nature of the current parent-child relationship. Third, these methodologies cannot be used with children and young adolescents. The strange situation is restricted to use with infants up to the age of 18 months while the Adult Attachment Interview can only be used with subjects who are at least 15 years old.

In order to address these limitations, we propose a model of parent-child relationships that is based on the notion that parents and children process attachment information at multiple levels. At the individual level, both the parent and the child have formed internal working models (IWMs) or expectations for the other person and for the self. For children, these models guide appraisals of the parent's availability and responsiveness and organize strategies for maintaining the relationship. For parents, expectations guide their evaluation of and reaction to the child's behavior. At the interpersonal level, parents and children engage in a series of interactions and communications and both send and receive signals. Problems in communication can occur both in terms of how clearly and congruently partners send signals and in terms of how sensitively and accurately signals are read. Finally, at the metacognitive level, the parent's capacity for monitoring self and other may facilitate communication and the degree to which IWMs are open to revision and updating. By adolescence, the child becomes increasingly capable of also monitoring self and other in the parent-child relationship (Kobak & Cole, 1994; Selman, 1980).

We believe that our levels of processing model can integrate constructs and findings from attachment research into a more comprehensive understanding of cognitive and emotional processes in parent-child relationships. In doing so, this model should address several major issues. First, it should provide clinicians with a guide to identifying attachment issues in parent-child relationships. Second, the model should account for the increased developmental complexity in attachment relationships that occurs during the postinfancy period. Third, the model needs to address the parent's ongoing contribution to the attachment relationship. Without a clear understanding of the parent's contribution, we believe that efforts to apply attachment theory and research to child psychopathology are seriously limited.

In this chapter, we describe our levels of processing (LOP) model and then use it to distinguish between secure, anxious, and distressed parent-teen relationships. These three types of relationships represent a continuum of risk for child and adolescent psychopathology and can serve as a heuristic guide to clinical assessment and treatment. Whereas in secure relationships cognitive and emotional processes operate to protect the child from the various stresses encountered over the course of development, in anxious relationships the child is vulnerable at times of stress and is at a higher risk of developing symptoms that require professional attention. By the time many children reach treatment, their parent-child relationships are no longer simply anxious, but may be actively distressed and these distressed relationships often become a major impediment to symptom reduction. Our LOP model provides a way to describe the dynamics of secure, anxious, and distressed parent-child relationships. These descriptions can provide the clinician with a guide for assessing children and their parents and for establishing treatment goals that increase security in the relationship.

LEVELS OF PROCESSING IN THE PARENT-CHILD RELATIONSHIP

An LOP model of parent-child relationships can be used to describe and integrate the major findings and constructs from the past two decades of attachment research, including IWMs (Bretherton, 1985), attachment strategies (Main, 1990), open communication (Bowlby, 1988), states of mind (Hesse, 1999), and reflective function (Fonagy & Target, 1997). We believe that an adequate understanding of parent-child relationships must consider the individual level at which IWMs of self and other organize feelings and cognitions in the relationship, the interpersonal level at which communication is exchanged, and the metacognitive level at which parents, and eventually children, become capable of establishing a perspective on IWMs and communication between self and other. In addition to integrating existing findings, a comprehensive LOP model of the parent-child relationship also points toward major gaps in researchers' understanding of parents and children.

The Individual Level: IWMs of Self and Other

At the core of attachment theory is Bowlby's (1969/1982) account of the child's attachment system and how it develops within the context of the parent-child relationship. According to the theory, children develop motivational or behavioral control systems that foster the formation and maintenance of a parent-child attachment bond (Cassidy, 1999). The emotional significance of this bond is evident in the child's enjoyment in maintaining contact with the parent and, conversely, in the extreme fear, anger, and sadness that accompany perceived threats to the relationship or disruptions of the bond (Bowlby, 1973). Bowlby also introduced the notion that individual differences in personality could be traced to the child's IWMs of their caregivers' availability. Children whose IWMs confidently forecast caregiver availability and responsiveness would feel secure, whereas those that lacked such confidence would feel anxious and, at times, angry.

Beginning in the 1960s, Ainsworth's (1978) studies of mothers and infants at home and in a laboratory situation illustrated the complex interplay between infants' IWMs and their strategies for maintaining the attachment relationship. Ainsworth found that infants' IWMs of their mothers' availability could be inferred from how infants organized their behavior in the strange situation (Ainsworth, Blehar, Waters, & Wall, 1978). Infants judged to be secure showed a pattern that reflected an IWM that confidently forecasted maternal availability in the novel situation created by a laboratory environment. These infants actively used the mother as a safe haven at times of distress and as a secure base for exploration. Infants judged to be anxious or insecure were restricted in the use of their mother as secure base and safe haven, reflecting underlying cognitive schemas or IWMs that forecast uncertainty or negative expectation about maternal response.

IWMs or expectations for the mother's availability organize the child's strategy for regulating the attachment system (Main, 1990) and for maintaining the attachment relationship (Main & Weston, 1982). IWMs serve as filters of both parent and child behavior in ongoing interactions, which guide appraisals of core issues such as whether the parent is perceived to be available and responsive to the child and whether the parent views him- or herself as a competent caregiver. These core appraisals of self and other in the parent-child relationship in turn organize emotion, cognition, and strategies for maintaining the attachment bond. For the most part, these appraisals and interpretations operate automatically and outside of awareness (Bowlby, 1980). In this respect, IWMs are similar to core cognitive schemas that form the basis for contemporary cognitive behavioral therapies (Safran & Segal, 1990).

Infant attachment patterns in the strange situation illustrate how IWMs organize feeling and behavior. Whereas infants who were confident in the mother's availability actively communicated distress and sought comfort, infants whose IWMs forecasted rejection or inconsistent response developed secondary strategies that either minimized or maximized attachment feelings and behavior (Main, 1990). It is clear then that IWMs carry enormous emotional significance for the child. If the child's IWM forecasts an available and responsive parent, he or she will feel secure and will enter situations with confidence, knowing that the parent would respond if called upon for help or support. Alternatively, if the child anticipates that the caregiver will be rejecting, neglecting, or physically inaccessible, he or she will feel anxious, angry, or sad.

During the toddler and early childhood periods of development, children are also forming an IWM of self. This IWM of self guides children's appraisals of their abilities to succeed in day-to-day challenges and to gain support from others. Both theory and research suggest that the appraisal of the parent as available supports an appraisal of the self as worthy of support (Bowlby, 1973) and as confident and competent in situations involving challenge (Sroufe, 1988). Thus, an IWM of the parent that forecasts parental availability supports the development of an IWM of the self that forecasts successful outcomes in challenging situations.

Our LOP model suggests that the construct of IWMs should be extended to parents as well as their children. From this perspective, not only are children's interpretations influenced by IWMs, but parents' interpretations of their children are guided by IWMs as well. Attachment researchers have only begun to consider parent's IWMs of the child (George & Solomon, 1999). Theoretically, parents' IWMs should guide parental behavior and regulate parents' caregiving behavioral system. The biological functions of the caregiving system include protecting the child and fostering the child's preparation for adult roles that ultimately increase the likelihood of reproductive success. In this respect, the parent's motivation to protect the child and facilitate the child's learning complements the child's need for the parent to serve as a safe haven from danger and a secure base to support exploration.

In contrast to the child, the parent's IWM of self precedes the development of the parent's IWM of the child. As a result, the parent's IWM of self may bias perceptions of the child and the development of an IWM of the child in complex ways. In situations where parents have an IWM of self as worthy and competent, they may be free to more fully attend and adapt to the needs of their child. Such a model of self may also increase the parent's abilities to manage the child's anger or oppositional bouts, both of which are an integral part of the child's growing capacities for self-regulation.

The Interpersonal Level: Reading and Sending Signals

The notion that individual differences in IWMs could be assessed in the first 18 months in the strange situation has captured the imagination of researchers interested in later periods of development (Crowell, Fraley, & Shaver, 1999; Hazan & Shaver, 1987; Main, Kaplan, & Cassidy, 1985). As a result, Ainsworth's patterns of attachment have been turned into a theory of personality across the life span. Unfortunately, this focus on IWMs as a core feature of personality has come at the expense of another aspect of Ainsworth's work that focused on the interpersonal communication between mothers and their infants (Kobak, 1999). For Ainsworth, the infant's IWM or expectations for a parent's availability went hand in hand with her observations of mother-infant interaction at the interpersonal level. Infants with IWMs that forecasted mothers' availability in the strange situation had mothers who had sensitively responded to their signals during normal day-to-day interaction during the first year of life. Thus, IWMs at the individual level were inextricably linked to a pattern of communication at the interpersonal level.

Although researchers have devoted considerable effort to assessing maternal sensitivity in parent-infant relationships, Bretherton (1999) noted that observation of interpersonal communication between parents and older children has been relatively sparse. The lack of research on interpersonal communication stems from both pragmatic and theoretical problems. Pragmatically, assessment at the interpersonal level requires observation of parent-child interaction and this type of research is time consuming and difficult. Theoretically, parent-child communication undergoes a dramatic transformation during early childhood, with the emergence of verbal communication and what Bowlby (1969/1982) described as the goal-corrected partnership phase of the attachment relationship (Marvin, 1999). With the emergence of the child as a partner in the relationship, communication consists of not only the parent reading and responding to the child's signals, but also the child reading and responding to the parent's signals.

For the most part, attachment research has failed to take into account the dramatic transformation of the parent-child relationship into a goal-corrected partnership. As children become capable of understanding parents' goals, delaying their own goals, and negotiating compromise, the criteria for a secure parent-child relationship shift from sensitive caregiving by parents in infancy to cooperation between parents and children by the end of early childhood (Thompson, 2000). The shift to a goal-corrected partnership places new importance on both the parent's and the child's abilities to use conversation to resolve goal conflicts and addressing the child's needs for safety and learning becomes an essential feature of a secure relationship. As a result, conversations that conform to Grice's criteria for cooperative or coherent discourse become essential to the child's security or appraisal of the parent's availability (Kobak & Duemmler, 1994). For a conversation to meet these criteria, both the parent and the child must effectively express their own concerns, acknowledge the other person's concerns, and establish a give-and-take relationship in situations involving goal conflicts.

The importance of parent-child communication has been demonstrated in studies of adolescents and their parents. The importance of both communicating goals and validating one's partner is assessed in Allen et al.'s (1994) Autonomy and Relatedness Coding System for parents and their teenage children. Allen found that relationships in which parents and adolescents demonstrate autonomous assertion of their position while also acknowledging their partner's perspective lead to higher levels of adolescent ego development and self-esteem (Allen, Hauser, Bell, & O'Connor, 1994). Similarly, mother-teen problem-solving interactions characterized by mothers dominating the conversation and by a mutual lack of perspective taking were associated with depressive symptoms in adolescents over a 9-month period (Kobak, Sudler, & Gambler, 1991).

The Metacognitive Level: Updating and Revising IWMs

During the past decade, a great deal of research has emerged from Mary Main's classifications of parents' "states of mind" with respect to attachment in the Adult Attachment Interview (AAI; Hesse, 1999). She found that parents who were "free to evaluate" their thoughts, feelings, and memories of their own parents were more likely to have infants who were judged secure in the strange situation (Main et al., 1985). This freedom to evaluate involves the ability to access and integrate memories about parents and to consider the effects of childhood memories on the self. Interview questions create opportunities for reflection and for reappraisal of IWMs. Main and Goldywn assessed parents' ability to successfully engage in this task with close analysis of the coherence of parents' discourse in the interview setting (see Hesse, 1999, for review).

Main's (1985) discovery of states of mind in the AAI introduced a new level of processing to researchers' understanding of the parent-child relationship. An autonomous state of mind depends on a metacognitive ability to access, monitor, and reappraise IWMs of self or other. The potential implications of this discovery extend far beyond adults reflecting about their childhood experiences in an interview setting. Theoretically, the metacognitive ability that Main described as an autonomous state of mind allows the parent to access information about IWMs, check IWMs for consistency, and, when appropriate, update and revise the IWMs of self and other that guide appraisals during day-to-day interactions.

Much of the processing of relationship information that occurs at the individual level with IWMs and at the interpersonal level through signaling and reading partners' behaviors occurs automatically, without need for reflection (Bowlby, 1980). When IWMs produce expectations for self and relationships that are confirmed, the models are relatively well adapted or tolerably accurate and, by operating automatically, they make fewer demands on cognitive and attentional resources. However, to remain well adapted, IWMs must be open to revision and updating in response to new information.

Bowlby stressed the importance of updating and revising IWMs primarily from the standpoint of the child. In the third volume of his attachment trilogy, Bowlby (1973, 1980) focused on the how the loss of an attachment figure involves gradually accommodating unwelcome information about the loss and revising and updating IWMs of self and the world accordingly. In later writings about the therapeutic process, Bowlby (1973, 1980) focused on the therapist's role in helping adults access and reevaluate their IWMs of self and other in light of new information. The common theme was that outdated IWMs can be the source of problems in adaptation. From this perspective, healthy development requires IWMs of self and other to be open to new information. The process of reevaluating automatic appraisals of an attachment figure or of the IWM from which the appraisals are derived requires some degree of metacognitive activity; expectations of self and others need to be accessed and evaluated.

Our LOP model suggests that the process of updating and revising working models is important not only in situations involving loss and psychopathology, but also as a part of normal development in parent-child relationships. It is hard to overemphasize the potential significance of parents' metacognitive ability to maintain a secure attachment relationship with their child. As the child develops, parents must continually update and revise their IWM of the child. Much of the challenge of parenting centers on balancing concerns for children's safety with concerns that children are learning skills that support their autonomy. An accurate IWM of the child allows parents to adjust their behavior to the child's particular needs and abilities at different ages. During the phase of early childhood, part of children's learning involves the parent gradually increasing expectations for children to accommodate their goals to fit with those of the parent (Kochanska, Aksan, & Koenig, 1995). These maturity demands (Baumrind, 1967) provide an important adjustment in the parent-child relationship that ultimately facilitates the child's learning of frustration tolerance and negotiation skills, both of which are important for maturation.

Our LOP model also points to the role that parents' metacognitive abilities may play in monitoring and repairing communications with the child. Parents' IWMs of their child are likely to be more accurate and result in more effective parenting when the IWMs result from their ongoing experience of reading their child's signals. When parents' IWMs are regularly updated, they more likely to respond to the child in a manner that is well adapted to the child's attachment and exploratory needs. Individual variation between children may also challenge parents to build an IWM of the child that is well adapted to that particular child's attachment and exploratory needs. However, in most circumstances, the parents' IWMs of the child should facilitate their appraisal of the child's needs in a way that leads to effective response and supports the child's appraisal of the parents' availability and responsiveness. Updated IWMs are likely to result in caregiving behavior that fosters the parent's sense of efficacy and the child's appraisal of the parent as available and responsive.

The notion of "reflective function" further expands the potential relevance of metacognition to secure parent-child relationships. Fonagy and Target (1997) defined reflective function as "the developmental acquisition that permits the child to respond not only to other people's behavior, but to his conception of their beliefs, feelings, hopes, pretense, plans, and so on" (p. 679). This capacity for mentalization enables children to "read" people's minds and to attribute mental states to others. Thus, the development of reflective function presupposes the child's ability to differentiate between self and other and to attribute intention to people. This mentalizing ability gives the child the capacity to realize that another person's behavior is open to interpretation. In this sense, reflective function creates the possibility of generating new information with which IWMs of self and other can be updated.

Fonagy and Target (1997) proposed that parents provide a mirror for children's experience and, to the extent that parents attribute intent to children, children will come to understand their own and others' experience in terms of mental states. What begins as parents' capacity to mentalize children's behavior eventually becomes a relationship in which children develop their own capacity for reflective function. Meins (1999) termed parents' capacity to mentalize their child's behavior as "mind-mindedness" and suggested that this metacognitive ability plays an important role in maternal sensitivity and the development of a secure attachment. Furthermore, Meins and her colleagues found longitudinal relations among mothers' "mind-mindedness" during infancy, infant attachment security, and subsequent measures of theory of mind when the children were 5 years old (Meins, Fernyhough, Russell, & Clark-Carter, 1998).

An LOP model not only integrates existing research, but, more importantly, points to the major gaps in researchers' understanding of parent-child attachment relationships. First, attachment research with older children and adults has focused on processes at the individual level of analysis and, in doing so, has neglected the interpersonal level of ongoing communication (Bretherton, 1999). Second, despite the promising work of Meins and colleagues (1998) and Fonagy (1999), the implications of metacognition for the parent-child relationship have barely begun to be explored. Third, attachment research has focused primarily on the child and not the parent; as a result, little is known about parenting motivation or how the parent's IWM of the child develops and influences the parent-child relationship. Finally, most research tends to focus on only one or two levels of analysis and, as a result, the systematic relationship among levels of processing has not been adequately addressed.

Despite these research limitations, levels of processing can serve as a valuable heuristic for clinicians working with distressed parents and their children. In the remainder of this chapter, we illustrate how, by taking into account the interrelation between the levels of processing, clinicians can be guided in the assessment and treatment of child and adolescent psychopathology. In this sense, it is useful to describe relationships as secure, anxious, or distressed. These more general descriptions provide the clinician with a guide for assessment that identifies the degree of distress in the relationship and with an overview of a family's strengths as well as weaknesses. Because clinicians often see anxious, or distressed relationships, it is useful to consider secure relationships as a way of illustrating how successful parent-child relationships can manage difficulties and cope with stress. Such a description can also be useful in establishing treatment goals as well as markers of improvement in therapy with more distressed parent-child relationships.

THE SECURE CYCLE IN PARENT-CHILD RELATIONSHIPS

The parent's IWM of self as a competent caregiver and the child's IWM of the parent as available and responsive lie at the heart of a secure parent-child relationship. These IWMs provide the basic schemas through which the parent and child interpret and respond to each other's behavior. The child's confidence in the parent's availability biases the child toward viewing the parent's behavior in a favorable light. Such an IWM promotes ongoing appraisals of parental availability and a feeling of security in the child. The parent's confidence in his or her ability to care for the child fosters engagement and allows the parent to find ways to balance acceptance of the child's needs with firm limits. Together, positive expectancies of self and other set the tone, or emotional climate, for how information is processed in the relationship.

Security at the individual level fosters open communication at the interpersonal level. As the child encounters difficulties, challenges, and potential conflict with the parent, confidence in the parent's availability allows the child to openly and directly communicate both negative and positive feelings at the interpersonal level (Bretherton, 1990). Direct communications from the child facilitate the parent's task of reading the child's signals and are less open to misinterpretation. As a result, the parent's response is more likely to be sensitive and appropriate. As children enter the phase of the goal-corrected partnership (Marvin, 1999), parental response to a child's signals often involves balancing meeting the child's requests with the parent's own goals and maturity expectations for the child (Baumrind, 1967). In the goal-corrected partnership phase, the parent gradually revises his or her IWM of the child to take into account the child's growing ability to tolerate frustration and to internalize parental rules. As a result, parent communications involve establishing a sense of cooperative partnership through negotiation and joint planning. Parents' IWMs are important for reading the child's signals and for guiding the parent in setting appropriate limits with the child. The parent's IWM of self as a competent caregiver enhances his or her ability to communicate limits clearly and consistently to the child.

Parent-child relationships are subject to ongoing adjustment and challenge as the child develops. Just as in parent-infant relationships, understanding the role of attachment in older children requires close analysis of the patterns of parent-child interaction. The following exchange taken from Haim Ginott's classic book on parenting illustrates how a secure parent-teen relationship would manage a conflict that is fairly typical of the adolescent period of development:

Mother walks into the house on Sunday evening after being away for the weekend. Her fifteen year old daughter Gloria pounces on her.

Gloria: "Mother! Wait 'til you see the dress that I bought. It's so gorgeous. I charged it to your account."

Mother: "There is to be no charging in department stores without permission."

Gloria: "But I didn't steal it, what are you so mad about?"

Mother: "There is to be no charging in department stores without permission!"

(Retreats to bedroom and closes door. Thinks to self, "She can't wear that hideous, mini-length ruffled horror, with a plum velvet sash, that looked like a masquerade costume.")

Gloria: (Knocks on door). "Please open up! Wait 'til you see it on me. It fits perfectly on me and it looks so feminine and romantic."

Mother: (Opens door and sees the plum lavender dress). "I can see why you are taken by the dress, but it's inappropriate for school and too expensive."

Gloria: "But isn't the color gorgeous?"

Mother: "Some people like that color, it's not one of my favorites."

Gloria: "Why! I thought you like this color."

Mother: "It's not one of my favorite colors for clothes, though I do like to use it in my paintings. I can see how much you love that dress. It's not going to be easy to return it, could you do it tomorrow afternoon?"

(Ginott, 1971, pp. 104–106)

Two aspects of this conversation typify a secure parent-child relationship at the interpersonal level. First, both partners remained engaged in the conversation, actively contributing their points of view. Second, the conversation remains cooperative in tone without either the child or parent resorting to angry, belittling, critical, or rude comments. In this exchange, the mother deserves much of the credit for maintaining a cooperative tone. Most evident is the mother's confidence in her self as a caregiver and her ability to work at repairing a violation of a rule about using her credit card. Her confidence is evident in her firm assertion of the rule about charging and her ability to contain her anger about the violation. For her part, the daughter, although absorbed with her own concerns about the dress, persists in trying to influence her mother, but is willing to modify her own goals in order to maintain cooperation in the relationship.

The mother also demonstrates how metacognition can contribute to maintaining a cooperative conversation. First, metacognition creates the possibility of taking into account multiple perspectives on self and other. At the most basic level, empathy with another person or reflective function involves moving beyond the self to consideration of alternative perspectives. This ability becomes a critical feature of the goal-corrected partnership phase of parent-child relationships and is a necessary skill for establishing cooperative conversation. In this conversation, the mother was able to, at several points, acknowledge the importance of the dress to her child. Second, metacognition can provide an opportunity to reflect on IWMs at moments when expectations are violated. As such, metacognition creates the possibility for accessing automatic appraisals of self and other and for subjecting those appraisals to evaluation. This reappraisal process creates the possibility of identifying misperceptions and apologizing, and the opportunity for the emergence of a new understanding of self and other. This mother was able at several points to reappraise her initial reaction to her daughter and to seek time out as a way of editing her reactions. Thus, in a secure relationship, reflective function makes it possible for both parent and child to accommodate the changes that accompany development in the parent-child relationship.

Open communication also creates new information with which IWMs can be updated and revised. When the child shares concerns and accomplishments with the parent, the parent's IWM of the child can be gradually altered to take into account the child's interests, concerns, sensitivities, and abilities. Furthermore, as parents communicate their own goals, children can revise their IWM of the parent to take into account the parent's concerns, rules, and habits. Updated IWMs of self and other in turn lead to communications in which both parent and child needs are anticipated and taken into account. IWMs of self and other that are tolerably accurate promote both the parent's and the child's confidence in the relationship, which, in turn, supports more direct and congruent signaling of the child's and parent's goals and a greater capacity to empathize with the other person. Updated IWMs that foster realistic confidence in self and other lead to the positive emotions associated with a secure relationship. At times of low stress, such models enhance enjoyment of the relationship. At times of high stress, favorable IWMs of self and other allow the child to view the parent as a potential coping resource and source of support. In short, the parent is viewed as a solution and not a problem.

Even the most secure parent-child relationships are challenged by mis-cued communication. The metacognitive level of processing can serve an important role in repairing such communications. Metacognitive process-ing can be triggered when the child's behavior violates the normal expec-tations derived from the IWM. In a secure relationship, the child's noncooperative behavior is likely to be seen as an exception to the rule and draw the parent's closer attention. Similarly, if a child's IWM biases appraisals of parent's behavior toward availability and responsiveness, a parental behavior that is seemingly inconsistent with the IWM will be ei-ther selectively ignored or reinterpreted. In both situations, behaviors on the part of the child or parent that are inconsistent with secure expecta-tions become opportunities for updating IWMs in ways that reduce the likelihood of similar misunderstandings in future interactions. In this re-spect, miscues and misunderstandings play the important function in se-cure relationships of triggering reappraisals of IWMs that support their revision.

Although the three levels of processing in our model represent concep-tually distinct aspects of parent-child relationships, in actual interactions between parents and children information is processed simultaneously at all three levels. Furthermore, how information is processed at one level in-fluences its processing at another level. The diagram in Fig. 6.1 illustrates how the different levels of processing interact in a secure parent-child relationship. Generally, in secure relationships the different levels of processing operate in ways that support each other. For example, at the in-dividual level represented by parent and child IWMs, confident expecta-tions support more direct signaling of needs by the child and a greater ca-pacity for perspective taking and empathy by the parent. As the child gets older and becomes more of a partner in the relationship, a secure IWM al-lows parents to more directly communicate their goals and allows the child to understand and empathize with the parent's perspective. At the metacognitive level, secure IWMs increase reflective function and empa-thy and facilitate reappraisal processes. These metacognitive abilities in turn can foster more open communication, which provides new informa-tion with which IWMs can be updated. Thus, secure IWMs at the individ-ual level, cooperative conversation at the interpersonal level, and reflec-tive function at the metacognitive level interact to create a virtuous cycle that allows IWMs to be updated and revised. More accurate IWMs, in turn, foster more open communication and better perspective taking. The relatively smooth interplay of the individual, interpersonal, and meta-cognitive levels provides both parents and children with a sense of confi-dence and allows them to approach developmental changes or stresses in the relationship with a sense of optimism.

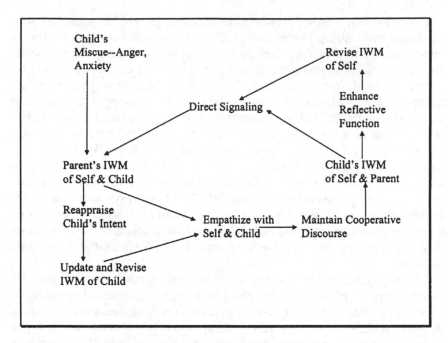

FIG. 6.1. The secure cycle.

The secure cycle facilitates an overall positive emotional climate in the parent-child relationship. When a relationship is secure, conflicts or disagreements are relatively short-lived and often produce opportunities for learning and accommodation within the relationship. Furthermore, disagreements are resolved through a process of negotiation providing both parent and child with an overall sense of a cooperative partnership. In these relationships, both parent and child derive a sense of mutual enjoyment and satisfaction from the relationship. As a result, the relationship is marked by exchanges of positive emotion and by containment of negative feelings.

LEVELS OF PROCESSING IN ANXIOUS PARENT-CHILD RELATIONSHIPS

In some parent-child relationships the kind of exchange that characterizes a secure cycle is notably absent. Whereas secure relationships are marked by negotiation at times of conflict and by warmth and positive affect at moments of low stress, insecure relationships are marked by a lack of cooperation and often by a lack of warmth or positive engagement. When children perceive their parents as unavailable or unresponsive, the way in which information is processed and exchanged between parent and child is fundamentally altered: Instead of approaching interactions with a feeling of security that is derived from confidence in the parent's availability, the insecure child approaches the relationship with feelings of anxiety and anger (Bowlby, 1973). Similarly, parents in insecure relationships may come to perceive their child's behavior as potentially threatening to their sense of competence and to their sense of efficacy in the caregiver role (Bugental, 1992).

Another example from Ginott illustrates the type of exchange that characterizes an anxious parent-child relationship. Floyd, age 13, enters the living room with a bouncing basketball:

Mother: "Get out of here with that. You'll break something!"

Floyd: "No, I won't!" (Ball hits lamp and sends it crashing)

Mother: "For crying out loud, you never listen to anything I say. You had to break something, didn't you? You are so stupid sometimes."

Floyd: "You broke the washing machine, what does that make you?"

Mother: "Floyd, you know better than to be rude."

Floyd: "You were rude first. You called me stupid."

Mother: "I don't want to hear another word from you. Go to your room this instant!"

Floyd: "Quit trying to boss me around. I'm not a kid anymore."

Mother: "To your room this instant!"

Floyd: "Go ahead, make me."

(Ginott, 1971, pp. 86–87)

This conversation is marked by a lack of cooperation between parent and child. The mother's reaction to Floyd's rule violation of bouncing a basketball in the living room is angry and accusatory. This type of response is more likely when the parent has developed negative expectations for the child and a corresponding sense of failure as a parent. These IWMs bias the parent toward perceiving the child's rule violation as threatening and increase the likelihood of more controlling or coercive types of response to the child. The mother's negative affect sets the tone for an exchange that is likely to elicit defensive responses from the child. As a result, the mother will have relatively little opportunity to state the rule that has been violated or initiate repair processes. Floyd will be given no opportunity to restore a cooperative relationship with his mother.

The child in this insecure relationship faces a dilemma: His IWMs create biases toward perceiving his mother as unavailable and, as a result, his appraisals and interpretations of her behavior are likely to create a sense of uncertainty or fear of rejection. Such appraisals are usually accompanied by a great deal of anxiety and anger (Bowlby, 1973). In Floyd's case, his immediate concern was to defend himself against his mother's accusations. His anger found expression in his retort, though his anxiety about his mother's availability remained hidden. This confrontation would ultimately have ended with either physical conflict or disengagement.

Although the immediate source of distress in the relationship could be terminated through disengagement, the child in this situation is likely to interpret this exchange as further evidence for an IWM that forecasts an unavailable and rejecting mother. These appraisals produce more permanent anxiety about the relationship. These negative feelings create a conflict for the child insofar as directly communicating these feelings may threaten the parent and further escalate conflict and the child's anxiety about the parent's availability (Main & Weston, 1982). To cope with this dilemma, Main (1990) suggested that children strategically alter their thoughts and feelings in order to maintain the attachment relationship. Floyd could dismiss his mother and focus his attention elsewhere or he could precipitate further conflict in order to maintain his involvement with his mother.

The notion of insecure or secondary strategies for regulating the attachment system is illustrated by Ainsworth's (1978) descriptions of insecure infant attachment patterns in the Strange Situation procedure. Infants classified as avoidant can be understood as having IWMs that forecast rejection from the parent. As a result, these infants strategically deactivate the attachment system and disengage from the parent at times of stress. In contrast, infants classified as ambivalent have IWMs that forecast inconsistent responding from the caregiver and, as a result, they strategically hyperactivate the attachment system in ways that serve to increase involvement with the parent (Kobak, Cole, Ferenze-Gillies, Fleming, & Gamble, 1993). These infant patterns of disengagement or pursuit at times of stress have also been identified in distressed marital relationships (Johnson, 1996) and may also characterize anxious parent-teen relationships.

Parents may develop complementary strategies for deactivating or hyperactivating the child's attachment system. These caregiving strategies may be most apparent when parents view the child's behavior as potentially threatening to their sense of competence or security. For instance, parents may shift their attention from or attempt to reduce their contact with the child or they may focus on achievement in ways that complement the child's deactivating strategy. Parents of children with hyperactivating strategies may adopt intrusive efforts to control the child's behavior or they may appear helpless and attempt to elicit increased involvement from the child. The goal of both types of parent and child strategies is to reduce the immediate perceived threat to the relationship and most insecure strategies will be maintained if they are effective in stabilizing the relationship.

Although insecure strategies serve to temporarily alleviate parent and child anxiety, they create a number of vulnerabilities for the parent-child relationship at all three levels of information processing. Figure 6.2 indicates how insecure IWMs create vulnerabilities at all three levels of processing. At the individual level, the child's insecure IWMs forecast lack of availability from the parent. At the interpersonal level, the child's insecure strategies distort and restrict communication. Children with deactivating strategies are likely to minimize or downplay feelings of distress, actively divert attention away from their difficulties, and disengage from interaction. Children with hyperactivating strategies may show distress in ways that make effective parental response more difficult and less effective. They may be prone to overinvolvement with parents in ways that ultimately prove ineffective and reduce overall exploration. As a result, parents are likely to have difficulty reading these children's signals and empathizing with their goals and needs.

Distorted communication may also foster parents' feelings of ineffectiveness and frustration and confirm negative expectancies derived from IWMs of self and child. As a result, child behaviors may be perceived as threatening to parents' sense of competence and parents' anxieties and worries about the child may be strategically altered. Without opportunity for sharing their concerns with other adults, parents may adopt strategies

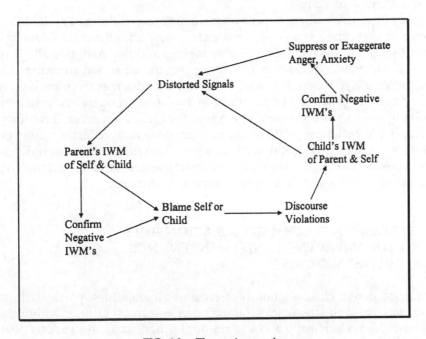

FIG. 6.2. The anxious cycle.

such as disengagement or overinvolvement to reduce their anxiety (Minuchin, 1974). Patterns of parental disengagement are likely to reinforce the child's IWM of an unavailable parent, whereas a pattern of overinvolvement may reinforce an IWM of an intrusive and inconsistently available parent.

As Fig. 6.2 illustrates, insecure strategies may also reduce parents' abilities to reflect upon and reappraise IWMs at the metacognitive level. Restrictions in parents' ability to think about IWMs of self and other are likely to interfere with their ability to take the child's perspective and to mentalize the child's behavior. This lack of awareness of the child's goals and intentions may make it more difficult for the child to use reflective function and to articulate his or her thoughts and feelings. Parents who lack support from other adults or who harbor doubts about their caregiving competence are more likely to perceive a child's anger or anxiety as threatening. As parents' anxiety increases, their ability to step back and monitor their own feelings or to consider alternative ways of interpreting the child's behavior decreases. As a result, they are more likely to respond to perceived threats in an automatic and defensive manner (Bugental, 1992) involving some form of flight or fight. These disengaged or coercive responses are likely to reinforce the child's appraisal of lack of parental availability and lead to further distorted expressions of attachment-related anxiety and anger.

Finally, as the child moves beyond infancy into childhood and adolescence, an insecure parent-child relationship may limit the child's development of communication, perspective-taking, and negotiation skills (Kobak & Duemmler, 1994). By restricting the parent's own capacities for empathy and reflective function, insecure strategies may limit the degree to which the parent-child relationship facilitates cooperative problem-solving and repair processes. As a result, the child's opportunities for developing emotion regulation, communication, and reflective function skills are reduced. The child's lack of experience with conflict resolution in the parent-child relationship may also limit the development of reflective function and the understanding of others' intentions.

DISTRESSED ATTACHMENT RELATIONSHIPS AND THE EMERGENCE AND MAINTENANCE OF CHILD SYMPTOMS

Insecure parent-child relationships create vulnerabilities, particularly at moments of high stress. Stressful experiences can occur both within the parent-child relationship and as a result of other situations, such as peer, school, or developmental difficulties. At times of stress, insecure attachments may increase the risk of psychopathology by limiting the support for the child and by reducing the parent's ability to understand and respond to the child's difficulties. If insecure strategies are successful in reducing anxiety about the parent's availability, stress can be managed without producing symptoms in the child. This explains why the majority of children in anxious attachment relationships do not develop psychopathology (Greenberg, 1999; Sroufe, 1988). Both parents and children in these relationships can manage school, peer, and emotional difficulties without the emergence of symptoms. Children with deactivating strategies may systematically shift their attention from difficulties to areas of competence and parents are likely to support these strategies. Children with hyperactivating strategies may excessively rely on their parents and these parents may become excessively involved. Both types of anxious strategies allow the child to cope with difficulties and to maintain a sense that the parent is available and, as a result, they allow the child to maintain some confidence in his or her ability to manage stress.

Risk of child psychopathology is substantially increased when the child's strategies for maintaining the relationship break down. Strategies for maintaining the attachment relationship are most likely to break down when stress reaches unusually high levels. Main and Hesse (1990) called attention to lapses in attachment strategies in the strange situation and linked these momentary lapses to infants' experiences with the parent as either frightened or frightening. In older children, breakdown in attachment strategies could result from severe difficulties in a parent's ability to serve as a caregiver, which may include depression, psychiatric difficulties, marital conflict, and threats to abandon the child. If the parent is having such severe trouble, the child's normal anxious strategies for ensuring parental availability may fail, creating increased anxiety in the child. Sources of extreme stress, trauma, or loss for the child may also overwhelm the child's coping strategies, exacerbating the child's already heightened anxiety.

When attachment strategies break down, the child is in a situation where distress is compounded first by the perceived threat to the parent's availability and then by the lack of coping strategies for managing this threat. This compounded fear situation is often accompanied by feelings of anxiety, anger, and sadness (Bowlby, 1973). Due to both the high level of negative affect and the lack of open communication with the parent, the child's attachment-related feelings are typically expressed in a distorted and problematic way that makes it difficult for the parent to understand or address the child's concerns. For instance, a child may express attachment-related anger through disruptive behavior in the home and in school settings. Alternatively, the child may show extreme withdrawal or disengagement from the parent and become noncommunicative.

The child's symptoms are often identified as problem behaviors. These may range from poor academic performance, disruptive behavior in school, and trouble with legal authorities to obsessive concern with appearance. These problem behaviors usually draw a parent's attention, and the parent then attempts to reduce the problematic behavior. Parents and children who have a secure relationship have an advantage in addressing these kinds of difficulties and often the child's problems prove to be an opportunity for increased understanding. Parents and children in distressed relationships, however, find managing problem behaviors more challenging. In distressed relationships, the child's disruptive or problematic behavior is more likely to threaten the parent's sense of competence and control (Bugental, 1992). Parents may respond to this sense of threat by increased efforts to control the child's behavior in coercive forms or by disengaging from caregiving responsibilities. Parental responses, in turn, serve to further confirm the child's fears that the parent is unavailable. This "symptomatic cycle" characterizes many families seeking treatment for child difficulties (Micucci, 1998).

In distressed relationships, the different levels of processing serve to perpetuate distress and symptomatic behavior in the child. At the individual level, the perceived threat to the parent's availability on the part of the child fuels negative feelings and may increase problematic behavior. For the parent, the child's behavior becomes a focus and efforts to control the problem result in an increased sense of failure. At the interpersonal level, communication is narrowly focused on the child's problematic behavior and more positive aspects of the relationship are diminished. The child's communications are often mistrustful and noninformative. At the metacognitive level, empathy and perspective-taking are reduced and the ability to repair noncooperative exchanges is lost. Thus, at a time when the parent would normally serve as a resource for the child in managing stress, the parent-child relationship may actually become a source of stress that further exacerbates the child's symptoms.

IMPLICATIONS FOR ASSESSMENT

By understanding the nature of secure, anxious, and distressed parent-child relationships, the clinician can be guided in both assessment and treatment of child psychopathology. From the standpoint of assessment, the clinician can determine a family's functioning along a continuum of risk; from the standpoint of treatment, attainable goals can be established that move the family toward more secure relationships and adaptive functioning. These goals can be shared with the family in order to define a treatment contract that builds on competence within the family and provides increased understanding of the child's symptoms. Furthermore, by considering multiple levels at which information is processed in the parent-child relationship, the therapist gains increased flexibility in identifying hidden strengths in the family and in choosing points at which to intervene.

Attachment-based assessment of child psychopathology begins with considering the possible connection between the child's symptoms and the perceived threats to parental availability. The goal of assessment is to locate the parent-child relationship on the continuum of risk, identify competent aspects of the relationship, and determine the association between the child's symptoms and the parent-child relationship. Not all child problems will necessarily be linked to anxious or distressed relationships. In more secure relationships, child difficulties may cause strain on the relationship, but parents find ways to support the child and repair ruptures in the relationship. In such relationships, the child's difficulties are likely to be contained and not contribute to the child's fears about parental availability. Despite difficulties, the parents in a secure relationship are likely to update and revise their IWM of the child while continuing to provide the child with a source of security and support. In these types of situations, parents or children may occasionally seek professional help, but these families can often benefit from advice and perspective on the child's difficulties and treatment is likely to be relatively brief.

In cases where the relationship between parent and child is more anxious or distressed, our LOP model provides a map for assessing the degree of distress. For instance, in observing parent-child communication, the therapist can assess the interpersonal markers of relationship distress such as lack of cooperation, negative exchanges, and lack of mutual understanding. Similarly, the therapist needs to assess the degree of reflective function shown by both the parent and the child. Here, parents' and children's abilities to acknowledge their assumptions, access the appraisals, and submit them to reevaluation and reappraisal provide areas of competence on which the partners can build. The capacity for reflective function can be gauged by observing communication. In more distressed relationships, empathy and accommodation are notably absent and are often replaced by accusatory communications or disengagement. The challenge of assessment is in accessing the IWMs that guide interpretation of behavior in the interaction.

Children's strategies for managing attachment anxiety often make it difficult for them to report on the painful feelings of hurt and rejection that fuel their anger and disengagement. Parents may also have difficulty acknowledging their sense of failure and lack of control with their child. It is often useful, therefore, to meet with parents and children separately. Individual assessments offer the therapist the opportunity to assess the parent's and the child's capacity for reflective function in the context of the safer and more controlled environment created by the therapist. Parents and children differ enormously in their capacities to monitor appraisals and reevaluate situations. Some parents may welcome the opportunity to discuss their thoughts and feelings about their child and about themselves in a caregiving role, but others may find such discussion threatening. Similarly, empathy and fondness for the child may vary and may indicate the level of distress in the relationship. Often, through the empathy provided by the therapist, both the parent and the child are capable of acknowledging some of the vulnerability and threat that motivates distorted and accusatory communications in the relationship. These sessions may also provide therapists with information that allows them to better determine the role that attachment and caregiving anxieties are playing in the child's symptomatic behavior.

Initial assessment of the family should take into account current stresses in the life of the child and in the family as a whole, as well as how these stresses are managed in the parent-child relationship. Family stresses ranging from economic hardship and marital conflict to deaths of grandparents and relatives may make demands on parents' and children's coping resources. In addition, it is important to assess the sources of support for the parent. A supportive adult attachment relationship can provide parents with an invaluable companion for managing their life stress and parenting difficulties. Alternatively, distress in adult relationships can be an additional source of distress for parents and can undermine their capacity for coping with children. After assessment of the family's sources of stress and support, the therapist and parent can set priorities for treatment and can determine whether parent-child treatment, marital therapy, or individual treatment for the parent is warranted.

In many cases in which parent-child treatment is chosen, our LOP model provides the basis for a treatment contract. A therapeutic contract should provide the parent and child with a rationale for treating the child's symptoms by reducing the level of distress in the relationship. The contract should begin by pointing out areas of strength in the relationship that may include positive examples of communication, empathy, or reflective function. It should then provide a link between anxious features of the relationship and the child's symptomatic behavior, in a way that emphasizes the significance of the parent to the child's emotional security and well-being. Finally, the contract should establish the number of sessions and emphasize that, as communication and understanding in the relationship improve, there should be a reduction in the severity of the child's symptoms.

IMPLICATIONS FOR TREATMENT

Attachment-based treatment has the general goals of interrupting the symptomatic cycle in family relationships and of increasing the parent's acceptance of the child and the child's confidence in the parent's availability. These general goals allow for a wide range of intervention techniques that increase the therapist's flexibility in promoting a more secure relationship. Our LOP model provides a way of organizing intervention techniques and specifying the curative mechanisms available to therapists. In addition, although the child's difficulties provide the central motivation for families seeking treatment, our attachment model suggests that changes in the relationship are likely to be the most effective and long-lasting result of treatment to the extent that they restore the parent's sense of efficacy as a caregiver. This sense of efficacy derives from changing the parent's IWM, or understanding, of the child, improving communication, and providing the parent with increased empathy and a greater capacity for reflective function that will, in turn, improve repair processes in the relationship.

The initial challenge facing therapists working with distressed parent-child relationships is to reduce the negative feelings and interpretations and increase the positive sentiment in the family. The therapist's relationships with the child and parent are essential for moving the family toward more positive feelings. The relationship that the therapist develops with the family needs to serve as a model of a secure relationship in a situation where such security is lacking. Thus, in initial interactions with the family, the therapist needs to model empathy and open communication so that the child and parent develop confidence in the therapist's availability and responsiveness. When a secure relationship develops, it is accompanied by feelings of safety, which make it possible for the parent and child to explore and examine their negative appraisals of each other and consider alternative points of view. The idea that security is a precondition for exploration and experimentation has been a central insight derived from the notion of the secure base function of the attachment relationship (Bowlby, 1988).

Once the therapist has established a secure base, most therapeutic techniques can be understood as guided by the therapist's effort to alter the child's and the parent's IWMs of each other from negative appraisals to more positive expectancies that facilitate engagement, communication, and increased understanding. The therapeutic technique of "reframing" (Minuchin & Fishman, 1981) involves having the therapist provide an alternative interpretation of the child's or the parent's behavior. In an attachment-guided approach, such reframing would emphasize the need for support or safety from the parent and the parent's desire to protect and nurture the child. These interpretations are guided by an understanding of parents' and children's motivations in secure relationships. The success of such interventions is dependent on the extent to which the therapist can help the parent understand negative child behaviors as distorted expressions of more positive attachment needs or, alternatively, on the extent to which the therapist can help the child understand controlling or angry parenting behavior as a distorted expression of legitimate caregiving concerns.

The success of reframing interventions is dependent on the extent to which the therapist has accessed attachment and caregiving needs with the child and parent. Thus, the therapist's ability to establish empathetic and reflective dialogue between the child and parent provides a rich source of new information that can be used in reframing the parent's and child's behavior and in opening communication. For instance, children's acknowledgment of their fears that their parent does not really care about them or parents' acknowledgment of frustration and despair over their inability to help their child can provide the foundation on which therapists can rest their argument for how important the parent is to the child and how important the child is to the parent. These alternative interpretations call attention to the significance of the attachment bond and may create the basis for a new understanding, on the part of the parent, of the child's symptomatic behavior. In addition, the therapist's empathy with both the child and the parent also provides a valuable model of the importance of empathy in maintaining open communication.

The ultimate goal of attachment-based therapy is to develop the parent's capacities for empathy and reflective function with the child, capacities that have been modeled by the therapist. Parents' ability to incorporate these capacities into their relationship with the child can be monitored in therapy with parent-child exchanges. The therapist can facilitate reflective function in the parent by intervening in exchanges that are miscued or lead to increased defensiveness and by asking the parent to stop and reflect on the thoughts and feelings that accompanied the negative interaction. Through repeated use of this stop-the-action technique, the therapist can increase the parent's ability to use reflective function to monitor, reappraise, and repair problematic communications with the child.

Videotaped replay of parent-child interactions offer another useful technique for developing parents' capacities for empathy and reflective function. Replay procedures offer some advantages for increasing parents' capacity for self-observation and reappraisal. By not having the child present, parents are given more opportunity for extended reflection on their thoughts and feelings during particular exchanges. This procedure also offers the opportunity for problem solving with the therapist and for discussion of alternative ways that the parent could manage the interaction. Videotaping also offers the therapist the opportunity to select for discussion interactions that are particularly promising and emphasize moments of positive change as well as more problematic interactions (Marvin, Cooper, Hoffman, & Powell, 2002).

Attachment-based treatment can work at all three levels of the parent-child relationship in order to find ways to disrupt the symptomatic cycle. By increasing the parent's ability to monitor communication with the child, to consider alternative perspectives, and to focus on the positive aspects of the relationship, the therapist gradually restores a sense of caregiving efficacy and competence to the parent. As parents feel more competent, they gain the ability to empathize, to repair interactions with the child, and to revise their IWM of the child. The parent's increased accessibility should gradually restore the child's confidence in the parent and should lead to more direct communication. Thus, when successful, therapy initiates confidence in the parent-child relationship that can be self-sustaining.

In this chapter, we sought to bridge the gap between attachment research and clinical treatment of child psychopathology. Much work remains to be done to test the relevance of our LOP model. On the research side, the different levels of processing need to be systematically assessed and markers of secure, anxious, and distressed relationships need to be identified. The LOP model highlights critical gaps in researchers' understanding of parent-child relationships and points toward understanding attachment and caregiving in the context of the parent-child relationship. To the extent that research methods assessing the quality of parent-child relationships are developed, these methods will be very useful to clinicians in assessing families seeking treatment and in understanding the link between attachment and child psychopathology.

For clinicians, our model provides a general map for assessing and treating distressed parent-child relationships. We view our LOP model as useful insofar as it can specify general principles that should guide assessment and treatment of child and adolescent psychopathology; it is not a standardized treatment for working with a specific age or diagnostic group. Thus, an important test of our model will be the extent to which it can formalize the assumptions that guide current standardized treatments. Hopefully the model will not only account for current techniques and intervention strategies, but it will also allow researchers and clinicians to explicate central curative processes and account for impasses in treatment. Moreover, an attachment-based framework should guide therapists in their work with populations and age groups for which there are currently no standardized treatment approaches.

REFERENCES

Ainsworth, M. D. S., Blehar, M. C., Waters, E., & Wall, S. (1978). *Patterns of attachment: A psychological study of the strange situation.* Hillsdale, NJ: Lawrence Erlbaum Associates.

Allen, J. P., Hauser, S. T., Bell, K. L., & O'Connor, T. G. (1994). Longitudinal assessment of autonomy and relatedness in adolescent-family interactions as predictors of adolescent ego development and self-esteem. *Child Development, 65,* 179–194.

Baumrind, D. (1967). Child care practices anteceding three patterns of preschool behavior. *Genetic Psychology Monographs, 75,* 43–88.

Bowlby, J. (1973). *Attachment and loss: Vol. 2. Separation.* New York: Basic Books.

Bowlby, J. (1980). *Attachment and loss: Vol. 3. Loss.* New York: Basic Books.

Bowlby, J. (1982). *Attachment and loss: Vol. 1. Attachment.* New York: Basic Books. (Original work published 1969)

Bowlby, J. (1988). *A secure base: Parent-child attachment and healthy human development.* New York: Basic Books.

Bretherton, I. (1985). Attachment theory: Retrospect and prospect. In I. Bretherton & E. Waters (Eds.), *Growing points in attachment theory and research* (Society for Research on Child Development Monograph No. 209, pp. 3–38). Waltham, MA: Blackwell.

Bretherton, I. (1990). Open communication and internal working models: Their role ion the development of attachment relationships. In R. A. Thompson (Ed.), *Nebraska Symposium on Motivation: Socioemotional development* (pp. 57–113). Lincoln, NE: University of Nebraska Press.

Bretherton, I. (1999). Updating the internal working model construct: Some reflections. *Attachment and Human Development, 1,* 343–357.

Bugental, D. (1992). Affective and cognitive processes within threat-oriented family systems. In I. E. Sigel, A. V. McGillicuddy-DeLisi, & J. J. Goodnow (Eds.), *Parental belief systems: Psychological consequences for children* (2nd ed., pp. 219–248). Hillsdale, NJ: Lawrence Erlbaum Associates.

Crowell, J. A., Fraley, R. C., & Shaver, P. (1999). Measurement of individual differences in adolescent and adult attachment. In J. Cassidy & P. Shaver (Eds.), *The handbook of attachment: theory, research, and clinical implications* (pp. 434–468). New York: Guilford Press.

Dozier, M., Stovall, K., & Albus, K. (1999). Attachment and psychopathology in adulthood. In J. Cassidy & P. Shaver (Eds.), *The handbook of attachment: Theory, research, and clinical implications* (pp. 497–519). New York: Guilford Press.

Fonagy, P. (1999). Psychoanalytic theory from the viewpoint of attachment theory and research. In J. Cassidy & P. Shaver (Eds.), *The handbook of attachment: Theory, research, and clinical implications* (pp. 595–624). New York: Guilford Press.

Fonagy, P., & Target, M. (1997). Attachment and reflective function: Their role in self-organization. *Development and Psychopathology, 9,* 679–700.

George, C., & Solomon, J. (1999). Attachment and caregiving: The caregiving behavioral system. In J. Cassidy & P. Shaver (Eds.), *The handbook of attachment: Theory, research, and clinical implications* (pp. 649–670). New York: Guilford Press.

Ginott, H. (1971). *Between parent and teenager.* New York: Avon Books.

Greenberg, M. (1999). Attachment and psychopathology in childhood. In J. Cassidy & P. Shaver (Eds.), *The handbook of attachment: Theory, research, and clinical implications* (pp. 469–496). New York: Guilford Press.

Hazan, C., & Shaver, P. (1987). Romantic love conceptualized as an attachment process. *Journal of Personality and Social Psychology, 52,* 511–524.

Hesse, E. (1999). The adult attachment interview: Historical and current perspectives. In J. Cassidy & P. Shaver (Eds.), *The handbook of attachment: Theory, research, and clinical implications* (pp. 395–433). New York: Guilford Press.

Johnson, S. (1996). *Creating connection: The practice of emotionally focused marital therapy.* New York: Brunner/Mazel.

Kobak, R. (1999). The emotional dynamics of disruptions in attachment relationships: Implications for theory, research, and clinical intervention. In J. Cassidy & P. Shaver (Eds.), *The handbook of attachment: Theory, research, and clinical Implications* (pp. 21–43). New York: Guilford Press.

Kobak, R., & Cole, H. (1994). Attachment and meta-monitoring: Implications for adolescent autonomy and psychopathology. In D. Cicchetti (Ed.), *Rochester Symposium on Development and Psychopathology: Vol. 5. Disorders of the self* (pp. 267–297). Rochester, NY: University of Rochester Press.

Kobak, R., Cole, H., Ferenz-Gillies, R., Fleming W., & Gamble, W. (1993). Attachment and emotion regulation during mother-teen problem-solving: A control theory analysis. *Child Development, 64,* 231–245.

Kobak, R., & Duemmler, S. (1994) Attachment and conversation: Toward a discourse analysis of adolescent and adult security. In D. Perlman & K. Bartholemew (Eds.), *Advances in personal relationships: Vol. 5. Attachment processes in adulthood* (pp. 121–149). London: Kingsley.

Kobak, R., Sudler, N., & Gamble, W. (1991). Attachment and depressive symptoms during adolescence: A developmental pathway analysis. *Development and Psychopathology, 3,* 461–474.

Kochansa, G., Aksan, N., & Koenig, A. L. (1995). Mother-child mutually positive affect, the quality of child compliance to requests and prohibitions, and maternal control as correlates of early internalization. *Child Development, 66,* 236–254.

Main, M. (1990). Cross-cultural studies of attachment organization: Recent studies, changing methodologies, and the concept of conditional strategies. *Human Development, 33,* 48–61.

Main, M., & Hesse, E. (1990). Parents' unresolved traumatic experiences are related to infant disorganized attachment status: Is frightening and/or frightened parental behavior the linking mechanism? In M. T. Greenberg, D. Cicchetti, & E. M. Cummings (Eds.), *Attachment in the preschool years* (pp. 121–160). Chicago: University of Chicago Press.

Main, M., Kaplan, N., & Cassidy, J. (1985). Security in infancy, childhood, and adulthood: A move to the level of representation. In I. Bretherton & E. Waters (Eds.), *Growing points in attachment theory and research* (Society for Research on Child Development Monograph No. 209, pp. 66–104). Waltham, MA: Blackwell.

Main, M., & Weston, D. R. (1982). Avoidance of the attachment figure in infancy: Descriptions and interpretations. In C. Parkes & J. Stevenson-Hinde (Eds.), *The place of attachment in human behavior* (pp. 31–59). New York: Basic Books.

Marvin, R. S. (1999). Normative development: The ontogeny of attachment. In J. Cassidy & P. Shaver (Eds.), *The handbook of attachment: Theory, research, and clinical implications* (pp. 44–67). New York: Guilford Press.

Marvin, R. S., Cooper, G., Hoffman, K., & Powell, B. (2002). The circle of security project: Attachment-based intervention with caregiver preschool child dyads. *Attachment and Human Development, 4,* 107–124.

Meins, E. (1999). Sensitivity, security and internal working models: Bridging the transmission gap. *Attachment and Human Development, 1,* 325–342.

Meins, E., Fernyhough, C., Russell, J., & Clark-Carter, D. (1998). Security of attachment as a predictor of symbolic and mentalizing abilities: A longitudinal study. *Social Development, 7,* 1–24.

Micucci, J. A. (1998). *The adolescent in family therapy*. New York: Guilford Press.

Minuchin, S. (1974). *Families and family therapy*. Cambridge, MA: Harvard University Press.

Minuchin, S., & Fishman, H. C. (1981). *Family therapy techniques*. Cambridge, MA: Harvard University Press.

Safran, J., & Segal, Z. (1990). *Interpersonal process in cognitive therapy*. New York: Basic Books.

Selman, R. (1980). *The growth of interpersonal understanding: Developmental and clinical analysis*. New York: Academic Press.

Sroufe, L. A. (1988). The role of infant-caregiver attachment in development. In J. Belsky & T. Nezworski (Eds.), *Clinical implications of attachment* (pp. 18–38). Hillsdale, NJ: Lawrence Erlbaum Associates.

Thompson, R. (2000). The legacy of early attachments. *Child Development, 71*, 145–152.

Attachment State of Mind and the Treatment Relationship

Mary Dozier
University of Delaware

Brady C. Bates
University of Delaware

Attachment state of mind refers to the way adults process attachment-related thoughts, memories, and feelings (Main & Goldwyn, in press). We argue in this chapter that the states of mind of clients as well as clinicians are central to the work of psychotherapy and other forms of mental health services for several reasons. First, the treatment relationship is often an attachment relationship: The client finds in the therapist someone who seems stronger and wiser than him- or herself. Thus, the client may interact with the clinician in ways that reflect expectations from other relationships. In clinical parlance, this is referred to as "transference." Second, although therapy does not ordinarily represent an attachment relationship for the clinician, the relationship is inherently interpersonal and involves caregiving. Therefore, the clinician's own state of mind affects his or her interactions with the client. Third, treatment is often directed at modifying the client's processing of attachment-related information as well as the client's expectations of, and interactions with, others. Thus, an objective of treatment is often modifying the client's state of mind, either directly or indirectly.

The way an individual thinks about attachment relationships and the processing of information related to these relationships constitute the individual's state of mind with regard to attachment. Although state of mind refers primarily to the processing of information from earlier attachment relationships, it is also associated with how current relationships are approached. The connection between state of mind and concurrent relationships has been looked at primarily in terms of parenting (van IJzen-doorn, 1995), but includes some study of peer, sibling, parent, and thera-pist relationships as well (Dozier, Cue, & Barnett, 1994; Dozier, Lomax, & Tyrrell, in press; Kobak, Cole, Ferenz-Gillies, Fleming, & Gamble, 1993; Kobak & Sceery, 1988; Tyrrell, Dozier, Teague, & Fallot, 1999).

MATERNAL STATE OF MIND AND INFANT ATTACHMENT SECURITY

Assessment of state of mind actually emerged from Main's (Main, Kaplan, & Cassidy, 1985) examination of similarities among mothers who had ba-bies with a common attachment classification. Main theorized that the ways mothers thought about their own attachment relationships should affect the way they responded to their infants' bids for reassurance. In dis-course regarding attachment relationships, mothers of babies with secure attachments tended to be able to freely evaluate their attachment experi-ences and showed evidence that they valued attachment. They were said to have autonomous states of mind. Presumably, autonomous mothers' valuing of attachment and their ability to freely evaluate their own experi-ences lead to their valuing their infants' expression of needs and ability to respond effectively to those needs. Mothers of avoidant babies tended to dismiss or devalue the importance of attachment relationships. They showed a lack of coherence in their discourse regarding earlier relation-ships through an inability to recall attachment-related memories or ideal-ization of caregivers in which global glowing impressions were unsup-ported by specific memories. These mothers with dismissing states of mind were presumed to be rejecting of their children's bids for reassur-ance as the result of their own discomfort with attachment needs. Mothers of resistant babies tended to become caught up in attachment-related ex-periences. Their incoherence took the form of rambling discourse or angry preoccupied speech. Presumably, these mothers with preoccupied states of mind had their own needs, which interfered with the ability to respond consistently to their infants' needs. Finally, mothers of infants with disor-ganized attachments were likely to appear unresolved with regard to a loss or trauma. Presumably, these mothers with unresolved states of mind behaved in frightened or frightening ways with their infants (Main & Hesse, 1990) as the result of their own unresolved experiences.

Empirical links between maternal state of mind and infant attachment have been well established (van IJzendoorn, 1995). Even when state of mind is assessed prenatally, it is predictive of babies' attachment classifi-cation (Benoit & Parker, 1994; Fonagy, Steele, & Steele, 1991; Ward & Carlson, 1995). Furthermore, links have been found between foster parent state of mind and foster infant attachment (Dozier, Albus, Stovall, & Bates, 2000), suggesting that the correspondence is mediated by maternal behaviors rather than by genetic factors shared by the dyad.

STATE OF MIND IN OTHER-THAN-PARENTING RELATIONSHIPS

State of mind has been associated with systematic differences in other types of relationships as well. For example, Kobak and Sceery (1988) examined the importance of state of mind for freshmen adjusting to their first year at college, a period that many students experience as distressing. Autonomous students reported low levels of distress and perceived others as highly supportive, relative to other students. In contrast, dismissing students perceived others as less supportive than did autonomous or preoccupied students. Preoccupied students reported the highest level of psychiatric symptoms.

Peers' ratings of these freshmen were also related to state of mind in systematic ways. The peers of autonomous students rated them as high in ego resiliency, low in anxiety, and low in hostility. Dismissing students were rated as more hostile than other students and preoccupied students were rated as more anxious than others.

Talking About Problems

When conducting an Adult Attachment Interview (AAI) with someone with a dismissing state of mind, the interviewer may feel uncomfortable. Despite the individual's claims that the interview topic was not troubling, there may be cues that the interviewer should not intrude in this area of attachment relationships. At times these cues are unmistakable, for example, "I told you that my family life was just fine! Why do you have to keep asking questions?!" Attachment theorists have assumed that this unwillingness to examine relationships reflects defensiveness. To provide evidence that these responses do in fact reflect defensiveness, Dozier and Kobak (1992) monitored the skin conductance of college students while they were being administered the AAI. It was reasoned that, if students with dismissing states of mind were indeed not bothered by the questions asked on the AAI, they should not show greater rises in skin conductance than others. On the other hand, if, as was expected, the interview was perceived as noxious by dismissing interviewees, there should be a greater rise for dismissing students than for others. Indeed, it was found that dismissing students showed significantly greater rises in skin conductance when asked about childhood incidences of distress. Despite making statements such as "I was rarely hurt" or "I'm sure my mother must have been there," their physiology belied their self-presentation.

The discomfort experienced by people with dismissing states of mind is, of course, not limited to the AAI. Presumably, state of mind reflects an information-processing strategy that was developed because appealing for help directly was not considered safe or effective. For example, the child who scraped his knee may have tried to look tough rather than risk the parent's saying, "I told you not to climb there" or "Get up, don't be a baby." This strategy involved denying both the child's own neediness and the parent's failure to care for the child.

When dismissing individuals are then asked to discuss their feelings about a relationship—by a significant other wanting to talk through problems, by a therapist, or by an AAI interviewer—their strategy for handling distress is challenged. To examine how people manage interactions with significant others, Dozier et al. (2001) asked clients to discuss a relationship issue with their significant others for 10 min while being videotaped. As expected, dismissing clients stayed off task more than other clients. Rather than avoiding the topic by changing the subject, though, they tended to reject their partners when their partners attempted to engage them in the discussion. Similarly, Kobak et al. (1993) found that dismissing teens showed more dysfunctional anger than other teens in problem-solving tasks with their mothers. We expect that this strategy of rejecting one's partner proves very effective in managing interactions. A pattern may develop in which partners of a dismissing person anticipate encountering rejection or anger if they bring up relationship issues. Indeed, relationships in which one individual wants to discuss relationship issues and the other avoids them at all costs have received much attention in the couples therapy literature (e.g., Berns, Jacobson, & Gottman, 1999), although not explicitly linked to dismissing strategies.

In contrast to people with dismissing states of mind, individuals with preoccupied states of mind do not avoid discussing problems and indeed may discuss them at great length. We have had the experience of interviewing individuals with preoccupied states of mind who would have discussed past experiences and problems for hours on end had they been allowed to. These individuals became so caught up in their memories and thoughts that they seemed to forget that the interviewer was in the room, as they appeared to relive past conversations or emotional experiences with attachment figures. Despite the amount of time they spend talking about their problems, though, preoccupied individuals seem to gain little insight into their problems or themselves. Indeed, as mentioned earlier, individuals with preoccupied states of mind report higher levels of psychiatric symptoms, especially anxiety, and not surprisingly are viewed as vulnerable and needy by their friends (Kobak & Sceery, 1988).

Individuals with unresolved states of mind have experienced loss or trauma so overwhelming that they experience a lapse in reasoning (e.g., insisting a dead person is really alive), discourse (e.g., use of eulogistic speech), or behavior (e.g., trying to get in the dead person's coffin) when talking about the event (Main & Goldwyn, in press). Although relatively little research has focused on how individuals with unresolved states of mind function in relationships, it is known that these individuals are more likely than others to be seen in psychiatric populations (Dozier, Stovall, & Albus, 1999; Fonagy et al., 1996).

Interviewing individuals with autonomous states of mind is often a pleasure. These individuals tend to discuss their attachment issues in an interesting and engaging way and their speech is vivid, fresh, and often insightful. Such individuals often have the capacity to talk about other relationships openly and nondefensively. During problem-solving situations with their spouses, for example, autonomous individuals tend to be accepting of their spouse's input, and to have happier marriages than others (Kobak & Hazan, 1991). Similarly, autonomous teenagers tend to show lower levels of dysfunctional anger and higher levels of problem-solving communication when working on a difficult problem with their mothers (Kobak et al., 1993). Whether it is during an interview such as the AAI, discussing relationship issues within a marital relationship, or in the context of a mother-adolescent problem-solving situation, individuals with autonomous states of mind appear well equipped to communicate clearly and effectively with significant people in their lives.

CLIENT STATE OF MIND AND TREATMENT

Given interpersonal behaviors linked with state of mind, it makes sense that state of mind proves to be an important variable affecting the way different people approach and use treatment. Treatment often involves acknowledging difficulties and asking for help, as well as talking about relationship issues. Findings converge from different populations and with different methodologies to suggest that state of mind affects how people ask for help, how treatment is used, and the effectiveness of treatment.

Asking for Help

Not surprisingly, people with dismissing states of mind tend to have difficulty asking for help or acknowledging the need for help, whereas those with preoccupied states of mind present themselves very openly as being in need (Dozier, 1990; Pianta, Egeland, & Adam, 1996). These findings have emerged in several contexts. Pianta et al. found that at-risk pregnant women with preoccupied states of mind reported more symptoms on the Minnesota Multiphasic Personality Inventory-2 (MMPI-2; Butcher, Dahlstrom, Graham, Tellegen, & Kaemmer, 1989) than other women. These findings are consistent with Kobak and Sceery's (1988) finding that college students with preoccupied states of mind reported more psychological symptoms on the Hopkins Symptom Checklist-90 (Derogatis, 1977) than students with either autonomous or dismissing states of mind.

To assess whether the greater likelihood of those with preoccupied states of mind to report symptomatology results from a reporting bias or actual symptomatology, Dozier and Lee (1995) obtained independent ratings of pathology for a group of clients with serious psychiatric disorders. Clients' symptomatology was rated following the administration of the AAI and following a quality-of-life interview. Additionally, the clinician working most closely with each client rated his or her symptomatology. Despite reporting less symptomatology themselves, clients with dismissing states of mind were assessed by all three sets of raters as more symptomatic than those with preoccupied states of mind. These findings suggest that reports of greater and lesser symptomatology by preoccupied and dismissing clients actually represent over- and underreporting, respectively.

State of Mind and Use of Treatment

Despite studying very different populations and using different methodologies, converging findings have emerged from several studies that have related state of mind to treatment use. First, Korfmacher, Adam, Ogawa, and Egeland (1997) examined differences in treatment use among pregnant mothers receiving home visitation services. The weekly home visits began when the mothers were 6 months pregnant and continued until the babies were 1 year old. Mothers with autonomous states of mind were more proactive in the help that they received, engaging in problem solving and supportive therapy more than others, whereas mothers with dismissing states of mind were least likely to engage in supportive therapy. Mothers with unresolved states of mind were especially likely to receive crisis interventions. The sample did not include enough preoccupied mothers to allow separate subgroup analyses.

In the Dozier (1990) study, clinicians rated the extent to which clients with serious psychiatric disorders used treatment effectively. Similarly to Korfmacher et al.'s (1997) finding, clients who were more autonomous were rated as more collaborative in the treatment process than those who were less autonomous. Clients who were more dismissing were rated as rejecting of treatment, whereas clients who were more preoccupied were rated as reaching out for help.

Together, these findings suggest that clients with autonomous states of mind have internal resources that allow them to approach treatment nondefensively and collaboratively. Dismissing clients appear least likely to acknowledge difficulties in previous or current relationships or to work on interpersonal problems. People with preoccupied states of mind tend to openly acknowledge difficulties in previous relationships: Indeed, by definition, they are caught up in these earlier relationship problems. Consistent with this, they tend to acknowledge and perhaps to exaggerate their current difficulties. Unresolved clients appear likely to have chaotic lives that make it difficult to sustain attention to matters other than the crisis at hand.

CLINICIANS' STATE OF MIND AND TREATMENT

Therapist state of mind has only begun to receive attention. However, what the therapist, or treatment provider, brings to the treatment relationship appears to be equally important as what the client brings. Taking as a parallel the mother's caregiving relationship with her infant, it is the mother's state of mind that affects her child's expectations of availability. Likewise, it may be the clinician's state of mind that affects the client's expectation of availability. The treatment relationship diverges from the mother-child relationship in an important way, however. The mother is helping the child establish expectations based on her availability. There is little in the way of preconceived notions of availability; rather, the child's expectations may be seen to accurately reflect the caregiver's history of previous availability. On the other hand, the therapist is forming a relationship with a client who has established expectations for relationships. Expectations of the therapist may have little to do with the therapist's actual availability, thus, the therapist must be more than sensitive to the client's needs. Being sensitive could involve simply providing confirmatory evidence for the client's worldview. Therapists must resist the pull to respond in kind to the client if they are to help the client change expectations.

Those therapists who can resist this pull are able to provide experiences for clients that fail to confirm the client's worldviews. In the context of a trusting, safe relationship, the therapist's gentle challenge can help clients make fundamental changes. Which therapists can resist the interpersonal pull that appears so powerful? It is expected that clinicians who themselves had autonomous states of mind would be most capable of resisting this interpersonal pull from clients and best able to provide interventions that challenged clients' worldviews.

To address this question, Dozier et al. (1994) followed 18 case managers in their interactions with their clients who had serious psychiatric disorders over a 3-month period. Both clients and case managers completed the AAI, with continuous scores for autonomous versus nonautonomous and preoccupied versus dismissing states of mind provided by the rating system. Interventions were rated for the extent to which they were psychological (e.g., thinking through problems with a roommate) versus practical (e.g., getting help with a bus schedule). Given other findings, it was expected that dismissing clients would behave in ways that discouraged clinicians from providing interventions of a more psychological nature, whereas preoccupied clients would behave in ways that encouraged such interventions. Consistent with expectations, clinicians with higher autonomy scores provided more challenging interventions than clinicians who had lower autonomy scores. Specifically, high-autonomous clinicians intervened in more psychological ways with dismissing clients and in more practical ways with preoccupied clients. Low-autonomous clinicians did just the opposite: They intervened in more practical ways with dismissing clients and in more psychological ways with preoccupied clients. We suggest that these interventions of the low-autonomous case managers are in keeping with clients' expectations and serve to perpetuate expectations of others. On the other hand, the interventions of the high-autonomous case managers provide clients with experiences that are incongruent with expectations.

Dozier et al.'s (1994) work was extended with a study of a select group of well-trained and well-supervised case managers and their clients (Tyrrell et al. 1999). Interestingly, nearly all clinicians in this very selective site had autonomous states of mind. Clinicians nonetheless varied in the extent to which they put aside attachment issues or were somewhat preoccupied with those issues. Most clients had nonautonomous states of mind, but again varied in the secondary strategy they used (i.e., preoccupied vs. dismissing). It was expected that clinicians might be better able to challenge clients if they differed from these clients with respect to the extent to which they put aside or were caught up in attachment issues. Outcomes were assessed in terms of the clients' quality of life, level of depression, number of hospitalizations, and global functioning. As predicted, clinicians who set aside attachment issues worked more effectively with clients who were more caught up in attachment issues, whereas clinicians who were more caught up in issues worked more effectively with clients who set attachment aside. These findings are consistent with other results in suggesting that challenge is a necessary aspect of treatment. We expect that this challenge can only occur in the context of a trusting relationship. When there is challenge but inadequate trust, the client could well choose to discontinue treatment.

STATE OF MIND AND GENERAL TREATMENT ISSUES

Main (1990) suggested that an autonomous state of mind could be considered primary. When an autonomous state of mind proves ineffective in handling distress, a secondary preoccupied or dismissing strategy is adopted, although the autonomous strategy remains primary. The implications are that, even though an individual may appear extremely dismissing of attachment or caught up in attachment issues, there is an underlying autonomous state of mind that nonetheless continues to exert influence at some level. If so, treatment can capitalize on this underlying need for connectedness and coherence.

Treatment of People with Autonomous States of Mind

Empirical data and anecdotal evidence suggest that treatment of persons with autonomous states of mind is often a rewarding, collaborative endeavor. It is easy to see how individuals with autonomous states of mind would get into therapy: Such individuals would be more likely than others to acknowledge difficulties and to recognize the need for obtaining help. An objective other, the therapist, is likely to share the same goals for treatment as the client and the two may often work together very productively to achieve those goals. Autonomous clients value the role that attachments have played in their development and value current relationships, both inside and outside of therapy. Their valuing of close relationships, willingness to seek help, and ability to view their situation nondefensively make it more likely that autonomous clients will invest emotionally in therapy and collaborate actively with their therapist in solving problems, both of which are central to a productive working alliance.

Treatment of People with Dismissing States of Mind

On the other hand, treatment of people with dismissing states of mind can often feel like a struggle for the dyad. There are a variety of circumstances under which the dismissing individual might enter treatment. Some of these circumstances involve coercion, such as meeting a court order to maintain custody of children or as a component of drug treatment, or to satisfy the marital partner's demands. Other circumstances, though, involve individuals willingly seeking out treatment, despite the fact that they may appear unwilling to deal with important issues. Kobak and Sceery's (1988) findings that dismissing freshmen reported more loneliness than other students in their transition to college are relevant here. Dismissing people are at risk for feeling alienated because they turn away from, rather than toward, others when they go through difficult times. Their dismissing strategy may, however, fail to inoculate them against a sense of being alone at such times. Seeking out of treatment reflects a partial breakdown of the dismissing strategy.

Even when the individual has chosen to enter therapy, the treatment provider may feel that he or she is working at cross purposes with the dismissing client. The therapist's first task is to begin building a trusting relationship with the client. This, in and of itself, is a complicated task and one that challenges the client's worldview. Dismissing clients have developed expectations that others will not be emotionally available when they are in need. Such clients may actively avoid addressing issues regarding their relationship with the therapist. We suggest that gentle challenge in the context of a trusting relationship is critical. An example of a technique that proves effective in reducing resistance is the paradoxical injunction, borrowed from family systems therapists. For example, the therapist might tell the client, "It is going to be important for you to hold onto your belief that I won't be there for you for awhile." In this example, the client is instructed not to give up on his or her resistance. The therapist has thus joined the client in that resistance. This intervention assumes that the client has an underlying need, however, to connect with someone, as suggested by Main (1990).

An example of a dismissing client is Susan, an adult psychotherapy client with major depressive disorder with whom one of the authors of this chapter worked. Susan was the single parent of a troubled adolescent girl, had undergone a painful divorce, and had no close friends and virtually no contact with her family. Despite the fact that Susan was clearly having trouble coping and had no one to confide in or comfort her, she initially kept conversations with the therapist focused on her daughter's troubles, refusing to acknowledge or discuss her own pain and difficulties. Early in the client-therapist relationship, when the therapist gently inquired about her own feelings, Susan replied that she was okay and that the problem was her daughter. Even when she became tearful, Susan insisted that she was "just fine." As Susan learned to trust the therapist over time, she slowly began to allow the therapist more into her own personal world. Eventually, Susan was able to cry in the therapist's presence and began to acknowledge that she felt rejected and worthless. As Susan's trust in the therapist grew, she also began to examine her beliefs about herself and her attachment figures.

A second example is that of Janie, an adult case management client with schizoaffective disorder. She had been hospitalized at the time her therapist was assigned as her case manager because she had become belligerent and out of control in a public place. When Janie learned that the therapist had been assigned as her case manager, she eyed her suspiciously at times when she assumed the therapist would not notice. When the therapist attempted to talk with her, she mumbled responses but made it clear that she neither wanted nor needed a case manager. The therapist made contact often, essentially disregarding her message that she did not need her help. Indeed, the therapist explicitly remarked that she planned to be there for Janie regardless of whether she acted as if she did not need help. The therapist talked openly with her about issues in her life that could be seen to bear some likeness to Janie's own issues. One of their frequent places for talks was the lawn of the hospital where they shared chicken gizzards, a favorite of Janie's. Gradually, Janie developed a trust in the therapist, which allowed her to begin questioning some of her strong and rigid assumptions about her relationships.

Treatment of People with Preoccupied States of Mind

Initially, treatment of clients with preoccupied states of mind may not appear to present a significant challenge for the treatment provider. Such individuals are often willing and eager to acknowledge difficulties in past and current relationships, as well as in their own functioning (Dozier, 1990; Kobak & Sceery, 1988; Pianta et al., 1996). However, the therapist does encounter problems when attempting to help these clients focus on and work through difficulties. Such clients often appear unable to focus coherently on the issues at hand. Whereas other clients' discussion of anger toward important others may seem productive, the discussion of anger by preoccupied clients often seems ruminative and unproductive. The treatment provider needs to help clients find ways to get beyond their anger and to focus productively on salient interpersonal issues.

Joann was a preoccupied client in individual psychotherapy for depression. When one of the authors of the present chapter became her therapist, Joann had recently separated from her alcoholic husband who had routinely beaten her. When she separated from her husband, her father invited her husband to move into his house. Over a period of months, Joann spent her therapy hour raging against her husband and father and their treatment of her, often yelling and jumping up out of her seat during these tirades. Despite her extensive discussions of how they had wronged her, Joann appeared to derive no sense of relief from or perspective on her own situation. Indeed, the more she raged, the worse she felt. Her therapist's job was to acknowledge the validity of her feelings, but also to get beyond the rage that was so preoccupying her.

Sylvia represents an example from the case management context. Immediately after Sylvia found that her therapist was her case manager, she became involved in an intense, noisy verbal exchange with a ward nurse that appeared to be for the therapist's benefit. For the next several weeks, she related one crisis after another to the therapist. When discharged to a group home, she called the therapist regularly to say that she was thinking about killing herself. The challenge for the therapist was to establish a relationship with Sylvia that respected her sense of vulnerability without revolving around her crises. They worked on this agenda explicitly, with her having a regular time to call the therapist daily, during which she discussed her successes in handling interpersonal issues. The issues of her vulnerability were not ignored, but were contained.

Treatment of People With Unresolved States of Mind

Individuals with unresolved states of mind need help in working through the unresolved issue. Exposure has proven to be effective in the treatment of unresolved trauma. We suggest that exposure, again in the context of a trusting relationship, will help the individual integrate the loss or abuse rather than engage in a dissociative process.

APPLICATION TO FOSTER CARE

Foster children arrive in the care of their foster parents sharing a key characteristic with adult clients: They have had relationship experiences that affect their expectations of parental availability. Indeed, when children are placed later than about 1 year of age into a foster home, they tend to behave in ways that suggest to foster parents that they are not needed. Even autonomous foster parents tend to respond in kind to children's behaviors. We expect that foster parents, like therapists, need to learn to respond therapeutically to their foster children. They need to provide nurturing care even when children are giving them the message that they do not need it. Dozier et al. (2000) found, surprisingly, that foster children placed with autonomous foster parents eventually develop secure attachments. We suspect that the autonomous foster parents' propensity to behave in nurturing ways eventually overcomes the child's resistance, that is, these autonomous foster parents may function in ways that challenge children's expectations of the world.

The way individuals think about attachment relationships plays an important role in their characteristic way of communicating about problems in both personal and professional relationships. Traditionally, clinicians have focused almost exclusively on understanding how clients' relationship histories have shaped their expectations and views of current relationships and consequently affected their behaviors with important people in their lives, including their relationship with their clinicians. Only more recently, though, have clinicians begun to consider how their own way of thinking about relationships affects the way they care for their clients. In concrete terms, both client and clinician state of mind matter. The consideration of both client and clinician state of mind is critically important as accumulating evidence suggests that there is a powerful interaction between client and clinician state of mind that affects the quality of service provided to clients and, perhaps, client outcomes. Practically speaking, clinicians need to be aware of whether clients tend to become caught up in attachment issues or whether they tend to set them aside. In addition, they also need to be aware of their own tendency to set aside or get caught up in attachment issues. Through their awareness of their own and their clients' states of mind, clinicians increase their chances of resisting the pull to respond in a way that confirms their clients' existing worldview. Such an awareness allows clinicians, within the context of a trusting relationship, to instead gently challenge or disconfirm their clients' worldview and encourage healthy changes in their clients.

AUTHOR NOTE

Support for this research was provided by NIMH grant 52135 to the first author. Correspondence concerning this article should be addressed to Mary Dozier, Department of Psychology, University of Delaware, Newark, Delaware 19716.

REFERENCES

Benoit, D., & Parker, K. C. H. (1994). Stability and transmission of attachment across three generations. *Child Development, 65*, 1444–1456.

Berns, S. B., Jacobson, N. S., & Gottman, J. M. (1999). Demand-withdraw interaction in couples with a violent husband. *Journal of Consulting and Clinical Psychology, 67*, 666–674.

Butcher, J. N., Dahlstrom, W. G., Graham, J. R., Tellegen, A., & Kaemmer, B. (1989). *MMPI-2: Manual for administration and scoring.* Minneapolis, MN: University of Minnesota Press.

Derogatis, L. R. (1977). *SCL-90 administration, scoring, and procedures manual: I.* Baltimore: Johns Hopkins University.

Dozier, M. (1990). Attachment organization and treatment use for adults with serious psychopathological disorders. *Development and Psychopathology, 2*, 47–60.

Dozier, M., Albus, K. A., Stovall, K. C., & Bates, B. C. (2000). *Attachment for infants in foster care: The role of caregiver state of mind.* Manuscript submitted for publication.

Dozier, M., Cue, K., & Barnett, L. (1994). Clinicians as caregivers: Role of attachment organization in treatment. *Journal of Consulting and Clinical Psychology, 62*, 793–800.

Dozier, M., & Kobak, R. R. (1992). Psychophysiology in adolescent attachment interviews: Converging evidence for dismissing strategies. *Child Development, 63*, 1473–1480.

Dozier, M., & Lee, S. (1995). Discrepancies between self- and other-report of psychiatric symptomatology: Effects of dismissing attachment strategies. *Development and Psychopathology, 7,* 217–226.

Dozier, M., Lomax, L., & Tyrrell, C. L. (2001). The challenge of treatment for adults using deactivating attachment strategies. *Attachment and Human Development, 3,* 62–76.

Dozier, M., Stovall, K. C., & Albus, K. E. (1999). Attachment and psychopathology in adulthood. In J. Cassidy & P. R. Shaver (Eds.), *Handbook of attachment: Theory, research, and clinical applications* (pp. 497–519). New York: Guilford Press.

Fonagy, P., Leigh, T., Steele, M., Steele, H., Kennedy, R., Mattoon, G., Target, M., & Gerber, A. (1996). The relation of attachment status, psychiatric classification, and response to psychotherapy. *Journal of Consulting and Clinical Psychology, 64,* 22–31.

Fonagy, P., Steele, H., & Steele, M. (1991). Maternal representations of attachment during pregnancy predict the organization of infant-mother attachment at one year of age. *Child Development, 62,* 891–905.

Kobak, R. R., Cole, H. E., Ferenz-Gillies, R., Fleming, W. S., & Gamble, W. (1993). Attachment and emotion regulation during mother-teen problem solving: A control theory hypothesis. *Child Development, 64,* 231–245.

Kobak, R. R., & Hazan, C. (1991). Attachment in marriage: Effects of security and accuracy of working models. *Journal of Personality and Social Psychology, 60,* 861–869.

Kobak, R. R., & Sceery, A. (1988). Attachment in late adolescence: Working models, affect regulation, and representations of self and others. *Child Development, 59,* 135–146.

Korfmacher, J., Adam, E., Ogawa, J., & Egeland, B. (1997). Adult attachment: Implications for therapeutic process in a home visitation intervention. *Applied Developmental Science, 1,* 43–52.

Main, M. (1990). Cross-cultural studies of attachment organization: Recent studies, changing methodologies, and the concept of conditional strategies. *Human Development, 33,* 48–61.

Main, M., & Goldwyn, R. (in press). Adult attachment classification system. In M. Main (Ed.), *Behavior and the development of representational models of attachment: Five methods of assessment.* Cambridge: Cambridge University Press.

Main, M., & Hesse, E. (1990). Parents' unresolved traumatic experiences are related to infant disorganized attachment status: Is frightening and/or frightened parental behavior the linking mechanism? In M. Greenberg, D. Cicchetti, & M. Cummings (Eds.), *Attachment in the preschool years* (pp. 161–182). Chicago: University of Chicago Press.

Main, M., Kaplan, N., & Cassidy, J. (1985). Security in infancy, childhood and adulthood: A move to the level of representation. In I. Bretherton & E. Waters (Eds.), *Growing points of attachment theory and research* (Society for Research in Child Development Monograph No. 50, pp. 66–104).

Pianta, R., Egeland, B., & Adam, E. (1996). Adult attachment classification and self-reported psychiatric symptomatology as assessed by the MMPI-2. *Journal of Consulting and Clinical Psychology, 64,* 273–281.

Tyrrell, C. L., Dozier, M., Teague, G. B., & Fallot, R. D. (1999). Effective treatment relationships for persons with serious psychiatric disorders: The importance of attachment states of mind. *Journal of Consulting and Clinical Psychology, 67,* 725–733.

van IJzendoorn, M. H. (1995). Adult attachment representations, parental responsiveness, and infant attachment: A meta-analysis on the predictive validity of the Adult Attachment Interview. *Psychological Bulletin, 117,* 387–403.

Ward, M. J., & Carlson, E. A. (1995). Associations among adult attachment representations, maternal sensitivity, and infant-mother attachment in a sample of adolescent mothers. *Child Development, 66,* 69–79.

Two Therapies: Attachment Organization and the Clinical Process

Arietta Slade
City University of New York

Attachment theory was first conceptualized by John Bowlby, a psychoanalyst and member of the British Psychoanalytic Society (Bowlby, 1969/ 1982, 1973, 1980, 1988). Attachment theory grew out of Bowlby's clinical work, beginning with his observation that the delinquent boys with whom he was working had all suffered early losses or traumatic abandonments (Bowlby, 1944). Despite its inherent links to psychoanalytic theory, Bowlby's belief that the need and predisposition to form life-sustaining attachments is what forms the core of human connectedness and his explicit rejection of drive theory led to his extrusion from the British Psychoanalytic Society and from the psychoanalytic literature as well. This regrettable chapter in psychoanalytic history today has been thoroughly reviewed by Holmes (1993, 1996), Karen (1998), and van Dijken (1996). It was not until three decades later, when first Mary Main and later Peter Fonagy began to translate the central tenets of attachment theory into concepts that were relevant to the clinical process, that psychoanalytically oriented clinicians began to consider some of the ways attachment theory might be applicable to developmental theory and clinical work (Ammaniti, 1999; Diamond & Blatt, 1994; Diamond et al., 1999; Eagle, 1995, 1997; Fonagy, 1999, 2000; Holmes, 1993, 1995, 1996; Lyons-Ruth, 1999; Slade & Aber, 1992; Slade, 1999a, 1999b, 2000).

My original training was in psychoanalytically oriented clinical psychology. However, I began conducting attachment research in the late 1970s and was trained in the Adult Attachment Interview in 1985. Over the course of the past decade, I have slowly come to appreciate the dramatic impact this way of thinking has had on my clinical work. This chapter is, in fact, an outgrowth of my effort to describe some of the ways that working as an attachment researcher and thinking in the terms of attachment theory has changed the way I understand and speak to my patients. I begin by sketching out what I consider to be the four basic assumptions and findings of attachment theory and research. I then consider some of the clinical implications of attachment theory, using my work with two long-term psychotherapy patients as a basis for this discussion.

ATTACHMENT THEORY AND RESEARCH: BASIC ASSUMPTIONS

The first basic assumption of attachment theory and research is that babies are highly motivated from birth to form, maintain, and preserve their primary relationships, because their emotional and indeed physical survival depends on it (Bowlby, 1969/1982). It was this notion, rooted in ethology, that led to Bowlby's breach with the British Psychoanalytic Society. As radical as this idea once seemed, it is now supported by a wealth of evidence from the domains of object relations theory, developmental psychology, clinical study, and basic neuroscience.

The second basic assumption of attachment theory is that infants do what is necessary emotionally, cognitively, and otherwise to maintain their primary attachment relationships (Belsky & Cassidy, 1994; Bowlby, 1988; Cassidy, 1999; Main, Kaplan, & Cassidy, 1985). Consequently, disruptions in these relationships often lead to lifelong disturbances in their sense of self, their sense of others, and their capacity to regulate, contain, and modulate their affective experience. This fundamental premise is at the heart of much current psychoanalytic thinking. Nevertheless, what is particular to attachment theory is its view that there is a specifiable and observable relationship between actual lived experience and the development of structures for thinking, feeling, remembering, and knowing in the child. This position is obviously complemented by recent infant research, namely the work of Stern (1985), Tronick (Tronick & Weinberg, 1997), and Beebe (Beebe, Lachmann, & Jaffe, 1997; Beebe & Stern, 1977).

Intrinsic to the third basic assumption of attachment theory and research is the notion that the child's biologically driven adaptations to the caregiver's actions and to the caregiver's mind lead to the development of regularly occurring and stable patterns of defense and affect regulation in relation to attachment (Ainsworth, Blehar, Waters, & Wall, 1978; Bowlby, 1969/1982, 1988; Cassidy, 1994; Cassidy & Kobak, 1988). Thus, rather than (as in traditional analytic theory) viewing defenses as arising out of the ego's efforts to fend off intolerable internal experiences, attachment theorists suggest that they arise as a function of the child's adaptation to what can be contained and tolerated within the relationship with the caregiver. From the beginning, infants live in relationships with specified boundaries and expectations; they quickly perceive and learn these boundaries and develop patterned ways of responding to their caregivers. These patterned responses slowly become internal representations that determine access to thoughts, feelings, and memories relevant to attachment (Main et al., 1985). Emotions and cognitions that threaten to disrupt primary relationships are defended against in ways that lead to the fragmented, distorted, representational models of insecure individuals (see also Crittenden, 1995, 1997). Although Bowlby's writings set the stage for the notion of attachment classification, these constructs were brought to life and substantially elaborated first in the work of Mary Ainsworth (Ainsworth et al., 1978) and later the work of Mary Main (Main, 1991, 1995; Main et al., 1985; Main & Hesse, 1990).

Ainsworth set out to research the normal development of mother-infant attachment; ultimately, she studied a group of mothers and infants over the first year of life, in an attempt to understand individual differences in the development of human attachment (Ainsworth et al., 1978). Her research culminated in the development of a laboratory separation procedure known as the "Strange Situation." In this seminal work, she was able to describe patterns of behavior and emotion upon reunion with mothers, which she linked to qualities of the mother-child relationship during the first year of life. This study of individual differences in the development of "felt security" offered confirmation for what I have termed the first and second basic assumptions of attachment theory (Ainsworth et al.), namely that children form attachment relationships that in their very nature reflect the vagaries and demands of that particular relationship. In addition, the documentation of the secure, avoidant, and resistant attachment organizations provided strong support for Bowlby's (1969/1982, 1973, 1988) notion that regularly occurring interactive experiences lead to the development of stable patterns of behaving and thinking in relation to one's primary attachment figures.

A decade later, Mary Main and her colleagues (George, Kaplan, & Main, 1996; Main et al., 1985) discovered that, just as patterns could be discerned in infants' reunion behavior in the Strange Situation, patterns of representation could be discerned in adult narrative accounts of early childhood attachment experiences. Using the Adult Attachment Interview (AAI), Main and her colleagues observed that some parents were able to access their thoughts, feelings, and memories regarding early attachment, regardless of how negative these memories were. She described these parents' representations of attachment as secure or autonomous.

Other parents' capacities to talk about and describe their early relationships were fragmented, incoherent, or somehow compromised; these representations of attachment were described as dismissing, preoccupied, or unresolved with respect to mourning or trauma. Importantly, adults were judged secure not because they had had easy or loving childhoods, but because they were able to discuss the nature of their early attachment relationships, however negative, in a coherent and integrated fashion.

Main and her colleagues (Main et al., 1985) also discovered that the organization of maternal attachment narratives predicted the quality of infant attachment. Mothers who were judged secure on the AAI had children who were themselves secure in the Strange Situation, whereas dismissing mothers had children who were insecure-avoidant and preoccupied mothers had children who were insecure-resistant. Main was later able to document a link between a mother's lack of resolution of mourning on the AAI and disorganization and disorientation in the child in the Strange Situation (Main & Hesse, 1990). These findings have been replicated by a number of researchers and provide evidence for the intergenerational transmission of attachment (Fonagy, Steele, & Steele, 1991; van IJzendoorn, 1995). This is the fourth basic assumption of attachment theory and research, namely, that the quality of a mother's organization of attachment (and, to some extent, the father's), profoundly influences the child's emerging representations of attachment.

Main (1991, 1995) focused attention on an individual's language in relation to attachment, as reflected in patterns of narrative. She made an explicit distinction between coherence and incoherence in narratives about attachment and between organized and disorganized narratives. She drew attention to the importance of listening closely to moment-to-moment changes in linguistic fluency, shifts in voice, lapses in meaning and coherence, and fragmentation of descriptions of early experiences of care, separation, and loss. Main linked narrative coherency to what she termed "metacognitive monitoring" (Main, 1991, 1995). Secure individuals, she suggested, are able to monitor their thinking without resorting to defensive exclusion or distortion and thus rely on a "single" model of metacognitive monitoring. They are able to monitor their "thinking about [their] thinking" without segregating aspects of conscious experience from each other. Insecure individuals must resort to "multiple" models in order to keep experiences that are painful and disorganizing out of consciousness.

Main's ideas about narrative coherency and metacognitive monitoring were to capture the interest of Peter Fonagy, who was the first psychoanalyst to bring them into the domain of current-day psychoanalytic thinking (Fonagy, 1999, 2000; Fonagy & Target, 1996, 1998). Fonagy and his colleagues (Fonagy, Steele, Steele, Leigh, Kennedy, Mattoon, & Target, 1995) suggested that the notion of metacognitive monitoring should be expanded to include the monitoring, understanding, and making meaning of feelings, desires, and intentions, that is, of mental states. They introduced the term "reflective functioning" to describe a process intrinsic to the human ability to make sense of another's behavior: the capacity to use the understanding of mental states to make sense of another's mind. This work has had an enormous impact on later psychoanalytic theory and is where one can see most directly the emerging interface between attachment theory and psychoanalytic psychology.

THE CLINICAL IMPLICATIONS OF ATTACHMENT
THEORY AND RESEARCH: TWO THERAPIES

There are a variety of ways to consider the implications of this body of theory and research for clinical work (cf. Slade, 1999a, 1999b, 2000). In the sections that follow I present my work with two patients, Rebecca and Rose, both of whom have been in long-term, twice weekly psychoanalytic psychotherapy for over 5 years. As will become clear later, my work with them provides an ideal opportunity to discuss how thinking about attachment organization and attachment processes can have a direct impact on clinical work.

The first woman I describe is Rebecca, whom I consider to be dismissing in relation to attachment; the second is Rose, whom I consider to be preoccupied in relation to attachment. The notions of detachment and enmeshment reflect opposite ends of an attachment continuum. Individuals who are dismissing of attachment maintain closeness by avoiding feelings, memories, or longings that might drive away their caregivers; Bowlby (1969/1982, 1973, 1988) called this "avoidance in the service of proximity." Preoccupied-enmeshed individuals maintain closeness via enmeshment in affect and in relationships, because the caregiver's availability can only be assured via affective engagement. Using thought to contain, regulate, or understand affective experience is very difficult for these individuals. At the midpoint in this continuum are secure individuals, who are able to balance intimacy and autonomy (Holmes, 1996), negative and positive memories and affects within the structure of a flexible, integrated representation of attachment. Affect and cognition are balanced and integrated (Crittenden, 1995, 1997; Slade, 2000).

Such profound differences in one's basic sense of self and of self in relation to others require very different approaches to treatment and lead to profoundly different transference and countertransference manifestations (Holmes, 1998; Slade, 1999a). This will become quite obvious as I describe my work with Rebecca and Rose.

Rebecca

Rebecca was in her early 30s when she began seeing me and her therapy continued for 5 years. Initially I saw her twice a week; after 3 years, regrettably, she cut back to once a week. Finally, 2 years later, she left treatment and moved to the west coast, although she continued to return regularly to visit her family.

A petite and animated woman with a quick wit and lively intelligence, Rebecca sought treatment shortly after the birth of her third daughter. Rebecca began her treatment stating that she wished to be a "better" mother. She knew intellectually that she had been poorly mothered, alternately emotionally abandoned and attacked by her mother, whose narcissism dominated her primary relationships. Rebecca was also able to articulate her own difficulties with mothering: She found it hard to tolerate closeness with her children. Although she had only a part-time job as an investment advisor (one she could manage from home), she often left the children with nannies and babysitters. Rebecca felt that she loved her children, but readily acknowledged that she could not sit or play with them for more than a little while at a time. She was content to take them out with her on errands, but she hated getting up with them in the morning and often went out for dinner in the evenings. Despite twinges of anxiety, she sometimes stayed away overnight and at times traveled without them. Occasionally she brought the children, but these trips were unbearable without the help of a nanny. Her husband's work led him to be absent much of the time.

What became clear was that, as much as she felt love and an intense devotion to her children, she could often be distant and unavailable. When she did spend long periods of time with them, she could be very tense and irritable. When she became angry or overwhelmed by mothering, she simply left the room and left the children's care to the babysitter. Indeed, she was rarely alone with the children without a babysitter.

Ironically, however, Rebecca worried about her children all the time. During the early years of our work together, she spent many of her sessions worrying about who would care for her children; indeed, the help changed constantly. Would she have a part-time and a live-in nanny, two part-time nannies, the warm young nanny, or the organized and tough older nanny? In essence, who could help provide some of the things that she could not give her children? Who could protect her children from the difficulties she herself had faced as a child?

Rebecca was the younger of her parents' two children. She grew up in the suburbs; her parents ran a successful film company that kept them traveling and away from home much of the time. She attended demanding private boarding schools and performed extremely well. At age 13,

Rebecca began using drugs; relatively and sometimes very heavy drug use continued throughout high school, college, graduate school, and her employment as a high-level stockbroker. She stopped taking drugs when pregnant with her first child. She had a series of steady boyfriends throughout adolescence and at 24 married a successful businessman. From the time she was 16 until she was 28, she had little contact with her family. She received little financial support from them and lived essentially an entirely independent life. However, after the birth of her first child, she moved into a house less than an hour's drive from her parents' home.

Rebecca had few memories of her early childhood; although she "knew" that her mother had a terrible temper and often erupted in rages, beating her children with whatever was at hand, Rebecca had no memories of these incidents. It was family lore, but it was not something she herself could remember. She also "knew" that she had been left, throughout her childhood, from infancy on, with various nannies and housekeepers. Some had been nurturing and caring, others had not, but her mother, clearly too narcissistically involved to care for her small children, simply absented herself, pursuing her work. However, neither the memories nor the feelings surrounding these early experiences were directly accessible to her, hence, my use of quotation marks.

Once her children were born, Rebecca saw her parents very regularly; interestingly, however, their visits were often no longer than half an hour, cool, and without any real talk or intimacy. Her mother's narcissism, coldness, and raw ambition made any close connection to Rebecca or her children impossible; moreover, her mother was evidently uncomfortable with her grandchildren's rambunctiousness and curiosity. And yet Rebecca could not imagine living anywhere else; nor could she imagine not remaining in close contact with her parents.

Rebecca had a way about her that I can only describe as "breezy"; she was elusive and cool. Apparently, little touched her. She "knew" that her experiences in early childhood had everything to do with the troubles she had as a mother and various limitations in her marriage, but she could not feel the connections. She reported that she never remembered being upset and yet described a childhood of, on the one hand, unrelenting loneliness and neglect and, on the other, of frightening losses of control by her mother. As part of her effort to keep her feelings at bay, Rebecca often spoke in the second person ("Well, you know, when your mother is screaming, you're scared") and there was an unshakable rationality to all that she did. She experienced her emotional life as something far away and inaccessible and often said to me: "So, yeah, I can't remember any of it, and I don't feel it so, what can I do?" When I gently challenged her leaving her children behind and tried to link her children's feelings (and symptoms) to her own feelings of abandonment as a child, she rather imperiously told me: "I've just got to do this, I have to do what I have to do."

Over the course of the first years of our work together, Rebecca began to think differently about her children's needs and about herself as a mother. Although she could still feel enormously uncomfortable when faced with the raw demands and needs of her young children, she recognized the roots of her withdrawal and of her feelings of needing space and distance. She began to turn her worry about the children into real explorations of what her children needed and felt and she developed a much more nuanced appreciation of her mother's psychology and of the complex nature of their interdependency. This did not necessarily mean that she was immune to her mother's capacity to hurt and disappoint; rather, she developed a language for the effect and depth of these hurts. As our work progressed, she created more distance between herself and her mother and struggled to establish her independence in a more genuine way. Her progress ultimately allowed her to move away and establish her family in a separate part of the country.

Sadly, events in Rebecca's life were to push this process even further along. Three years into her treatment, Rebecca gave birth to her fourth child, a son. He was born blind and had numerous medical difficulties. I received a call from Rebecca within hours after she received this devastating news; she asked me to come to the hospital as quickly as I could. That evening, at her bedside, was probably the first time I saw Rebecca cry. She tried to be breezy, but she was overcome, as was I.

In the 2 years that followed, Luke permeated Rebecca's coolness. From the moment of his birth, Rebecca kept Luke close to her and protected him from impingements. She defended him in the face of insensitive comments from neighbors and friends and she worried greatly about his feelings about himself and about his development. Luke was a winning and bright boy who charmed everyone around him, despite his various medical problems, and he found his way into Rebecca's heart, more than anyone else in her life ever had. Rebecca was willing to let him wake her up in the morning, to let him sleep in her bed when he was frightened, and was much more sensitive to his separation anxiety and need for her than she had been with her older children. Although she acknowledged that her son's experience of her was always one of her "darting away"—leaving and coming back again and again—she was able to mother this child in a way that was very new for her.

For at least the first 2 years of Luke's life, Rebecca's grief over his differentness brought her closer to her own losses and loneliness; it certainly allowed her to be a more available mother. Clearly, the work we had done prior to Luke's birth set the stage for this, but Luke himself was suddenly a huge catalyst. Still, these events did not, of course, change her completely. She rode out what she called "patches" of anxiety and sadness with stoicism, waiting for the time when she could return to "normal" functioning. She cut back her therapy sessions to once a week after her son was born, clearly because she could not bear to confront her grief regularly. She was able to acknowledge this quite openly.

Of course, there were many ways in which she still found it difficult to listen to her own internal experience. About a year after her son's birth, Rebecca came in complaining of yet another round of physical illness, in particular hair and weight loss. For a young woman, she was ill with surprising frequency, with colds, viruses, and more serious problems that seemed to suggest that her immune system was not functioning properly. She began the session by telling me that she had seen an internist that morning. He suggested that her symptoms might be the result of stress. She reported this, noting that she actually did not feel stressed and was fairly "happy," just losing weight, not eating, and so on. When I pushed her to think about what might be going on, about why she was once again sick in a nonspecific and mysterious way, she shrugged her shoulders and said something to the effect that it must be her way of expressing feelings that she could not let out any other way. I said simply that I thought it was her body's way of crying. She nodded, in a way that surprised me for its depth of feeling.

We then began to talk about how physical ailments were the only way she could as a child or as an adult get her mother's attention. Her mother could not tolerate her needs and could never comfort her. Her father kept his distance. Speaking directly in the language of attachment, I said: "Imagine what it must have been like to be frightened, or worried about what was going to happen, or angry at your mother's rages. Who could you turn to, who would hear you, who would protect you?" Only her body could cry and seek comfort. Interestingly, Luke, with all his physical difficulties, was the only one of her children most able to permeate her remove.

After Luke's birth, Rebecca's oldest child began crying out in her own way. Rebecca was ambivalent about seeking treatment for her, perhaps because it was painful to consider how she had repeated her childhood experience in her mothering. She finally sought treatment for Chloe when Luke was 1 year old. After a dyadic session in which Chloe had repeatedly hit and punched Rebecca, Rebecca said: "You are really angry at me," to which Chloe replied: "You were a bad Mommy when I was a baby." Referring to work from her own treatment, in which I had suggested to Rebecca that she emotionally absent herself from her children whenever she became angry at them, she replied to Chloe: "I used to get very angry at you and then I would leave you alone, and that made you feel very badly." Chloe then replied: "I thought that you were going to come back and shoot me." Rebecca was then able to apologize to Chloe for leaving her to hold her anger alone and was able to put the child's anger and fear in a context. Chloe then announced they'd talked enough, and began singing "Full moon Mommy . . . I love my Mommy." With the powerful metaphor of the full moon, Chloe described the joy and relief of telling her mother this terrible secret in a way that brought closeness and reparation.

Unfortunately, this stability was short-lived. Just as Chloe was beginning to make some progress with her own anger and grief and as Luke was beginning to transition into a special education program, her husband was transferred, requiring that the whole family move to California. This effectively ended Rebecca's treatment, as well as Chloe's. Once again, she became swept up in the demands of moving, leaving the children with the huge task of adapting to a new life and of coping with the loss of their caretakers, other family, and so on. The older children became symptomatic again and Luke grew more insistent and demanding. Unfortunately, it was another year before things settled down again.

This is the exemplar of Main's (Main & Hesse, 1990) dismissing pattern of attachment: a rigid "story" that cannot be linked or adapted to real and felt memories. This accounts for the cool and unemotional feel of her sessions and the intellectualization and detachment that at times characterized the work. Intense memories and emotions were experienced as faint "blips" in her consciousness or as twinges of discomfort or anxiety in her daily life. For the most part, however, these were excluded from her felt self-experience and existed only as intellectual formulations that did not in any way lead to change or internal reorganization. Main (Main & Hesse, 1990) described such narratives as "incoherent" in the following sense: Although rife with contradictions ("My mother beat me, but I don't remember being upset"), they lack any tension or affect around the resolution of these inconsistencies.

Rebecca stayed as close to her significant objects as she could without threatening these relationships with the intensity of her inner life. This is precisely what Bowlby (1969/1982, 1973, 1988) meant by "avoidance in the service of proximity." Rebecca maintained proximity to her parents, hoping for some closeness and finding a way to partake of whatever they had to give, without mucking up the waters with her anger and vulnerability. She stayed as close to her children as she could bear. These were her efforts to come to terms with buried longings and needs; they were, however, doomed to failure. She found it difficult to bear the feelings behind her defenses and painful to engage with them in a felt and genuine way. When she first began her treatment, she could not "hold" her own experiences in mind, let alone those of her children, but her avoidant proximity seeking allowed her to find some comfort and solace, however limited.

Whereas Rebecca's older children were certainly insecure in their attachment to her, Luke had a chance of being secure. Mary Main observed similar phenomena in her longitudinal study; several insecure mothers had children who were seriously ill in their first years of life. Main found that these children were secure and hypothesized that the threat of loss in these situations was so great as to override the parents' detachment (M. Main, personal communication, June, 1985). The same may well have happened with Luke.

It is my impression that my steadiness and availability gradually created small and subtle changes. Rebecca became more available to her children (especially after Luke's birth) and more demanding of care and stability from her husband. Naturally, her coolness and detachment extended to the transference. Although I felt that she trusted me in a real, but limited, way (manifested, for instance, in her desperate call from the hospital after Luke was born), I always had the sense that it was terribly difficult for her to be present and known. She was attached to me in an avoidant way: She needed me, but it was hard to acknowledge that I mattered and that she depended on me. Throughout the treatment, she avoided the service of proximity. She was very comfortable keeping the sessions on the level of advice and, although she made what I would consider gestures with regard to really working deeply, there was rarely a ripple left where we had broken the surface. She did not appear to have any overt or conscious reaction to separations and vacations and, with some regularity, she "forgot" or had to reschedule appointments; for 6 months after Luke's birth, she was willing to have only phone sessions. In these ways, she managed the relationship and its intrinsic demands for closeness and reflection. In this way, too, she continued to enact her experience of separation, abandonment, and loss. It would have taken a much longer and more intense treatment to permeate her rigid defenses against intimacy and authenticity. At the same time, it is worth noting that, now 5 years after termination and despite the great geographic distance between us, Rebecca is still in regular contact. As has always been the case, I am indeed important to her, but once again this is best managed at a distance.

Needless to say, Rebecca was often able to make me feel dismissed and demeaned, as she maintained her detached and at times arrogant facade. I sometimes felt ridiculously emotional when I was trying particularly hard to reach her (Dozier, 1990; Dozier, Cue, & Barnett, 1994; Holmes, 1998; Slade 1999a); it was possible to reach her only through the cool entrees she preferred. In her need to avoid painful emotions, she was often successful in getting me to back away from themes of loss and abandonment and to fall into a cool and rational treatment that felt empty and hollow. I often felt deadened, reflecting, I suspect, the bleakness of her internal world.

One could think of Rebecca as having schizoid or narcissistic features, both of which would be correct characterizations. Moreover, it would be possible to see her breeziness and detachment as "resistance" in the traditional sense, but I do not think it was. The fight against letting her deeper feelings emerge was not generated primarily by the need to protect herself from unacceptable unconscious wishes and fantasies. The fight was driven, rather, by her perception that, if she was needy, sad, or angry, she would drive away those she needed and loved. Her rage and anxiety could never be directly acknowledged, although in her case such feelings were often expressed through somaticizing or, indirectly, in a kind of imperiousness and arrogance. Acknowledgment of her "true" self was quite difficult (Winnicott, 1965).

Rose

A completely different picture is presented by Rose, a woman who would clearly be described as preoccupied in relation to attachment. Rose, a strikingly beautiful woman who now in her early 40s, has been seeing me twice weekly for the past 6 years. Her prior treatment history included a 14-year course with a psychiatrist, which began in her early 20s. Rose now lives with her husband of 10 years and their two daughters, ages 7 and 9. Rose sought treatment for a wide range of concerns and anxieties within weeks of moving to a community local to my practice. The nature of these concerns will be obvious shortly.

Rose and her younger sister were for the most part raised alone by Rose's mother, for whom the description "toxic and abusive" would be an understatement. She was enraged, needy, punishing, and entirely wrapped up in herself. She left her daughters alone frequently and actually put them in an orphanage when she had major surgery, despite the fact that there were relatives available to care for them nearby. Even more salient, however, was her vicious and unrelenting criticism, which would today unquestionably be considered a form of emotional abuse. Rose was saddled with household chores and with the care of her younger sister, whom she grew to torment in the same way her mother tormented her. She never had a quiet moment; her mother continuously interrupted her moments of solitude (particularly reading) with demands, criticism, and scorn. Even today, her mother, now 70 years old, can be remarkably vicious and is unhappy and malcontent. Although there are many other salient aspects of Rose's history, including her father's abandonment of the family when she was 6 years old and various other childhood losses and traumas, I will have to limit my discussion of other details due to space limitations. It is sufficient to say that Rose's childhood experience was one of abandonment, neglect, and covert and overt emotional abuse.

One of Rose's mother's typical assaults when Rose was a child was the following: "If you had a brain, you'd be dangerous!" This statement speaks to what Rose was denied as a child and still struggles mightily to find as an adult: a mind of her own.

Rose carries numerous psychiatric diagnoses. She clearly has border-line and narcissistic features and she meets the criteria for a rapid cycling bipolar disorder, as well as for a generalized anxiety disorder. She has a severe binge eating disorder and has gained 65 pounds since adopting her daughter 7 years ago. She is being treated with a combination of a mood stabilizer and an SSRI. During the early years of her treatment with me, she insisted on participating in specific structured in- and outpatient treatments for her eating disorder. None had any long-term effect and we have now mutually agreed that she needs to address her eating problems at the psychological level. She has multiple somatic complaints as well, some of which are tied to her obesity and are increasingly serious. Rose's psychiatric and medical history clearly documents the link noted by many researchers between the diagnosis of a major psychiatric disorder, insecure attachment, physical vulnerability, and early trauma (Adam, Keller, & West, 1995; Fonagy et al., 1996; Goldberg, 2000; Lyons-Ruth & Jacobvitz, 1999).

Intense neediness, unrelenting feelings of chaos and frenzy, and an overwhelming sense of badness characterize Rose's clinical presentation, even after 6 years of treatment. Continuing to this day, Rose routinely demands advice, guidance, and support from me. She has wanted me to come to her home (to move in, in fact!), to tell her what to eat, how to manage her children, where to buy her clothes, who to hire as a housekeeper. She often asks for extra sessions. Early in the treatment, she called me at home at 9:00 on a Saturday morning and asked if the day she'd planned was too crazy. "Just tell me what to do!" was and still is a frequent (and often enraged) plea.

Just as compelling as Rose's neediness is her sense of chaos. Rose's daily life, particularly in the early years of her work with me, was absolutely frenetic and disorganized. Even now, although to a somewhat lesser extent, tasks, errands, and commitments pile up and clamor at her; she has absolutely no sense of how to order or prioritize the most rudimentary aspects of her day. Every plan she makes gets put through the grinder: Should she really do this, does it make sense, and so forth. She was always late, always "crazed," and had always forgotten something important, like her wallet. Just beneath the surface lay tremendous rage, which would erupt at anyone (including her children) who blocked her chaotic, desperate run. This is not a busy woman with a full day; this is a car skidding relentlessly out of control. (Ironically, she has had a number of car accidents, two of them quite serious.)

Embedded in every communication is Rose's sense of shame, envy, humiliation, inadequacy, rage, and badness. Her sessions are a litany of how terrible her life is, how inadequate she is, and how utterly desperate and hopeless she feels: "I am fat," "I have no friends," "My phone never rings," "My children hate me (or won't listen to me, aren't getting the same things other children are, etc.)," "I am bald" (her hair is thinning), "I am ugly," "My husband is critical," and so on.

As one might imagine, Rose's children are both showing many signs of emotional trouble, as a direct result of the kind of impulsive, chaotic, and enraged parenting they have received, but Rose worries little about their emotional life; indeed, she is terrified of their feelings and their inner lives. Instead, she scans the environment constantly for concrete clues as to how to mother them and desperately adjusts her mothering according to what other parents are doing. For example, after hearing that another mother in the school had hired a nanny for her children who spoke Chinese and French in order to expose them to these languages, Rose became obsessed with doing the same thing. She feels envious and diminished when she hears how other families spend their holidays; her rituals feel empty and hollow and her children have nothing. She often hovers anxiously in the hall at her children's school, desperate for information on how other mothers spent their weekend, what playdates they have arranged, and so on. Sadly, these discussions invariably make her feel envious and excluded and confirm her sense that in the realm of parenting she has failed dismally: She is a bad mother.

Food and eating are often among her most pressing concerns. Since having her first child, Rose has been binge eating on a regular, often nightly basis. Food was not a new problem, of course, and Rose likely had a subclinical eating disorder prior to her child's arrival. In any event, the weight gain of 65 pounds and feeling of being utterly out of control has been devastating to her. Rose used to pride herself on her looks and her clothes and now often wears nothing but sweat clothes. Sometimes she leaves the house without combing her hair. Rose gets up in the middle of the night like clockwork. She experiences her binge eating as something that happens to her, not as something tied to her feelings of rage, affect hunger, and shame. She just wants it fixed, and relentlessly seeks advice on finding the right (again concrete) method to do this, but throughout, she continues bingeing, sometimes at an alarming rate.

Rose's chronic affective dysregulation is exemplified not only in her experience of life, but also in the fragmented, incoherent, and inchoate nature of her mentation. In sessions, she jumps from subject to subject, worry to worry, often without a clear path from one to the next. I often have the sense of organization, defense, and meaning being dashed apart by upsurges of raw, negative affect.

Rose tries to manage her dysregulation by desperately searching for a way to externally regulate her experience. She wants someone, often me, to tell her what to do and, most often, she wants concrete solutions. Clearly, it is her fervent hope that these concrete solutions will eradicate her sense of emptiness, inadequacy, and rage and will give some sense of order to her fragmented, ruptured inner world. What is most striking in this regard is her absolute avoidance and rejection of reflection. She quite simply never reflects, never wonders, never pauses: Indeed, as I describe later, she fights it. I have often thought of Winnicott's (1965) notion of "going on being" while sitting with Rose. This is a woman who can never let herself contemplate at all and who conveys in the very structure of her language the degree to which experiences of selfness or of having a mind were continuously fragmented and dissolved by her mother's attacks. She cannot find a story that contains or helps her; she cannot reflect on any aspect of what makes her who she is.

This sense of being overwhelmed by raw and unmodulated affect that cannot be contemplated, ordered, or reflected on is typical of individuals Main (Main et al., 1985) described as preoccupied in relation to attachment. So too is Rose's absolute dependence on the real caregiver, whose presence she guarantees by continuous distress and disorganization. Like the resistant infant, Rose never feels adequately soothed and is never able to develop a sense of the caregiver as at once separate but nevertheless internally available and sustaining. Rose also presents a clear example of what Fonagy and his colleagues (Fonagy et al., 1995) referred to as "low reflective functioning." As is evident in her remarkably concrete mentation, she is particularly prone to relying on what Fonagy and Target (1996) referred to as the "psychic equivalence mode": What she experiences is what is real. That she is fat, has no friends, her husband hates her, and so on is what is real to her. She has no sense of others' realities, other perspectives, or other interpretations.

Rose is the kind of empty, enraged, needy, and sometimes heartbreaking patient clinicians are all familiar with, whose damage is great and deep. The challenge of working with Rose is not understanding her; rather, it is finding a way to help her make sense and meaning of her inner life, finding a way to develop a rudimentary "reflective capacity." In essence, this means helping her understand that her sense of herself and of her relationships is only a "sense" and that there are many other ways of experiencing and managing her reality. This is the only route to her developing a sense of herself as anything other than bad and damaged, separate from her mother and her mother's hatred.

In the early years of treatment, Rose shunned reflection outright. Complex, abstract solutions and meanings were anathema to her. Instead, she demanded to be "fixed." Rose took almost no solace from my words. My attempts to understand, contain, and very rarely interpret her experience in light of her history seemed futile: Although she seemed to find some transient meaning in what I had to say, moments of reflectiveness quickly gave way to her sense of desperation and inadequacy. Nothing ever stuck; we always seemed to be starting anew. Often she actively fought my attempts to understand her: What I said was not right, she already had done "anger work" on her relationship with her mother, and so on.

As time passed, there were windows or fragments of reflective functioning. She began to identify her mood crashes, the black holes of anaclitic, narcissistic vulnerability and despair. At rare moments, she could recognize the events or interactions that triggered these states. Someone had snubbed her or she had felt worried about her daughter, but it was terribly hard for her to consider that what had worried her and thus triggered her despair (or, often, her eating) could be interpreted in a variety of ways and did not require immediate action.

As an example, one of Rose's close friends had a child, Milly, about the same age as Rose's daughter. Milly and her mother were extremely close; indeed, they were inseparable and shared a bed every night. Rose was devastated to hear that Milly had shared her mother's bed and was convinced that the fact that her child did not sleep with her every night meant that she did not really love her and was not attached to her. It also meant, of course, that she was a bad mother: This was reality as far as Rose was concerned.

When I first heard stories like this, I wondered out loud at her interpretation of the situation, to no avail. Finally, I one day asked her if her "mishugena meter" was working. (Mishugena is a Yiddish word that loosely translates as "nuts" or "crazy.") She looked at me, puzzled. I said: "You know, like on the TV show 'Queen for a Day,' when they measure the applause for each contestant to see who wins. The one who gets the most applause on the applause meter wins. Don't you have a meter that tells you when something's mishugena?" She laughed (a good sign with her) but then went back to argue that so and so was really a better mother. I often used that metaphor in our work together, but it was not until years later that she began to use that metaphor herself, as a way of standing back from a rigidly held conviction of her own badness and playing with it. Indeed, playfulness has often been the only way I can get her to imagine an abstract or complex alternative to her very concrete way of seeing things (cf. Fonagy & Target, 1996, 1998; Winnicott, 1971).

Rose's capacity for any kind of sustained reflection or meaning making has been significantly constrained by her anxiety about thinking. She clearly believes, to use her mother's phrase, that to use her brain, to think, to make linkages, to find meaning, is very dangerous. Any understanding within a session leads to a frantic desire to escape and obliterate, leading to continuous shifts—often within a single session—between fragments of reflection and the return to desperate, concrete action. For her, ideas are reality and are thus terrifying calls to enactment or denial.

Rose rarely remembered what I had said in sessions; often she forgot from one moment to the next and she never remembered from session to session. Although an emphasis on reflection has clearly been at the heart of my work with her, about 6 months ago I finally said to her: "You know, I've noticed that you want me to be a particular kind of mother, like the mother who fixes your doll when it's broken. But you won't let me be the kind of mother I can really be, the mother who helps you make sense of things. You don't hang onto to the things we make sense of from session to session and you can't remember what I've said. You go back to wanting me to be the kind of mother who just fixes what is broken." I had often made comments to the effect that she could not internalize my concern for her, that she could not keep me in mind, but I had never put it quite like this, linking the two states and the two mothers together.

That comment was to have a subtle but clear impact on our subsequent work. Several days later she came into the session and remarked. "I was thinking about what you said last time." This was a simple statement, but a huge step forward for her. She had often in the past mentioned that something I had said made sense to her, but that she had "forgotten" it and would I please tell her again. Now she herself was providing the link between sessions.

Gradually, she began to carry her thinking from session to session; these were the very first stages of creating a coherent narrative within the context of treatment (Holmes, 1993; Slade, 2000). Within a few months, she had actually begun to recognize the kinds of situations that would trigger her intense despair and anxiety, and would lead to her bingeing. This was an extraordinary accomplishment. For years she had rejected the notion that anything psychological was at the root of her eating. She could not describe her feelings upon awakening during her trip to the kitchen or while she was eating. She could not identify anything in the day that made her want to drown her feelings in food. Now, however, for the first time, she began to identify what led to her mood crashes and began to tie these to her eating and attacks of self-hatred and anxiety. She described a weekend in which she had slowly succumbed to bingeing and for the first time she was able to trace the beginnings of her feelings of shame and affect hunger through to her eating binge.

This is not to say that recognizing the link between her mental life and her behavior offered an immediate palliative. In fact, recognizing her feelings often led to her enacting them, as the boundary between thought and action is often very fluid for her. For instance, Rose and I were recently engaged in a rare moment of reflection on the link between the onset of her bingeing and the birth of her daughter. Sensing her openness to seeing the connections, I delicately approached the subject of what it might have meant to her to have a daughter and to be the mother of a daughter, in light of all she had experienced as her mother's daughter. She played with the implications of this for 2 or 3 minutes, which was an enormous advance. Suddenly, she shifted gears and looked at me, almost belligerent. "Well, what do you want me to do? Give her back?"

The horror and guilt she obviously felt at momentarily realizing the power and depth of her rage and ambivalence toward her daughter was intolerable, even as an idea. It was too real for her. Immediate, concrete action was the only solution. She cannot feel these feelings and hold onto any tenuous sense of herself at all, let alone feel like a barely adequate mother. Using her brain and locating meaning is indeed dangerous. Her statement also speaks to what she must have known, but could never have allowed herself to understand: that in her mother's mind was the wish to destroy her, to, at the very least, give her back.

When Rose said this to me, I looked at her with mock exasperation and said, with a humorous inflection, "Yes, that was just what I had in mind!," at which moment she let out with a full laugh, as did I. At that moment, I was "marking" her concrete mentation (Gergely & Watson, 1996) and refusal to think both in my facial expression and my playful reply. She got it and she laughed. Slowly, and increasingly with humor, she has begun to recognize her pull to action; even now, however, she cannot always interrupt her retreat.

It hardly needs to be said that hers is a primitive transference, hence, my comment about the "fixing" versus the "thinking" mother. I am the desperately sought-after object whose goods she cannot metabolize and to whom she returns again and again, always hungry, never sated.

The work with Rose has been very difficult. I struggle in virtually every session not to yield to her concrete demands, although, just as in work with children, this is sometimes the necessary thing to do. I struggle not to feel overwhelmed and swamped by her affect and not to binge on the concrete details of her life as a way of keeping from drowning in her emotion. I struggle not to feel hopeless about the depth of her damage or about ever being able to help her find some sense of meaning in her experience and thus some capacity to regulate and manage it. I struggle continuously to keep thinking and to maintain a reflective stance (see Holmes, 1998; Slade, 2000).

Rose is slowly finding fragments of meaning and fragments of story. Meaning is what gives life to everyday experience and what contributes to success in treatment. She creates mininarratives that she is able to hold onto for longer periods of time, resisting the impulse to obliterate them in action and enactment. Not thinking once saved her from her mother's rage; now, however, it keeps her from having a mind, a body, and a self of her own.

CONCLUDING REMARKS

At the beginning of this chapter, I proposed that there are four basic assumptions of attachment theory. The stories of Rebecca and Rose, together and individually, provide a way of understanding how these four assumptions come alive in individual life histories and thus are central to clinical work. Both Rebecca and Rose developed highly organized and patterned ways of being, thinking, and feeling in relation to their primary objects that preserved their relationships to troubled, unsatisfying, and unavailable mothers. Their primary attachments (which both women still hold onto, to this day) involved adaptations that significantly distorted the development of feeling (in Rebecca's case) and thinking (in Rose's case) and allowed for a compromised sense of closeness, one at the expense of intimacy, the other at the expense of autonomy. Both adaptations determined a particular sense of self and of self in relation that powerfully inhibited the development of satisfying relationships and profoundly limited the development of a full, productive, and meaningful sense of self. Both stories provide powerful evidence for the intergenerational transmission of attachment, in all its complexity and nuance. The story of these two therapies also makes it evident that such adaptations profoundly shape the course and essential functions of therapeutic work.

Being dismissing in relation to attachment, as exemplified here by Rebecca, means that the individual maintains proximity to the caregiver (or to the therapist) by avoiding feelings, memories, or longings that might drive her away. Presumably, this mode of affect regulation was the only way Rebecca could guarantee her mother's attention to her needs, that is, by muting or disguising them. Main (1995) suggested that mothers of avoidant children (who presumably become dismissing adults) turn away from their children's attachment needs because they are too painful and evocative of their own disappointments and losses (see also Fraiberg, 1980). This was clearly the case with Rebecca's mother and then with Rebecca herself. As seen from Chloe's outburst, this insures that the child will experience the expression of intense emotion as leading to rejection and maternal unavailability. As a function of these early relational experiences, the structures Rebecca had available to her for regulating affect were rigid and inflexible; she did everything necessary to keep threatening affects at bay. Her internal world of objects and affective experiences seemed barren and she found it very difficult to remember or describe painful experience, other than in dissociated, cutoff ways. To remember or describe in a different way would have threatened the very fabric of her primary relationships and might have led to profound disruptions in their ability to receive even the most rudimentary emotional care.

Jeremy Holmes, a British psychiatrist who has written extensively about the clinical applications of attachment theory, noted that the aim of treatment with such patients is to help them "break stories" (Holmes, 1998). Dismissing individuals tell rigid stories that have been expunged of all memory and feeling. The job of the therapist is to open narrative to real and felt experience, which then makes these stories agents of change. To do this, the therapist must override the deadening experience of being locked out of stories or of being made to feel ridiculous and demeaned, without at the same time feeling intrusive and disrespectful of necessary boundaries. Certainly my aim with Rebecca was to find a way to help her experience herself and her inner life in a real and vital way. Her defenses against doing so were very powerful and, under the pressure of her child's disability and the intense feelings it engendered, they became even more so.

In sharp contrast, preoccupied individuals, as exemplified here by Rose, maintain proximity to the caregiver or transference object via distress and disorganization. For Rose, this was presumably the only way she could guarantee the mother's attention to her needs and thus guarantee her own survival. Mother and child were united in distress and by the mother's inability to regulate and modulate her experience or to see her as separate. For Rose to function as separate from her mother, to develop her own structures for regulating affect and experience, would threaten the very fabric of the mother-child relationship; once separate, Rose might have challenged her mother's cruelty and narcissism and thus deflated her fragile self-esteem. For Rose, internalized structures for regulating affect states remained ineffectual and tenuous, leaving her to continuously experience extreme affective dysregulation, which she could not contain, organize, or defend against in any coherent way. Here attachment theorists posit that the mother's failure to respond consistently, along with her particular sensitivity to and resonance with the baby's distress, underlies this structural deficit in the modulation of affect (Cassidy, 1994; Cassidy & Berlin, 1994). Interestingly, we see this resonance to distress in Rose's mother as well as in Rose herself. These deficits were evident in Rose's narrative, manifested as: (a) the fragmentation of experience by intrusions of intense affect and (b) the reliance on primitive, action-based defenses and on concrete thinking, which together distort and fractionate descriptions of self and relational experience.

Holmes (1998) suggested that the aim of treatment with such patients is to help them "make stories." The countertransferential "pull," however, when faced with such intense and unmodulated affect and with such levels of disorganization and fragmentation, is for therapists to create stories themselves. It was so tempting to want to explain things to Rose, as a means of quieting her chaos, but this only resulted in further fragmentation of meaning, as she clung to externally provided meaning as a substitute for hard-won, authentic integration. Instead, I had to struggle to become the bridge to thinking, providing the memory, the sense of time, and the cohesion that allow stories to slowly emerge. The emergence of fragments of coherent narrative were the result.

Underlying the core deficits manifested by both Rebecca and Rose (which may or may not be most usefully thought of as categories) are significant impairments in the reflective function (Fonagy et al., 1995). Dismissing individuals disavow internal experience and, in a sense, refuse to reflect on it. To do so would be to dissolve long-held boundaries between the internal world of memories, feelings, and fantasies and conscious experience. In contrast, preoccupied individuals are swamped and overwhelmed by internal experience. They cannot reflect on or mentalize their internal experience in any coherent way. Often this results in concrete, distorted, bizarre, or self-serving understanding of mental states. Indeed, the notion of preoccupation may be understood as a general failure to find meaning, organization, and predictability in affective experience via language and thought. In the absence of the reflective capacity, there are no stories that can coherently represent the inchoate, terrifying, fragmented, and sometimes bizarre state of the inner world of the self or the caregiver.

I am very aware of how differently I have written about Rebecca and Rose in an effort to make coherent stories out of both treatments. In the sections on Rebecca, I struggled to find words that bring this cool and intellectual treatment to life, just as I struggled against my own feelings of deadness and frustration with Rebecca and sought to insert emotion, vitality, and passion into the work. Similarly, in the sections on Rose, I struggled not to overwhelm the reader with a sense of raw emotion, chaos, dysregulation, and fragmentation. The language in these sections is rife with feeling, with episodic memories threatening to burst forth in a pell-mell and unintegrated fashion, with my efforts at organization and containment needing to be constantly renewed. Even in the act of writing about Rebecca and Rose, reliving my experiences in the room, I struggled to contain and bound the projections and projected identifications that are intrinsic to working in the realm of disordered attachments. The differences that are inherent in my presentation of both stories cannot help but convey the tremendous differences in these two treatments and, in particular, differences in my aims, my experience of transference and countertransference phenomena, and my function in relation to their inner worlds.

My experience of finding the story in these two therapies brings to mind the work of Crittenden (1995, 1997), who noted that, as a function of early attachment experiences, children come to rely on cognition and affect in different ways. Whereas secure children rely on cognition and affect in a complex, flexible, and integrated way, insecure children favor one at the expense of the other; thus, avoidant children rely heavily on cognitive and attentional strategies, whereas resistant children rely on affect as a means of solving problems and maintaining proximity. What I am suggesting here (and what is further implied by Fonagy's [Fonagy et al., 1995] work on the reflective function) is that there is a defensive aspect to these choices: Avoidant children are fearful of emotion and of its effects on their primary relationships and their own sense of self, whereas resistant children are frightened of the internal and relational effects of knowing and thinking. These defensive adaptations profoundly influence the development of a therapeutic relationship.

Before leaving the question of attachment organization, it is important to mention that there are aspects of disorganized or unresolved attachment in the clinical presentations of both Rebecca and Rose. Although it is unclear whether either would meet the full criteria for unresolved attachment (Main & Hesse, 1990), both sometimes rely on dissociative defenses. Furthermore, both can be quite frightening to their children, as a function of their own early traumatizing and damaging relationships. To some extent, they have both failed to resolve these traumas, as manifested in the fragmentation of thinking and feeling inherent in their case histories (Herman, 1992; Lyons-Ruth & Jacobvitz, 1999). As noted by Main and Hesse and as delineated in a volume on attachment disorganization edited by Solomon and George (1999), these are the hallmarks of unresolved or disorganized attachment in adults. Certainly, Rebecca dissociated when her affects in relation to her children became intolerable and she could be frightening to her children, as a function of both her dissociation and her flashes of anger (witness Chloe's fantasy). The extremes of fragmentation in Rose's mentation also point to ongoing dissociative processes. Rose is often frightening to her children, who are themselves showing signs of significant disorganization in relation to attachment, as a function of her rages and irrationality.

As a final note, I would like to underscore the link that emerges in these two cases between attachment insecurity and disturbances in the proper functioning of the immune system. Both of these women were often ill and both sought care from doctors in ways that reflect their experiences of needing and receiving care. Although these difficulties can be seen as stemming from profound disruptions in the development of self-care and self-regulation, various researchers have also suggested links between the chronically elevated stress levels (as measured by heart rate and cortisol secretions) of insecure individuals and the development of proper immune system functioning (Gunnar, Brodersen, Krueger, & Rigatuso, 1996; Hertsgaard, Gunnar, Erickson, & Nachmias, 1995; Spangler & Grossman, 1993). These two clinical stories point again to the link between the experience and regulation of bodily states, the early mother-child relationship, and physical health (see also Goldberg, 2000).

I have used these two cases to illustrate some of the ways I think of early attachment experiences and attachment organization in my work with adult patients. Clearly, there are many ways to think about Rebecca and Rose and many ways to describe the complexity of the clinical process in each of these two therapies. What I have described here in no way encompasses my understanding of either case, but I do hope that I have been able to capture some of the understanding and organization provided by an appreciation of attachment processes, as they are manifested in the quality of intrapsychic life, language, affect, and thought. It has not escaped my attention that these are cases with which I have had, relatively speaking, less success than I would have liked. Although, consistent with Diamond and her colleagues' recent report (Diamond et al., 1999), there was some evidence of shifts in attachment organization and reflective functioning with both patients, I would have to say that, relative to healthier patients in long-term psychotherapy, it was limited. I would also have to say that, although they both certainly became attached to me, these attachments were necessarily compromised; it took continuous effort on my part to provide a vital thinking and feeling secure base. With some patients, attachment themes come and go and take on more or less salience over the course of treatment, but, as clinicians have known for nearly a century, the more salient attachment issues are, the more salient early trauma, early disruption in care, and pronounced insecurity in patterns of thought and language, the more challenging the work.

REFERENCES

Adam, K. S., Keller, A. S., & West, M. (1995). Attachment organization and vulnerability to loss, separation, and abuse in disturbed adolescents. In S. Goldberg, R. Muir, & J. Kerr (Eds.), *Attachment theory: Social, developmental and clinical perspectives* (pp. 309–342). Hillsdale, NJ: Analytic Press.

Ainsworth, M. D. S., Blehar, M. C., Waters, E., & Wall, S. (1978). *Patterns of attachment: Psychological study of the strange situation.* Hillsdale, NJ: Lawrence Erlbaum Associates.

Ammaniti, M. (1999). How attachment theory can contribute to the understanding of affective functioning in psychoanalysis. *Psychoanalytic Inquiry, 19*, 784–796.

Beebe, B., Lachmann, F. M., & Jaffe, J. (1997). Mother-infant interaction structures and presymbolic self and object representations. *Psychoanalytic Dialogues, 7*, 133–183.

Beebe, B., & Stern, D. N. (1977). Engagement-disengagement and early object experiences. In N. Freedman & S. Grand (Eds.), *Communicative structures and psychic structures* (pp. 35–55). New York: Plenum Press.

Belsky, J., & Cassidy, J. (1994). Attachment: Theory and evidence. In M. Rutter & D. Hay (Eds.), *Development through life* (pp. 373–402). Oxford: Blackwell.

Bowlby, J. (1944). Forty-four juvenile thieves: Their character and home lives. *International Journal of Psycho-Analysis, 25,* 19–52.

Bowlby, J. (1973). *Attachment and loss: Vol. 2. Separation.* New York: Basic Books.

Bowlby, J. (1982). *Attachment and loss: Vol. 1. Attachment.* New York: Basic Books. (Original work published 1969)

Bowlby, J. (1988). *A secure base: Parent-child attachment and healthy human development.* New York: Basic Books.

Cassidy, J. (1994). Emotion regulation: Influences of attachment relationships. In N. A. Fox (Ed.), *The development of emotion regulation: Biological and behavioral considerations* (Society for Research in Child Development Monograph No. 240, pp. 228–249). Chicago: University of Chicago Press.

Cassidy, J. (1999). The nature of the child's ties. In J. Cassidy & P. R. Shaver (Eds.), *The handbook of attachment theory and research* (pp. 2–31). New York: Guilford Press.

Cassidy, J., & Berlin, L. J. (1994). The insecure/ambivalent pattern of attachment: Theory and research. *Child Development, 65,* 971–991.

Crittenden, P. M. (1995). Attachment and psychopathology. In S. Goldberg, R. Muir, & J. Kerr (Eds.), *Attachment theory: Social, developmental and clinical perspectives* (pp. 367–406). Hillsdale, NJ: Analytic Press.

Crittenden, P. M. (1997). Patterns of attachment and sexual behavior: Role of dysfunction versus opportunity for creative integration. In L. Atkinson & K. Zucker (Eds.), *Attachment and psychopathology* (pp. 47–93). New York: Guilford Press.

Diamond, D., & Blatt, S. (1994). Internal working models and the representational world in attachment and psychoanalytic theories. In M. Sperling & W. Berman (Eds.), *Attachment in adults: Clinical and developmental perspectives* (pp. 72–98). New York: Guilford Press.

Diamond, D., Clarkin, J., Levine, H., Levy, K., Foelsch, P., & Yeomans, F. (1999). Borderline conditions and attachment: A preliminary report. *Psychoanalytic Inquiry, 19,* 831–884.

Dozier, M. (1990). Attachment organization and treatment use for adults with serious psychopathological disorders. *Development and Psychopathology, 2,* 47–60.

Dozier, M., Cue, K., & Barnett, L. (1994). Clinicians as caregivers: Role of attachment organization in treatment. *Journal of Consulting and Clinical Psychology, 62,* 793–800.

Eagle, M. (1995). The developmental perspectives of attachment and psychoanalytic theory. In S. Goldberg, R. Muir, & J. Kerr (Eds.), *Attachment theory: Social, developmental and clinical perspectives* (pp. 123–153). Hillsdale, NJ: Analytic Press.

Eagle, M. (1997). Attachment and psychoanalysis. *British Journal of Medical Psychology, 70,* 217–229.

Fonagy, P. (1999). Points of contact and divergence between psychoanalytic and attachment theories: Is psychoanalytic theory truly different? *Psychoanalytic Inquiry, 19,* 448–480.

Fonagy, P. (2000). Attachment and borderline personality disorder. *Journal of the American Psychoanalytic Association, 48,* 1129–1146.

Fonagy, P., Leigh, T., Steele, M., Steele, H., Kennedy, R., Mattoon, G., Target, M., & Gerber, A. (1996). The relation of attachment status, psychiatric classification, and response to psychotherapy. *Journal of Consulting and Clinical Psychology, 64,* 22–31.

Fonagy, P., Steele, M., & Steele, H. (1991). Maternal representations of attachment during pregnancy predict the organization of infant-mother attachment at one year. *Child Development, 62,* 880–893.

Fonagy, P., Steele, M., Steele, H., Leigh, T., Kennedy, R., Mattoon, G., & Target, M. (1995). Attachment, the reflective self, and borderline states: The predictive specificity of the Adult Attachment Interview and pathological emotional development. In S. Goldberg, R. Muir, & J. Kerr (Eds.), *Attachment theory: Social, developmental and clinical perspectives* (pp. 223–279). Hillsdale, NJ: Analytic Press.

Fonagy, P., & Target, M. (1996). Playing with reality: I. Theory of mind and the normal development of psychic reality. *International Journal of Psychoanalysis, 77,* 217–233.

Fonagy, P., & Target, M. (1998). Mentalization and the changing aims of child psychoanalysis. *Psychoanalytic Dialogues, 8,* 87–114.

Fraiberg, S. (Ed.). (1980). *Clinical studies in infant mental health.* New York: Harper & Row.

George, C., Kaplan, N., & Main, M. (1996). *The Adult Attachment interview protocol* (3rd ed.). Unpublished manuscript, University of California, Berkeley.

Gergely, G., & Watson, J. (1996). The social biofeedback model of parental affect-mirroring. *International Journal of Psychoanalysis, 77,* 1181–1212.

Goldberg, S. (2000). *Attachment and development.* London: Arnold.

Gunnar, M., Brodersen, L., Krueger, K., & Rigatuso, J. (1996). Dampening of adrenocortical responses during infancy: Normative changes and individual differences. *Child Development, 67,* 877–889.

Herman, J. L. (1992). *Trauma and recovery.* New York: Basic Books.

Hertsgaard, L., Gunnar, M., Erickson, M. F., & Nachmias, M. (1995). Adrenocortical responses to the Strange Situation in infants with disorganized/disoriented attachment relationships. *Child Development, 66,* 1100–1106.

Holmes, J. (1993). *John Bowlby and attachment theory.* London: Routledge.

Holmes, J. (1995). Something there is that doesn't love a wall: John Bowlby, attachment theory and psychoanalysis. In S. Goldberg, R. Muir, & J. Kerr (Eds.), *Attachment theory: Social, developmental and clinical perspectives* (pp. 19–45). Hillsdale, NJ: Analytic Press.

Holmes, J. (1996). *Attachment, intimacy and autonomy.* New York: Aronson.

Holmes, J. (1998). Defensive and creative uses of narrative in psychotherapy: An attachment perspective. In G. Roberts & J. Holmes (Eds.), *Narrative in psychotherapy and psychiatry* (pp. 49–68). Oxford: Oxford University Press.

Karen, R. (1998). *Becoming attached: First relationships and how they impact our capacity to love.* Oxford: Oxford University Press.

Lyons-Ruth, K. (1999). Two person unconscious: Intersubjective dialogue, enactive relational representation, and the emergence of new forms of relational organization. *Psychoanalytic Inquiry, 19,* 576–617.

Lyons-Ruth, K., & Jacobvitz, D. (1999). Attachment disorganization: Unresolved loss, relational violence, and lapses in behavioral and attentional strategies. In J. Cassidy & P. R. Shaver (Eds.), *The handbook of attachment theory and research* (pp. 520–554). New York: Guilford Press.

Main, M. (1991). Metacognitive knowledge, metacognitive monitoring, and singular (coherent) vs. multiple (incoherent) model of attachment: Findings and directions for future research. In C. Parkes, J. Stevenson-Hinde, & P. Marris (Eds.), *Attachment across the life cycle* (pp. 127–160). London: Routledge.

Main, M. (1995). Recent studies in attachment: Overview, with selected implications for clinical work. In S. Goldberg, R. Muir, & J. Kerr (Eds.), *Attachment theory: Social, developmental and clinical perspectives* (pp. 407–475). Hillsdale, NJ: Analytic Press.

Main, M., & Hesse, E. (1990). Lack of mourning in adulthood and its relationship to infant disorganization: Some speculations regarding causal mechanisms. In M. Greenberg, D. Cicchetti, & M. Cummings (Eds.), *Attachment in the preschool years: Theory, research, and intervention* (pp. 161–182). Chicago: University of Chicago Press.

Main, M., Kaplan, N., & Cassidy, J. (1985). Security in infancy, childhood and adulthood: A move to the level of representation. In I. Bretherton & E. Waters (Eds.), *Growing points of attachment theory and research* (Society for Research in Child Development Monograph No. 209, pp. 66–107). Chicago: University of Chicago Press.

Slade, A. (1999a). Attachment theory and research: Implications for the theory and practice of individual psychotherapy with adults. In J. Cassidy & P. R. Shaver (Eds.), *The handbook of attachment theory and research* (pp. 575–594). New York: Guilford Press.

Slade, A. (1999b). Representation, symbolization and affect regulation in the concomitant treatment of a mother and child: Attachment theory and child psychotherapy. *Psychoanalytic Inquiry, 19,* 797–830.

Slade, A. (2000). The development and organization of attachment: Implications for psychoanalysis. *Journal of the American Psychoanalytic Association, 48,* 1147–1174.

Slade, A., & Aber, J. L. (1992). Attachments, drives and development: Conflicts and con-
vergences in theory. In J. Barron, M. Eagle, & D. Wolitzky (Eds.), *Interface of psychoanalysis
and psychology* (pp. 154–186). Washington, DC: American Psychological Association.

Solomon, J., & George, C. (Eds.). (1999). *Attachment disorganization.* New York: Guilford
Press.

Spangler, G., & Grossmann, K. E. (1993). Biobehavioral organization in securely and insecurely attached infants. *Child Development, 64,* 1439–1450.

Stern, D. N. (1985). *The interpersonal world of the infant.* New York: Basic Books.

Tronick, E. Z., & Weinberg, M. K. (1997). Depressed mothers and infants: Failure to form
dyadic states of consciousness. In L. Murray & P. Cooper (Eds.), *Postpartum depression and
child development* (pp. 54–81). New York: Guilford Press.

van Dijken, S. (1996). *The first half of John Bowlby's life: A search for the roots of attachment theory.*
Doctoral dissertation, University of Leiden.

van IJzendoorn, M. H. (1995). Adult attachment representations, parental responsiveness,
and infant attachment: A meta-analysis on the predictive validity of the Adult Attachment Interview. *Psychological Bulletin, 117,* 387–403.

Winnicott, D. W. (1965). *Maturational processes and the facilitating environment.* New York: International Universities Press.

Winnicott, D. W. (1971). *Playing and reality.* London: Tavistock.

An Antidote to Posttraumatic Stress Disorder
The Creation of Secure Attachment in Couples Therapy

Sue Johnson
University of Ottawa

Attachment theory is about belonging and the power of emotional bonds in human families. These are the ties that bind people together in space and endure over time (Ainsworth, Blehar, Waters, & Wall, 1978). These bonds provide children and adults with a secure base in which to develop and grow. Much of the literature details how a lack of secure connection with others adversely influences the optimal development of personality, including how people see the world, regulate affect, process information, and communicate with others. This theory is not just about belonging, however, it is also about how attachment bonds are evolutionary survival mechanisms that offer protection and a safe haven from life's adversities (Bowlby, 1969/1982). A sense of secure connection with others is most pertinent in the face of danger and loss. The lack of such connection not only leaves us unprotected in the storms of life and specifically influences how we deal with such storms, but can, in itself, be aversive and even traumatic. Attachment theory has been called "a theory of trauma emphasizing physical separation, whether threatened or actual, and extreme emotional adversity" (Atkinson, 1997, p. 3).

The field of couples and family therapy has focused on alleviating the distress of intimate bonds that have gone awry. This chapter addresses not only how a more satisfying connection with a life partner can be fostered in therapy, but how such therapy can help create a safe haven where old wounds and hurts can be healed and how a life partner can be a resource in this healing.

Bowlby stated (1973) that, when a person is confident that an attachment figure will be available when needed, "that person will be much less prone to either intense or chronic fear than will an individual who has no such confidence" (p. 202). There is now clear evidence that secure attachment fosters the development of positive strategies for dealing with environmental stressors (Mikulincer, Florian, & Weller, 1993). If the creation of such safe connection tends to protect us from life's perils, it also offers a potent healing environment when those perils overtake us. Couples therapy, particularly a couples therapy that focuses on the creation of the emotional accessibility and responsiveness that are the building blocks of secure attachment, such as emotionally focused couples therapy (EFT), may then be able to help couples create such an environment.

Mental health professionals see many people who have encountered life's perils and been traumatized by them and the trauma literature demonstrates that trauma that is of human design is particularly difficult to deal with and recover from. In a clinical assessment in a marital and family therapy clinic, a client, Carol, said, "I can't be touched. I don't like the water in the shower hitting my skin. I don't like my child grabbing me and even sitting on the couch with David, my husband, is hard. I have been burned. The only way to feel safe is to be alone, to be invisible." As she spoke, her husband, David, sat and wept. Carol had grown up in a hostile world, without the protection of parents and in a setting where she was emotionally and sexually abused by those she depended on. She is now seriously anorexic and dealing with the symptoms of posttraumatic stress disorder. This client was referred to our clinic because the treatment of her anorexia and her other symptoms had not been effective. It seems that her unhappy relationship with her husband was undermining the impact of her daily group therapy sessions and his distancing from her had, in fact, been the main precipitating factor in her eating disorder. She said, "I decided I must be too big, so I got rid of as much of me as I can."

The tragedy of trauma inflicted by the people we need the most is that it not only wounds us but contaminates our future connections with others, connections that might allow us to heal from such wounds. It is hard to recover from what Herman (1992) called "violations of human connection," such as sexual and physical abuse in childhood, without the corrective experience of a secure bond, but it is extremely hard to create this kind of bond with any attachment figure after such a violation. Trauma increases the need for protective attachments and, at the same time, renders those attachments direct sources of danger. In my clinic, we try to help couples like David and Carol not only to become less distressed in their relationship but also to create the trust and safe emotional engagement typical of secure bonds, which will then promote healing in the traumatized partner.

In Celtic myth and story, life is dark. In this vision we all stand in a dark, narrow place with our backs against a wall and wait for a dragon who, inevitably, comes to destroy us. There is no escape. The only question is how well we fight. In our time, there is perhaps another question, the question of whether we fight alone or whether someone stands beside us in the dark. Trauma is like a dragon that comes in the dark and floods us with helplessness. There are very limited ways for us to respond to this dragon. If the one we love the most is able to stand beside us, the dragon seems smaller, the dark is less terrifying, and we can fight for our lives. If we are alone in the dark, the trauma will likely overwhelm us and its impact will be magnified. We do not seem to be designed to face trauma and overwhelming fear alone; we most often disassociate and numb out until another stands beside us. The lack of a safe attachment exacerbates and perpetuates the effects of trauma

ATTACHMENT AND TRAUMA

The essence of attachment theory is that emotional connection with significant others offers us comfort, reassurance, and protection in the face of the adversities of life. A secure attachment with another becomes an inner resource, a source of trust in the self and the world that promotes resilience and a sense that danger and fear can be dealt with. Those who see the world through the lens of secure attachment, if they do experience trauma, are less likely to develop posttraumatic stress disorder (PTSD; Alexander & Alexander, 1994); they can manage distress and trauma by acknowledging their distress, engaging in constructive actions, and turning to others for support (Bowlby, 1988; Mikulincer & Florian, 1998). For children and adults, secure bonds are the primary defense against trauma-induced psychopathology (Finkelhor & Browne, 1984; van der Kolk, 1996). However, for those who grow up with insecure attachments and who are also then traumatized by attachment figures, there is no safety anywhere. Close relationships become flooded with trauma cues rather than being potential safe havens. After such violations of human connection, as Mary Main pointed out, significant others become simultaneously a "source of and solution to danger" (Main & Hesse, 1990, p. 163). This creates a double bind that is, to a certain extent, present in all couples conflict where individuals need emotional support from the attachment figure with whom they are in conflict with or threatened by (Gottman, Coan, Carrere, & Swanson, 1998; Kobak & Duemmler, 1994). However, this bind is particularly poignant in trauma survivors who do not know whether to flee toward attachment figures or from them. Organized constructive responses to one's partner and interactions that foster new learning are then almost impossible. Attachment, and experience in general, then become, as Main and Hesse suggested, chaotic or "disorganized."

Those who have been traumatized by significant others in childhood cannot rely on the caring touch that "tranquillizes the nervous system" (Schore, 1994, p. 244) or the confiding that allows them to give meaning and structure to difficult experiences (Pennebaker, 1985). Activities that soothe and comfort other couples, such as love making, are sources of threat. People then must find ingenious ways to cope with a dangerous world; they become hypervigilant, distrustful, and hyperaroused or they numb out and become hypoaroused. In very distressed attachment relationships, which in themselves can be considered traumatic (Atkinson, 1997) with a small *t*, styles of hyperactivation (anxious attachment) and deactivation (avoidant attachment style) develop. In the symptoms of PTSD, this lack of affect regulation is even more pronounced with dramatic swings between hypo- and hyperarousal. Affect regulation has been identified as a central factor in both development of the attachment styles enacted with loved ones (Simpson & Rholes, 1998) and the constellation of symptoms that make up PTSD.

The symptoms of PTSD are not rare. If other sources of trauma such as combat, natural disaster, rape, and assault are omitted and the focus is on childhood sexual abuse (CAS), it is estimated that 20% of female children are sexually abused in their own families by a family member (Badgley et al., 1984; Russell, 1984) and approximately 5% report father-daughter incest (Finkelhor, 1984). Boys are also victimized, but in smaller numbers. Such victims are disproportionally represented in patient populations. A large proportion of outpatients displaying a wide range of symptomatology are incest survivors (24–44%), as are hospitalized but nonschizophrenic adolescents and children (Lundberg-Love, Marmion, Ford, Geffner, & Peacock, 1992; Kirschner & Kirschner, 1996). Survivors are also vulnerable to revictimization: Russell (1986) found that 68% of survivors had been the victims of rape or attempted rape. The symptoms of PTSD, which tend to be "particularly severe and long-lasting" when the stressor is "of human design," arise as a result of exposure to a stressor that involves "intense fear, helplessness, and horror" involving actual or threatened injury to the self or another (*Diagnostic and Statistical Manual of Mental Disorders*, 4th Ed.; American Psychological Association, 1994). These symptoms are detailed in the following sections.

Persistent Reexperiencing of Traumatic Events

Persistent reexperience is not remembering; it is being in the traumatic situation rather than in the present. In the novel *The English Patient* by Michael Ondaatje (1993), the experience of a young nurse making love with a sapper who is a bomb disposal expert is described in the following terms. She feels "invisible" to him because his eyes are always on "what is dangerous"; everything else is "periphery." She feels it is necessary to teach him to make a noise, to "admit his whereabouts in the darkness" (p. 126). This echoes the voice of Carol, the clinic patient, who stated that she had never been "present" when making love to her spouse; he was peripheral. She had experienced every sexual contact in their 10-year marriage as a reoccurrence of her sexual trauma. The quote from the novel also emphasizes the impact the symptoms of PTSD have on partners. If at key moments of emotional engagement the trauma survivor is "there rather than here," that is, he or she is neither accessible nor responsive, this inevitably evokes attachment insecurity and separation distress in the partner.

Avoidance and Numbing

Avoidance and numbing symptoms have been found to be particularly important in defining the quality of intimate relationships for trauma survivors (Riggs, Byrne, Weathers, & Litz, 1998) and there is a consensus that they are also harder to treat than the reexperiencing symptoms. Avoidance here involves detachment, dissociation, and restricted affect. The literature on marital distress now clearly identifies lack of emotional engagement and distance as the most significant factor in the development of distress and marital disruption, rather than factors such as angry disagreements or the inability to resolve issues (Gottman, 1991, 1994; Gottman & Levenson, 1986). One of the pernicious effects of numbing is that it then restricts opportunities to form new kinds of attachments and limits the restoration of relational capacities that is considered key to recovery from trauma (Harvey, 1996; McCann & Pearlman, 1990). It also alienates the partner, who may become not only maritally distressed but also vicariously traumatized (Solomon et al., 1992).

Physiological Hyperarousal

Physiological hyperarousal often manifests as extreme irritability and free-floating anger as well as hypersensitivity to ambiguous or negative cues. The clinical and research literature on trauma emphasizes that the main effect of trauma is the loss of the ability to regulate affective states (van der Kolk, 1996). This generally impaired affect regulation then results in extreme fight, flight, and freeze responses to what appear, from the outside, to be relatively innocuous stimuli. Trauma inflicted by attachment figures in childhood is so pernicious and long-lasting in its effects that it is beginning to be defined in terms of inescapable shock and as a special kind of Type II trauma or complex PTSD (Herman, 1992).

The *DSM-IV* stresses impaired relationships with others as a key associated feature of PTSD and the symptoms noted earlier have obvious implications for a person's ability to create and sustain a close relationship. The recent research on couple relationships stresses not only the crucial importance of sustained emotional engagement for stability and satisfaction but also the impact of absorbing states of negative affect (where everything leads in and nothing leads out) on the generation and maintenance of relationship distress (Gottman et al., 1998). Marriages seem to succeed or fail as a function of how well couples handle negative affect. If affect is the music of the attachment dance (Johnson, 1996), the loss of affect regulation as a result of trauma can be expected to wreak havoc on close relationships. Survivors' relationships are often defined by intense anger, shame, and fear. If the first two features, anger and shame, are considered, the difficulties that survivors face in creating supportive relationships become clear.

Bowlby distinguished (1973) between the anger of hope and the less functional anger of despair. The anger of hope protests the negative behavior of attachment figures and often modifies their behavior. As Gottman and Krokoff (1989) noted, appropriately expressed anger promotes marital satisfaction over time. The anger of despair, more typical of survivors' relationships, is intense and persistent and drives the other away. Loss of control over such anger also impacts survivors' efficacy; not only can they not trust others, they cannot trust themselves. As Carol stated, "The rage happens suddenly; it sweeps me away. I can't predict it. I have to run away and space out. I think I'll hurt David and the children. I must be bad." This kind of anger, together with a more hostile attributional bias and general anger proneness, is typical of insecure attachment styles (Mikulincer, 1998a), but is particularly apparent in survivors' relationships. Even if the partners of survivors try to be responsive, they tend to become alienated, particularly if they do not understand the survivors' trauma, and they then withdraw, thus confirming all the survivors' worst abandonment fears. Shame also makes it difficult for survivors to reveal and disclose themselves. The nature of shame is to "hide and divide" (Pierce, 1994). This sense of the self as defective and therefore unentitled to love or caring and, in fact, deserving of punishment blocks not only disclosure and sharing but also the ability to respond to others' caring. As Carol said, "His empathy makes my stomach turn. It can't be for me." It has been noted that survivors often take the caregiver role but find it difficult to be the recipient of it (Kirschner & Kirschner, 1996), no matter how sensitively responsive the partner is.

It is not difficult, considering the symptoms described previously, to understand why distressed relationships are a significant part of the aftermath of trauma and why couples therapy is being advocated more and more as a crucial facet of trauma treatment (Johnson & Williams-Keeler, 1998; Reid, Wampler, & Taylor, 1996), although there are as yet very few published empirical studies of couples therapy with this population. There has been a recognition for many years that a new safe attachment was probably the crucial context for healing in trauma, but most often this relationship was assumed to be with a therapist who would see a client for a few hours a week. Although there has been a growing recognition that survivors need social support, the concept of using the real attachments in a survivor's life as an active source of healing is relatively recent. This concept has evolved from the recognition that trauma survivors are caught in a vicious cycle, namely, that the lack of any vestige of secure attachment perpetuates the effects of trauma and prevents healing and the effects of trauma perpetuate relationship distress and the lack of a secure base. Pragmatically, if the spouse is not part of the solution to the trauma survivor's problems, this partner generally becomes part of the problem.

Because working models of attachment affect the strategies people use for dealing with distress and challenge, it is to be expected that attachment style, or the habitual form of engagement with others that is associated with particular working models, would mediate the effects of trauma. Attachment insecurity generally makes people vulnerable to symptomatology (Cicchetti, Toth, & Lynch, 1995) and secure individuals seem to suffer fewer symptoms after trauma (Alexander & Anderson, 1994; Mikulincer et al., 1993). Mikulincer et al. (1993) studied responses to traumatic experience and related these responses to attachment style. They found that those with anxious attachment styles were more distressed during missile attacks in the Gulf War and those with avoidant styles were more hostile and had higher levels of somatization. Mikulincer et al. (1995) made the point that a sense of attachment security is a personal resource that gives a sense of efficacy and teaches that life's adversities are manageable. Insecure attachment styles have also been associated with more anger proneness and less anger control (Mikulincer, 1998a), mirroring the hyperarousal symptoms of PTSD. Both anxious-preoccupied and avoidant individuals also exhibited a stronger fear of death and seemed less able to regulate this affect (Mikulincer, Florian, & Tolmacz, 1990).

In terms of the link between trauma, particularly physical and sexual abuse, and the evolution of an individual's attachment style, the experience of trauma has been particularly associated with disorganized attachment in children (Main & Hesse, 1990) and with a fearful-avoidant style in adults' (Alexander, 1997; Shaver & Clarke, 1994). Alexander (1993) noted that 58% of women who were incestuously abused during childhood were fearful (a much higher percentage than the usual 20% found in Bartholomew & Horowitz, 1991). Brennen, Shaver, and Tobey (1991) suggested that these styles, disorganized (as defined by the Adult Attachment Interview, which focuses on past relationships with parents) and fearful-avoidant (as defined by self-report questionnaires focused on present relationships), are analogous. Fearful-avoidants tend to vacillate between hostility toward and distancing from and preoccupation with and longing for closeness; thus, their attachment behaviors seem disorganized and conflicted. Shaver and Clarke pointed out that fearful-avoidants have the most negative self-concepts, are most likely to be depressed, and, in fact, on every measure of mental health are the worst off. Shaver, Collins, and Clarke (1996) characterized the appraisal of self in fearfuls as "helpless and hopeless" (p. 49). If trauma occurs in the context of rejection and isolation and results in a fearful-avoidant attachment style, this style will then ongoingly and negatively influence relational capacities. Couples therapists may then most often be dealing with partners who have been traumatized and have also never had the resources of a safe attachment with which to cope with that trauma.

The fearful-avoidant style that seems to characterize many trauma survivors not only involves a negative sense of self-worth and of others' dependability, but may also be the most difficult model to update and modify. Contradictory, automatic, rigidly held models that lack coherence and are infused with intense negative affect such as fear are harder to change (Main, Kaplan, & Cassidy, 1985) and more likely to pull for confirming responses from others. This style also involves difficulty in metamonitoring in relationships (Kobak & Cole, 1991), that is, in stepping outside and forming a coherent view of relationships. It is hard to revise what one cannot access, coherently articulate, or evaluate. In general, insecure attachment styles act to constrict and narrow how cognitions and affect are processed and thus to constrain behavioral responses; this may be particularly true in the case of survivors and may help to explain why victims of trauma are likely not only to have distressed relationships that help to maintain the symptoms of PTSD but also to be retraumatized.

THE MARITAL BOND AS RECOVERY ENVIRONMENT

Van der Kolk, Perry, and Herman (1991) suggested that the ability to derive comfort from another human being predicts more powerfully than trauma history whether symptoms improve and whether self-destructive behavior can be regulated. What does the creation of a more secure attachment with a partner offer a trauma survivor?

First, a more secure bond with a partner creates a safe haven that helps survivors regulate their grief, anger, and fear in a positive self- and relationship-enhancing way. Attachment theory is primarily a theory of affect regulation (Feeney, 1998). The way in which an individual engages with attachment figures reflects strategies that have been learned as ways of dealing with negative affect. A safe haven with a partner helps survivors deal with emotionally loaded reexperiencing symptoms such as nightmares, intrusive thoughts, and flashbacks in a constructive way. Turning to one's partner for comfort then begins to replace other negative affect regulation strategies such as self-mutilation or dissociation. If the taming of fear is the most basic goal in the treatment of trauma (Foa, Hearst-Ikeda, & Perry, 1995), the natural inborn antidote to fear in primates is contact comfort. The availability of the spouse also lessens the need for numbing and dissociation and allows fear to be confronted. Spouses then become allies against the incursions of trauma, rather than cues for traumatic memories and secondary victims.

Apart from providing alternative affect regulation strategies and so lessening PTSD symptomatology, a safe relationship generally contains distress and renders emotions such as shame and grief endurable. The empathy of a loving partner counteracts shame and allows survivors to deal positively with issues such as the need for high levels of control of closeness and touch. The essence of attachment theory is perhaps that attachment relationships are physiological and emotional regulators; they organize emotional life and the representations of the world associated with that life. Attachment theory began in the study of bereavement and the physical and functional disorganization it brings (Hofer, 1984). A safe attachment with a spouse allows survivors to grieve and to come to terms with loss, allowing loss to become ground rather than figure, periphery rather than center stage. As Holmes (1996) suggested, a key task of psychotherapy is to "give sorrow words"; it is easier for individuals to feel sorrow when they are held and supported by those they love.

Second, to be connected and also secure is foreign territory for many survivors. Such a relationship offers a corrective emotional experience that shows that a secure base is possible, that others do not always betray, and that trust is possible. Working models of attachment concerning others can then be revised. Safety allows people to be more open to new evidence, articulate tacit attitudes, and consider alternative perspectives (Kobak & Cole, 1991). As Bowlby (1969/1982, 1973, 1980) suggested, this connection then buffers survivors against further incursions of the trauma and allows them to break cycles of abuse that may have spanned generations. Abused women who manage to create positive relationships with their spouses are, for example, less likely to abuse their own children (Egeland, Jacobvitz, & Sroufe, 1988).

Third, once a safe base has been established, this safety then facilitates the continued reprocessing and integration of traumatic experience. Affective states can be used as cues to attend to incoming information rather than alarm signals that prime hyperarousal or numbing. Intense fight and flight responses are contained so there is time to assess and construct meaning. The negative effects of behavioral inhibition and secrecy can be replaced by the positive effects of confiding in a trusted other (Penne-baker, 1985). Such confiding promotes cognitive reorganization and helps individuals find new meaning in traumatic events. The acceptance of the partner, for example, can legitimize and validate the pain of a survivor in a powerful way.

Fourth, all approaches to the treatment of trauma emphasize the need to address the negative sense of self that often follows this experience. Many survivors blame themselves for what happened to them and have powerful negative working models of self. They not only feel unworthy, as is typical in those with fearful and preoccupied attachment styles, but feel personally to blame for their fate and actively mistrust and hate them-selves. It is perhaps less painful to define themselves as inherently flawed and responsible for the evil that has befallen them than to tolerate the helplessness of traumatic experience (Pagels, 1988). To be seen and ac-cepted by a partner after spending most of their life in hiding is a transformative experience for survivors. The psychotherapy literature has focused on the therapist as a source of validation for clients. However, at-tachment theory might suggest that, if the acceptance of the therapist is like a 20-watt light bulb, the validation offered by a spouse might be com-pared to a stadium floodlight. The spouse can hold up a mirror that re-flects not toxicity and shame, but a sense of self that not only is worthy of love and comfort, but also is empowered and can be trusted to handle in-ner states, master the effects of trauma, and repair attachment disruptions. As David said to Carol, "Come out here and listen to my voice, not to that cruel voice that tells you how bad you are and to go hide. We can fight that voice together." The reprocessing of traumatic experiences can in fact build an intense and powerful bond between partners that then becomes a protective barrier against retraumatization.

The most obvious question that now arises is how to help survivors of "violations of human connection" that have deeply wounded them and infused every human contact with fear create a secure connection with a partner. An appropriate couples intervention would have to pay particu-lar attention to the processing, regulation, and integration of affect and it would have to focus explicitly on the creation of a secure bond rather than on other couples interventions such as teaching negotiation skills. The process of the therapy would have to be focused on creating the emotional connection that trauma therapists suggest is the "primary protection against feelings of helplessness and meaningless" (McFarlane & van der Kolk, 1996, p. 24).

Emotionally focused couples therapy (EFT; Greenberg & Johnson, 1988; Johnson, 1996), as its title suggests, focuses on partners' emotional responses and how these responses organize attachment behaviors. The goal of this therapy is to help partners explore and expand the emotions that underlie the positions they take with each other in the interactional cycles that define the relationship. EFT sees marital distress through the lens of separation distress and insecure attachment and helps couples shift their interactional positions in the direction of accessibility and responsiveness so that a secure bond can be established. This approach to couples therapy is now one of the best delineated and most empirically validated models in the field (Alexander, Holtzworth-Munroe, & Jameson, 1994; Baucom, Shoham, Mueser, Daiuto, & Stickle, 1998; Johnson, Hunsley, Greenberg, & Schindler, 1999), demonstrating impressive treatment effect sizes and stable recovery rates from relationship distress. Key change events in EFT have been identified, as well as the kinds of clients who are most suited to this form of couples therapy (Johnson & Greenberg, 1988; Johnson & Talitman, 1997). EFT has been used with depressed partners, families, and, more specifically, it has been adapted and used with partners who are dealing with PTSD as a result of past physical and sexual abuse, violent crime, natural disasters, chronic and terminal illness, and a small number of combat veterans (Johnson & Williams-Keeler, 1998).

The process of therapy in EFT is mapped into nine steps. In the first four of these steps, couples deescalate their negative cycles of interaction, such as critical pursuit followed by defensive withdrawal. In the middle phase of therapy (steps 5–7), they shift their interactional positions toward increased accessibility and responsiveness; for example, withdrawn partners reengage and critical partners risk being vulnerable and open and asking for their attachment needs to be met. This shift culminates in bonding events that then redefine the safety of the connection between partners. These changes are consolidated in the last two steps of therapy and a recent 2-year follow-up suggests they are then relatively stable (Clothier, Manion, Gordon Walker, & Johnson, 2002). With trauma couples a psychoeducational component concerning the nature of trauma is included and the couples are helped to frame the trauma in ways that do not continue to damage the relationship, as suggested by Figley (1989). Trauma symptoms are linked to negative interactions in the relationship and both partners are framed as being victimized by them. The partners are encouraged to stand together against the common enemies of the echoes of trauma and the cycles of interaction that isolate them from each other and perpetuate attachment insecurity. The process of therapy also tends to be longer (30 sessions rather than 12–15) for traumatized couples and the survivor is often also in individual therapy of some kind. There is more and more recognition that trauma victims often need more than one kind of intervention or modality because of the encompassing and multidimensional nature of their problems.

An observer would typically see an EFT therapist creating a secure base in the session by attuning to and collaborating with the partners and then exploring the leading edge of couples' emotional experience, beyond automatic reactive emotions to key attachment responses. The therapist is a process consultant, respectfully following and leading the clients as they reshape and redefine their relationships. The therapist might differentiate, heighten, and explore a partner's anger until the vulnerability underlying that anger emerges. She/he then shapes new interactions by asking partners to share these underlying feelings with their spouses and encouraging the spouses to respond. A withdrawn partner, for example, might for the first time be able to express his fear of his traumatized wife's rage and how it inhibits his desire to support her. A full description of EFT interventions is beyond the scope of this chapter and may be found elsewhere (Johnson, 1993, 1996, 1999; Johnson & Greenberg, 1995). A shorthand image of EFT might be that it is a therapy where experiential humanists, such as Rogers and Perls, meet systemic therapists, such as Minuchin and Fishman (Minuchin & Fishman, 1981; Perls, 1973; Rogers, 1951).

The process of change as the couple journeys toward more secure connection and how this process counters the effects of trauma is now illustrated in an excerpt of a couples therapy session with Carol and David. Another excerpt of a couples session where the couple relationship evokes and then provides a secure base for dealing with a traumatic flashback can be found in the literature (Johnson & Williams-Keeler, 1998). It is worth noting that David and Carol were dealing with trauma that was essentially unaddressed, therapeutic efforts having focused on her eating disorder. This couple had completed the first stage of change in EFT; they had deescalated the negative cycles of criticize-withdraw and withdraw-withdraw that had taken over their relationship and recognized the role of Carol's trauma in defining their relationship. The second stage of change, where couples shift their interactional positions, had progressed and David had reengaged and become much more accessible and responsive. The task now was for Carol to become more open, vulnerable, and connected to her spouse and begin to ask for her attachment needs to be met. This is called a "softening" in EFT and has been empirically linked to successful change (Johnson & Greenberg, 1988). At this point the echoes of trauma usually intensify as survivors risk emotional engagement with their partners. The main themes that emerge are the fear of closeness and difficulties with affect regulation in general, the risk involved in creating new trusting interactions, the effect of the echoes of trauma on the partner (David), and the survivor Carol's struggle with self-disgust and shame and how this struggle impacts the relationship. Following is a session excerpt:

David: I have to watch everything I say. I can't get through to her. So she's right, I do still withdraw. I get to where I give up.

Therapist: You would like to comfort her. (David nods empathically.) It feels sad not to be able to reach for her when you know she is hurting?

David: (Very softly, looking at his wife, who is staring at the floor.) I'd really like to hold her, to make it better.

Therapist: Can you tell her, David? (Motioning with her hand towards Carol.)

David: Let me hold you, just let me be there. (He stretches his arms out to her; Carol turns in her chair so her shoulder is towards him and looks away.)

Therapist: What is happening, Carol? David is reaching for you, do you see him? (She nods.) What is happening right now?

Carol: I feel irritated. (She glances at David and then turns to the therapist.) See, he's crying now. I'm obviously toxic. He should stay away.

Therapist: When you see him reach for you, you feel irritation and you feel afraid that you might hurt him? Is that right?

Carol: Yeah. I can't handle nice things, my stomach twists, I have nowhere to put it. (David weeps.) (Carol turns to the therapist.) You see, I'm a disappointment no matter what!

Therapist: What happens to you when he reaches and tells you that he wants to help?

Carol: (Long silence. She answers in a flat voice.) Don't know (pause) well, I get this "ping" feeling.

Therapist: Ping, hum, like is that alarm? (She nods.) Do you believe him?

Carol: No, so I'm mad. And yes, and it's scary. He might get close. He might want sex, and I'll disappoint him. I should be able to respond to him. I'm untreatable.

Therapist: So "ping" is anger. No one ever protected you and David sometimes withdraws too. And "ping" is fear. People you have trusted have burned you. Closeness is just so scary, the alarm goes off.

Carol: I should be over all this. I'm defective. I feel better giving to David. It's hard for me to, well, I don't like receiving.

Therapist: Aha. All this anger and fear. The "ping" comes and you can't take anything in, can't put food in your mouth or let David give to you, comfort you. It's all too scary.

Carol: I want to crawl under the rug. I can't breathe. (She grips the chair arm. Her hands are shaking.)

Therapist: It's okay, Carol. You're here, in my office. No one will hurt you here. This is so hard. You needed this alarm system, it probably saved your life. You so needed comfort, especially when your mum died and those who came close hurt you so badly, terrified you. All you could do was try to be invisible, hide, stay away and get smaller.

Carol: Yes, not eat. The more I eat, the more I feel.

Therapist: Aha. And if David comforts you, and you let him come close and touch you, let him see you, it might feel like those other times . . . and so the alarm goes off.

Carol: My memory is tangible. I can still feel his hands on me. I can still hear his laughter and I feel sick. The only way out is less of me.

Therapist: Was there ever a time when all this shame and fear and anger didn't step between you and David, when the dragon didn't step between? When there was another way out?

Carol: In the very beginning maybe. I still trust David more than anyone. But, if I feel upset, everyone is the enemy.

Therapist: So what would you like from him now, Carol?

Carol: I'd like him to be there and let me go through this and be there, but not too close right now.

Therapist: You can't let him comfort you right now, but you want him to stand beside you while you fight the dragon? (She agrees and nods her head.) Tell him. (The therapist motions with her hand.)

Carol: (She turns, makes eye contact with David, tears and speaks very softly.) Stand with me. . . . Can I ask you?

David: (To the therapist.) She is worth fighting for. (He turns to Carol.) You are worth fighting for.

Carol: (She smiles and turns to the therapist.) He's my boomerang. He keeps coming back. He gives me courage.

David: It's easier, now that I understand what is going on. I do hold back. . . . I'm sometimes. . . . I don't know what to do, how she'll react. I get overwhelmed, kind of numb. But I'm here. I'm here for the long haul.

As this excerpt suggests, when David offers Carol a safe haven, the violation of human connection she has experienced prevents her from responding. There is no way to him and to secure attachment but through her trauma and its aftermath.

Carol and David have made considerable progress. They can now sometimes eat together; Carol is no longer consumed with shame if David sees her put food in her mouth. Carol has agreed to go for individual therapy and work specifically with her trauma experiences. They hold hands as they walk back to the parking lot after sessions and he sees her rage as part of the trauma and does not become injured by it. He is more responsive to her and she can tell him when she can be touched and when she "has no skin" and must be alone. She can also break the one rule of survival in her family, which was "keep your mouth shut," and tell him when she is flooded with fear. She says, "I take little steps. . . . The closer I get the scarier it is, but . . . it's happening. I never really expected to be, well, attached. Thank God he's still here."

If a couples therapy intervention can help couples like David and Carol create a secure base from which to deal with trauma and, implicit in this process, revise working models of self and other and affect regulation strategies, can couples therapy help couples deal with trauma with a small t? Specifically, can couples therapy help partners deal with specific incidents that have defined the key relationship in their lives as insecure? As Simpson and Rholes (1994) observed, the quality of a relationship seems to be "unduly influenced by those occasions when one member of a couple is seriously distressed and the other either provides proximity or fails to do so" (p. 22). Intense versions of such incidents, which Johnson and Whiffen (1999) termed attachment injuries, result in obsessive rumination and often lead to clinical depression in the injured spouse. This spouse brings up the incident again and again, at times of conflict and at times of potential risk taking or intimacy. The other spouse, often not understanding the significance of the incident and despairing of finding any kind of closure around it, avoids and defends. These incidents tend to occur when a partner is particularly vulnerable at crucial moments of attachment need, experiencing abandonment, rejection, and betrayal. For example, a strong, rather dominant wife comes home from a minor operation just before which the surgeon informed her that if the worst scenario occurred she could die. Her husband responds to her walking into the house after the operation by saying, "Oh good, you're home. I'm off to bed." and going to sleep. The next morning, the wife overhears a conversation between her husband and a young female colleague where he is supportive and empathic and offers all kinds of assistance to this young woman. The marriage goes up in flames. The wife becomes highly symptomatic. Our experience is that this kind of incident becomes a touchstone that, until resolved, defines the relationship as insecure for the injured spouse and erodes the positives in the relationship; such incidents cannot be bypassed or left behind. Unless placed in an attachment context, these incidents are often hard to understand and exceedingly hard to resolve (Johnson, Makinen, & Millikin, 2001).

In EFT, where attachment is the theoretical map used to guide interventions, such incidents are focused on and, most often, resolved. The process of resolution goes through the following steps: The therapist names and clarifies the cycle of protest and complaint followed by defense and distance that characterizes the dialogue around this issue and spreads to the rest of the relationship; the injured party, with the help of the therapist, accesses the emotions that color the incident and places them in an attachment framework. The other partner is supported to frame the incident in terms of his or her attachment significance to the injured spouse and to acknowledge the injured partner's pain; the therapist supports this other partner to become more accessible and access fears and working models that block that accessibility; injured spouses are then able to walk through the incident with the therapist beside them, share their sense of loss and attachment fears, and take the risk of asking for their attachment needs to be met. When the other partner responds to this, a bonding event occurs that redefines the attachment in the relationship. Once attachment security is no longer an issue, other pragmatic problems and issues are relatively easy to deal with. Once attachment security is established, partners can use their relationship to help them regulate negative affective states and are less vulnerable to destructive attempts at self-regulation such as substance abuse and eating disorders (van der Kolk, 1996).

Does the therapist have to adapt couples therapy to partners with different attachment styles to build a secure base? It is unlikely that all trauma survivors or distressed couples with specific attachment injuries are fearful-avoidants as described by Bartholomew and Horowitz (1991). The change process then differs somewhat depending on partners' styles (Johnson & Whiffen, 1999). From an attachment point of view, change in relationships is assumed to arise from compelling emotional experiences that disconfirm past fears and biases (Collins & Read, 1994) and allow working models to be elaborated and revised (Fiske & Taylor, 1984). In the middle stage of EFT, key shifts in interactional positions occur that shape empathic responsiveness and challenge working models of self and other. As Rothbard and Shaver (1994) suggested, the lack of fit between working models and reality has to be extremely apparent for change to occur. Events that are inconsistent with existing models require more attention and processing (Planalp, 1987). The more closed and diffuse the models, the more the therapist has to direct attention to these disconfirming events, block discounting attributions, and track and clarify how partners are processing each element of the event. How do such change events, where partners own and coherently articulate attachment needs and fears to their spouse, impact working models? First, this process involves an expansion of a partner's sense of self, as when a wife says, "Maybe I can talk about my needs; I do not always have to stand alone." Second, the other partner shifts his appraisal of his spouse ("She isn't so dangerous; she was scared all the time, not just angry") and, when he responds, his sense of self expands ("She needs me. I am important to her and I can give her what she needs"). Third, as he reassures her, her beliefs about the responsiveness of others are challenged and his acceptance and reassurance also increase her sense of self-worth. These events, which usually end in bonding sequences of confiding and comforting, rewrite the script for the relationship and redefine it as a safe haven. New dialogues allow models to be updated and revised and new cycles of behavior confirm new expanded models.

Partners with different styles encounter specific difficulties in this process. Avoidant partners require that the therapist help them to stay connected to present emotional experience. Such partners may then move from the "numbness" expressed earlier in therapy to formulating a sense of intimidation and shame. New emotions often emerge at this point, such as a sense of isolation that has never surfaced before or attachment longings that have always been inhibited. The therapist slows down if emotions become too overwhelming and focuses and reflects on the process, affirming how difficult this process is for the individual. It is necessary to monitor exits into rationalizations and content-oriented instrumental issues that derail the process of engagement. These exits are highly aversive for the other spouse, especially if he or she is anxiously attached. Avoidant partners can now begin to articulate their interactional position and the associated model of attachment. For example, "I guess I have always been hiding. I was never going to let anyone close enough to hurt me again. The only thing to do was to numb out and go on. Now I don't know how to open up." As emotions change, so new action tendencies emerge (e.g., grief gives rise to a desire to be comforted) and these individuals can directly share their attachment needs with their partners and ask for help to become more engaged.

Anxious partners tend to revert to blaming the other when their emotions become overwhelming and the therapist has to support them and redirect the process. Anxious partners' inability to tolerate ambiguity or uncertainty makes it difficult for them to be open to new responses from their spouses. They find ways to discount new information. The therapist invites the person to continue to process new cues. A therapist might state, "It's hard for you to believe him as he says that he's intimidated; he doesn't know how to please you, so he just freezes up. You see him as so powerful, as choosing to shut you out, but he's actually intimidated by you." At this stage in therapy, these partners have to risk asking for their newly articulated attachment needs to be met. These risks fly in the face of their working models and fears of rejection and abandonment. They must be allowed to take small steps and helped to regulate their affect as well as being given direction in interactional tasks. For example, the therapist might say, "Can you ask him to hold you?" and, if the person refuses, the therapist explores the emotion and the beliefs that inhibit this response and revises the task, asking, "Can you tell him how hard this is?" Although the process of creating secure attachment varies somewhat according to where partners start from, the change process always involves new formulations of key emotional responses related to attachment and new interactions based on these new formulations that foster responsiveness in both spouses.

The creation of secure attachment through couples therapy is of course not possible for all survivors of trauma. Some are so badly scared that they cannot ever tolerate a close relationship. Others handle their wounds in ways that preclude the kind of processes described here; for example, EFT is not suited to violent couples. However, for many couples, traumatized by big T events or struggling with the little t of helplessness in the face of specific attachment injuries, couples therapy, especially if it uses an attachment perspective, would seem to be a logical and crucial part of treatment. EFT is not the only couples and family therapy that uses an attachment model to understand and change relationships. Byng-Hall in England (1995) and Diamond and Siqueland in Philadelphia (1995) also use attachment theory as a guide to modifying family relationships. The strength of attachment theory is that it looks both within and between, to how people organize their experience of relatedness and how patterns of interaction confirm and create that experience.

How can recovery from trauma be defined? It would necessarily contain many elements. A list of such elements might include authority over remembering and the ability to construct a continuous coherent life narrative, affect tolerance, self-esteem and cohesion, the assignation of new meanings to the trauma, and the capacity for trust and creation of safe attachment (Harvey, 1996). It seems that the creation of safe attachment is the basic building block on which all the other elements stand and is, in fact, a prerequisite to the development of these other elements. It may be that the words *treatment* and *antidote* offer a distorted frame, because they imply that professionals must create an intervention and implement it in order to "cure" someone. Perhaps it is more accurate to acknowledge that secure attachment between intimates is nature's way of protecting us from the terrors of life and helping us when we are wounded by these terrors. What therapists have to do is to help people access this natural process and face the dragon of trauma together.

REFERENCES

Ainsworth, M. D. S., Blehar, M. C., Waters, E., & Wall, S. (1978). *Patterns of attachment: A psychological study of the strange situation.* Hillsdale, NJ: Lawrence Erlbaum Associates.

Alexander, J. K., Holtzworth-Munroe, A., & Jameson, P. (1994). The process and outcome of marital and family therapy: Research review and evaluation. In A. Bergin & S. Garfield (Eds.), *Handbook of psychotherapy and behavior change* (4th ed., pp. 595–607). New York: Wiley.

Alexander, P. C. (1993). The differential effects of abuse characteristics and attachment in the prediction of long-term effects of sexual abuse. *Journal of Interpersonal Violence, 8,* 346–362.

Alexander, P. C. (1997). Application of attachment theory to the study of sexual abuse. *Journal of Consulting and Clinical Psychology, 60,* 185 195.

Alexander, P. C., & Alexander, C. L. (1994). An attachment approach to psychotherapy with the incest survivor. *Psychotherapy, 31,* 665–675.

American Psychological Association. (1994). *Diagnostic and statistical manual of mental disorders—DSM-IV* (4th ed.). Washington, DC: American Psychological Association.

Atkinson, L. (1997). Attachment and psychopathology: From laboratory to clinic. In L. Atkinson & K. Zucker (Eds.), *Attachment and psychopathology* (pp. 3–16). New York: Guilford Press.

Badgely, R., Allard, H., McCormick, N., Proudfoot, P., Fortin, D., Oglivie, D., Rae-Grant, Q., Gelinas, P., Penin, L., & Sutherland, S. (1984). *Sexual offences against children (Vol. 1).* Ottawa: Canadian Government Publishing Centre.

Bartholomew, K., & Horowitz, L. M. (1991). Attachment styles among young adults: A test of a four category model. *Journal of Personality and Social Psychology, 61,* 226–244.

Baucom, D., Shoham, V., Mueser, K., Daiuto, A., & Stickle, T. (1998). Empirically supported couple and family interventions for marital distress and adult health problems. *Journal of Consulting and Clinical Psychology, 66,* 53–88.

Bowlby, J. (1973). *Attachment and loss: Vol. 2. Separation.* New York: Basic Books.

Bowlby, J. (1982). *Attachment and loss: Vol. 1. Attachment.* New York: Basic Books. (Original work published 1969)

Bowlby, J. (1988). *A secure base.* New York: Basic Books.

Brennen, K., Shaver, P., & Tobey, A. E. (1991). Attachment styles, gender and parental problem drinking. *Journal of Social and Personal Relationships, 8,* 451–466.

Byng-Hall, J. (1995). Creating a secure family base: Some implications of attachment theory for family therapy. *Family Process, 34,* 45–58.

Cicchetti, D., Toth, S., & Lynch, M. (1995). Bowlby's dream comes full circle. *Advances in Clinical Child Psychology, 17,* 1–75.

Clothier, P., Manion, I., Gordon Walker, J., & Johnson, S. M. (2002). Emotionally focused marital therapy for the parents of chronically ill children: A two year follow-up. *Journal of Marital & Family Therapy, 28,* 391–399.

Collins, N., & Read, S. (1994). Cognitive representations of attachment: The structure and function of working models. In K. Bartholomew & D. Perlman (Eds.), *Attachment processes in adulthood* (pp. 53–92). London: Kingsley.

Diamond, G., & Siqueland, L. (1995). Family therapy for the treatment of depressed adolescents. *Psychotherapy, 32,* 77–90.

Egeland, B., Jacobvitz, D., & Sroufe, A. (1988). Breaking the cycle of abuse. *Child Development*, *59*, 1080–1088.

Feeney, J. A. (1998). Adult attachment and relationship-centered anxiety: Responses to physical and emotional distancing. In J. A. Simpson & W. S. Rholes (Eds.), *Attachment theory and close relationships* (pp. 189–220). New York: Guilford Press.

Figley, C. R. (1989). *Healing traumatized families*. San Francisco, CA: Jossey Bass.

Finklehor, D. (1984). *Child sexual abuse: New theory and research*. New York: Free Press.

Finklehor, D., & Browne, A. (1984). The traumatic impact of child sexual abuse: A conceptualization. *American Journal of Orthopsychiatry*, *55*, 530–541.

Fiske, S. T., & Taylor, S. E. (1984). *Social cognition*. New York: Random House.

Foa, E. B., Hearst-Ikeda, D., & Perry, K. J. (1995). Evaluation of a brief behavioral program for the prevention of chronic PTSD in recent assault victims. *Journal of Consulting and Clinical Psychology*, *63*, 948–955.

Gottman, J. (1991). Predicting the longitudinal course of marriages. *Journal of Marital and Family Therapy*, *17*, 3–7.

Gottman, J. (1994). An agenda for marital therapy. In S. Johnson & L. Greenberg (Eds.), *The heart of the matter: Perspectives on emotion in marital therapy* (pp. 258–296). New York: Brunner/Mazel.

Gottman, J. M., Coan, J., Carrere, S., & Swanson, C. (1998). Predicting marital happiness and stability from newlywed interactions. *Journal of Marriage and the Family*, *60*, 5–22.

Gottman, J., & Krokoff, L. J. (1989). The relationship between marital interaction and marital satisfaction: A longitudinal view. *Journal of Consulting and Clinical Psychology*, *57*, 47–52.

Gottman, J., & Levenson, R. (1986). Assessing the role of emotion in marriage. *Behavioral Assessment*, *8*, 31–48.

Greenberg, L., & Johnson, S. M. (1988). *Emotionally focused therapy for couples*. New York: Guilford Press.

Harvey, M. R. (1996). An ecological view of psychological trauma and trauma recovery. *Journal of Traumatic Stress*, *9*, 3–23.

Herman, J. L. (1992). *Trauma and recovery*. New York: Basic Books.

Hofer, M. A. (1984). Relationships as regulators: A psychobiologic perspective on bereavement. *Psychosomatic Medicine*, *46*, 183–197.

Holmes, J. (1996). *Attachment, intimacy, autonomy: Using attachment theory in adult psychotherapy*. Northvale, NJ: Aronson.

Johnson, S. M. (1993). *Healing broken bonds: A marital therapy training video*. (Available from the Ottawa Couple and Family Institute, #201, 1869 Carling Ave., Ottawa, Canada K2A 1E6)

Johnson, S. M. (1996). *The practice of emotionally focused marital therapy: Creating connection*. New York: Brunner/Mazel.

Johnson, S. M. (1999). Emotionally focused couples therapy: Straight to the heart. In J. Donovan (Ed.), *Short term couple therapy* (pp. 13–42). New York: Guilford Press.

Johnson, S. M., & Greenberg, L. (1988). Relating process to outcome in marital therapy. *Journal of Marital and Family Therapy*, *14*, 175–183.

Johnson, S. M., & Greenberg, L. (1995). The emotionally focused approach to problems in adult attachment. In N. Jacobson & A. Gurman (Eds.), *Clinical handbook of couples therapy* (pp. 121–141). New York: Guilford Press.

Johnson, S. M., Hunsley, J., Greenberg, L., & Schindler, D. (1999). Emotionally focused couples therapy: Status and challenges. *Clinical Psychology: Science and Practice*, *6*, 67–79.

Johnson, S. M., Makinen, J., & Millikin, J. (2001). Attachment injuries in couple relationships: A new perspective on impasses in couples therapy. *Journal of Marital and Family Therapy*, *27*, 145–155.

Johnson, S. M., & Talitman, E. (1997). Predictors of success in emotionally focused marital therapy. *Journal of Marital and Family Therapy*, *23*, 135–152.

Johnson, S., & Whiffen, V. (1999). Made to measure: Adapting emotionally focused couples therapy to couples attachment styles. In M. Whisman & D. Snyder (Eds.), Affective and developmental considerations in couples therapy [Special issue]. *Clinical Psychology: Science and Practice, 6,* 366–381.

Johnson, S. M., & Williams-Keeler, L. (1998). Creating healing relationships for couples dealing with trauma: The use of emotionally focused therapy. *Journal of Marital and Family Therapy, 24,* 25–40.

Kirschner, S., & Kirschner, D. (1996). Relational components of the incest survivor syndrome. In F. Kaslow (Ed.), *Handbook of relational diagnosis and dysfunctional family patterns* (pp. 407–419). New York: Wiley.

Kobak, R., & Cole, H. (1991). Attachment and meta-monitoring: Implications for adolescent autonomy and psychopathology. In D. Cicchetti & S. Toth (Eds.), *Disorders and dysfunctions of the self* (pp. 267–297). Rochester, NY: University of Rochester Press.

Kobak, R., & Duemmler, S. (1994). Attachment and conversation: Toward a discourse analysis of adolescent and adult security. In K. Bartholomew & D. Perlman (Eds.), *Attachment processes in adulthood* (pp. 121–149). London: Kingsley.

Lundberg-Love, P. K., Marmion, S., Ford, K., Geffner, R., & Peacock, L. (1992). The long term consequences of childhood incestuous victimization upon adult women's psychological symptomatology. *Journal of Child Sexual Abuse, 1,* 81–102.

Main, M., & Hesse, E. (1990). Parent's unresolved traumatic experiences are related to infant disorganized attachment status. In M. Greenberg & D. Cicchetti (Eds.), *Attachment in the preschool years* (pp. 161–182). Chicago: University of Chicago Press.

Main, M., Kaplan, N., & Cassidy, J. (1985). Security in infancy, childhood and adulthood: A move to the level of representation. In I. Bretherton & E. Waters (Eds.), *Growing points of attachment theory and research* (Society for Research on Child Development Monograph No. 50, pp. 66–104). MA: Blackwell.

McCann, I. L., & Pearlman, L. A. (1990). *Psychological trauma and the adult survivor.* New York: Brunner/Mazel.

McFarlane, A. C., & van der Kolk, B. A. (1996). Trauma and its challenge to society. In B. A. van der Kolk & A. C. McFarlane, et al. (Eds.), *Traumatic stress: The effects of overwhelming experience on mind, body, and society* (pp. 24–46). New York: Guilford Press.

Mikulincer, M. (1998a). Adult attachment style and individual differences in functional versus dysfunctional experiences of anger. *Journal of Personality and Social Psychology, 74,* 513–524.

Mikulincer, M. (1998b). Attachment working models and the sense of trust: An exploration of interactional goals and affect regulation. *Journal of Personality and Social Psychology, 74,* 1209–1224.

Mikulincer, M., & Florian, V. (1998). The relationship between adult attachment styles and emotional and cognitive reactions to stressful events. In J. Simpson & W. S. Rholes (Eds.), *Attachment theory and close relationships* (pp. 143–165). New York: Guilford Press.

Mikulincer, M., Florian, V., & Tolmacz, R. (1990). Attachment styles and fear of death: A case of affect regulation. *Journal of Personality and Social Psychology, 58,* 273–380.

Mikulincer, M., Florian, V., & Weller, A. (1993). Attachment style, coping strategies and posttraumatic psychological distress: The impact of the Gulf War in Israel. *Journal of Personality and Social Psychology, 64,* 817–826.

Minuchin, S., & Fishman, H. C. (1981). *Family therapy techniques.* Cambridge, MA: Harvard University Press.

Ondaatje, M. (1993). *The English patient.* New York: Vintage Books.

Pagels, E. (1988). *Adam, Eve and the serpent.* New York: Random House.

Pennebaker, J. W. (1985). Traumatic experience and psychosomatic disease: Exploring the psychology of behavioral inhibition, obsession and confiding. *Canadian Psychology, 26,* 82–95.

Perls, F. (1973). *The gestalt approach and eye-witness to therapy.* Ben Lomond, CA: Science and Behavior Books.

Pierce, R. A. (1994). Helping couples make automatic emotional contact. In S. M. Johnson & L. S. Greenberg (Eds.), *The heart of the matter: Perspectives on emotion in marital therapy* (pp. 75–107). New York: Brunner/Mazel.

Planalp, S. (1987). Interplay between relational knowledge and events. In R. Burnett, P. McGhee, & D. Clarke (Eds.), *Accounting for relationships* (pp. 175–191). New York: Methuen.

Reid, K. S., Wampler, R. S., & Taylor, D. (1996). The alienated partner: Responses to traditional therapies for adult sex abuse survivors. *Journal of Marital and Family Therapy, 22,* 443–453.

Riggs, D., Byrne, C., Weathers, F., & Litz, B. (1998). The quality of the intimate relationships of male Vietnam veterans: Problems associated with posttraumatic stress disorder. *Journal of Traumatic Stress, 11,* 87–101.

Rogers, C. (1951). *Client centered therapy.* Boston: Houghton Mifflin.

Rothbard, J., & Shaver, P. (1994). Continuity of attachment across the life span. In M. Sperling & W. Berman (Eds.), *Attachment in adults* (pp. 31–71). New York: Guilford Press.

Russell, D. E. (1984). *Sexual exploitation: Rape, child sexual abuse and workplace harassment.* Newbury Park, CA: Sage.

Schore, A. N. (1994). *Affect regulation and the organization of self.* Hillsdale, NJ: Lawrence Erlbaum Associates.

Shaver, P., & Clarke, C. (1994). The psychodynamics of adult romantic attachment. In J. M. Masling & R. F. Bornstein (Eds.), *Empirical perspectives on object relations theory* (pp. 105–156). Washington, DC: American Psychological Association.

Shaver, P., Collins, N., & Clarke, C. (1996). Attachment styles and internal working models of self and relationship partners. In G. Fletcher & J. Fitness (Eds.), *Knowledge structures in close relationships: A social psychological approach* (pp. 25–61). Mahwah, NJ: Lawrence Erlbaum Associates.

Simpson, J., & Rholes, W. S. (1994). Stress and secure base relationship in adulthood. In K. Bartholomew & D. Perlman (Eds.), *Attachment processes in adulthood* (pp. 181–204). London: Kingsley.

Simpson, J., & Rholes, W. S. (1998). Attachment in adulthood. In J. Simpson & S. Rholes (Eds.), *Attachment theory and close relationships* (pp. 3–21). New York: Guilford Press.

Solomon, Z., Waysman, M., Levy, G., Fried, B., Mikulincer, M., Bennenishty, R., Florian, V., & Bleich, A. (1992). From front line to home front: A study of temporary traumatization. *Family Process, 31,* 289–302.

van der Kolk, B. (1996). The complexity of adaptation to trauma. In B. van der Kolk, A. McFarlane, & L. Weisaeth (Eds.), *Traumatic stress* (pp. 182–213). New York: Guilford Press.

van der Kolk, B., Perry, C., & Herman, J. (1991). Childhood origins of self-destructive behavior. *American Journal of Psychiatry, 148,* 1665–1671.

10

Toddler-Parent Psychotherapy for Depressed Mothers and Their Offspring: Implications for Attachment Theory

Dante Cicchetti
Sheree L. Toth
Fred A. Rogosch
Mt. Hope Family Center, University of Rochester

Attachment theory provides a powerful perspective for investigating the nature of the relationship between caregiving experiences and developmental outcomes (Ainsworth, Blehar, Waters, & Wall, 1978; Crittenden, 1992; George & Solomon, 1999; Main, Kaplan, & Cassidy, 1985; Sroufe, 1983; Sroufe & Fleeson, 1988). John Bowlby consistently articulated the potential of attachment theory for contributing to an understanding of the pathways through which early experiences of caregiving could eventuate in mental health or in psychopathology. Moreover, Bowlby believed that attachment theory could provide a framework for implementing therapeutic interventions (Bowlby, 1977a, 1977b, 1988).

In the last decade, investigators have increasingly directed their efforts toward understanding and modifying attachment relationships in high-risk and psychiatric populations (Cicchetti & Greenberg, 1991; Cicchetti, Toth, & Lynch, 1995; Crittenden, 1992; Lieberman & Pawl, 1990; van IJzendoorn, Juffer, & Duyvesteyn, 1995). In fact, examinations of attachment relationships in atypical populations have resulted in the identification of additional patterns of attachment organization not evident when normal groups of youngsters were observed (Crittenden, 1988; Main & Solomon, 1990; Solomon & George, 1999a; Vondra & Barnett, 1999). Thus, the utilization of attachment theory to elucidate developmental processes in atypical populations holds much promise not only for modifying theoretical conceptualizations derived from normal populations, but also for informing psychotherapeutic interventions.

In this chapter, we begin by summarizing research that has found that youngsters with depressed parents are at risk for the development of insecure attachment relationships. We then review some representative interventions that have been informed by attachment theory. This theoretical and empirical exposition serves at the backdrop for describing the attachment-informed intervention, toddler-parent psychotherapy (Lieberman, 1992), that we provided to depressed mothers and their toddlers. We then present outcome data on the efficacy of the preventive intervention. Finally, in order to provide a more fine-grained analysis of the implementation and course of the preventive intervention, we examine two case studies, incorporating information on the mothers' representational models of their childhood attachment relationships, their representations of their child, and the mother-child attachment relationship prior to the provision of intervention. Follow-up information on these same constructs after completion of the intervention also is examined. The presentation of these case studies is framed so as to inform issues relevant to theoretical conceptualizations of attachment. Before turning to our specific intervention, we provide a framework for understanding why offspring of depressed mothers are at risk for the development of insecure attachment relationships and, therefore, why the provision of an attachment-informed intervention is considered to be important.

ATTACHMENT IN OFFSPRING OF DEPRESSED MOTHERS

Mothers who suffer from major depressive disorders are likely to struggle with the demands of providing early care for their infants. The features of the disorder, including anhedonia, difficulty in negative affect regulation, feelings of worthlessness, helplessness, and hopelessness, sleep disturbances, and decrements in role functioning conspire to generate an early relational context that may impair the development of the mother-child relationship and consequent child adaptation. Moreover, depressive disorders frequently have evolved from difficulties in mothers' own childhood attachment experiences.

Linkages between disturbances in parent-child relations and the emergence of depression have been made by theoreticians operating in the traditions of psychoanalytic and object relations theory (see, e.g., Abraham, 1911; Arieti & Bemporad, 1978; Bowlby, 1980, 1988; Jacobson, 1971; Mahler, 1968; Sandler & Joffe, 1965). Additionally, many retrospective studies have found that depressed adults report histories involving inadequate or abusive parental care (Bemporad & Romano, 1992).

Insecurity in childhood attachment relationships thus not only may contribute to mothers' depressive disorders, but also may influence the manner in which they are able to relate to their young offspring via the operation of the mothers' internal working models of attachment relationships. In attempting to understand the effects of maternal depression on the attachment relationship with a child, the issue of psychological unavailability must be considered. From the perspective of attachment theory, physical absence of a caregiver may be much less important than the child's experience of the parent as psychologically unavailable. Moreover, during periods of parental depression, children are likely to be confronted with caregivers who are inconsistent, unpredictable, insensitive, hostile, or intrusive (Cohn, Matias, Tronick, Lyons-Ruth, & Connell, 1986; Cummings & Cicchetti, 1990; Egeland & Sroufe, 1981; Lyons-Ruth, Zoll, Connell, & Grunebaum, 1986). Such behavior in depressed caregivers may interfere with the capacity to relate to their child in a way that promotes the development of a secure attachment relationship.

Because children with depressed parents are especially likely to be faced with the psychological unavailability of parents, the role of depression in contributing to insecure attachment relationships has been a fertile area of inquiry. To date, the results of existing studies have varied with respect to the effect of maternal depression on the quality of attachment. In view of the heterogeneous outcomes evidenced by children with depressed mothers, developmental researchers have been confronted with the challenge of specifying the processes underlying this diversity (Teti, Gelfand, Messinger, & Isabella, 1995).

In general, investigations of attachment security in infants, toddlers, and preschoolers with depressed caregivers suggest that offspring of depressed mothers are more likely to evidence increased rates of insecurity (cf. Gaensbauer, Harmon, Cytryn, & McKnew, 1984; Lyons-Ruth, Connell, Grunebaum, & Botein, 1990; Radke-Yarrow, Cummings, Kuczynski, & Chapman, 1985). However, findings regarding attachment insecurity vary as a function of sample characteristics (e.g., depressed poverty-stricken mothers vs. depressed middle-socioeconomic-status mothers, hospitalized vs. community samples of depressed mothers), as well as transient versus more prolonged exposure to maternal depression (cf. Campbell, Cohn, & Meyers, 1995; Frankel & Harmon, 1996; Murray, 1992; Teti et al., 1995). Additionally, issues such as the presence or absence of other supportive individuals (e.g., nondisordered fathers) or the overall family context in which the depressed mother resides are likely to exert a major impact on the child's ultimate functioning (Cicchetti, Rogosch, & Toth, 1998; Downey & Coyne, 1990).

The investigation reported in this chapter was conceived in view of remaining questions regarding the effects of maternal depression on child development and, more specifically, on the mother-child attachment relationship, as well as the potential for intervention to foster a positive relationship. We sought to examine the effects of maternal depression on child development in a relatively high-functioning group of mothers and, furthermore, to evaluate the efficacy of a preventive intervention in promoting mother-child attachment security. The intervention was predicated on the importance of addressing the interplay among maternal representational models of their attachment experiences in childhood, the mother's representations of her child, and the quality of the developing attachment relationship between mother and child. Before directing our attention to this program, we next examine representative interventions that have been provided to foster attachment security in order to provide a framework within which to conceptualize the provision and evaluation of our intervention.

APPLICATIONS OF ATTACHMENT THEORY
TO PREVENTIVE INTERVENTIONS

Although a number of attachment-informed interventions have been developed, they typically have involved the provision of treatment to multiproblem populations (cf. Egeland & Erickson, 1990; Erickson, Korfmacher, & Egeland, 1992; Lyons-Ruth et al., 1990). Consequently, an array of services has been provided in order to meet the extensive needs of the families being served. This diversity in service provision has made it difficult to evaluate outcomes that may be attributed to changes in representational models versus results that may be due to other factors, such as a reduction of environmental stressors. Therefore, the application of attachment-informed interventions to populations with more circumscribed problems, such as mothers suffering from a major depressive disorder without co-occurring poverty and its associated risk factors, can be informative through more effectively isolating the specific factors that influence outcome.

In the area of attachment, theoreticians continue to grapple with whether modifying parental attachment organization, including their representations of their child, will result in behavioral change, as evidenced by improved parenting, or, conversely, whether improving parenting also may, independent of attention to parental attachment representations, result in relationship improvements between parent and child. To date, efforts to prevent or correct the development of insecure attachment between infant and caregiver have taken one of two stances (van IJzendoorn et al., 1995). One approach targets intervention at the behavioral level by seeking to improve parental sensitivity directly; the other method seeks to alter maternal representational models that are seen as precursive to the capacity to exhibit sensitivity. Stated simply, these approaches can be conceptualized as either behavioral or representational in their theoretical foci; parental sensitivity is a skill that can be taught according to behaviorally informed interventions, whereas in representational models of therapy, sensitivity is thought to occur as an outgrowth of the development of more positive internal working models.

In a meta-analysis of 12 studies of the effectiveness of preventive or therapeutic interventions in enhancing parental sensitivity or children's attachment security, van IJzendoorn et al. (1995) concluded that interventions were more effective in improving maternal sensitivity than in fostering children's attachment security. Moreover, longer, more representationally based intensive interventions appeared to be less effective than short-term behaviorally focused interventions. These conclusions, however, must be tempered by the absence of measures of parental representation, even in studies that sought to modify parental representation. Moreover, as noted by van IJzendoorn et al., if interventions fail to change parental representations, then intervention effects may not endure or may even be counterproductive when youngsters come to expect parental sensitivity that does not continue into future developmental periods because the parent learned only how to be sensitive for a specific point in development. In accordance with this thinking, parental responsivity to child needs may be more likely promoted in later periods of development if the parent has developed a more secure attachment organization through developing more positive working models of relationships. Additionally, only 2 of the 12 studies included in the meta-analysis utilized a more insight-oriented approach to intervention (Erickson et al., 1992; Lieberman, Weston, & Pawl, 1991), thereby precluding any extensive analysis of the efficacy of such approaches. Moreover, eight of the studies were targeted at low-income families, consequently increasing the likelihood of multiple stressors being present. With such multiproblem populations, behaviorally based approaches may be the most effective, whereas families who do not have to struggle with an array of life stressors and survival needs might benefit from more insight-oriented approaches.

In an important investigation that elucidates the use of a behavioral approach, van den Boom (1994) sought to promote secure attachment in well-functioning mothers and their infants who were drawn from lower socioeconomic backgrounds and who were selected based on their scores on a dimension of negative emotionality. A skills-training format that emphasized the acquisition of maternal sensitive responsiveness was utilized beginning when infants were 9 months old and lasting 3 months. Although this intervention did not seek to modify maternal representations of infants or internal working models, but focused instead on teaching mothers how to respond sensitively to their infants, the intervention was effective in enhancing maternal responsiveness and stimulation, in improving child sociability and cognitive sophistication during exploration, and in promoting secure attachments. With respect to the issue of enduring effects of intervention, improved parental responsiveness and child cooperation were found at age 3 (van den Boom, 1995). These findings were interpreted as indicating that maternal sensitivity is causally related to infant attachment security and that maternal sensitivity can be acquired through skills training (van den Boom, 1994).

Although the van den Boom (1994) study supports the utility of modifying parental behavior (e.g., sensitivity) in order to improve attachment security, maternal representations of the infants were not assessed. It is especially important to determine whether modifying parental behavior can also alter parental representations of the infant. Additionally, because the mothers in this sample were generally well functioning, despite their lower class membership and the stressors associated with financial pressures, the applicability of a skills-oriented approach such as this to less well-functioning mothers who are struggling with more serious conditions such as major psychopathology and histories of inadequate care remains to be determined.

Moreover, the type of maternal insecurity that is present may affect mothers' receptivity to various intervention strategies. Bakermans-Kranenburg, Juffer, and van IJzendoorn (1998) provided two types of short-term intervention to mothers with insecure attachment organizations. One of the interventions focused on the provision of information about sensitive parenting whereas the other also incorporated discussions about the mothers' early attachment experiences. These investigators found that maternal sensitive responsiveness was enhanced by the intervention, regardless of the type of maternal attachment insecurity or the type of intervention provided. However, mothers classified as insecure-dismissing tended to profit the most from feedback on sensitive parenting, whereas mothers classified as insecure-preoccupied tended to benefit the most from adding discussions about their childhood attachment experiences (Bakermans-Kranenburg et al.). Although these results must be viewed as preliminary given the constraints in reaching statistical power imposed by small sample size, they are consistent with an earlier investigation that elucidated differential responsivity to intervention as a function of attachment organization (Dozier, 1990).

Two interventions targeted specifically at offspring of depressed mothers sought to assess attachment security. Gelfand, Teti, Seiner, and Jameson (1996) found that a home-based intervention designed to improve maternal self-efficacy was not effective in improving attachment security in offspring. Similarly, Cooper and Murray (1997) also evaluated four types of intervention for mothers with postpartum depression. Mothers were assigned randomly to either routine primary care, nondirective counseling, cognitive-behavioral therapy, or attachment-theory-guided dynamic psychotherapy. With the exception of the primary care condition, all treatment groups evidenced fewer relationship difficulties with their children postintervention. However, improvements in attachment security did not occur. Thus, studies with diverse populations have yet to demonstrate consistently the ability of attachment-informed therapies to foster attachment security. Moreover, the relation between enhancing maternal attachment organization and subsequent improvements in offspring attachment security has not been examined.

A PREVENTIVE INTERVENTION FOR TODDLERS WITH DEPRESSED MOTHERS

Theoretical Background and Description of the Intervention

In view of the potential challenges to the development of secure attachment relationships that confront children with depressed caregivers, the continued provision and evaluation of preventive interventions for this population are extremely important. Although it is not uncommon for depressed women to receive therapeutic interventions for their depression that involve pharmacological treatments, individual therapy, or both, it is much less likely that such interventions recognize the woman as a mother and, consequently, address the relationship that is forming between mother and child. Unfortunately, disregard for this evolving relationship may result in greater risk for the emergence of an insecure attachment relationship and associated developmental difficulties for the child. Inattention to relational issues in depressed mothers, in turn, may serve to perpetuate maternal depression, as the caregiver may be confronted with current and future child behavior problems and the associated guilt resulting from the fear that her depression has interfered with effective parenting.

In the investigation reported in this chapter, an intervention approach that emanates from the rapidly growing field of infant mental health (Stern, 1995; Zeanah, 1993) was developed with the goal of improving the early mother-child relationship in women who had experienced a major unipolar depressive disorder at some time subsequent to the birth of their child. This intervention, referred to as toddler-parent psychotherapy (TPP), has its origins in the work of Selma Fraiberg, who described the pernicious influences that an unresolved parental past can exert on the evolving parent-child relationship (Fraiberg, Adelson, & Shapiro, 1975). Lieberman and her colleagues provided this form of intervention to

Latina mothers and their children who had insecure attachments (Lieberman et al., 1991).

In the work described in the current chapter, the theoretical underpinnings and techniques embodied by TPP (Lieberman et al., 1991) were applied to the provision of a preventive intervention for depressed mothers and their toddlers. In reflecting back on the two previously discussed approaches to improving attachment security (e.g., behavioral vs. representational), TPP clearly can be viewed as a representational intervention.

In TPP, mothers and their toddlers are seen in joint therapy sessions. It is through the observation of the toddler-mother dyad that therapeutic insights into the influence of maternal representation on parenting can be gained. In the language of attachment theory, TPP is designed to provide the mother with a corrective emotional experience in the context of the relationship with the therapist. Through empathy, respect, concern, accommodation, and positive regard, an environment is provided for the mother and toddler in which new experiences of self in relation to others and to the toddler can be internalized. Thus, if the mother has a generalized negative representational model of self and relationships, a therapeutic goal is to help the mother's models become more specific with regard to various relationship partners. Evolving positive representations of the therapist can be utilized to contrast with maternal representations of self in relation to parents. As the mother is able to reconstruct representations of self in relation to others through the therapeutic relationship, she also is able to reconstruct representations of herself in relation to her child. Thus, in this intervention, parallel processes occurring among the mother, child, and therapist all reflect relationship experiences that can result in modifications at the representational level for the mother and the child.

Within the therapeutic sessions, the therapist strives to alter the relationship between mother and toddler. Toward this end, therapists must attend to both the interactional and the representational levels as they are manifested during the therapy sessions. Maternal representations that have evolved from the mother's relationship history are viewed as affecting the character of the interactions between mother and child. Furthermore, interactions and toddler behaviors also evoke maternal representations of prior relationship experiences that influence the mother's reactions to the toddler and her experience of self. As such, seemingly ordinary behaviors between mother and toddler during therapy sessions are regarded as behavioral manifestations of representational themes. Through the use of observation and empathic comments, the therapist works toward helping the mother to recognize how her representations are manifested during her interactions with her toddler, thereby allowing for the clarification of distorted perceptions and alterations of how she experiences and perceives her toddler and herself. The therapist also attends to the nature of the interactions that occur between the mother and the toddler, the mother and the therapist, and the therapist and the toddler. Interactions in one relationship pair tend to elicit parallel interactions in other relationship pairs. Thus, the attention to parallel processes in interactions across relationships and the influence of representations on these interactions provide templates for modifying maternal representations as they are enacted behaviorally in the mother-child relationship.

To summarize, TPP seeks to highlight, clarify, and restructure the dynamic balance between representational and interactional contributions to the quality of the relationship between mother and child. Moreover, it is expected that the modified maternal representations that develop with regard to mother and child will also affect the mother's interactions with other relationship figures. In TPP, therapeutic change is seen as a result of increasing maternal understanding regarding the effects of prior relationships on current feelings and interactions. By expanding positive representations of the self and of the self in relation to others, it is expected that maternal sensitivity, responsivity, and attunement to the child will improve and maternal satisfaction with other relationships will increase.

Participants and Recruitment

Participants in this preventive intervention were recruited for a longitudinal study designed to evaluate the efficacy of a preventive intervention (TPP) for toddlers of depressed mothers and to examine the effects of maternal depression on child development, including child attachment. The sample included 168 mothers and their toddlers (86 boys and 82 girls). At the time of enrollment, the average age of the toddlers was 20.47. Of the toddlers, 102 had mothers with a history of major depressive disorder that minimally involved a major depressive episode occurring at some time since the toddler had been born. The remaining 66 children had mothers with no current or prior history of major psychiatric disorder. Maternal age ranged from 22 to 41 years ($M = 31.62$, $sd = 4.51$).

In order to minimize co-occurring risk factors that may accompany parental depression (Campbell, Cohn, Flanagan, & Popper, 1992; Downey & Coyne, 1990), the families were not of low socioeconomic status. Specifically, parents were required to have at least a high school education and families could not be reliant on public assistance. A community sample of mothers with a history of depressive disorder was recruited through referrals from mental health professionals and through notices placed in newspapers, community publications, and medical offices and on community bulletin boards. In addition to having a child of approximately 20 months of age, mothers in the depressed groups had to meet *Di-*

agnostic and Statistical Manual of Mental Disorders (American Psychiatric Association, 1987) criteria for a major depressive disorder occurring at some period since the birth of their toddlers. The depressed mothers also had to be willing to accept random assignment to either the intervention or the nonintervention group following completion of baseline assessments. Among depressed mothers, 92.8% had been depressed during the postpartum period. Only 12.4% had been depressed exclusively in the postpartum period since the toddler was born. Forty-six depressed mothers were randomly assigned to receive the TPP intervention. The length of the intervention period averaged 57 weeks (SD = 9.81) and ranged from 41.7 to 78.93 weeks. The mean number of intervention sessions conducted was 45.63 (SD = 11.38) and ranged from 30 to 75.

Recruitment of control group mothers without a history of psychiatric disorder was achieved by contacting families living in the vicinity of the families of depressed mothers. Names of potential families with a toddler of the targeted age were obtained from birth records. In addition to the same demographic characteristics required for families with depressed mothers, the control group mothers were screened for the presence or history of major psychiatric disorder using the Diagnostic Interview Schedule III-R (DIS-III-R; Robins et al., 1985) and only mothers without a current or past history of major psychiatric disorder were retained. Thus, this control group constitutes a "super normal" comparison group, given the prevalence of psychological disturbance in the general population.

Participants in the depressed intervention (DI), depressed control (DC), and nondepressed control (NC) groups were comparable on a range of basic demographic characteristics. Mothers were predominantly Caucasian (92.4%) and minority representation did not differ across groups. Maternal education also was comparable across groups. Overall, 53.8% of the mothers were college graduates or had received advanced degrees. Family socioeconomic status based on Hollingshead's (1975) four-factor index also was consistent across groups: 73.4% were ranked in the two highest socioeconomic group status levels (IV and V). Although the age of the toddlers was equivalent across groups, minor differences in maternal age were present, with mothers in the DC group being somewhat younger (M = 30.46) than mothers in the NC group (M = 32.51). Neither group differed from the DI group (M = 31.81). Although the majority of mothers in all groups were married, not surprisingly, the rate of marital instability at the baseline was higher in the two depressed groups. The percentage of mothers in the DI and DC groups who were married was 81.4% and 79.6%, respectively, contrasting with 98.4% in the NC group. By postintervention follow-up, there were no new cases of separation or divorce in the DI or DC groups; however, two mothers in the NC group had separated from their spouses. The groups also were equivalent in terms of the number of children in the family (M = 1.96), the percent of toddlers who were in childcare (48.1%), and working mothers (61.4%).

Finally, as expected, the current level of depressive symptoms as measured by the Beck Depression Inventory (BDI) was higher in the DI (M = 15.30) and DC (M = 17.33)groups than in the NC group (M = 2.42). The DI (76.7%) and DC (77.8%) groups both evidenced a high rate of comorbidity with other psychiatric disorders (including, for example, anxiety disorders, posttraumatic stress disorder, obsessive-compulsive disorder, bulimia, and substance abuse disorders), but these rates were equivalent for the two depressed groups. The DI (14%) and DC (11%) groups also were equivalent in terms of the percentage of mothers who were depressed exclusively during the postpartum period.

Baseline assessments occurred when toddlers were approximately 20 months of age and depressed mothers were randomly assigned to the intervention group or the nontreatment control group. Postintervention assessments occurred subsequent to the child turning 3 years old, when the DI group had completed the course of intervention.

Maternal Functioning

Baseline assessments of maternal functioning revealed that, as hypothesized, mothers with a history of major depressive disorder evidenced substantial emotional, cognitive, interpersonal, and representational liabilities (Cicchetti et al., 1998). Extensive analyses of baseline measurements were conducted and differences between the depressed mothers randomized to the preventive intervention (DI) and nonintervention (DC) control group, in contrast with the normative group of nondepressed mothers (NC) were examined (Cicchetti et al.). Consistently, across diverse measurements, the two groups of depressed mothers were found to be indistinguishable, verifying the effectiveness of the randomization procedures. Importantly, the DI and DC groups were both found to be consistently different from the NC group and, in all cases, the depressed groups were found to have less adaptive functioning. Although not all mothers in the depressed groups were experiencing a depressive episode at the beginning of the investigation, it was apparent that vulnerabilities in the two groups were substantial and continued beyond the confines of depressive episodes.

In findings published on the microsystem contextual features co-occurring with maternal depression (Cicchetti et al., 1998), families with depressed mothers were found to evidence greater stress and more frequent parenting hassles. Depressed mothers also reported significantly less social support, in terms of receiving less self-validation, less companionship, and less tangible assistance in their daily lives. The marriages of depressed mothers also were less harmonious and satisfying and greater levels of conflict were reported in the families of depressed mothers in general. Thus, support was obtained for characterizing the families in which young offspring of mothers with major depression are developing as stressful, poorly supported, and high in disharmony and marital distress, all features detrimental to facilitating optimal child development and secure attachment relationships (Coyne, Downey, & Boergers, 1992; Cummings & Davies, 1999; Downey & Coyne, 1990). Furthermore, both groups of depressed mothers reported higher levels of negative affect and lower levels of positive affect than mothers in the NC group. These findings underscore the adverse emotional climate in which the toddler offspring of depressed mothers are immersed.

Maternal Depression and Child Functioning

In a paper on contextual influences in maternal depression (Cicchetti et al., 1998), the extent to which maternal depression and associated contextual features were related to two outcomes in the toddler offspring, emergent behavior problems and attachment security, was examined. Contextual distress was related to higher levels of behavior problems in the toddlers, however, this was true for toddlers of both depressed and nondepressed mothers. Importantly, maternal depression was more uniquely related to attachment insecurity than was contextual distress. These findings emphasize that maternal depression contributes to risk for compromised early adaptation in the toddlers of depressed mothers and that this result is not attributable to the contextual distress associated with maternal depression. Rather, features of the affective presentation of depressed mothers were more likely to account for these attachment security differences (Cicchetti et al.; see also Seifer, Sameroff, Dickkstein, Keitner, & Miller, 1996).

In accordance with the organizational perspective on development in offspring of depressed mothers (Cicchetti & Schneider-Rosen, 1986; Cicchetti & Toth, 1998), findings also have been attained regarding aberrations in the emergent self-organization of the toddlers of depressed mothers, as observed in a laboratory mirror-rouge paradigm (Cicchetti, Rogosch, Toth, & Spagnola, 1997). The mirror-rouge paradigm relies on the presence of mark-directed behavior involving touching the nose after a spot of rouge has been applied as the criterion for self-recognition (Lewis & Brooks-Gunn, 1979). Although toddler offspring of depressed mothers were comparable to children of nondepressed mothers in terms of making expected cognitive maturational advances involving self-recognition and emergent self-awareness, unique differences were found in terms of the affect associated with the self among the toddler offspring of depressed mothers. Specifically, affect associated with the self was more likely to evidence a shift from positive to negative upon self-recognition among toddlers of depressed mothers. Thus, even at a very early age, toddlers of depressed mothers were more likely to have negative affect associated with the self, a potential early precursor to later vulnerability for depression.

The variability inherent in the affective environments of depressed mothers provides an important entrée for further examining the relation between variations in maternal affect and differential outcome in their toddlers (Field, 1989; Murray, 1992; Tronick & Weinberg, 1997). Depression group analyses demonstrated that toddlers who had not achieved visual self-recognition and also displayed changeable affect from pre- to post-rouge administration had mothers who reported lower levels of positive affect. The association between maternal affect with both toddler unstable affect and the absence of visual self-recognition provides evidence that low-level maternal positive affect may impede aspects of early self-knowledge, particularly when toddlers exhibit affective instability. This same group of toddlers of the depressed mothers who changed affect and did not self-recognize also were reported to be more insecurely attached. The relation between maternal report of low attachment security and the absence of the attainment of visual self-recognition is congruent with the predictions from the organizational perspective that attachment security and self-knowledge are linked (Cicchetti & Schneider-Rosen, 1986; Cicchetti & Toth, 1998).

Intervention Efficacy

Given the centrality of attachment organization to early personality development and competent adaptation, a critical question involved whether the toddlers of a middle class group of depressed mothers would evidence heightened rates of attachment insecurity at baseline. At baseline and at postintervention completion at 36 months, attachment was assessed via the attachment Q-set, a measure that has been found to provide a valid assessment of attachment (AQS; Waters & Deane, 1985). Mothers were given detailed instructions and training on how to complete the AQS prior to the baseline assessment and were asked to observe their child for 2 weeks before completing the AQS. In accordance with the findings of others, toddlers with depressed mothers evidenced higher rates of insecurity than toddlers of nondepressed mothers. Subsequently, the effectiveness of the attachment-theory-based intervention for fostering attachment security of toddlers of depressed mothers was examined (Cicchetti, Toth,

& Rogosch, 1999). Although, at baseline, the toddlers in the DI and the DC groups evidenced equivalent rates of insecure attachment and both groups had higher rates of insecure attachment than the NC group, at follow-up the DC group continued to have higher rates of insecure attachment than the NC group. In contrast, the DI group at postintervention follow-up was not significantly different from the NC group in terms of the rate of insecure attachment. For toddlers who had taken part in the intervention, there had been greater maintenance of secure attachment organization among those who were initially secure, as well as a greater shift from insecure to secure attachment groupings (see Cicchetti et al.). These findings demonstrate the efficacy of TPP in promoting secure attachment organization among young offspring of depressed mothers and are among the first in the literature to demonstrate the effectiveness of a preventive intervention for altering attachment organization.

The results also confirm the heightened risk of insecure attachment in offspring of depressed mothers, even in this sample of families with middle to high socioeconomic status and consequently fewer social risks hindering development. Furthermore, the findings indicate that attachment organization is malleable and can be improved through the provision of a preventive intervention formulated from attachment theory. Factors that might influence the patterns of change resulting from the intervention also were examined. Child gender was not associated differentially with continuity versus change in attachment organization. The influence of further maternal major depressive episodes occurring between baseline and postintervention follow-up assessments also was examined for the potential of further severe depression to impact the efficacy of the TPP preventive intervention. However, the presence versus absence of subsequent depressive episodes did not account for improvements in toddler attachment organization. Moreover, although mothers in the DI and DC groups continued to report higher mean levels of depressive symptomatology relative to the NC group, change in attachment organization had nonetheless been effected through the TPP preventive intervention. Thus, directing preventive intervention efforts at the level of the mother-child dyad had demonstrable effects on improving the developmental competence of these offspring, even though maternal depression did not appear to be uniquely altered by the intervention.

It could be argued that strange situation classifications would provide a more stringent test of the efficacy of the intervention. In our view, however, the utilization of the AQS is not a limitation; rather, it is a different method for assessing attachment. Numerous studies have documented the reliability and validity of the AQS as a measure of attachment security when completed by trained raters (Waters, Vaughn, Posada, & Teti, in press). Maternal Q-sets also have been shown to relate to strange situation classifications (Vaughan & Waters, 1990), as well as in theoretically expected ways to maternal internal working models and child security (Eiden, Teti, & Corns, 1995). Thus, the AQS has demonstrated validity as a method for assessing attachment, even when completed by mothers.

It is unlikely that the maternal reports were biased because the Q-set method, unlike face-valid, self-report measures, requires the respondent to make forced-choice decisions across items, thereby reducing potential for biased responding. Moreover, mothers were not informed as to what constitutes secure attachment and they were unaware of our experimental hypotheses. In addition, mothers were neither trained in attachment theory nor knowledgeable about the security and dependency criterion ratings for the AQS. Consequently, it is improbable that demand characteristics affected maternal ratings of attachment security. In this regard, the nondidactic nature of the intervention provided becomes important. Unlike interventions that strive to teach sensitive responding or utilize modeling, the TPP intervention never provided such techniques.

These findings underscore the necessity of preventing the coalescence of a multitude of risk factors associated with maternal depression that may conspire to undermine adaptation. The ongoing examination of the toddler strange situation data that were collected at baseline and postintervention will further elucidate the impact of TPP on attachment organization.

The effects of the preventive intervention also have been examined in terms of other aspects of toddler development, specifically, cognitive development (Cicchetti, Rogosch, & Toth, 2000). At baseline, no differences were found among the DI (111.12), DC (109.48), and NC (111.39) groups in terms of scores on the mental development index of the Bayley scales of infant development (Bayley, 1969). However, at postintervention followup, significant group differences emerged for cognitive abilities. Specifically, whereas the DI and NC groups continued to be equivalent, a relative decline in IQ was found in the DC group. On the Weschler Preschool and Primary Scale of Intelligence-Revised (WPPSI-R) full scale (FSIQ) and verbal scale (VIQ) IQ tests, both the DI (FSIQ = 107.09; VIQ = 104.21) and NC (FSIQ = 107.41; VIQ = 103.70) groups evidenced higher scores as compared to the DC (FSIQ = 100.78; VIQ = 97.50) group; a marginal treatment effect in the same direction also was found for performance IQ. Thus, the preventive intervention appeared to be effective in maintaining normative cognitive advances in the DI group, relative to the NC group, whereas a decline in cognitive advances was observed in the DC group, in the absence of the preventive intervention. The findings in this middle-class sample are congruent with results obtained in the literature. For example, in a longitudinal investigation of a large heterogeneous sample, the National Institute of Child Health and Human Development (NICHD) Early Child Care Research Network (1999) discovered that children whose mothers reported depressive symptoms performed more poorly on measures of cognitive and linguistic functioning at 36 months of age than children of mothers who never reported depressive feelings. Interestingly, maternal sensitivity was found to moderate the depression group differences in expressive language. Specifically, a composite rating of maternal sensitivity displayed during free play observations was found to be a better predictor of positive developmental outcomes among children whose mothers reported feeling depressed. Furthermore, Kaplan, Bachorowski, and Zarlengo-Strouse (1999), in an examination of a low-risk sample, discovered that the child-directed speech segments produced by mothers with high levels of depressive symptomatology did not promote associative learning in 4-month-old infants. Finally, Egeland and Sroufe (1981), in a longitudinal study of high-risk infants from low-socioeconomic-status backgrounds, found a substantial decline in cognitive development between 9- and 24-month assessments in offspring of psychologically unavailable mothers.

Additionally, the effect of continued severe maternal depression on child cognitive development within the DI and DC groups was examined (Cicchetti et al., 2000). In both groups, approximately 30% of the depressed mothers experienced subsequent major depressive episodes based on DSM-III-R (1987) criteria in the period between baseline and postintervention follow-up. An interaction was found between presence versus absence of subsequent depressive episodes and treatment group. Specifically, in the DI group, no differences were observed in cognitive scores at follow-up depending on whether mothers did or did not have subsequent depressive episodes. In contrast, in the DC group, toddlers of mothers who experienced subsequent depressive episodes evidenced the lowest full scale and verbal IQs; in fact, these differences were 15 IQ points lower for the DC group.

These findings emphasize the continued risk that offspring of depressed mothers face in the absence of intervention as these mothers continue to struggle with their depressive disorders. The findings also demonstrate the efficacy of the preventive intervention in safeguarding successful cognitive development among offspring of depressed mothers, irrespective of continued depressive episodes in these children's mothers. Maintenance of an adaptive cognitive developmental trajectory as a result of the preventive intervention may prove particularly beneficial for the DI children as they face the later stage-salient issue of successful adaptation to school. Thus, our evaluation of TPP for toddler offspring of depressed mothers has demonstrated the efficacy of this attachment therapy intervention in improving both child cognitive functioning and security of attachment.

CLINICAL CASE MATERIAL

Background Information

Now that a theoretical and research perspective on maternal depression and attachment has been presented, the framework for a clinical intervention described, and its efficacy demonstrated, we turn our attention to two cases that received the TPP preventive intervention for toddlers with depressed mothers. The cases reported herein constitute a subsample of those included in the empirical investigation of the effectiveness of TPP for depressed mothers and their toddlers reported previously, however, the cases chosen are representative of the broader sample (Cicchetti et al., 1999; Cicchetti et al., 2000). In order to elucidate issues of relevance to attachment theory, we chose depressed mothers with different types of insecure attachments prior to the initiation of the intervention. The toddlers of each of these mothers also had insecure attachments prior to the provision of intervention. Clinical psychologists holding doctoral degrees supervised all cases and the fidelity of the intervention was monitored through regular supervisory review of videotapes of sessions, therapist process notes that were reviewed weekly, and therapist completion of questionnaires that were reviewed at 6-month intervals by Dante Cicchetti, who was not involved in ongoing case supervision.

This clinical case material is presented in order to address several questions with relevance to attachment theory: (a) In order to be effective in fostering attachment security between parent and child, does an attachment-informed mode of therapy need to alter maternal representations, maternal behavior, both representations and behavior, or neither?; (b) how consistent is information attained through semistructured interviews such as the Adult Attachment Interview (AAI) or Parent Attachment Interview (PAI) with material revealed during an ongoing course of therapy?; (c) does maternal attachment organization affect mothers' ability to benefit from certain forms of intervention?; and (d) how does the clinical intervention described herein inform attachment theory? After the clinical case material is presented, it is synthesized and its implications for questions about attachment theory are examined.

To provide a context within which to conceptualize the course of treatment, information on measures designed to evaluate attachment-relevant issues also is provided. Specifically, at baseline and at the conclusion of the intervention we include information from the strange situation (Ainsworth & Wittig, 1969), the AAI (George, Kaplan, & Main, 1984), and the PAI (Bretherton, Biringen, Ridgeway, Maslin, & Sherman, 1989).

Measurement of Attachment

A number of methods for assessing the quality of attachment and for measuring parent representations of attachment figures are currently being utilized (Crowell, Fraley, & Shaver, 1999; Solomon & George, 1999b). Although much work has focused on the assessment of attachment in the early years of life, theoreticians and researchers have also been addressing the measurement of attachment across the life span. In order to provide a context for understanding the measurement of the quality of attachment used in the evaluation of the preventive intervention that we discuss in this chapter, we briefly describe the methods utilized to measure quality of attachment and parent representations of attachment figures and their toddler.

The strange situation (Ainsworth & Wittig, 1969), a 21-min laboratory procedure, designed to elicit low-level stress and activate the attachment behavioral system, was administered prior to the intervention when children were 20 months old and following the provision of intervention when children were 3 years old. The Ainsworth et al. (1978) coding system allows for the classification of three major attachment categories, including secure (Type B), insecure-avoidant (Type A), and insecure-ambivalent (Type C). The quality of attachment relationships is considered to be the result of the history of interactions with the primary caregiver and each attachment strategy has been linked with particular aspects of the caregiving history. Secure attachments have been related to a history of maternal warmth, sensitivity, and responsivity. In contrast, insecure-avoidant attachments have been associated with histories involving parental rejection, emotional unavailability, or harsh caregiving and insecure-ambivalent attachments have been related to histories of inconsistent caregiving (Ainsworth et al.; Belsky, 1999; Cassidy & Berlin, 1994; Isabella, 1993; Sroufe & Waters, 1977). A fourth attachment classification, insecure-disorganized-disoriented (Type D), was developed as a result of work with atypical populations, where infants and toddlers could not be easily categorized by the previously described classifications (Main & Solomon, 1990; Solomon & George, 1999a; Vondra & Barnett, 1999). Youngsters with Type D attachments do not possess organized coping strategies with respect to attachment figures. Rather, they exhibit contradictory features of several strategies (e.g., strong proximity seeking followed by strong avoidance) or a disordering of expected temporal sequences or appear to be dazed and disoriented upon reunion with their caretakers.

Mothers' state of mind with respect to their caregiving experiences during their own childhoods were assessed prior to and following the provision of the intervention through the AAI (George et al., 1984). This interview is comprised of questions that ask the mother to describe and reflect on significant attachment-related experiences that have affected her development. Based on adults' descriptions of childhood experiences, four different patterns of attachment organization can be coded. These patterns were constructed to be congruent with the infancy-toddlerhood patterns previously described. A free-autonomous classification (F) is viewed as analogous to the secure infant pattern, whereas the dismissing classification (Ds) is consistent with the infant insecure-avoidant pattern and the preoccupied-entangled classification (E) is associated with the infant insecure-ambivalent pattern (Main, 1996). The unresolved classification (U) is consistent with the disorganized-disoriented pattern of infancy and can be coded in conjunction with either the two insecure or the one secure classification.

Similar to the patterns described during the early years of life, these adult attachment organizations also have been related to various experiences of early caregiving. The free-autonomous or secure adult attachment pattern is viewed as emerging from a loving, supportive parenting experience. These individuals are clear and coherent when describing their experiences, have ready access to attachment-related information, and are able to integrate cognition and affect as these domains relate to early attachment experiences. Individuals with dismissing patterns of attachment have had childhood experiences involving parental rejection. Consequently, their representational models are structured to defend against this pain. During their interviews, the effects of early relationships on subsequent development are minimized and parents may be defensively idealized. Overall, attachment-related information is excluded from awareness and attachment experiences are processed without integrating affect. These individuals tend to be distant, terse, and incoherent when discussing attachment. The preoccupied-entangled pattern is linked with childhood experiences involving a reversal of the parent-child role, guilt, and inconsistency. Such individuals tend to be consumed by their childhood memories and they have a great deal of unresolved affect regarding their parents. Although they have ready access to attachment-related information and associated affects, these affects are not effectively integrated with their cognitions. Ambivalence is prominent in processing attachment-related experiences. Finally, individuals who display lapses in the monitoring of discourse or reasoning while discussing loss or abuse experiences may be classified as unresolved-disoriented-disorganized.

The PAI (Bretherton et al., 1989) also was administered pre- and postintervention to examine how parents describe their attachment relationships with their offspring. Unlike the AAI, which asks parents to reflect on their own histories of caregiving during childhood, the PAI asks them to answer questions designed to elucidate their representations of their child. A rating scale was designed to assess the mother's sensitivity and insight concerning her relationship with her child (Biringen & Bretherton, 1988). High scores are awarded if the interview conveys maternal sensitivity and appropriateness to child communication and if the mother has insight into her own and her child's behavior and personality. An assessment of consistency between maternal general statements and actual descriptions of occurrences between her and her child must be made in coding the PAI. Low scores are coded if a mother is able to describe appropriate parenting, but reports her own behavior as being at variance with such statements. Low scores also are assigned if a mother is unable to make connections between her and her child's behavior, if she presents as helpless to modify her own or her child's behavior, or if she consistently refers to the child as a possession. If the mother describes insensitive behavior in relation to her child, but can state what is wrong, she is given a less extreme low score on the PAI.

Now that the measures used to examine pre-and postintervention attachment organization have been described, we present two cases in which the mother-child dyads have received TPP. Throughout these case presentations, excerpts from interviews and contacts with the mothers and toddlers are provided; these are direct quotations.

Case Number 1: Rita and Karen[1]

Rita, the 32-year-old mother of 18-month-old Karen, was referred to the TPP program by her psychiatrist, whom she was seeing in order to monitor her antidepressant medication. Although Rita's psychiatrist saw her monthly and was viewed as a support by Rita, psychotherapy was not being provided, nor was any therapeutic work occurring on the relationship between Rita and Karen. Rita had a history of major depressive disorder dating to adolescence and had been on antidepressant medication for a year prior to her pregnancy with Karen. Rita had continued on her medication throughout her pregnancy and expressed considerable fear that the medication had somehow harmed Karen.

On the AAI, Rita described a history replete with intergenerational violence. She reported that her biological father raped her mother after her

---

[1]All names and identifying details have been altered to protect the anonymity of participants.

mother informed him that she wanted a divorce and that he was put in jail for trying to murder her mother the night that Rita was conceived. In describing this, Rita stated, "So I wasn't exactly a planned or wanted child to begin my life with, but my mother always loved me very much and she never let me forget that." Rita reported that she had never met her biological father and that her mother had been involved with her stepfather from the time of her birth, eventually marrying him when Rita was 8 years old. Rita went on to state that she had never met her biological father because "he was never allowed to come to visit because he, he was kinda violent." As Rita continued to describe her childhood years, it also was apparent that "violence" was a characteristic shared by her stepfather:

> My stepfather was a very, uh, domineering, demanding, perfectionist-type person, which, believe it or not, some of my personality traits came from. He used to, I don't know how to say it, I never actually had to say it, um . . . beat me. If the rug was wrinkled, I'd get smacked. If I didn't wash out a coffee cup, I'd get smacked. Um, at one point, we took my mother to the hospital a number of times because he'd beat her. . . . At one point my stepfather hit me hard enough to knock my, my jaw out of place, and, um, refused to take me to get medical help. So consequently for about a week, my, my jaw was, dislocated. But eventually it went back together and, and, I still can talk (laughs).

Despite the fact that Rita stated, "My mother was always very loving and very caring. She was always there. I mean, she was always my best friend," the veracity of this memory was contradicted at several points in the AAI. Early on, Rita stated that her mother "worked quite a lot, actually." Later in the interview, when questioned about what she did when she was hurt physically, Rita reported an incident in which she was helped by a neighbor because "my mother must have been at work." Rita goes on to state:

> Once my mother married my stepfather, our relationship changed somewhat. She wasn't as accessible as she had always been. My stepfather would get jealous of, if, if, I had a private conversation with my mother, he thought we were talking about him. Then, 20 minutes later, they'd be in a fight and then I'd be in a fight and I'd get the shit kicked out of me.

The extent of Rita's mother's "unavailability" is underscored by her description of purchasing a blouse when she was approximately 11 years old:

> I tried on the blouse and my mother said she thought it looked fine. Well, when my father saw the blouse, that was it. I was a sleazebag. I looked like a prostitute. I was going to hell. And . . . my mother, she never said anything.

She didn't stick up for me. But at the same time, I understood, because if she did she'd get beat up. And then after she got beat up, I'd get beat up.

Elaborating on one such incident of abuse that resulted in her mother being hospitalized, Rita related the following:

It was very scary one night. My parents were doing their usual arguing and I was making a cake in the kitchen. My stepfather started slapping my mother around and I got involved in it. I musta been 12 or 13. I was standing in the middle between them so he wouldn't hurt her and, this particular night, I threatened to call the police. He pulled the phone outta the wall and he slapped my mother, I wanna say so hard he slapped her into another time zone. She crawled under the table and she pulled me under and she kept saying, "Quiet! Quiet! They won't find us here!" I kept trying to get away, to pull her up, and tell her, "Mom! He's right here and he can see us!" But she was in another, somewhere else. We went to the hospital and I was told under no uncertain terms was I allowed to speak to anyone about what happened. And I had to go home with him. And I was so afraid. I thought he was gonna kill me that night. . . . Um, I made it through that night. My mom came home the next day and, uh, we went on.

Most significantly, with regard to maternal unavailability, Rita reported that a neighbor sexually molested her when she was 4 or 5 years old, prior to her mother's marriage to her stepfather. Although Rita described her mother as "always being there for her," Rita did not inform her mother of the sexual abuse until she reached adulthood.

Despite the years of abuse that she endured and her choice of words to describe her childhood memories of her stepfather, such as "impossible," "degrading," "horrifying," "disillusionment," and "humorous," Rita recalled that when her stepfather died when she was 23, "when they lowered the casket . . . I felt like they shoulda just thrown me in." This statement suggests considerable unresolved loss for Rita. Moreover, in explaining her choice of a positive adjective for her stepfather, Rita also evidenced a subtle lapse in her discourse that suggested that she continued to view her stepfather as alive and that she felt guilty over her anger toward him: "Well, he did have some good points. I had ta give him a good point. I promised I would . . . try always, whenever I said things, that were bad, that I would always try to say something good, at the end. And, Dad, I'm still tryin."

In reviewing Rita's preintervention AAI, it is clear that she continued to struggle with considerable confusion stemming from her childhood years. Rita's inability to resolve her childhood experiences was especially evident in her discussion of her stepfather's death. After stating that she continued to have difficulty dealing with his death, Rita, in an emotion-laden voice, stated:

> You have a lotta confused thoughts, you know? . . . Um, finally when, when you've reached the point after so many years when you can say to each other that you love each other and that you're sorry for the things you've done, and then he's no longer there. . . . I was in a lot of pain. I was angered. I was, I felt, I felt, uh, guilty. I felt guilty because I had wished him dead earlier. Not now. Not once we knew each other, in, in a normal sense. But, uh, relieved. Relieved because I knew that he couldn't get me anymore. He couldn't get to my mother anymore. Very confusing.

The confusion that emerged as Rita discussed her childhood abuse and the death of her abusive stepfather results in the classification of Rita's AAI as unresolved-disorganized. In accord with recommendations regarding providing an alternate forced classification for AAIs that are categorized as unresolved-disorganized (Main, 1995), Rita's AAI also has features that are consistent with a preoccupied-entangled classification. Specifically, Rita's experience of a weak mother who failed in protecting her from abuse, the role reversal in relation to her mother, her seeming inability to move beyond a sense of self as entangled in her childhood relationships, and her guilt and conflicted feelings over anger toward her parents are consistent with a preoccupied-entangled attachment organization.

In reviewing the preintervention strange situation of Rita and Karen, Karen presents as quite wary of the stranger. Although Karen did not protest Rita's departure, when alone during the second separation her facial expression was disoriented and freezing and stilling were noted. Although disorganized-disoriented behavior cannot be classified in the absence of the mother, these occurrences were interesting and atypical of more securely attached toddlers. Additionally, other disorganized-disoriented indices were observed. During the first reunion with Rita, Karen made an aborted approach toward Rita. She made little eye contact with Rita and shared positive affect between mother and toddler was not evident. During the second reunion, Karen approached Rita with a wide-mouthed smile, but backed away and eventually engaged in a sideways approach to Rita. Again, no shared positive affect was present. With regard to attachment classification, Karen meets criteria for a disorganized-disoriented attachment pattern. When trying to force Karen into one of the three organized attachment categories, as recommended by Main and Solomon (1986, 1990), her attachment is most consistent with that of insecure-avoidant.

On the PAI, Rita's representations with respect to Karen prior to the initiation of the TPP intervention were not very positive. When asked about her thoughts and feelings while she was pregnant, Rita responded:

I resented it. I hated it. It was terrible. When I found out that I was pregnant, I was horrified. Now all my, my, all my plans and goals and everything had to be rearranged. . . . It bothered me that all my independence was taken away. . . . When Karen was born and, and they gave me Karen, I looked at her, and I handed her to my husband, and I said, "Here, you wanted her. Take her."

In describing what Karen was like in the early months, Rita stated, "She would never eat. I had to force-feed her all the time. But, um, other than that, she was, she still is, wonderful. She was a great baby from the beginning. She never got sick." Rita also expressed fear that Karen would be "deficient" due to the medication Rita had taken during her pregnancy. Rita described a situation, prior to when Karen could talk, where she felt that Karen was manipulative because she had gone to her father to get more milk for her bottle after Rita had told her "no." Despite some of these negative statements, Rita was able to report that there were times when she felt close to Karen, though the vignette that she described involved a time when only she could make Karen stop crying following an injury when Karen was around a year old: "This is the first real attachment here. Mommy's the only one who can make it okay just by holding me. So I felt close and it started to get better from that." Rita also was able to articulate the kind of parent that she did not want to be: "I don't wanna get angry like my father. I don't wanna hit her. I don't want, I don't wanna say things to her that are gonna damage her for the rest of her life." Rita also described how Karen tried to comfort her when she was sad: "She kept trying to hug me. She wanted to make it all better." In reflecting on similarities and differences in her own childhood and in how she relates to Karen, Rita stated, "I will never let her think or believe, for a minute, that I hate her, or that she was unwanted. Although I may have resented the fact that I was pregnant, it doesn't mean that she wasn't wanted. Once she was here, I had nothing but love for her." The contradictory nature of this statement and Rita's prior statement about not wanting Karen are consistent with her preoccupied-entangled AAI classification.

Near the end of the PAI, Rita reflected that she expected that Karen would be headstrong as an adolescent and that they would have difficulties when Karen rebelled. This statement seems to stem from Rita's difficulties in extricating herself from family enmeshment.

Overall, Rita's PAI reflects a moderate level of sensitivity and insight. Although Rita's early representations of Karen were not positive, she attained a more positive view of Karen over time. Of concern, however, is the fact that many of the positives that she described in relation to Karen pertained to situations in which Karen meets Rita's needs (e.g., comforting Rita, not being sick, etc.) rather than to an unconditional acceptance of Karen. Additionally, these positive memories were associated with times when Karen made Rita feel important, thereby validating her as a person. Rita was able to articulate her fear, as well as her desire, that she would not repeat those aspects of her own childhood parenting experiences that she found to be damaging, thereby demonstrating insight into the influence of her own experiences on her parenting.

Course of Intervention for Rita and Karen

Although project staff explained to all mothers that assignment to the intervention was random, when contacted and offered the intervention Rita sounded disappointed and asked if the research assistants had found "something wrong" with her parenting and decided that she "needed the intervention." The random assignment was again described and Rita readily agreed to take part in the intervention.

Rita arrived for the first session with Karen and her mother, stating that her mother provided all transportation as Rita did not drive. The dependency and ongoing entanglement with her mother was readily apparent. During her first individual session with the therapist, Rita stated that Karen was her only child, but that she was 3 months pregnant. Rita reported taking Nardil for her depression while pregnant with Karen. She reportedly tried to stop the medication when learning of her second pregnancy, but her depressive symptoms returned. Rita also reported that she had been married for 8 years and that her husband Mark was a loving, supportive man.

During the initial dyadic session, Rita described Karen as being happy "all the time" and stated that she did not understand how she and Karen could be related, given their discrepancy in mood. Rita further expressed her envy of Karen's happiness, along with her concern over the possibility that Karen could be harmed, thereby losing her innocence and happiness. She described herself as a survivor of her own childhood and wondered how she had avoided becoming a "major drug addict." Rita also stated that she believed that, if she could only understand how she survived her childhood, she could ensure Karen's survival. Despite the fear that seemed to be underlying Rita's comments, many of her answers appeared rehearsed and relied on jargon belying her emotional experiences.

Rita alluded to the occurrence of childhood molestation, stating, "My troubles began when my mom let me go down the street to visit neighbors." She quickly averted the intense affect associated with this statement by reflecting, "Well, you know, a child never tells their mother until much later and then the mom has all that guilt to bear. How will Karen ever tell me if something goes wrong?" Rita's guilt for "hurting" her mother by being molested underscored her lack of resolution regarding this occurrence. Both as a child and as an adult, she feels responsible for protecting her mother. Her feelings of devastation due to the molestation and guilt over needing to protect her mother were actively in conflict, yet she was unable to express anger toward her mother for being unavailable and not protecting her.

During Rita's discussion of her childhood, Karen brought a triangular block to Rita, stating, "Slide." Rita responded by saying, "Yes, it looks like a slide, but it's a block." Karen then brought Rita a handful of crayons and tried to give them all to her. Rita responded by saying, "Mommy can't hold everything. You give everything to mommy, but she can't hold it all." This simple statement suggests that Rita is overwhelmed by Karen's needs, the typical needs of a toddler. Moreover, her unresolved fear that Karen will be somehow harmed, just as Rita was as a child, exacerbates her feelings of being overwhelmed.

Over the course of therapy, the pervasive influence of Rita's childhood experiences on her parenting of Karen became very clear. Rita stated that during her childhood her mother had attempted suicide several times and that Rita learned to avoid upsetting her mother out of fear of causing her to harm herself. At the time of her entrance into therapy, Rita and her husband rented a home from her mother that was adjacent to her mother's home. Rita also relied on her mother for all of her transportation needs, as Rita had not renewed her driver's license when she was pregnant with Karen. It appeared that the prospect of parenthood served to further the enmeshment between Rita and her mother. Rita had extreme difficulty in asserting herself in any way, a characteristic that was again seemingly attributable to her stance in relation to her mother. She chose to blame herself and to experience guilt when she had any strivings for self-care or self-determination.

During early dyadic sessions, Karen generally avoided interacting with Rita. Karen's play was disconnected and haphazard and her motor skills seemed awkward. She was difficult to engage and she often would stare off into space for long periods of time, a presentation consistent with the disorganized-disoriented classification of the strange situation. Although Rita reported that she feared her use of medication had resulted in developmental delays for Karen, she simultaneously expressed fear that Karen would be "smarter" than her. At these times, she seemed oblivious to Karen's needs and her tone was characterized by veiled anger. Rita also shared that she often "did not feel like Karen's mother" because her own mother had tried to fill that role and Rita resented this.

Therapy sessions focused on helping Rita to resolve her conflicted emotional experiences, to assert herself, and to thereby become freer to parent Karen and to enjoy Karen's developmental progress. A significant component of this process involved helping Rita to recount childhood experiences and to express her anger, rather than holding onto her feelings of responsibility for her mother and guilt for failing to meet all of her mother's needs. As stated earlier, Rita was very concerned about her ability to protect Karen from harm and, more significantly, worried that Karen would not share information with Rita if she were ever hurt. Clearly, this fear stemmed from Rita's unresolved issues regarding her own victimization and her acceptance of responsibility for failing to inform her mother of her abuse. At this point in therapy, Rita demonstrated minimal insight that her decision not to tell her mother of her trauma most likely stemmed from a little girl's accurate perception that her mother would be unable to deal with the information. During one session in which Rita was discussing her childhood abuse and her fears that Karen would experience similar trauma, Karen utilized a puppet to tell Rita, "The puppet is biting me," to which Rita responded, "What are you doing biting my Karen? Stay away from my Karen!" Karen's choice of safety themes mirrored Rita's preoccupation with ensuring Karen's well-being and provided Rita with an opportunity to metaphorically rescue Karen, something Rita's own mother had been unable to do.

A significant point in therapy occurred approximately 3 months into the course of treatment, when Rita recounted a conversation in which her mother stated how Rita had the ideal situation having her mother live next door to her. Rita reportedly responded by saying, "I think the ideal situation would be to live in Alaska." Karen, picking up on the tension between mother and grandmother, began repeating, "Alaska, Alaska," a chant that she would echo in future months whenever she perceived conflict between her mother and her grandmother. This incident reflected Rita's early desire to disengage from her enmeshment with her mother and the courage to take the steps to tell her mother of her feelings, thereby confronting and freeing herself from her years of internalized anger.

Despite this breakthrough early in therapy, 1 year after beginning TPP, Rita had resolved very little of the emotional pain from her childhood. Therefore, the therapist consistently and gently continued to help Rita make connections between her early childhood, her current relationship with her mother, and her relationship with Karen. Difficulties that emerged with regard to Karen's eating behavior at 33 months of age provided a window of opportunity to solidify some of these linkages. Upon inquiry, Rita reported that meal times were very stressful for her as a child because "that was the time when you were told what you did wrong during the day." Consequently, Rita stated that she was not interested in food and often resisted eating, resulting in instances of her being force-fed. The therapist helped to draw parallels between the power struggles in her family of origin and her power struggles with Karen. Rita resonated to these linkages and devised creative solutions to make meal time a less stressful and more enjoyable experience for Karen.

Rita's ability to recognize such parallels and to strive to avert repeating negative patterns of parenting also seemed to give her the energy to set limits with her mother, reduce the enmeshment, and move toward more autonomous functioning. A second noteworthy occurrence in therapy emerged when Rita stated, "I've chosen to . . ." This active voice indicated the first time Rita had expressed her ability to initiate an action, rather than to view herself as a passive victim of the actions of others.

As Rita continued to assert herself, her mother became increasingly rejecting of her. At one point, Rita reported asking her mother if she were aware of how hesitant Rita was to upset her. Her mother responded by stating that, of course she was aware of this and that, in fact, she expected that Rita should "never be angry, never be upset, and never be sad." Rita was helped to label the anger that such a response aroused in her and eventually began to feel less responsible for her mother's feelings.

Rita continued to progress with regard to disentangling herself from her childhood issues. Approximately 3 months prior to termination, the therapist was trying to help Rita express the issues that continued to underlie her mother's intrusiveness. Rita responded, "Frankly I don't care what my mother's issues are because it is not my responsibility to fix them!"

Analysis of Case 1

When Rita began in TPP, she had accepted her family's portrayal of her as the "sick, helpless family member." She believed that she was unable to meet Karen's needs and that Karen would "pass her up" intellectually. This conceptualization resulted in a preoccupation with her own issues to the detriment of being emotionally available to Karen. Additionally, in many ways Rita resented the innocence and "undamaged" state of her toddler.

Despite Rita's attempts to extricate herself from a dysfunctional family system, she continued into adulthood believing that she was responsible for her mother's emotional well-being. Rita's mother intruded in all aspects of Rita's life, trying to ensure that Rita would continue to "need" her and that she would remain as her daughter's emotional protector. In many ways, the birth of Rita's first child increased her insecurity and reawakened fears from her own childhood.

Over the course of therapy, Rita was helped to recognize her conflictual feelings and to examine how they were affecting her parenting of Karen, as well as other aspects of her life. The fact that Rita had married a kind, understanding man, even in the absence of having dealt with her childhood issues, is interesting and a clear departure from what might be expected based on her attachment organization. Moreover, the presence of such a supportive mate may have helped Rita commit to the hard work that was needed for her to progress in therapy. Of course, trying to understand how Rita was able to break away from her childhood to marry such an individual is an interesting question. In late adolescence, Rita left home and went to live in a community approximately 2 hrs from her family. For approximately a 3-year period, Rita ended all contact with her stepfather and called but did not visit her mother. Rita returned home only when her mother begged her to visit her stepfather, who had fallen ill. It was during her separation from her family that Rita initiated her relationship with her future husband.

Baseline measures of attachment revealed significant insecurity in both maternal attachment and in the mother-child attachment relationship. Although Rita's representations of Karen as expressed on the PAI were not wholly positive, some insight into the role of her own history and a desire not to repeat negative caregiving with Karen was evident and represented a positive sign that she might be able to develop a positive relationship with Karen. Moreover, Rita had a prolonged history of depressive illness that was active and clinically significant at the time of her entrance into the TPP program. Even so, she had married a nonabusive, supportive man who may well have been a factor in helping her to utilize the intervention effectively. However, the fact that this relationship was initiated during a period when Rita was living apart from her family of origin points to her striving for independence and health. Although her husband was not involved directly in TPP therapy, he accepted and encouraged Rita's involvement.

At the termination of therapy, Rita and Karen were again seen in the strange situation. Although there were similarities between the strange situations conducted at 18 and 36 months of age, there were also significant differences. To begin, Karen's affect was much more positive, she made more eye contact with Rita, and there was considerable synchrony of affective tone between mother and daughter. Although Karen again took no real notice of her mother's departure, upon reunion she approached her mother immediately and offered her a puzzle. The aborted approaches noted at 18 months were no longer evident. Overall, a much more positive relationship was exhibited and Karen was classified as securely attached to her mother. Interestingly, however, some remnants of the 18-month strange situation continued. Most notably, when alone, Karen appeared to be very subdued and unfocused. In fact, when her mother tried to leave for the second separation, Karen softly stated with downcast eyes, "But I'll be all alone." This simple statement, with its accompanying shift in affect upon mother's departure, hearkens back to Rita's statement at the burial of her stepfather, when she too was faced with a loss: "They shoulda thrown me in, too." One cannot help but wonder about the pervasiveness of fears of aloneness that seem to be crossing generations and hope that the achievements evidenced during Rita's involvement in therapy will, ultimately, be enough to sustain her and her daughter on their positive trajectories.

In reviewing Rita's follow-up PAI, a much more positive representation of Karen emerged. Although Rita's memories of her disappointment upon learning of her pregnancy and her reactions immediately following Karen's birth had not changed, her postintervention stance in relation to Karen was much more positive. The adjectives that she chose to describe Karen were all positive and she was able to provide considerable detail to support her adjective choice. Moreover, her affect in describing various interactions with Karen, even those reflecting more difficult situations, was generally appropriately accepting and sensitive to Karen's needs.

Finally, Rita's postintervention AAI, though continuing to contain elements of unresolved abuse, was classified as free-autonomous. Although some preoccupying anger about her childhood continued to be present, the postintervention AAI differed from the previous AAI with respect to Rita's presentation of a more balanced view of her early experiences, as well as in her descriptions of her efforts to resolve conflicts with her mother.

Case 2: Donna and Hallie

Donna learned of the TPP program through her psychiatrist, who was treating her pharmacologically for depression. However, Donna did not feel that she derived any support from her psychiatrist. She was very enthusiastic about participating in the intervention when she was called and informed that this was an option for her. Donna began her initial session by informing the therapist that she had been out of work for several months because she was hospitalized for 30 days and then attended a 12-week day treatment program for her depression. During that period, she had relied heavily on her own mother for support in parenting Hallie. At the time of Donna's entrance into TPP, Hallie was 22 months old.

During the preintervention AAI, Donna described a chaotic childhood in which she moved approximately 10 times prior to the age of 12. She reported that her parents divorced when she was 8 years old and that they married other partners when she was 9. She further stated that, after living with her mother and stepfather, she had moved in with her biological father, who was an alcoholic, when she was 12 years old.

Donna's preintervention AAI was marked with inconsistencies. Although early in the interview she stated that she was closer to her father than to her mother when she was young, she later contradicted this by saying, "I don't think I was ever close to my father." Moreover, despite descriptions of her childhood relationship with her mother containing words such as "loving," "security," "sensitivity," "closeness," and "bonding," she later described an incident involving abuse:

> One time, my mother hit me because she didn't want me to go somewhere. She was sick and she wanted me to stay with her. I can remember my mother getting really mad at me and then she slapped me across the face. And I, I ended up falling asleep and when I woke up I had like this bloody nose. . . . When my grandparents got back they saw me like that and they ended up taking me for 6 weeks to their house. I was about 5 years old.

Donna went on to report that, when she was ill, "She [her mother] ignored me. You know, she was a very soothing mother, but not when it came to that. She would just um, I think she would get mad at me when I would complain a lot about if I was sick or if I hurt myself. . . . She would get mad cause she couldn't handle it."

Interestingly, despite the clear emotional and physical abuse embodied in these memories, Donna appeared to have no sense of this. Rather, she described these occurrences matter-of-factly and with no recognition that these memories did not support the loving, caring mother image that she had created.

In reflecting on her wishes for Hallie in the future, Donna stated that she wanted Hallie "to love ME." Donna further stated that she wanted Hallie to "have a father. . . . So I'm hoping that, you know, someday she will have somebody that cares about both of us." Donna's neediness and the importance of Hallie's guaranteed love came through loudly in these statements.

Donna's inability to provide details of her childhood experiences and her apparent disregard for the impact of her childhood experiences are consistent with a dismissing attachment organization. Although it is not clearly apparent that Donna is dealing with unresolved loss, the examples of disorganization in her discourse and her descriptions of abuse by her father and mother result in the additional classification of unresolved. Thus, Donna's AAI results in a dismissing-unresolved-disoriented classification.

The baseline strange situation for Donna and Hallie was marked by considerable avoidance on the part of Hallie toward her mother. Although Hallie initiated some shows of toys to her mother across a distance, she never made eye contact with Donna and there was no positive affective sharing. When Donna exited, Hallie made no note of her departure; her search behavior for Donna also was extremely low, verging on nonexistent. She continued her play during Donna's absence. At reunion, Hallie looked at Donna briefly, then looked down. She did not smile, nor did she approach her mother. Finally, Hallie made a distance show of play food to Donna, who responded, "You're eating it, you're supposed to drink it." For the second separation, Hallie again took no notice of her mother's departure. Upon Donna's return, no eye contact was made and Hallie continued playing. Almost 2 min into the reunion, Hallie looked at her mother and showed her a toy. Positive affect was again absent. During periods with the stranger, Hallie was more interactive and engaging. Hallie's classification at the time of the baseline strange situation was clearly consistent with an insecure-avoidant attachment.

When queried on the PAI, Donna stated, "I felt really good when I was pregnant . . . bubbly, I kind of had a bubbly personality." However, this positive representation of her unborn child apparently changed abruptly. When asked what Hallie was like during the early months, Donna replied:

> She was miserable. She cried all the time. I went back to work when she was 6 weeks old and then she started sleeping through the night. But as a newborn, she was very fussy. Before 6 weeks I had a really hard time going to sleep because she was up every 2 hrs. . . . Usually newborns are supposed to sleep.

When asked what she thought Hallie would be like as a 2-year-old, Donna stated, "I was hoping that she wouldn't be the same." It also was clear that Donna considered Hallie's caring for her to be a positive characteristic: "For a toddler, she's very sensitive to my feelings. Not so much now, but when she was younger she'd come up to me and try to comfort me." Additionally, Donna stated, "Hallie's like the complete opposite from me. She's very ambitious and assertive." Generally, Donna's representations of Hallie were not positive. Although Donna was happy at the thought of having a baby, her positive affect appeared to be based on her desire to have unconditional love. When it became clear that a baby could not meet her needs, Donna became increasingly distant from and resentful of Hallie. Donna's score on the PAI is quite low, as she demonstrated minimal sensitivity to Hallie's needs and little insight into how her personality impacted on her parenting of Hallie. Despite some recognition of appropriate parenting practices, Donna's reports of physical punitiveness and emotional abuse toward Hallie do not reflect an incorporation of this understanding.

Course of Intervention for Donna and Hallie

At the initiation of treatment, Donna resided with her mother and Hallie in an apartment. Donna had moved in with her mother following Donna's hospitalization for depression. Donna's hospitalization was sudden and Hallie was faced with the unexpected disappearance of her mother.

Donna stated that, without her mother's assistance, she would not have been able to keep Hallie and that Hallie would have been placed in foster care. Donna was not married at the time of Hallie's birth and Hallie's father had left the state upon learning of Donna's pregnancy. Donna was employed as a sales clerk on a full-time basis and Hallie attended full-time daycare. Despite a seemingly distant relationship from Donna and Donna's lack of knowledge regarding parenting, Hallie presented as developmentally advanced, both socially and with respect to verbal skills. Her advanced development was most likely attributable to the fact that she had been in daycare since she was 3 months old.

In the initial TPP session, it became clear that Donna had low confidence in her parenting skills and that she became easily frustrated with Hallie. At these times, Donna was negative and rejecting of Hallie. For example, when Hallie had difficulty leaving the therapy session, Donna made threatening comments such as, "All right. Do you want me to leave you here?"

During the early phase of treatment, Donna presented as extremely overwhelmed and confused. She stated that being a single parent was very difficult for her: "I love her and could never give her up, but I don't know how to do it. I don't know anything, I don't do anything with her like playing with her or teaching her anything." Donna also had difficulty organizing details of her past and routinely described various individuals and events in opposing terms. For example, whereas at one moment she described how terrible being in the hospital had been and how it had not helped her, she later stated, "The hospitalization really helped me." Similarly, although in the same session Donna recalled that her family members never visited her during her hospitalization, she later reported that her family was very supportive of her. Donna appeared to be unaware of the contradictory nature of these statements. She was equally inconsistent with her stories about her childhood. For example, despite stating that her mother was neglectful of her as a child and only marginally supportive during Donna's hospitalization, she also emphasized how close she and her mother had always been. These contradictory statements are consistent with the idealization that was noted during the preintervention AAI.

Donna's presentation was very adolescent-like, yet it also appeared that she had been placed in the role of caretaker for family members, both during childhood and in her adult years. Donna reported that she was attending counseling with her father to help him recall the years he "lost" due to his alcoholism.

Donna was physically punitive, as well as emotionally abusive, to her daughter. Donna described a situation during Thanksgiving dinner where Hallie dropped her plate onto the floor, hitting her grandmother's foot. Donna reported that her mother became very angry and that Donna responded by taking Hallie upstairs and spanking Hallie "hard and let-[ting] her cry herself to sleep."

In general, the relationship between Hallie and Donna was quite distant, an interactional style that validates the observations found in the preintervention strange situation. During sessions when Hallie attempted to engage the therapist in play, Donna appeared to be jealous, stating, "See? This is how she always is. She likes everyone but me. She lets other people do things for her, but won't let me." Donna vacillated between ignoring Hallie's rare bids for attention and being overly intrusive in her interactions with Hallie. In one poignant session, Hallie approached Donna with some pretend soup that she had made. Upon tasting the soup, Donna exclaimed, "Yech Hallie, this is awful. Make something that I like." This vignette not only illustrated Donna's rejection of Hallie, but also portrayed the role reversal that permeated their relationship. Moreover, scenarios such as this contributed to Hallie's ambivalence toward her mother. For example, Hallie engaged in very contradictory behaviors: "Mommy, I'm going to cook you dinner. I'm going to make you your favorite meal. . . . I'm not cooking this for you. I'm going to eat it all."

As therapy progressed, Donna became increasingly able to deal with her childhood experiences and to recognize their continued role in her life. In discussing her involvement in her father's therapy, she stated, "It's such a crock. He chooses not to remember because he doesn't want to have to face what it was that he did to me." Donna also became better able to recognize the fact that her mother had not been there for her as a child, but stated that the recent support provided by her mother had contributed to healing some of her childhood wounds. As Donna reflected on such issues, she also began to link her parenting of Hallie with her own childhood experiences: "I often go into rages with Hallie just like my mother did with me. I know that this makes Hallie fear me and I feel awful afterward."

As Donna grappled with improving her relationship with Hallie, she also struggled with her own pain. For example, when telling the therapist that she had begun reading bedtime stories to Hallie and how much Hallie enjoyed this, she wistfully commented that she wished someone had done things like that for her when she was a child. Rather than having her needs met, Donna was expected to care for her mother and was made to feel guilty if she did not do so. In this regard, she described having to make a decision about which parent she wanted to live with when she was 12 years old. When she chose her father, she stated that her mother had made her feel guilty and that she feels guilty to this day. As the therapist helped Donna to question the appropriateness of some of her parents' actions during her childhood, she became increasingly able to modify her own stance in regard to Hallie.

During therapy, Donna began to set appropriate limits with Hallie and, consequently, to attain more desired behaviors from her. This, in turn, resulted in a growing attachment with and emotional attunement to her daughter. As Hallie developed more security and trust in the structure of her environment, she was able to trust more in her interpersonal relationship with her mother. Over the course of treatment, the relationship between Hallie and her mother blossomed, with both Donna and Hallie enjoying their interactions with each other. In fact, near the end of treatment, Donna reported that she was no longer sending Hallie to daycare on her day off because she wanted to be able to spend more time with her.

Interestingly, the improvements evidenced in the mother-child relationship also appeared to reflect gains in other areas of Donna's life. Donna was able to end her involvement in frequent and unfulfilling romantic liaisons, striving rather to meet and maintain a relationship with a caring man. She also left her job as a sales clerk, became certified as a nurse's aid, and planned to complete a degree as a registered nurse. Although Donna continued to experience difficulties in her relationship with her own mother, she was able to establish her role as Donna's parent, thereby ending her subservience to her mother on that dimension.

Analysis of Case 2

Donna entered TPP with a major depressive disorder, a history of childhood abuse, and an insecure relationship with her child. Donna presented as somewhat immature and demonstrated minimal insight into the role of her childhood experiences on her parenting.

For several months into TPP therapy, Donna's therapist questioned whether Donna would be able to benefit from treatment due to her extremely limited parenting repertoire. To use Donna's words in the latter stages of treatment, she "was in a fog" when she started therapy. Donna had many ephemeral relationships, choosing to end difficult involvements rather than work on improving them. In retrospect, it was clear that Donna's 13-month relationship with her therapist was one of the longest and most important in her life.

Initially, Donna's therapist considered her parenting of Hallie to be so impaired that the therapist felt that the parenting needed to improve before there would be any hope of a more positive relationship developing between mother and child. Rather than trying to teach Donna how to parent, however, Donna's therapist sought to help Donna reflect on how she had felt when she was treated poorly as a child and to help her link these observations to how Hallie might feel. This strategy was effective in bringing about some changes in parenting, which resulted in modifications in Hallie's responsivity to and bids for attention from Donna. As Donna began to see the beginnings of a positive relationship with her daughter, she became increasingly motivated to engage in positive interchanges with Hallie. Much of the taunting and negativity toward Hallie that Donna exhibited during the early phases of therapy disappeared and mother and daughter began to enjoy their time together. Donna was able to acknowledge and reflect on these changes and proudly commented that Hallie now seemed to like being with her. This case is interesting in that attending to historical relationship issues for Donna resulted in a change in her parenting, as well as in an improved attachment relationship with Hallie.

During the follow-up strange situation when Hallie was 3 years old, some important changes were noted. Although Hallie presented as a child who exhibited rather muted affect with her mother, more positive affective interchanges were noted. When Donna first separated from Hallie, Hallie took little notice of the departure. Upon Donna's return, Hallie looked at her mother, then stated, "I did the puzzle all by myself." Donna responded positively to this statement, at which point Hallie smiled. Overall, there were more eye contact and positive affective interchanges between mother and child than had been noted during the baseline strange situation. During the second reunion, Hallie stated, "I want you to play with me Mommy." Although some remnants of avoidance remained, at follow-up the relationship between Donna and Hallie appeared to be much more positive and Hallie was classified as having a secure attachment organization.

In reviewing the follow-up PAI that Donna completed, little change in her representation of her relationship with Hallie could be found. She continued to have difficulty providing any specific details to support her report of various occurrences and little positivity was noted in her descriptions of her interactions with Hallie. This lack of change in Donna's representation of Hallie, despite Hallie's secure attachment relationship and Donna's overall progress during the course of therapy, with regard to both improved parenting and increased insight regarding the effect of her history on her parenting of Hallie, is informative and hearkens back to the question raised regarding representation, parenting, and attachment security. Based on this case, it appears that an attachment-informed intervention was able to impact parenting and attachment security in the absence of actually modifying the mother's representations of her child or of her own representations of attachment.

Interestingly, despite positive changes noted during the course of therapy, Donna's postintervention AAI continued to be classified as insecure-dismissing. In fact, Donna appeared to be even less open in the post-intervention AAI than she had been in the AAI administered prior to the initiation of the TPP intervention. It is important to note that the post-AAI does not reflect the progress noted in Donna's open discussions of the adverse effects of her childhood on her adult development that she had shared during therapy sessions. Nonetheless, it is interesting that neither the PAI nor the AAI support the changes in Donna's conceptualization and understanding of her childhood experiences that she had shared with the therapist during intervention sessions. Given that the interviewers for the AAI and PAI were, unlike the therapist, individuals that Donna did not have a relationship with, these differences between interview and therapy interactions may reflect the operation of specific working models of relationship rather than general working models.

SYNTHESIS OF CASE HISTORY MATERIAL: COMPARISONS OF TWO CASE STUDIES

These case studies were chosen to illustrate consistencies, as well as divergences, between them. With regard to similarities, both mothers suffered from a history of a major depressive disorder, both were receiving medication for their depressive disorders, and both were first-time mothers. Both women also reported a history of physical abuse, although Donna did not have a history of sexual molestation. Both Rita and Donna were members of the middle class, with Donna being in the lower range of middle income. Both Rita and Donna received some education after graduating from high school, but, whereas Rita obtained a college degree, Donna did not. Rita was employed part time, but Donna worked full time. Perhaps most significantly, Donna was a single mother who continued to live with her mother. Interestingly, although Rita was married, both women shared very enmeshed, dependent relationships with their mothers and both women entered therapy with idealized views of their mothers, despite childhoods marked by abuse. However, prior to her participation in the TPP intervention, Rita's attachment organization was preoccupied, whereas Donna's was dismissing. Interestingly, the primary and significant difference between Rita and Donna pertains to the former's ability to form and sustain positive and supportive relationships.

The parallels between the memories reported by Donna and Rita are striking. Both women exhibited a need to protect their mothers, even from their own anger. Additionally, the mothers of both women appear to have used their daughters to meet their own needs, to the detriment of being emotionally available to their offspring. Unlike Rita, however, Donna was much less able to provide specific memories of childhood occurrences, relying instead on global generalizations of occurrences to support her idealized view of her mother.

Like Rita, Donna described an alcoholic father who rejected her when he remarried when she was 9. This is reminiscent of Rita's report about the "loss" of her mother due to her stepfather's jealousy of her mother's affection for her. Thus, both women were placed in situations where the sexual partner of a parent seemed to displace their role as an important person in their parent's life. Moreover, it appears that both girls (and later women) tried to win back the affections of their parent by trying to minimize the adversity to which they had been subjected and by idealizing the parent that they felt most likely to "be there" for them.

Rita possessed considerably more insight into the role of her childhood experiences on her parenting than Donna, a factor that may have contributed to differences in their modifications of their representations of their children. Additionally, the fact that Rita had been able to establish a positive relationship with her spouse constitutes a major difference between the two mothers. In this regard, the preintervention AAI classifications of Rita and Donna are important to consider. Although both women had elements of unresolved loss, Rita was insecure-preoccupied, whereas Donna was insecure-dismissing. Prior research has suggested that individuals with dismissing attachments are more resistant to intervention (Dozier, 1990).

IMPLICATIONS FOR ATTACHMENT THEORY

The case material presented in this chapter provides insight into the questions raised earlier. Therefore, we turn our attention to these issues.

The first question was: In order to be effective in fostering attachment security between parent and child, does an attachment-informed mode of therapy need to alter maternal representations, maternal behavior, both, or neither? A clarification of the role of representational models in behavioral change can be gained from these case studies. At the time that TPP was initiated, both Rita and Donna seemed to lack some basic knowledge of parenting skills. However, rather than trying to teach techniques to the mothers, the therapists providing TPP sought to help the mothers understand the role that their own caregiving experiences, and subsequent representations of attachment, exerted on their current relationship with their child. For Rita, improved parenting followed her development of increased sensitivity to Karen, even though parenting skills were not taught directly. Increased sensitivity was observed during therapy sessions and a secure attachment was coded at the postintervention assessment. Rita's representations of Karen similarly improved at the postintervention assessment.

Interestingly, Donna's therapist initially was so concerned about the poor quality of parenting being provided to Hallie that she asked her supervisor whether TPP would be effective in resulting in any positive change. Despite these misgivings, Donna's therapist concluded that, as Donna's relationship with and investment in her daughter improved, her actual parenting mirrored these changes. In essence, for Donna and Hallie, improved parenting and increased security appeared to occur in tandem. However, improvements were not noted in the postintervention assessment of maternal representations of Hallie, suggesting that modified representations are not necessarily a prerequisite for improved parenting or for increased attachment security. It is important to note that, for Rita, improvements in security in all domains occurred (AAI, PAI, strange situation), whereas, for Donna, initially classified as insecure-dismissing on the AAI, increased security was present only in Hallie's postintervention strange situation. The continuance of insecure representations of attachment history and of her child in the context of an intervention that resulted in increased maternal sensitivity and child attachment security provides an important addition to the literature.

Because TPP was not a parenting-skills-focused intervention, it is not possible to comment on whether improving parenting alone, in the absence of addressing attachment, would result in more positive dyadic attachment or in more positive maternal representations. However, we can state that, at least for these cases, focusing on improving representations and the security of attachment was related to improved parenting, even though parent training was not provided. Moreover, although one of the cases appears not to have resulted in the modification of maternal representation of the child or of the mother's state of mind regarding attachment history, increased child attachment security was noted nonetheless. Importantly, the active utilization of parent memories and affective responses as they arose in the therapy sessions in response to the child served as a means to improve the parent-child relationship despite differences in the extent to which maternal representational models were changed.

These observations possess some important implications for the provision of interventions to various populations. Because therapists observed that both mothers felt more positively toward their offspring and were more sensitive to their needs, it is not improbable that the improvements attributable to the TPP would be sustained in the future, even as new challenges to parenting occur over development. Thus, although attachment-informed interventions are generally likely to be more time intensive, the benefits derived from such interventions also may be more enduring. The enduring effects of the TPP intervention are being evaluated through follow-up assessments conducted at the childrens' ages of 4 and 5 years.

The second question was: How consistent is information attained through semistructured interviews such as the AAI or PAI with material garnered during an ongoing and relatively lengthy course of therapy? Although the AAI involves accessing memories of childhood and is subject to criticism that it does not actually measure the mother's attachment relationship with her own attachment figures during childhood, but rather the mother's current views of the attachment relationship, the current clinical material lends support to the continuance of insecure models of attachment across generations. Not only can similar patterns be seen with respect to the childhoods of both Rita and Donna, but the beginnings of role reversal and parentification are also evident in both of their toddler offspring at baseline. Thus, despite the fact that the AAI may not accurately measure the attachment that was present during childhood, the details recalled by these women, both in their AAI interviews and over an extended course of weekly therapy, lend credence to the attachment classification derived from the AAI. Additionally, the insecurity evidenced in both toddlers during the baseline strange situations confirms the development of insecurity in these offspring. Although therapists had no knowledge of the data obtained via interview or observational measures, their observations of initial difficulties, as well as their evaluations of improvements in the relationships between both mothers and their toddlers, generally mirrored those obtained during research assessments. In fact, the similarity between the information presented in the AAI and the therapists' assessments of the mothers' attachment history is extremely concordant, especially with respect to both women's tendency to overidealize their caregivers. Additionally, although they did not possess knowledge of strange-situation-derived attachment classifications, the concordance between therapists' observations of mother-child interaction and strange situation attachment classifications were similarly quite consistent. A discrepancy did emerge between therapist observations of Donna's presentation in therapy and her continued insecure-dismissing classification on the postintervention AAI, as well as the lack of change on the postintervention PAI. Despite the fact that Hallie's postintervention strange situation was coded secure and supports the belief that improvements in therapy did occur, it is interesting that neither Donna's postintervention PAI nor her AAI contain indices of security. This finding calls for a cautionary note in concluding that intervention has not been effective in individuals with dismissing attachment organizations, as they may change in some areas but not others. Rather, alternative means of assessing change may be needed in these cases. For Donna, it may be the case that implicit affective models and procedural knowledge about attachment relationship strategies had been altered; however, change may not have been achieved at the cognitive linguistic level of representation.

In summary, the utility of the semistructured assessments of adult attachment seem to reveal a depth of information commensurate with that derived from a long-term therapeutic relationship, underscoring the importance of these measures in more basic research endeavors, as well as the potential applicability and generalizability of such research to clinical arenas. In cases involving insecure-dismissing attachment, however, the veracity of interview information needs to be further assessed, as a more long-term and trusting relationship may reveal information not accessible in semistructured interviews conducted by unfamiliar researchers.

The third question was: Does maternal attachment representation differentially affect mothers' ability to benefit from intervention? Although our ability to address this question is limited by the provision of a single form of intervention, differences in the baseline attachment organization of the mothers described can provide some insight into this question. In this case report, both mother-child dyads appeared to benefit from the provision of the TPP intervention with respect to the emergence of postintervention child attachment security. However, Rita, the mother classified as insecure-preoccupied on the preintervention AAI, appeared to make more progress with respect to modifying her stance in relation to representations of attachment with others and with her child than did Donna. It may be that Donna's insecure-dismissing attachment organization was less amenable to a form of therapy that, by its nature, required a focus on relationships and a trusting therapeutic connection. This conceptualization cannot be wholly accepted, however, as Donna appeared to benefit from the intervention according to her therapist's reports. Longitudinal assessments may be particularly helpful in elucidating this issue, as it may be that intervention effects are more enduring in dyads where maternal representation also has been modified toward security.

The fourth and final question was: How does this case study approach inform attachment theory? The clinical material presented in this chapter provides support for the potential malleability of attachment relationships. Despite seemingly insurmountable obstacles to the development of secure attachment patterns between mother and child and even though both dyads were considered to be insecure via the baseline strange situations, over the course of intervention, significant improvements were noted in the attachment relationships between mother and toddler.

In addition to information on the malleability of attachment relationships, the case material presented also informs questions raised in the meta-analysis of van IJzendoorn et al. (1995). Because a representationally based form of intervention was effective in modifying representations in only one of the dyads, although both offspring evidenced increased security of attachment, the need for research into the mechanisms whereby attachment security is affected is underscored. In this regard, we echo van IJzendoorn et al.'s call for the importance of examining issues other than maternal sensitivity in order to elucidate pathways that eventuate in attachment security.

Although not raised earlier as one of our primary questions, the existence of generalized versus more specific representational models of relationships also emerges in this clinical material. The fact that Rita was able to form a positive relationship with her spouse, despite not having resolved her childhood experiences with an abusive stepfather and an emotionally unavailable mother, suggests that she did not generalize a negative representation to all of her interactions, but, rather, was able to respond to alternate relationship figures more objectively. Conversely, Donna, who had a dismissing stance in regard to relationship figures, generalized this model to all potential partners. Interestingly, it was Rita who evidenced modified representations of her own attachment history and of her child and her child that developed a secure attachment, whereas, for Donna, changes in her representations were not evident. It may be that Rita's representation of her child was more modifiable as a function of an overall more open model of relationships.

In this chapter, we have presented empirical data on the efficacy of an attachment-informed intervention in promoting secure attachments in toddlers with depressed mothers. To our knowledge, this is one of the first interventions for depressed mothers that has been shown to modify security of attachment. We have furthermore supplemented our group data by examining the course of treatment with two depressed mothers and their offspring. The presentation of this clinical material has provided a more qualitative window on the process of TPP and its effect on attachment security. The case material also provided a more in-depth examination of the utility of an attachment-informed intervention for reducing the insecurity for which the offspring of depressed mothers have been shown to be at risk.

Because the number of risks present in the clinical target group were minimized, the potential effectiveness of such an intervention could be assessed without clouding interpretations with more comprehensive and less attachment-specific interventions. Additionally, the present chapter underscores the importance of determining which aspects of the parent-child relationship can be affected by the provision of an attachment-informed intervention, as well as understanding the durability of various intervention outcomes. Finally, support for the potential malleability of attachment relationships, in addition to the consistency between research measures and material obtained over the course of therapy, was provided. Based on our quantitative as well as qualitative data, we believe that the provision of attachment-theory-informed therapies holds considerable promise for preventing the consolidation of insecure attachments in children at risk due to maternal depression.

ACKNOWLEDGMENTS

The work reported in this chapter was funded through a grant and a Scientific MERIT Award received from the Lifecourse Prevention Branch of the National Institute of Mental Health (MH45027). We acknowledge the therapeutic skills of Barbara Fox, Michelle Parker, Kristina Rauscher, Elizabeth Sather, and Jodi Steigerwald, the therapists who provided treatment to the mothers who took part in this preventive intervention. We also thank the mothers and children who participated in this project for sharing their lives with us and for having the courage to move beyond difficult experiences. Finally, we thank Dr. June Fleeson Sroufe for her assistance in coding AAIs and Dr. Nancie Spector for her comments on an earlier draft of this manuscript.

REFERENCES

Abraham, K. (1911). Notes on the psycho-analytical investigation of manic-depressive insanity and allied conditions. In *Selected papers on psychoanalysis*. New York: Basic Books.

Ainsworth, M. D. S., Blehar, M. C., Waters, E., & Wall, S. (1978). *Patterns of attachment: A psychological study of the strange situation*. Hillsdale, NJ: Lawrence Erlbaum Associates.

Ainsworth, M. D. S., & Wittig, B. A. (1969). Attachment and the exploratory behavior of one-year-olds in a strange situation. In B. M. Foss (Ed.), *Determinants of infant behavior* (Vol. 4, pp. 113–136). London: Methuen.

American Psychiatric Association. (1987). *Diagnostic and statistical manual of mental disorders* (3rd ed., revised). Washington, DC: Author.

Arieti, S., & Bemporad, J. (1978). *Severe and mild depression*. New York: Basic Books.

Bakermans-Kranenburg, M. J., Juffer, F., & van IJzendoorn, M. H. (1998). Interventions with video feedback and attachment discussions: Does type of maternal insecurity make a difference? *Infant Mental Health Journal, 19*, 202–219.

Bayley, N. (1969). *The Bayley scales of infant development*. New York: Psychological Corporation.

Belsky, J. (1999). Interactional and contextual determinants of attachment security. In J. Cassidy & P. R. Shaver (Eds.), *Handbook of attachment: Theory, research, and clinical applications* (pp. 249–264). New York: Guilford Press.

Bemporad, J. R., & Romano, S. J. (1992). Childhood maltreatment and adult depression: A review of research. In D. Cicchetti & S. L. Toth (Eds.), *Rochester Symposium on Developmental Psychopathology: Vol. 4. Developmental perspectives on depression* (pp. 351–376). Rochester, NY: University of Rochester Press.

Biringen, Z., & Bretheron, I. (1988). *The insight/sensitivity scale for evaluating parent attachment interviews*. Unpublished manuscript, University of Colorado Health Services Center, Denver.

Bowlby, J. (1977a). The making and breaking of affectional bonds. *British Journal of Psychiatry, 130*, 201–210.

Bowlby, J. (1977b). The making and breaking of affectional bonds. *British Journal of Psychiatry, 130*, 421–431.

Bowlby, J. (1980). *Attachment and loss: Vol. 3. Loss, sadness, and depression*. New York: Basic Books.

Bowlby, J. (1988). *A secure base*. New York: Basic Books.

Bretherton, I., Biringen, Z., Ridgeway, D., Maslin, M., & Sherman, M. (1989). Attachment: The parental perspective. *Infant Mental Health Journal, 10,* 203–220.

Campbell, S. B., Cohn, J. F., Flanagan, C., & Popper, S. (1992). Course and correlates of postpartum depression during the transition to parenthood. *Development and Psychopathology, 4,* 29–47.

Campbell, S. B., Cohn, J. F., & Meyers, T. (1995). Depression in first-time mothers: Mother-infant interaction and depression chronicity. *Developmental Psychology, 13,* 349–357.

Cassidy, J., & Berlin, L. (1994). The insecure/ambivalent pattern of attachment: Theory and research. *Child Development, 65,* 971–991.

Cicchetti, D., & Greenberg, M. (Eds.). (1991). Attachment and developmental psychopathology [Special issue]. *Development and Psychopathology, 3*(4).

Cicchetti, D., Rogosch, F. A., & Toth, S. L. (1998). Maternal depressive disorder and contextual risk: Contributions to the development of attachment insecurity and behavior problems in toddlerhood. *Development and Psychopathology, 10,* 283–300.

Cicchetti, D., Rogosch, F. A., & Toth, S. L. (2000). The efficacy of toddler-parent psychotherapy for fostering cognitive development in offspring of depressed mothers. *Journal of Abnormal Child Psychology, 28,* 135–148.

Cicchetti, D., Rogosch, F. A., Toth, S. L., & Spagnola, M. (1997). Affect, cognition, and the emergence of self-knowledge in the toddler offspring of depressed mothers. *Journal of Experimental Child Psychology, 67,* 338–362.

Cicchetti, D., & Schneider-Rosen, K. (1986). An organizational approach to childhood depression. In M. Rutter, C. Izard, & P. Read (Eds.), *Depression in young people, clinical and developmental perspectives* (pp. 71–134). New York: Guilford Press.

Cicchetti, D., & Toth, S. L. (1998). The development of depression in children and adolescents. *American Psychologist, 53,* 221–241.

Cicchetti, D., Toth, S. L., & Lynch, M. (1995). Bowlby's dream comes full circle: The application of attachment theory to risk and psychopathology. In T. Ollendick & R. Prinz (Eds.), *Advances in clinical child psychology* (Vol. 17, pp. 1–75). New York: Plenum Press.

Cicchetti, D., Toth, S. L., & Rogosch, F. A. (1999). The efficacy of toddler-parent psychotherapy to increase attachment security in offspring of depressed mothers. *Attachment and Human Development, 1,* 34–66.

Cohn, J. F., Matias, R., Tronick, E. Z., Lyons-Ruth, K., & Connell, D. (1986). Face-to-face interactions, spontaneous and structured, of mothers with depressive symptoms. In T. Field & E. Z. Tronick (Eds.), *Maternal depression and child disturbance: New directions for children development* (pp. 31–46). San Francisco: Jossey-Bass.

Cooper, P., & Murray, L. (1997). The impact of psychological treatment of postpartum depression on maternal mood and infant development. In L. Murray & P. Cooper (Eds.), *Postpartum depression and child development* (pp. 201–220). New York: Guilford Press.

Coyne, J. C., Downey, G., & Boergers, J. (1992). Depression in families: A systems perspective. In D. Cicchetti & S. L. Toth (Eds.), *Rochester Symposium on Developmental Psychopathology: Vol. 4. Developmental perspectives on depression* (pp. 211–249). Rochester, NY: University of Rochester Press.

Crittenden, P. M. (1988). Relationships at risk. In J. Belsky & T. Nezworski (Eds.), *Clinical implications of attachment theory* (pp. 136–174). Hillsdale, NJ: Lawrence Erlbaum Associates.

Crittenden, P. M. (1992). Quality of attachment in the preschool years. *Development and Psychopathology, 4,* 209–241.

Crowell, J. A., Fraley, R. C., & Shaver, P. R. (1999). Measurement of individual differences in adolescent and adult attachment. In J. Cassidy & P. R. Shaver (Eds.), *Handbook of attachment: Theory, research, and clinical applications* (pp. 434–465). New York: Guilford Press.

Cummings, E. M., & Cicchetti, D. (1990). Attachment, depression, and the transmission of depression. In M. T. Greenberg, D. Cicchetti, & E. M. Cummings (Eds.), *Attachment during the preschool years* (pp. 339–372). Chicago: University of Chicago Press.

Cummings, E. M., & Davies, P. T. (1999). Depressed parents and family functioning: Interpersonal effects and children's functioning and development. In T. Joiner & J. C. Coyne (Eds.), *The interactional nature of depression: Advances in interpersonal approaches* (pp. 299–327). Washington, DC: American Psychological Association.

Downey, G., & Coyne, J. C. (1990). Children of depressed parents: An integrative review. *Psychological Bulletin, 108*, 50–76.

Dozier, M. (1990). Attachment organization and treatment use for adults with serious psychopathological disorders. *Development and Psychopathology, 2*, 47–60.

Egeland, B., & Erickson, M. F. (1990). Rising above the past: Strategies for helping new mothers break the cycle of abuse and neglect. *Zero to Three, 11*, 29–35.

Egeland, B., & Sroufe, L. A. (1981). Attachment and early maltreatment. *Child Development, 52*, 44–52.

Eiden, R., Teti, D. M., & Corns, K. M. (1995). Maternal working models of attachment, marital adjustment, and the parent-child relationship. *Child Development, 66*, 1504–1518.

Erickson, M. F., Korfmacher, J., & Egeland, B. (1992). Attachments past and present: Implications for therapeutic intervention with mother-infancy dyads. *Development and Psychopathology, 4*, 495–507.

Field, T. M. (1989). Maternal depression effects on infant interaction and attachment behavior. In D. Cicchetti (Ed.), *Rochester Symposium on Developmental Psychopathology: Vol. 1. The emergence of a discipline* (pp. 139–163). Hillsdale, NJ: Lawrence Erlbaum Associates.

Fraiberg, S., Adelson, E., & Shapiro, V. (1975). Ghosts in the nursery: A psychoanalytic approach to impaired infant-mother relationships. *Journal of the American Academy of Child Psychiatry, 14*, 387–421.

Frankel, K. A., & Harmon, R. J. (1996). Depressed mothers: They don't always look as bad as they feel. *Journal of the American Academy of Child and Adolescent Psychiatry, 35*, 289–298.

Gaensbauer, T. J., Harmon, R. J., Cytryn, L., & McKnew, D. (1984). Social and affective development in infants with a manic-depressive parent. *American Journal of Psychiatry, 141*, 223–229.

Gelfand, D. M., Teti, D. M., Seiner, S. A., & Jameson, P. B. (1996). Helping mothers fight depression: Evaluation of a home-based intervention program for depressed mothers and their infants. *Journal of Clinical Child Psychology, 25*, 406–422.

George, C., Kaplan, N., & Main, M. (1984). *Attachment interview for adults*. Unpublished manuscript, University of California, Berkeley.

George, C., & Solomon, J. (1999). The development of caregiving: A comparison of attachment theory and psychoanalytic approaches to mothering. *Psychoanalytic Inquiry, 19*, 618–646.

Hollingshead, A. (1975). *Four-factor index of social status*. Unpublished manuscript, Yale University, New Haven, CT.

Isabella, R. (1993). Origins of attachment: Maternal interactive behavior across the first year. *Child Development, 64*, 605–621.

Jacobson, E. (1971). *Depression: Comparitive studies of normal, neurotic, and psychotic conditions*. New York: International Universities Press.

Kaplan, P. S., Bachorowski, J., & Zarlengo-Strouse, P. (1999). Child-directed speech produced by mothers with symptoms of depression fails to promote associative learning in 4-month-old infants. *Child Development, 70*, 560–570.

Lewis, M., & Brooks-Gunn, J. (1979). *Social cognition and the acquisition of self*. New York: Plenum Press.

Lieberman, A. F. (1992). Infant-parent psychotherapy with toddlers. *Development and Psychopathology, 4*, 559–574.

Lieberman, A., & Pawl, J. (1990). Disorders of attachment and secure base behavior in the second year: Conceptual issues and clinical intervention. In M. Greenberg, D. Cicchetti, & M. Cummings (Eds.), *Attachment beyond infancy* (pp. 375–397). Chicago: University of Chicago Press.

Lieberman, A. F., Weston, D., & Pawl, J. H. (1991). Preventive intervention and outcome with anxiously attached dyads. *Child Development, 62,* 199–209.

Lyons-Ruth, K., Connell, D., Grunebaum, H., & Botein, S. (1990). Infants at social risk: Maternal depression and family support services as mediators of infant development and security of attachment. *Child Development, 61,* 85–98.

Lyons-Ruth, K., Zoll, D., Connell, D., & Grunebaum, H. (1986). The depressed mother and her one-year-old infant. In E. Tronick & T. Field (Eds.), *Maternal depression and infant disturbance* (pp. 61–82). San Francisco: Jossey-Bass.

Mahler, M. (1968). *On human symbiosis and the vicissitudes of individuation: Vol. 1. Infantile psychosis.* New York: International Universities Press.

Main, M. (1995). Recent studies in attachment: Overview, with selected implications for clinical work. In S. Goldberg, R. Muir, & J. Kerr (Eds.), *Attachment theory: Social, developmental, and clinical perspectives* (pp. 407–474). Hillsdale, NJ: Analytic Press.

Main, M. (1996). Introduction to the special section on attachment and psychopathology: 2. Overview of the field of attachment. *Journal of Consulting and Clinical Psychology, 6,* 237–243.

Main, M., Kaplan, N., & Cassidy, J. C. (1985). Security in infancy, childhood and adulthood: A move to the level of representation. In I. Bretherton & E. Waters (Eds.), *Growing points of attachment theory and research* (Society for Research in Child Development Monograph No. 209, pp. 66–104). MA: Blackwell.

Main, M., & Solomon, J. (1986). Discovery of a disorganized/disoriented attachment pattern. In T. B. Brazelton & M. W. Yogman (Eds.), *Affective development in infancy* (pp. 95–124). Norwood, NJ: Ablex.

Main, M., & Solomon, J. (1990). Procedures for identifying infants as disorganized/disoriented during the Ainsworth strange situation. In M. Greenberg, D. Cicchetti, & E. M. Cummings (Eds.), *Attachment during the preschool years* (pp. 121–160). Chicago: University of Chicago Press.

Murray, L. (1992). The impact of postnatal depression on infant development. *Journal of Child Psychology and Psychiatry and Allied Disciplines, 33,* 543–561.

National Institute of Child Health and Human Development Early Child Care Research Network. (1999). Chronicity of maternal depressive symptoms, maternal sensitivity, and child functioning at 36 months. *Developmental Psychology, 35,* 1297–1310.

Radke-Yarrow, M., Cummings, E. M., Kuczynski, L., & Chapman, M. (1985). Patterns of attachment in two-and-three-year-olds in normal families and families with parental depression. *Child Development, 56,* 884–893.

Robins, L., Helzer, J., Orvaschel, H., Anthony, J., Blazer, D., Burnam, A., & Burke, J. (1985). The diagnostic interview schedule. In W. Eaton & L. Kessler (Eds.), *Epidemiologic field methods in psychiatry* (pp. 143–170). New York: Academic Press.

Sandler, J., & Joffe, W. G. (1965). Notes on childhood depression. *International Journal of Psychoanalysis, 46,* 88–96.

Seifer, R., Sameroff, A. J., Dickstein, S., Keitner, G., & Miller, I. (1996). Parental psychopathology, multiple contextual risks, and one-year outcomes in children. *Journal of Clinical Child Psychology, 25,* 423–435.

Solomon, J., & George, C. (1999a). The measurement of attachment security in infancy and childhood. In J. Cassidy & P. R. Shaver (Eds.), *Handbook of attachment: Theory, research, and clinical applications* (pp. 287–316). New York: Guilford Press.

Solomon, J., & George, C. (1999b). The place of disorganization in attachment theory: Linking classic observations with contemporary findings. In J. Solomon & C. George (Eds.), *Attachment disorganization* (pp. 3–32). New York: Guilford Press.

Sroufe, L. A. (1983). Infant-caregiver attachment and patterns of adaptation in preschool: The roots of maladaptation and competence. In M. Perlmutter (Ed.), *Minnesota Symposium in Child Psychology* (Vol. 16, pp. 41–83). Hillsdale, NJ: Lawrence Erlbaum Associates.

Sroufe, L. A., & Fleeson, J. (1988). The coherence of family relationships. In R. A. Hinde & J. Stevenson-Hinde (Eds.), *Relationships within families: Mutual influences* (pp. 27–47). Oxford: Oxford University Press.

Sroufe, L. A., & Waters, E. (1977). Attachment as an organizational construct. *Child Development, 48,* 1184–1199.

Stern, D. N. (1995). *The motherhood constellation: A unified view of parent-infant psychotherapy.* New York: Basic Books.

Teti, D. M., Gelfand, D., Messinger, D., & Isabella, R. (1995). Maternal depression and the quality of early attachment: An examination of infants, preschoolers, and their mothers. *Developmental Psychology, 31,* 364–376.

Tronick, E. Z., & Weinberg, M. K. (1997). Depressed mothers and infants: Failure to form dyadic states of consciousness. In L. Murray & P. Cooper (Eds.), *Postpartum depression and child development* (pp. 54–81). New York: Guilford Press.

van den Boom, D. C. (1994). The influence of temperament and mothering on attachment and exploration: An experimental manipulation of sensitive responsiveness among lower-class mothers with irritable infants. *Child Development, 65,* 1457–1477.

van den Boom, D. C. (1995). Do first-year intervention effects endure? Follow-up during toddlerhood for a sample of dutch irritable infants. *Child Development, 66,* 1798–1816.

van IJzendoorn, M. H., Juffer, F., & Duyvesteyn, M. G. C. (1995). Breaking the inter-generational cycle of insecure attachment: A review of the effects of attachment-based interventions on maternal sensitivity and infant security. *Journal of Child Psychology and Psychiatry, 36,* 225–248.

Vaughn, B. E., & Waters, E. (1990). Attachment behavior at home and in the laboratory: Q-sort observations and strange situation classifications of one-year-olds. *Child Development, 61,* 1965–1973.

Vondra, J. I., & Barnett, D. (Eds.). (1999). *Atypical patterns of attachment in infancy and early childhood among children at developmental risk* (Society for Research in Child Development Monograph No. 258). Malden, MA: Blackwell.

Waters, E., & Deane, K. E. (1985). Defining and assessing individual differences in attachment relationships: Q-methodology and the organization of behavior in infancy and early childhood. *Monographs of the Society for Research in Child Development 50*(1–2, Serial No.), pp. 41–65).

Waters, E., Vaughn, B. E., Posada, G., & Teti, D. (in press). *Patterns of secure base behavior: Q-sort perspectives on attachment and caregiving in infancy and childhood.* Mahwah, NJ: Lawrence Erlbaum Associates.

Zeanah, C. (Ed.). (1993). *Handbook of mental health.* New York: Guilford Press.

Author Index

A

Aber, J. L., 181, *206*
Abraham, K., 230, *271*
Achenbach, T. M., 34, 35, 39, *45*, 124, *131*
Adam, E., 171, 172, 177, *180*
Adam, K. S., 193, *203*
Adelson, E., 51, *64*, 235, *273*
Adelson, J., 109, *132*
Aguilar, B., 39, *45*
Ainsworth, M. D. S., 3, 4, 6, 17, 20, *20*, 54, 62, 67, *92*, 97, 98, 99, 100, 104, 106, 107, *131*, 141, 142, 154, *164*, 182, 183, *203*, 207, 225, 229, 245–246, 246, *271*
Aksan, N., 146, *165*
Albus, K., 13, 22, 139, *164*, 169, 171, 174, 178, *179*, *180*
Alexander, J. K., 217, *225*
Alexander, P. C., 202, 209, 213, *225*
Allan, S., 97, 112, *131*, *133*
Allard, H., 210, *225*
Allen, J. P., 11, *20*, 144, *164*
Alpern, L., 8, 23, 74, 88, *93*
Altermeier, W. A., III, 50, *62*
Altman, M., 51, 52, 53, 60, *64*
Ambrosini, P. J., 34, *45*
Ammaniti, M., 181, *203*
Anderson, C. L., 209, 213, *225*
Andrews, M., 68, *92*
Anthony, J., 238, *274*
Arend, R. A., 86, *93*
Arieti, S., 230, *271*
Asquith, P., 113, *135*
Atkinson, L., 5, 10, 11, 12, *21*, 207, 210, *225*
Atwood, G. E., 11–12, 23, 73, 77, 80, *93*
Auerbach, J., 51, 52, 53, 60, *64*
Aynsley-Green, A., 51, *64*

B

Bachorowski, J., 244, *273*
Badgely, R., 210, *225*
Bakermans-Kranenburg, M. J., 11, 12, 24, 25, 54, *64*, 69–70, *94*, 234, *271*
Baldwin, A. L., 84, *92*
Baldwin, C. P., 84, *92*
Barbero, G., 51, *62*
Barnett, D., 7, 8, 9, 12, *21*, 69, *92*, 229, 246, *275*
Barnett, L., 168, *179*, 191, *204*
Barriga, A., 123, 124, *131*, *132*
Bartholomew, K., 213, 222, *225*
Barton, M. L., 50, 58, *62*
Bates, B. C., 169, 178, *179*
Bates, J. E., 61, *62*
Baucom, D., 217, *225*
Baumrind, D., 132, 146, 148, *164*
Bayley, N., 61, *62*, 241, *271*
Beckwith, L., 44, *45*
Beebe, B., 182, *203*
Behar, L., 32, *45*
Bell, K. L., 144, *164*
Belsky, J., vii, 6, 7, 9, *21*, 30, *46*, 182, *203*, 246, *271*
Bemporad, J. R., 230, *271*
Bennenishty, R., 211, *228*
Benoit, D., 10, 11, *25*, 50, 53, 57, 58, 59, 60, 61, *62*, *63*, 168, *179*
Berenson-Howard, J., 52, *63*
Berkowitz, C. D., 51, *62*
Berlin, L., 89, *92*, 200, *204*, 246, *272*
Berns, S. B., 170, *179*
Bernstein, V., 36, *47*
Biederman, J., 38, *46*
Biringen, Z., 246, 248, *271*, *272*
Bithoney, W. G., 52, *62*
Black, M. M., 52, *63*

277

Subject Index